Housing Policy in the UK

Public Policy and Politics

Series Editors: Colin Fudge and Robin Hambleton

PUBLISHED

Danny Burns, Robin Hambleton and Paul Hoggett, *The Politics of Decentralisation: Revitalising Local Democracy*

Stephen Glaister, June Burnham, Handley M. G. Stevens and Tony Travers, *Transport Policy in Britain*

Christopher Ham, *Health Policy in Britain: The Politics and Organisation of the National Health Service* (fifth edition)

Ian Henry, *The Politics of Leisure Policy* (second edition)

Peter Malpass and Alan Murie, *Housing Policy and Practice* (fifth edition)

Robin Means, Sally Richards and Randall Smith, *Community Care: Policy and Practice* (third edition)

David Mullins and Alan Murie, *Housing Policy in the UK*

Gerry Stoker, *The Politics of Local Government* (second edition)

Marilyn Taylor, *Public Policy in the Community*

Kieron Walsh, *Public Services and Market Mechanisms: Competition, Contracting and the New Public Management*

FORTHCOMING

Rob Atkinson and Simin Davoudi with Graham Moon, *Urban Politics in Britain: The City, the State and the Market* (second edition)

Robin Hambleton, *Reinventing Local Governance*

Christopher C. Hood and Helen Z. Margetts, *The Tools of Government in the Digital Age*

Housing Policy in the UK

David Mullins and Alan Murie

**with Phil Leather, Peter Lee, Moyra Riseborough
and Bruce Walker**

First published 2006 by
PALGRAVE MACMILLAN
Houndmills, Basingstoke, Hampshire RG21 6XS and
175 Fifth Avenue, New York, N.Y. 10010
Companies and representatives throughout the world

PALGRAVE MACMILLAN is the global academic imprint of the Palgrave Macmillan division of St. Martin's Press, LLC and of Palgrave Macmillan Ltd. Macmillan® is a registered trademark in the United States, United Kingdom and other countries. Palgrave is a registered trademark in the European Union and other countries.

ISBN-13: 978–0–333–99433–7 hardback
ISBN-10: 0–333–99433–7 hardback
ISBN-13: 978–0–333–99434–4 paperback
ISBN-10: 0–333–99434–5 paperback

This book is printed on paper suitable for recycling and made from fully managed and sustained forest sources.

A catalogue record for this book is available from the British Library.

Library of Congress Cataloging-in-Publication Data
Mullins, David, 1955–
   Housing policy in the UK / David Mullins and Alan Murie.
      p.   cm. — (Public policy and politics)
   Includes bibliographical references and index.
   ISBN 0–333–99433–7 (cloth)
   1. Housing policy—Great Britain.   2. Great Britain—Social policy.
   I. Murie, Alan.   II. Title.   III. Series.
   HD7333.A3M82 2006
   363.5′610941—dc22   2005056101

10   9   8   7   6   5   4   3   2   1
15   14   13   12   11   10   09   08   07   06

Printed and bound in China

Contents

List of Tables

List of Figures

Preface

Housing Policy in the UK aims to provide a readable introduction to key issues that affect housing in the UK. It reflects the multidisciplinary tradition in housing studies and draws on material on the history, politics, economics and management of housing. All of these disciplines help to explain the contemporary debates on housing and show how housing policy has developed.

This book is a successor to the successful textbook *Housing Policy and Practice* by Peter Malpass and Alan Murie. That text was first published in 1982 and was substantially revised in four subsequent editions (1987, 1990, 1994 and 1999). *Housing Policy in the UK* takes forward the account in the earlier book but has adopted a new framework for the selection of material. The history of housing policy up to 1997 is dealt with briefly in Chapters 2 and 3. Chapter 3 focuses on the 18 years of Conservative government and Chapter 4 charts the development of Labour's approaches to housing after 1997. Readers are therefore provided with a general historical context covering the whole of the twentieth century and a more detailed account of housing policy developments since 1979.

Chapters 5–10 explore key developments in each form of housing tenure. These chapters emphasize the links between policies on different tenures and internal fragmentation within the main tenures. There is comprehensive consideration of the social rented sector, reflecting its importance to people on housing professional development programmes and to housing policy makers and practitioners. The discussions include organizational management reform and modernization, regulation, the finance of social housing, the role of the non-profit sector and changing approaches to housing management.

Finally, Chapters 11–14 explore the increasing links between housing policy and other key areas of policy in the days of 'joined-up government'. The cross-cutting themes of housing and social care, neighbourhood renewal and private sector renewal are covered with reference to the major policy reforms of Supporting People, social inclusion, the Sustainable Communities Plan and the Regulatory Reform Order.

While our title is *Housing Policy in the UK* it is not possible to provide a full account of developments in each UK jurisdiction. Rather we stress the importance of the national and spatial context in the development and working out of policies. This is done by providing examples of developments at the city, regional and national levels to illustrate the substantial differences that exist in the role and nature of housing and the institutional forms that have emerged. The impact of devolution and the emergence of regionalism in housing policy are also discussed.

We would like to acknowledge the influence of Peter Malpass, particularly in relation to the historical chapters. The presentation of some arguments reflects his contribution to the field of study and his longstanding collaboration with Alan Murie, including joint authorship of successive editions of *Housing Policy and Practice*. We gratefully acknowledge the chapters contributed by colleagues at the Centre for Urban and Regional Studies, whose expertise enabled a more comprehensive and informed approach than could have been achieved without them: Chapter 8, Bruce Walker; Chapter 11, Moyra Riseborough; Chapter 12, Peter Lee; and Chapter 13, Philip Leather.

DAVID MULLINS
ALAN MURIE

The authors and publishers are grateful to the following for permission to reproduce copyright material in this work: Palgrave Macmillan and Peter Malpass for Tables 2.1, 2.2, 2.3 and 3.1 and Figure 2.1; Taylor and Francis for Table 9.4; The Policy Press for Table 12.3 and Figure 10.2; Key Haven Press Inc. and the Housing Corporation for Figure 10.1. Thanks also to Palgrave Macmillan and Peter Malpass for Tables 2.5, 3.2, 3.4 and 3.5, Springer Science and Business Media for Table 9.1 and Open University Press/McGraw-Hill Publishing Company for Figure 9.2 for permission to include adapted versions of copyright material.

Chapter 1

Introduction

This book is concerned with housing and housing policy in the UK. It makes reference to the long historical development of policy but focuses on the very rapid changes that have occurred since 1979. In this period there have been important breaks with what went before: privatization has enhanced the dominance of owner-occupation; the private and social rented sectors have undergone major changes; patterns of governance and housing finance have been radically reviewed; and regional and local inequalities and changing patterns of demand for housing have been acknowledged in the policy process.

Housing has a number of distinctive characteristics that make housing policy different from other public policies. Housing is a highly durable and flexible product, but has a fixed location and a high cost relative to current income. It is has a long life and key elements of the housing situation reflect patterns of investment of 60–100 years earlier. While dwellings can be modernized and modified the legacy of previous policy periods is very strong – new additions to the housing stock amount to some 1 per cent per annum. Consequently the nature of housing problems and housing services is slow to change and is much more determined by the past than are social services, education, health and especially social security, where dramatic change is more feasible in a short time scale.

The state has never been the principal provider of housing in the UK – at its peak council housing accounted for about one in three dwellings. Instead the majority of the construction and management of housing has been carried out by the private sector. Nevertheless in the twenty-first century housing remains an important contributor to social welfare and continues to involve a wide range of organizations and professions in the state, voluntary and private sectors.

Housing policies and housing tenures

Two key terms are used throughout this book: housing policy and housing tenure. Consequently it is important at the outset to offer brief definitions. The word policy is notoriously difficult to define with any precision (Hill, 1997). A starting point is to say that it generally implies action in relation

1

to a particular problem. Policy implies change that is consciously planned and brought about with some objective in view. At election time, manifestos set out politicians' policies for dealing with the problems they believe are important for their party. Policies of this sort involve many other actors in translating manifestos and turning them into actions. Policy therefore implies a process, involving the initial recognition of a problem to be addressed, a planning or policy-making stage, and the execution or implementation of the policy, which may itself be followed by appraisal or evaluation of the success of that policy (Hogwood and Gunn, 1981).

All kinds of organization have policies, although they may not be explicit or formally set out. The focus in this book is generally on state housing policy at the national, regional and local levels. State intervention affects all parts of the housing system by regulating and supporting important aspects of the market, such as the housing association sector, new housing development, the improvement of older houses and neighbourhoods and the financing of house purchases. Intervention may be direct, through the provision of housing, or indirect, through regulation, subsidies and incentives (see Chapter 8)

Housing tenure describes the legal status of and the rights associated with different forms of housing ownership and occupancy. Tenure has come to be regarded as a significant indicator of people's position in the housing market and society. Tenure has also had a wider impact in terms of the design and built form of urban areas and the development of the welfare state (Kemeny, 1981). There are four main types of tenure in the UK: owner-occupation, council renting, housing association renting and private renting. These convenient labels assume huge importance in political debates on housing but have analytical limitations. Tenure categories embrace numerous differences – for example different home owners own different types and size of dwelling and have different levels of indebtedness. The heavily mortgaged recent purchaser of an older terraced house in an inner-city area of a northern city is in a very different position from the outright owner of a modern detached suburban property in South-East England. Research by Burrows (2003) suggests that around half of the poorest households now live in owner-occupied homes. Equally council housing has very different meanings for a tenant living in an unpopular tower block and a tenant of a traditionally built house with a large garden.

Housing policy includes measures designed to modify the quality or quantity of housing, its price and ownership, access to it and management of it. Different countries have different approaches to housing and housing policy. Housing patterns do not simply reflect countries' stage of economic growth and development, the logic of industrialism or the operation of the market. Because of the durability of housing, the housing stock reflects past patterns of economic development and employment. This is particularly true in the UK and other European countries where many of the dwellings available today were built during much earlier phases of economic development to house very different communities working in different places. Housing, and especially better-built housing, remains long after its original relationship to places of work has gone. In most places local employment in shipyards or docks, coal mines or heavy manufacturing has completely vanished, and the properties now house people working in different localities and different parts of the economy.

Because industrialization and urbanization occurred at a relatively early stage in the UK the dislocation between housing and current place of employment is particularly striking. Neighbourhoods have gone through a number of transitions in terms of their economic function, accessibility and desirability, and the nature of the population living there. The complexities of this situation are much greater than was the case 50 years ago and in comparison with those in recently industrialized countries.

Modernization and change

Some writers have viewed the development of housing policy as a process of modernization; for example modernization of tenure (Harloe, 1985) or modernization of institutional frameworks (Mullins, Reid and Walker, 2001). In this book we view modernization as a continuous process of adjusting and adapting the housing system to external changes, such as economic growth or changes in society and politics. As noted earlier the high cost, durability, fixed location and long life of housing stock usually make adjustment a very gradual process. However there have been periods of more rapid adjustment, for example in the Victorian era, rapid economic growth and urbanization was accommodated by subdividing properties and cramming people into the existing housing stock.

As the economic base has changed – for example with the decline of older industries, deindustrialization and the move towards a more service-based economy – the housing system has constantly had to catch up. The existing stock has been adapted through market processes and public policy, and new housing has been developed to meet modern requirements and changing needs. But it is important to recognize that modernization is not simply a technical process of adaptation, but also involves bargaining between the various actors and interest groups involved. For example private landlords were dominant throughout the nineteenth century, but then their financial interests were challenged by public health interventions and alternative types of provision. The term modernization should not be taken as implying just one 'modernizing' pathway. Different approaches have been developed in different countries to reflect the interests and power of different groups.

A more specific notion of modernization is offered by Malpass (2004), who refers to the modernization of tenure as a consistent theme in UK policy. The modernization of housing in the UK has involved the demise of private landlordism. For most of the twentieth century there was little political support for private landlordism (Englander, 1983) but much for local authority housing provision and owner-occupation. The modernization of the housing sector partly involved the replacement of private landlordism with more appropriate forms of provision that were better equipped to respond to the needs of the population.

Policy change also involves institutional change. In the twentieth century the UK differed from many other countries in that it developed strong capacities in central and local government. The institutional capacity developed in one period had a real impact later, enabling local authorities to meet the housing needs of a third of the population by 1979, supporting Esping-Andersen's (1990) view of the path-dependent nature of welfare states. More recent modernization of social housing has involved a move away from these institutions, and the roles and capacities of other players such as housing associations and building societies have been transformed. The modernization process has involved a continuous interaction between national frameworks for policy and groups of institutions – such as local authorities and housing associations – exploiting their capacity to influence those frameworks and meet their own strategic aims. Later chapters of this book show how this dynamic framework has produced significant differences in housing conditions and provision in different territories and regions of the UK, and in different cities and towns. Given this fact, it is insufficient to focus only on national top-down processes of change if we want to understand the scope and impact of housing policy.

It is important to consider the modernization of different aspects of the policy process. This requires attention to changing housing needs in respect of the physical condition of the housing stock, space standards, changing demographic patterns and overcrowding. Other important considerations are changes in housing tenure and political tenure strategies, and the exercise of housing choice, including choice that relates to the size and condition of dwellings and tenure. Organizational considerations include change in the public and private sectors, in central and local government, and in the procurement, production, financing and management of housing. Finally there have been changes in the politics of housing, and political debates on housing have reflected the changing aspirations of and demands by the various social classes and groups.

The modernization of housing policy has not been a steady progression. The appropriate ways to modernize have always been contested politically, for example giving priority to different housing tenures. Progress has also been interrupted by dramatic events such as wars and economic recessions and the resultant limitations on public finance and private investment. It is essential to recognize that these differences affect national and local policies alike. What happens at the local level is affected by both national and local policies and practices, changes in local political control, local economic circumstances and local patterns of demographic change.

UK housing in an international context

While historical legacies influence the housing available in different countries, housing provision is also affected by key events and institutional and governance arrangements. These arrangements reflect the distinctive historical and political circumstances of individual countries and regions. Such factors distinguish the UK system but also account for the differences among countries, and among regions and cities in the UK.

Table 1.1 provides some basic comparisons between the UK housing system and those in other European countries. The UK has a very high level of owner-occupation in comparison with many of these countries, as well as a relatively low proportion of private rented housing. However there are no uniform patterns and this is a consequence of different policy traditions. The high level of owner-occupation in the UK is partly the result of governments' deliberate promotion of home ownership and the privatization of state housing

Table 1.1 *Dwelling stock by tenure, selected European countries, 1980 and 1999 (percentage of total stock)*

	Rented		Owner-occupied		Other	
	1980	*1999*	*1980*	*1999*	*1980*	*1999*
Belgium	38	23	59	74	3	3
Denmark	41	45	52	51	8	4
West Germany	55	57	43	43	2	0
Spain	21	13	73	81	6	6
France	41	38	47	54	12	8
Ireland	24	18	76	79	0	3
Netherlands	58	48	42	52	0	0
Austria	43	41	52	56	5	3
Portugal	39	28	52	64	5	8
Finland	29	30	61	60	10	10
UK	45	31	55	69	0	0

Sources: ODPM *Housing Statistics*; EU *Housing Statistics*.

in recent years. In Spain and Portugal it is more the product of historical and rural traditions and the lack of major public intervention. The high level of private renting in Switzerland reflects support from banks, financial institutions and large businesses, whilst in Germany it is the product of postwar subsidies for social rented housing. Subsidies were provided to private landlords in return for housing people in need for a fixed period of time; once this period expired they were free to choose their own market niche and much of this housing has become part of the private rented sector.

Institutional arrangements and the meaning of home ownership vary considerably among countries. Differences relate to the legal basis of ownership and to the rights and responsibilities associated with land and the property built on the land. There are differences, for example, among countries' legal processes for exchanging the ownership of property and their institutional and organizational arrangements for registering titles and carrying out property transactions. These differences mean that the term home ownership has different meanings in different places according to their history and legal and institutional arrangements. These differences also exist within the UK, notably in relation to the different rights and sale processes for home owners in Scotland and differences between the ownership of flats and houses.

There are also considerable differences among European states in terms of institutional structure and social rented housing (Stephens *et al.*, 2002). In the UK most social rented housing has traditionally been provided by local authorities, but in recent years there has been a significant shift to the non-profit sector. This sector comprises charitable and non-charitable housing associations with different origins and histories, with the largest growing group consisting of new associations set up to manage homes transferred from local authorities (see Chapter 9). New towns were formerly landlords, but their housing stock has now been transferred to local authorities or housing associations. Other public sector organizations also play an important part, for example the Northern Ireland Housing Executive and Communities Scotland (previously Scottish Homes) are non-departmental public bodies that own and manage housing. Finally there is a small public sector that falls outside the social rented sector and mainly provides housing for employees, the largest example being the Ministry of Defence Housing Executive.

The historical provision of social housing largely by the public sector in the UK increased the potential for housing policy to be an arena for local and national competition between parties and interests. In this respect the shift of provision to the non-profit sector is interesting since this sector is treated as private for public spending purposes and is less subject to local authority or political party influence. It has been argued that in comparison with France, for example, the political debate on housing policy has always been more confrontational and competitive in the UK (Duclaud-Williams, 1978). Similarly it has been suggested that the different approaches to social rented housing in the UK and the Netherlands is partly attributable to the broad base of political support for non-profit housing organizations in the Netherlands, which has been much less the case in the UK (Murie and Priemus,1994).

Differences within the UK

In international comparisons the UK is usually treated as a single regime type that is characterized by high levels of home ownership alongside a substantial public rented sector. However there have long been significant differences within the UK, notably between Scotland and England, and to a lesser extent between Northern Ireland, Wales and the English regions. Furthermore the recent devolution of power to legislative assemblies in Scotland and Northern Ireland, to an assembly with administrative and scrutiny powers in Wales, and to appointed regional assemblies in the regions of England might be expected to reduce further the uniformity of regime type. Against these divergent forces must be weighed macroeconomic policy, European legislation and globalization, which may result in convergence over time. Evidence for convergence includes the emergence of similar policy responses, such as support for home ownership and local authority stock transfer throughout the UK. We also need to question whether internal differences provide a sufficient basis for assuming that more than one regime exists in the UK.

We shall now review the distinctive housing traditions in different parts of the UK and the debates on convergence and divergence. Figure 1.1 shows the changing tenure patterns in the four UK jurisdictions between 1971 and 2003. It is apparent that despite the different patterns that prevailed in 1971 (with higher levels of owner-occupation in England and Wales and more local authority housing in Scotland), the trajectory of change has been similar in each jurisdiction, with growth in home ownership and housing association accommodation and a decline in local authority and private renting.

Northern Ireland had a distinctive housing policy in the period between the passage of the Government of Ireland Act of 1921 and 1972 (Paris, 2001). During that time there was a separate government in Northern Ireland and its housing policy did not seek to achieve parity with that in the rest of the UK. There was no Westminster scrutiny and little discussion about housing. Very considerable differences emerged in relation to the nature of rent control legislation and subsidies, but this is too complex a matter to be

Figure 1.1   *Changing tenure mix, UK, 1971–2003 (per cent)*

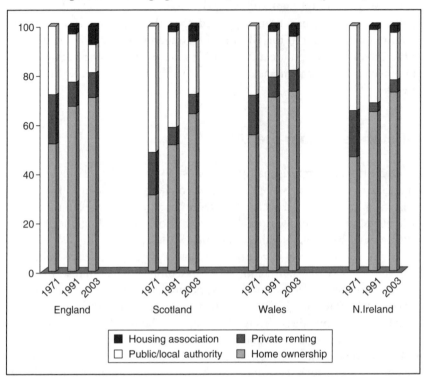

Note: The Northern Ireland Housing Executive appears here as a public/local authority
Source: Data from *Housing Statistics* (ONS), 2004.

covered in our account of the development of UK housing policy prior to 1972 (Chapter 2). Housing became an arena for sectarian politics, and this was one of the factors that contributed to the change in governance arrangements in 1971. Housing responsibilities were then transferred from local authorities to a new province-wide Northern Ireland Housing Executive (NIHE). The latter also took over the stock of the Northern Ireland Housing Trust, which between 1945 and 1971 had built homes for 48 000 households (Murie and Birrell, 1971).

Direct rule of Northern Ireland from Westminster has been in place for the majority of the period since 1972. There has been some convergence of policy, with a tendency to adopt very similar policies to those being pursued in England, although relatively higher levels of public expenditure on housing have been maintained. In the 1950s and 1960s housing in Northern Ireland was more distinct from the rest of the UK than it is today, although the existence of the Northern Ireland Housing Executive and the absence of local authority housing means that Northern Ireland remains distinctive. The Northern Ireland Legislative Assembly created a separate administration, which was more strongly Northern Ireland based than in much of the period since direct rule was in place. However the suspension of the assembly after 2002 delayed any impact this might have had and policy subsequently developed broadly in line with that in England.

Scotland also had a distinctive housing policy in the past, but based less on the formal devolution of power than on differences arising from its separate legal system and legislation (Sim, 2004). Housing and urban problems produced a local and national politics that generated what in effect was an independent administration and welfare state (Paterson, 1994). Local political differences in Scotland were strongest between the wars and in the 1950s and 1960s. The tradition of having a separate civil service and administrative infrastructure based in Edinburgh continued throughout the postwar period. However after the 1960s policy was increasingly centralized in Whitehall, national political and public expenditure agendas for housing became more intrusive and the extent of Scottish policy difference was reduced, but the distinctive planning and subsidy frameworks remained.

In Wales there has not been a tradition of separate legislation, and even with the establishment of the Welsh office the tendency was for Wales to follow English practices, both in legislation and in the adoption of guidance (Smith *et al.*, 2001). In many respects the differences that did exist were similar to those in the English regions. Administration from Westminster was *laissez faire*, wedded to the view that housing was the responsibility of local government and avoided the minefield of overly close central government involvement. Until the 1970s legislation tended to be enabling, with limited enforcement duties, a lack of scrutiny of what was actually happening and no strong regional authority in relation to housing. Consequently the tenure structures, policies and practices in different parts of England and Wales differed, and in some cases were as different as those between them and Scotland or Northern Ireland.

In many respects the important break point in terms of differences within the UK may not have been the introduction of devolution in 1998 but rather the centralization of policy in the mid 1970s. Until then, with the partial exception of Northern Ireland, there was continuity in allocating administrative responsibility for housing services to local authorities (rather than the various organizations that fulfilled this task in other countries). This allowed local politics and local differences to influence policy.

By the time of devolution the system had become more centralized and the differences between local policies began to reduce. Since then privatization policies have been similar throughout the UK, and changes in housing tenure have followed similar trajectories (Figure 1.1). Although Scotland continues to have less owner-occupation and more social housing than other parts of the UK, some of the English regions and cities throughout the UK still have a considerable amount of social housing, suggesting that differences are partly related to cities and regions rather than nations.

Other forces are tending to 'renationalize' housing policy and reduce local differences. These include national policies on economic management. For example taxation, inflation management and economic policy all operate at the national level. Housing Benefit has increased in importance and is administered on a common basis across the UK. The growing trend for home ownership has exposed local housing systems to broader market and institutional influences, such as interest rate policy, mortgage lenders' policies and housing developers' approaches to design and marketing. Finally, Europeanization and globalization are sources of regulatory and policy convergence and fewer matters that affect housing are subject to local decision making than was the case 40 years ago.

In conclusion it seems unlikely that devolution will exert a sufficiently strong influence to overwhelm the nationalizing, unifying and converging forces. Nevertheless past legacies will remain and differences in organizational capacity and resources, legal systems, politics, administrative traditions and local and regional economies will cause some divergence. However the overall trend is likely to be towards convergence, especially where market-based organizations are becoming dominant, along with privatization and macroeconomic policies. Our account of the impact of devolution on the non-profit sector in Chapter 9 reveals a similar tendency for convergence, despite different starting points and individual institutional changes. At the European level some differences remain because welfare systems, taxation systems and social security systems differ, but if these systems begin to converge in response to global pressures, the distinctiveness of housing systems will decline, reinforcing common patterns such as residualization and marketization.

Policy structures and networks

The structures through which housing policy is made include market mechanisms and local and regional networks of agencies. This reflects wider trends in governance, with hierarchies increasingly being displaced by markets and networks (Thompson *et al.*, 1991). The role of local authorities as enablers rather than providers encapsulates this change, their function being to coordinate private sector providers and social housing networks rather than engage in direct provision (Goodlad, 1993). In this less hierarchical world the central government still plays a key role in terms of policy making and providing a framework for the enactment of policy by a variety of agencies operating at the national, regional and local levels. As noted above, devolution has changed the institutional framework for housing in Scotland, Northern Ireland and Wales, while in England regional bodies have become more significant and have drawn power from others. But it is at the local level that implementation takes place and local authorities, housing associations, private sector and voluntary organizations now constitute networks through which housing policy is delivered (Reid, 1995). These networks are not agents of central government and the way in which they interpret policy and use resources varies. This reflects the different meaning of central policy for different localities, and the varying objectives of different organizations (Lowe, 2004).

When considering difference it is also important to consider the ways in which policy has engaged with and affected different groups in society. Morris and Winn (1990) have analyzed the effect of housing policies on social divisions based on class, race and gender, and conclude that housing studies has suffered from a lack of sociological input. Similarly Harrison and Davis (2001) argue that disability, ethnicity and gender should be at the centre of any analysis of housing policies and practices. Their analysis of housing policies from 1979 to 1997 shows that the residualisation of social housing had consequences for many disabled people, single parents and substantial numbers of people from minority communities who relied on non-market provision. 'One intepretation is that, at the same time as the sector's status and relative quality declined it also became more receptive to these groups (albeit not in an unproblematic or uneven way' (ibid., p.15).

The central government has distinct aims, objectives and preoccupations in relation to housing. These are tied to its concern with economic regulation, capital accumulation, investment and taxation. These influences on policy are discussed in the next three chapters, which summarize the history of housing policy in the UK prior to 1979 (Chapter 2), under the Conservative governments between 1979 and 1996 (Chapter 3) and under Labour governments since 1997 (Chapter 4). Each of the governing parties has had a distinctive agenda for housing policy. This is described in relation to home ownership (Chapter 5), private renting (Chapter 6) and social housing (Chapters 7–10).

The identification of policy as a key driver of change in housing does not mean that it has been the sole driver. Changes in the wider economic, political, demographic and social environment, including the impact of war, have had a profound effect. Changes in the structure of the housing market and the legacy from earlier periods of development are affected by public policy, but they also reflect the operation of the market and interactions between a number of factors. External factors such as economic and demographic change have exerted an independent and sometimes more powerful influence than policy on the shape and functioning of the housing system. This is exemplified by the 'Right to Buy' scheme (Chapter 5), the growing dependence of the social housing sector on private finance (Chapter 8), and the influence of local demographic and housing market change on social housing letting policies (Chapter 10). Economic and demographic factors are particularly important in the supply of new private housing and the different costs to users of similar types of older private housing in different markets (Chapter 13).

The importance of both policy and non-policy drivers of change and their continuous interaction suggests the need for a holistic explanation of housing and housing policy. The 'whole systems approach' to policy has gained considerable support in specific policy areas such as 'Supporting People' (Chapter 13). Another approach emphasizes the complex interplay of factors leading to stability or change, for example in relation to approaches to letting social housing (see Chapter 10). We shall return to explanations of policy change in the increasingly fragmented public policy environment in Chapter 14.

Chapter 2

The Origins of Housing Policy

Most accounts of housing policy in the UK link its development to nineteenth-century industrialization and urbanization (for example Gauldie, 1974; Merrett, 1979; Burnett, 1986; Malpass and Murie, 1999). The state and philanthropic organizations had taken action in the preindustrial era with Poor Law and alms house provision, but it was the scale and concentration of problems brought about by industrialization that gave rise to new housing legislation and policy instruments.

A higher standard of housing was necessary for two reasons. First, there was a need for a healthy population to provide the labour force for modern industry, and good-quality housing within easy reach of the new factories was essential for the effective working of the economy. Second, inadequate and unsanitary housing not only posed a risk to the health of those on low incomes, but also the failure to house the population adequately posed wider problems for society as a whole. The market had responded to the demand for housing following industrialization and urban growth by packing the new workforce into increasingly unsanitary accommodation with inadequate facilities. Without intervention the health of society and the efficiency of industry would be put at risk.

While these factors established the preconditions for policy they do not explain why policy took the form it did. International comparisons show that countries with similar preconditions developed different forms of housing provision underpinned by different legislation and different institutional and financial arrangements. The form of housing policy cannot be explained by need alone, nor by industrialization and urbanization. The additional factor is political action: arguing the case for intervention, political coalitions to make such arguments carry weight, action to change the national legislative and financial framework, action to develop and deliver policies and, at the local level, actions by organizations that make and deliver housing policy. Once we recognize the importance of political action it is also evident that the development of housing policy is embedded in wider social, institutional and historical contexts. The political coalitions that have influenced housing policy, wider aspects of public policy, and the development of the welfare state have differed among countries, as have the economic, cultural and demographic contexts. The institutions developed around housing have

13

been shaped by these factors and have in turn helped to shape political and policy debates. The distinctiveness of policy regimes reflects this process and contributes to shaping the alternative routes that policies are likely to take.

Any long-term historical account is faced with the problem of identifying significant dates that can be associated with systemic change. For the purposes of this book we have selected two key turning points that relate both to changes of government and to significant philosophical changes in the approach to housing policy, particularly in relation to public housing provision. The 1915–19 break point is selected because the introduction of rent control in 1915 signalled the start of a long period of regulation of private rents and the introduction of exchequer subsidies in 1919 heralded a long phase of growth of council housing. The year 1979 is selected as the second turning point because the ensuing decade was an era of privatization, individualization and demunicipalization, with the first decline in direct state provision of housing since 1919, a shift from subsidizing construction to assisting with rent payments and a change in the role of local authorities from housing providers to enablers. These turning points are some what arbitrary and there were important continuities in policy: for example the argument for exchequer subsidies and the growth of council housing before 1919, and changes to housing subsidies and the move towards a more residual housing policy prior to 1979.

Housing policy prior to 1915

The first tentative steps towards a housing policy were made in the period prior to 1915. What emerged fell far short of a coherent housing policy, but it did involve the development of public health measures and set the direction for what was to follow. Small, insanitary, ill-maintained dwellings were not a new phenomenon, but the problem was exacerbated by the increasing concentration of the population in towns and industrial areas. There was an explosion in the growth of industry and the migration of people in search of employment. Neither of these was phased or controlled, and there were no attempts to manage the consequences in terms of water supply and waste disposal. Local and national governmental institutions were not capable of responding to the needs created by rapid urbanization and industrialization. Nor did those in positions of administrative and political power regard it as natural that they should respond. Consequently industrial pollution of residential areas added to the problems arising from residential growth and the inadequacy of the housing stock.

The basis for the organization of housing provision was the private landlord. Poverty and bad housing conditions were inextricably linked, or as Merrett (1979, p. 4) puts it, 'The working class lived in slums because they could afford nothing else.' Affordable dwellings had poor water and sewerage services, and were small, damp, badly ventilated, deprived of daylight and sometimes structurally unstable. In areas of high demand (near to places of work), rents were driven up and considerable overcrowding resulted when people sublet their accommodation in order to pay the rent.

A state of inaction

In view of subsequent experiences, an important question is why a housing policy did not emerge sooner. Throughout Ireland, then part of the UK, an more interventionist housing policy and land reform were established well before 1915 in response to strong nationalist political demands and the land reform movement (Fraser, 1996). In mainland Britain, however, the government was unwilling to incur the costs and bear the responsibility of providing dwellings, intervene in the free market in housing or provide assistance that might encourage dependency and erode people's commitment to family and work. While the threat of civil disturbance and the need to sustain a productive work force subsequently influenced the development of a wider housing policy, the strongest nineteenth-century influence was the lack of adequate sanitation. This posed a real threat to the health of all classes, and the 'health of the towns problem' arose from the threat of cholera and other diseases, rather than concern about the inadequacies of housing provision. Gauldie (1974) argues that powers did exist to intervene to affect housing conditions, but were not used, that it was inefficiently, dishonestly or inadequately used, reflected the attitude of the administrators rather than inadequacies of the law.

While legislative reform was needed, existing powers could have been used to prevent the worst excesses of slum landlords. But these powers rested with a system of local government that had been devised prior to industrialization and the change in population distribution. In the nineteenth century local government was characterized by administrative confusion and a proliferation of *ad hoc* bodies with specific but limited responsibilities. Improvement commissions, highways boards, health boards and sanitary authorities often operated within different boundaries and were frequently in dispute with each other and with local councils over responsibility for specific tasks. Local councils did not make effective use of their powers in respect of cleansing and maintaining pure water supplies. Pressure from manufacturing interests as well as cupidity and corruption meant that councils chose to ignore matters that were within their control.

A report by the Royal Sanitary Commission in 1871 revealed that powers were not being used, and this was blamed on the permissive nature of the law, the absence of inspection and poor local administration. In the 1870s local government reorganization produced a more coherent and uniform structure, with increased responsibilities and fewer *ad hoc* bodies. Coordination by the central government was also improved through the creation of the Local Government Board in 1871 to manage services previously divided between departments. The Local Government Act of 1888 set up county councils, the London County Council and county borough councils. In 1894 urban and rural district councils were established to replace the old urban and rural sanitary authorities.

The Public Health Acts of 1872 and 1875 divided the country into sanitary areas, each with a medical officer of health who laid down standards, procedures for land purchase and legal machinisms for the abatement of nuisances. The Public Health Act of 1890 extended the 1875 Act and made councils responsible for the interior arrangement of houses: the ventilation of rooms, the paving and drainage of premises, segregation of the sexes, an adequate water supply for water closets, the structure of floors, hearths and staircases, the height of rooms and the designation of dwellings fit for human habitation. Councils also had the power to control the construction of houses and to govern their use and repair. Within a generation public health legislation went from scratch to a modern, comprehensive code that enabled local authorities to control housing conditions.

The Public Health Acts did not obviate the need for housing legislation. The Public Health Act of 1875, under which local authorities made their housing by-laws, and various local Acts that individual authorities used to undertake particular schemes provided housing powers. These powers were related to individual dwellings and did not extend to slum areas or combatting shortages and overcrowding by building new dwellings. Thus the need for a permanent housing authority remained unmet.

Towards a housing policy

As in subsequent periods, the Victorian approach to housing problems was not simply polarized between state and market, but also involved the voluntary sector. In the late nineteenth century there were various experiments to tackle aspects of the problem. From the 1830s a number of housing schemes were developed by investors who were willing to accept below-market rates of return for housing working-class tenants; these schemes have been described as 'philanthropy and 5 percent' (Ashworth, 1954, p. 67). While there were many types of provider, two main types are usually distinguished: charitable trusts endowed by wealthy individuals, such as George Peabody in London and Edward Guinness in London and Dublin; and limited-profit model dwelling companies, such as the Improved Industrial Dwellings Company founded by Sir Sydney Waterlow in London, who raised funds by issuing shares and loan stock that paid below-market dividends (Malpass, 1998).

Table 2.1 *Principal housing and public health legislation, 1848–1914*

1848 *Public Health Act*: established the General Board of Health and enabled local boards to be set up.

1851 *Labouring Classes' Lodging Houses Act*: first Act to permit local authorities to provide housing, but very widely ignored. *Common Lodging Houses Act* (amended in 1853): provided for control and monitoring of private common lodging houses.

1866 *Labouring Classes' Dwelling Houses Act*: permitted local authorities and model dwellings companies to borrow at cheap rates from the public works loans commissioners.

1868 *Artisans' and Labourers' Dwellings Act (Torrens Act)*: authorities given the power to demolish individual unfit houses. No compensation for owners and no municipal rebuilding (amended to provide compensation in 1879).

1872 *Public Health Act*: created urban and rural sanitary authorities throughout the country.

1875 *Artisans' and Labourers' Dwellings Improvement Act (Cross Act)*: permitted local authorities to purchase and clear areas of unfit housing. Local authorities permitted to build on the cleared sites, but had to sell within 10 years (amended in 1879 to limit compensation).

1875 *Public Health Act*: established principles for the purchase of land by local authorities and set up framework for the extension of local building by-laws.

1885 *Housing of the Working Classes Act*: consolidating Act.

1890 *Public Health Act*: extended the 1875 Act.

1890 *Housing of the Working Classes Act*: consolidated and amended earlier legislation. Part I dealt with areas of unfit and insanitary housing and rebuilding powers; Part II dealt with individual unfit houses; Part III dealt with local authority powers to build housing for general needs.

1900 *Housing of the Working Classes Act*: amended the 1890 Act to give the London metropolitan boroughs the power to use Part III of the Act (in addition to the London County Council).

1909 *Housing and Town Planning Act*: ended the obligation of the authorities to sell houses in redevelopment areas within 10 years. Authorized the authorities to prepare town planning schemes.

Source: Malpass and Murie (1999).

These experiments were limited in impact and failed to attract sufficient investment to make a real dent in the housing problem, particularly outside London. They were targeted mainly at better-off working-class people with more reliable wages. The dwelling style and management regime were generally unpopular. Merrett (1979, pp. 18–19) concludes that 'The most vital achievement of the philanthropic movement was its failure. It demonstrated for those who had eyes to see that laissez-faire contradictions were not to be resolved by laissez-faire responses.'

By the 1880s the problem of affordability had gained official recognition. The Royal Commission on the Housing of the Working Classes, appointed in 1884, concluded that 'through poverty, the failure of local authorities to protect their interests and the success of the landlord class in exploiting their need, the working people in the UK were as a class ill-housed to the point of destitution' (quoted in Gauldie, 1974, p. 289). The failure of both free enterprise and charitable endeavour strengthened the hand of the labour movement, which 'emerged to take a leading part in the agitation for better housing' (Wohl, 1977, p. 317).

This agitation resulted in a stream of legislation that gave powers to and later funding for local authorities to engage in direct housing provision. The Housing of the Working Classes Act of 1890 gave local authorities the discretionary power to build for general needs but did not provide subsidies that would make such housing affordable to the intended working-class clientele. The Housing and Town Planning Act 1909 authorized local councils to establish town planning schemes for specific areas of new development and to define density, road width and land use zones.

By 1915 some key elements of housing policy were in place and the structure of local government had been established. Councils had the power to replace slums and to build for general needs, arrangements had been made for municipal borrowing at favourable interest rates, and arrangements to compensate owners had been developed. However there was no duty to remove slums or to rehouse those displaced by demolition of insanitary homes. Where municipal housing was provided, rents were high. There was no obligation to subsidize rents by levying a charge on local ratepayers, although Merrett (1979) argues that some indirect subsidization took place by under-valuation of municipal housing sites.

Local responses to the new powers varied. In the period 1890–1914, 179 urban authorities received loan sanction to build. By 1914 local authorities had built only 24 000 dwellings nationally, just 500 of which were in rural areas (ibid.) Prior to 1915 housing policies tended to address the symptoms of the housing problem rather than its underlying causes. Without effective subsidy arrangements the poor did not benefit fully from attempts at improvement. For most of the nineteenth century, state intervention in the supply of housing was successfully resisted; shortages were apparent in many parts of the country and overcrowding was increasing. In short, 'no real reform in housing was achieved by legislation during the nineteenth century' (Gauldie, 1974, p. 240). Public health reforms had some impact but they were unable to address key problems on their own. This strengthened the case for a public housing policy to control the activities of private landlords and develop a subsidized housing service to break the link between poverty and bad housing.

The proposal for the subsidization of housing by the exchequer must be seen in this context. The first report calling for this was issued in 1909 (Wilding, 1972), but it was not until 1912 that the first bill was drawn up and it did not pass the committee stage. Other bills and proposals emerged in 1912–14. According to Wilding (ibid.), in 1914 the Liberal government was preparing legislation that would include grants to urban authorities for housing. It appears that the First World War delayed the introduction of exchequer subsidies and that the key factors leading to subsidies were not war and wartime pledges, or the impact of the rent control legislation of 1915, but political pressures prior to 1919 and the switch of investment away from the housing sector by those who had traditionally provided rented property.

An evolving housing policy: 1915–45

The First World War brought about major changes to society and housing in the UK. Social change arose from the expectations of those who had survived the carnage. Demands for housing were more strongly articulated and the state was now more inclined to respond. It was also necessary to address the backlog of housing production, which had been in decline for most of the decade before 1914 and had slowed further during the war. Wartime measures had embroiled the state in housing policy in ways that had not been envisaged and this period marked a turning point in housing policy and state intervention (Table 2.2).

Housing between the wars

A feature of the interwar period was extensive house building in both the public and the private sector. Private sector output was above 100 000 dwellings per year after 1925, and above 250 000 per year in 1934–38. Local authority output averaged a little more than 50 000 per year throughout the interwar period. This was very high compared with the pre-1914 municipal building rates, but private construction outstripped it, especially in the 1930s (Figure 2.1).

Rent control

The introduction of rent control in 1915 was a temporary measure to prevent profiteering by landlords during wartime, and is generally attributed

Table 2.2   *Principal housing legislation, 1915–39*

1915	*Increase of Rent and Mortgage Interest (War Restrictions) Act*: – rents and interest rates fixed at their August 1914 levels.
1919	*Housing and Town Planning Act (Addison Act)*: introduced exchequer subsidies for local authority houses. Local liability fixed at 1 d; exchequer met any remaining deficit. Withdrawn in 1921.
1919	*Housing (Additional Powers) Act*: extended subsidies to private builders of working-class housing.
1920	*Increase of Rent and Mortgage Interest (War Restrictions) Act*: continued principle of control but permitted certain increases.
1923	*Housing Act (Chamberlain Act)*: introduced a new subsidy with fixed exchequer liability and no mandatory rate contribution. Intended mainly to stimulate private builders. Withdrawn in 1929.
1923	*Increase of Rent and Mortgage Interest Restrictions Act*: Introduced decontrol of rent at next change of tenancy.
1924	*Housing (Financial Provisions) Act (Wheatley Act)*: introduced a new, higher subsidy with mandatory rate contribution. Withdrawn in 1933.
1930	*Housing Act (Greenwood Act)*: intended to promote slum clearance; new subsidy calculated on the number of people rehoused from clearance areas. Permitted local authorities to operate rent rebates.
1933	*Housing (Financial Provisions) Act*: withdrew subsidies for all new housing, except that for slum replacement. All authorities required to produce five-year clearance plans. *Rent and Mortgage Interest Restrictions (Amendments) Act*: extended decontrol.
1935	*Housing Act*: new subsidies to help relieve overcrowding. Local authorities required to operate one Housing Revenue Account, and permitted to pool rent and subsidies.
1936	*Housing Act*: major consolidating Act.
1938	*Housing Act*: introduced a single subsidy of £5.10s for slum clearance and relief of overcrowding.
1939	*Rent and Mortgage Interest Restriction Act*: reintroduced rent control on all but the highest-value properties.

Source: Malpass and Murie (1999).

to the Glasgow rent strike of 1915 and wider threats of civil disturbance (Melling, 1989). The Increase of Rent and Mortgage Interest (War Restrictions) Act of 1915 was only intended to continue until six months after the end of the war, but was maintained by legislation in 1919 and 1920. In 1920 the range of properties subject to control was extended.

Once rent control had been introduced it was not easy to remove. Doing so could lead to major rent increases, especially in areas suffering the

Figure 2.1 *Number of dwellings built in England and Wales, 1920–39*

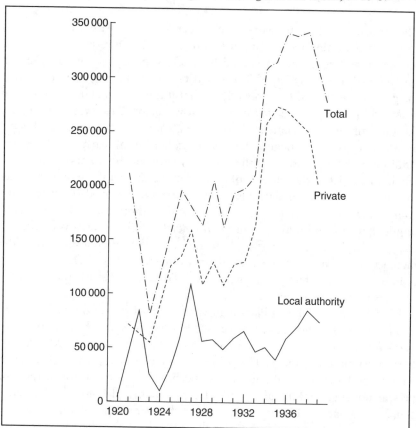

Source: Malpass and Murie (1999).

effects of economic depression, and the political consequences of this were not to be contemplated. In addition the fall in real wages during the war had reduced effective demand. Relaxation of controls would not necessarily affect shortages, but could contribute to social and industrial unrest.

Nevertheless in 1923 arrangements for decontrol on vacant possession were introduced. The changes in Scotland, England and Wales were similar, but there were significant differences in Northern Ireland due to political factors. Legislation in 1933 and 1938 further relaxed rent control but dwellings with the lowest rateable values remained under control. Finally, with the outbreak of the Second World War in 1939, decontrol by vacant possession was abolished and control was extended to virtually all privately rented housing. Rent control had become part of the landscape and had a long-term influence on investment behaviour by private landlords.

The emergence of council housing

The influence of growing working-class demands is apparent in a report in 1917 by a Committee of Inquiry into industrial unrest, which recommended that 'arrangements should be made of policy as regards housing' (quoted in Merrett, 1979, p. 32). Lloyd George famously declared during the general election of December 1918 that if the government was returned it would build 'homes fit for heroes'. However progress was slow due to disputes among government departments, and between them and local authorities. No significant steps were taken until early 1919, when Addison became president of the Local Government Board and Minister of Health. In 1919 further threats of unrest led the cabinet to announce a plan to build half a million dwellings over a three-year period. However this could only be achieved by involving local authorities, and this would require a means of limiting councils' financial liability. This was eventually achieved by an exchequer subsidy to make up the difference between the income from rents and the cost of providing the houses. Orbach (1977) argues that the key factor encouraging the Treasury to release the necessary funds was fear of Bolshevism.

The Housing and Town Planning Act of 1919 (the Addison Act) imposed a duty on local authorities to survey the housing needs in their areas, make plans for the provision of houses and, with the consent of the Ministry of Health, to build dwellings. The Ministry was also to approve rents, which were to be fixed by local authorities and based on the controlled rents of prewar housing, making allowances for the quality of houses and circumstances of tenants. This Act introduced exchequer subsidies to meet all the losses incurred by local authorities in excess of a specified local tax (in England and Wales the product of a one penny rate and in Scotland four fifths of that rate).

Demands for high-quality homes with three bedrooms, a parlour, separate bathroom and piped hot water were considered by the Tudor Walters Committee, which in 1918 made recommendations about estate layout and model house plans (Swenarton, 1981). An official housing manual issued to local authorities in 1919 provided guidance on minimum room sizes, cooking and heating arrangements and general design.

The cost of new housing was high in 1919 and 1920 as a consequence of inflation during the brief postwar economic boom. Councils competed in the open market for scarce materials and skilled labour, and rapidly escalating costs led to local authorities being accused of extravagance. This was the pretext for cutting the housing programme in July 1921. Because the government did not expect the private sector to respond sufficiently, temporary arrangements for public provision were still needed.

The remainder of the interwar period saw periodic subsidy revisions, with different schemes producing different quantities and qualities of council housing.

The Housing Act of 1923 (the Chamberlain Act) introduced a fixed-sum subsidy for new local authority and private working-class housing. Before building, local authorities had to convince the Ministry of Health that private enterprises did not want to undertake the work. More generous subsidies were available for approved slum clearance schemes. Local authorities also had the power to sell dwellings they had built and to provide and guarantee mortgages. The change from the Addison to the Chamberlain Act involved a switch from a deficit to a unit subsidy. The consequences of inefficiency or rising costs fell on local authorities.

The Housing (Financial Provisions) Act of 1924 (the Wheatley Act), introduced by the first Labour government, increased the level of subsidy and extended the repayment period from 20 to 40 years. This subsidy was not available to private enterprises and there was no requirement to prove that building did not compete with the private sector, but local authorities had to provide a subsidy from their rates of at least 50 per cent of the exchequer subsidy. Because average rents were fixed in relation to the controlled rents for prewar houses, a large rate subsidy was necessary.

From 1924 until 1929, when the Chamberlain subsidies were terminated (the Wheatley subsidies operated until 1933), local authorities could build under the Chamberlain Act – with a lower exchequer subsidy but no compulsory rate subsidy – or the Wheatley Act. In all 75 300 dwellings were built by local authorities under the former and 504 500 under the latter. This 'established the local authorities as part of the permanent machinery for providing working-class houses' (Bowley, 1945, p. 40).

Slum clearance

The Housing Act of 1930 (the Greenwood Act) marked a shift in policy focus from housing shortage to housing conditions, with attention now being given to slum clearance. All local authorities with populations in excess of 200 000 were required to produce five-year plans for slum clearance and replacement. 'Improvement Areas' could be declared where wholesale clearance was inappropriate and properties could be rehabilitated. Over a hundred statutory Improvement Areas were declared and substantial rehabilitation was completed, although some regarded this as a 'second best' method of dealing with slums.

The Greenwood Act was explicitly designed to rehouse lower-income tenants living in slum areas and unable to afford Wheatley Act rents. Councils were required to rehouse (or arrange rehousing for) all those displaced by slum clearance. More generous subsidies were provided for 40 years to cover the costs of each person rehoused, with an additional subsidy for the cost of acquiring and clearing sites. Local authorities were also required to make rate fund contributions and could fix reasonable rents and provide rent rebates. In urban areas the new subsidy exceeded the Wheatley subsidy when rehousing more than four persons. For the first time there was an explicit package in place to channel housing resources to lower-income households.

At the same time the government was moving the responsibility for building new homes for general needs to the private sector. Public spending was to be constrained to slum clearance, and general needs housing could only be built in exceptional cases (Gilbert, 1970). The Wheatley Act subsidy was abolished under the Housing Act of 1933. Further legislation in 1935 introduced a statutory duty for local authorities to survey overcrowding and provided limited subsidies for building to reduce overcrowding. But the definition of overcrowding excluded all but the severest cases and only 24 000 houses were built in the first four years of the implementation of this legislation (Bowley, 1945).

Between 1932 and 1939 the number of dwellings built each year by local authorities in slum clearance programmes rose from 2400 to 74 000. In total 265 500 dwellings were completed. Slum clearance was accompanied by a reduction of the size of new dwellings, thus bringing prices within the means of poorer households and reducing public expenditure. These lower-standard properties included utilitarian and ill-designed flats and estates on the edge of cities, where there was poor access to jobs, schools and community facilities.

As intended the private sector did pick up responsibility for general needs housing and built at very high rates between 1934 and 1939. However 74 per cent of these dwellings were intended for sale and only 15 per cent were for rental. These had a ratable value of £13 or less, which put them in the working-class market. (Bowley, 1945). Thus during a period when local authorities could have continued to build high-volume, high-quality homes and benefit from low construction costs and a low cost–income ratio, their role had shifted to housing those who the private sector could not, and moreover in lower-quality homes than under previous Acts.

Reaching poorer households

In the interwar years local authorities were building for households that would not otherwise obtain modern dwellings of a high standard. But for most of this period the ability of the poorest households to benefit from this was limited by the rent levels. Housing management practice involved eviction if rent arrears accumulated, and in order to avoid this a minimum income requirement was not uncommon in tenant selection. The switch to slum clearance ended this exclusion and improved the prospect of the poorest households obtaining council housing.

Local authorities were encouraged to build smaller, cheaper houses, to set 'reasonable' rents and to provide rent rebates for poorer tenants. In 1932 the Committee on Local Expenditure argued that instead of 'wasting' public money on subsidies for tenants who could afford an economic rent, subsidies should be used to provide lower rents for the poor. However, despite circulars to local authorities advising them to adopt this policy, 'a very large proportion of local authorities ignored the Ministry of Health's advice on the rent problem' (Bowley, 1945, p. 125). Local authorities still regarded better-off households as better potential tenants, and differential rents were unpopular among tenants because of means testing, and because assistance for low-income tenants meant higher rents for other tenants.

In 1935 the government introduced an important change to the rules governing council housing accounts. Previously the accounts for houses built under each Act had to be kept separate and had to balance. Under the 1935 Housing Act the authorities were required to consolidate all accounts into one Housing Revenue Account, which must be balanced annually. This meant that subsidies could be pooled to fund rebates to poorer tenants. Local reluctance to introduce a rebate scheme persisted, but one unanticipated effect – arising from inflation – was that the rents for new houses could be kept down by subsidizing them from surpluses accumulated by charging higher rents than needed for cheaper, older houses. Rent pooling emerged as a key means to facilitate new construction without the high rents or subsidies needed when each scheme had to cover its own costs, and this remained a significant advantage of council housing until new building was ended in the 1980s (Malpass, 1990).

On balance and despite these changes, in the interwar years council housing did not generally benefit the worst off. The exchequer subsidies were not large enough to bring rents within the reach of those in marginal economic situations. In addition the wages of tenants tended to be low and there were few people who did not need a subsidy. General poverty meant that a gap continued to exist between rents and wages. The central government preferred to reduce public expenditure than to respond to this. The only alternative was to make rate contributions above the statutory minimum and keep rents down. This did occur, especially in Scotland, but some local authorities viewed any rate subsidy as undesirable.

The policy legacy

During the interwar period housing policy paid more attention to quality, quantity and price. The provision of housing to the working class had shifted decisively from philanthropic organizations to local authorities, but by default the private rented sector continued to provide for many. The objectives of the policy framework established by the central government changed over time, reflecting political and economic developments. By the late 1930s local authorities were being manoeuvred into a more residual role, leaving general needs provision to the private sector. Nevertheless council housing consisted almost wholly of modern dwellings, most of which were much more attractive than those on offer in the private rented sector. Tenure transfers, clearance and renovation activities were changing the private rented sector, but it still compared unfavourably with council house tenancy and home ownership. At the same time a continued role was being played by the voluntary sector. Malpass (2000a) notes that a significant number of new housing societies were established in the early decades of the twentieth century, including the so-called 'front line' housing societies set up to improve slum housing, such as the William Sutton Trust (Garside, 2000) and COPEC in Birmingham (Gulliver, 2000). There was also significant growth in home ownership, facilitated by legislative and tax arrangements.

By 1938 the proportion of dwellings rented from private landlords had fallen to 58 per cent, compared with 90 per cent in 1900. Thirty-two per cent of dwellings were owner-occupied and 10 per cent were publicly owned. Over 50 per cent of owner-occupied dwellings had been built before 1919, and approximately one million rented dwellings had been sold to owner-occupiers in the period prior to 1938 (DoE 1977). According to Cullingworth (1966), in 1939 there was a rough balance between the number of houses and the number of families. Between 1919 and 1939, 4.1 million houses had been built. The net increase of about 3.7 million dwellings was accompanied by an increase of about 2.25 million households. Cullingworth concludes that 'the overall housing situation had improved very greatly' (ibid., p. 26). The housing shortage had been relieved and the condition of the dwelling stock improved by the addition of new council housing, private building and the removal of substandard dwellings.

By 1939 housing policy had taken a recognizably modern form and state intervention looked permanent. In spite of resistance to local authority housing, once established the exchequer subsidies had survived and local authorities had established a long-term role as housing providers. But other issues remained unresolved. Baths were not a statutory requirement in subsidized housing until 1923 (1936 in the case of non-subsidized housing) and space was reduced, especially after 1933. Changes to the subsidies had an effect on what was built. The average floor areas achieved in 1919–20 were never bettered in the rest of the interwar period, and in later years more non-parlour houses and more two-bedroom houses were built. Increased density, lower layout and design standards and cheaper finishes were all employed to save money. In 1927, 1929 and 1932 the government issued circulars calling on local authorities to build the cheapest type of house, and after 1930 standards fell further and more blocks of flats were built. The standard of these flats and their residential environment were far inferior to the spacious, leafy cottage estates of the early 1920s. In contrast to housing built with the full Wheatley subsidy, 'many of the estates built in the 1930s were to become the ghettos of the 1960s' (Merrett, 1979, p. 57).

Moreover considerable deprivation remained in the older private sector stock (Titmuss, 1950). In Hull in 1943 and Bootle in 1939, 40 per cent of houses were without baths. In York in 1939 about 66 per cent of working-class houses were without baths. In Stepney in 1939, 90 per cent of families had no bathroom. In Salford in 1943, 52 per cent of houses lacked baths. In Glasgow in 1944 about 50 per cent of the population had no bath and one third had to share a lavatory with anything up to six families. One third of all houses in the Scottish burghs and cities had no private water closet in (1944). In Birmingham in 1946 nearly 25 per cent of dwellings had no bathroom, nearly 33 per cent had no bath and 1 per cent lacked a separate lavatory. In rural areas in 1939 about 30 per cent of the population lived in houses that were not connected to or within easy access of a water main, and nearly 50 per cent of households were without a fixed bath in 1947.

A mature housing policy: 1945–79

As Figure 2.2 indicates there were four phases in housing production between 1945 and 1979:

- Between 1945 and 1953 the principal objective was to increase the supply of dwellings: slum clearance was held in abeyance and local authorities dominated housing construction.
- Between 1954 and 1964 high output continued but the contribution made by local authorities fell and private production expanded.
- In 1964 these was an increase in output, sustained for a short period.
- In the 1970s output was relatively low, heralding the policies of the 1980s.

Figure 2.2   *Number of dwellings built in the UK, 1949–79*

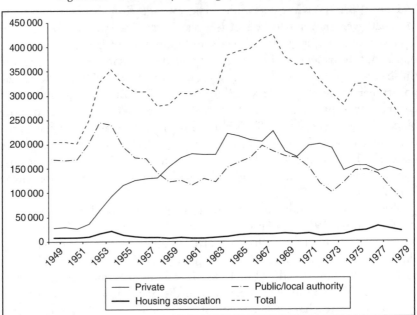

Source: Data from *Housing and Construction Statistics* (ODPM).

Housing in the welfare state

During the Second World War housing production was severely curtailed. Shortages associated with the redeployment of labour and materials away from house building and repair were exacerbated by severe bomb damage, resulting in evacuation and homelessness. Nearly four million houses in the UK were either damaged or destroyed and repair work on damaged dwellings was often only temporary. Unlike during the First World War there was a net population increase of a little over a million. Meanwhile 700 000 homes were lost and the housing stock was in poorer physical condition (Titmuss, 1950).

The postwar Labour government established a more comprehensive welfare state, including national insurance, a national health service and a national education system. It implemented some of the recommendations made by the civil servant William Beveridge in his wartime report on social insurance and allied services. Beveridge had named squalor as one of the 'five great evils' that his proposed reforms were designed to address: 'we haven't now anything like enough houses or good enough houses. Dealing with squalor means planning town and countryside and having many more and better houses' (Beveridge, 1943, p. 86). However his influential report, which had focused on the establishment of a national insurance system, had only an indirect impact on housing.

Malpass (2004) argues that although housing was a key part of the reconstruction plans it was not among the innovations associated with the welfare state during and after the Second World War. Rather than a radical new approach to housing a temporarily expanded role for local authorities was planned, with more generous exchequer subsidies until the major shortages occasioned by the war were over. At that point the part played by the market would increase. In practice this is largely what happened, although the share of the housing stock controlled by municipal authorities continued to increase until 1979.

To augment traditional building the erection of prefabricated dwellings – provided and owned by the central government but managed by local authorities – started in 1944, and 124 455 'prefabs' had been erected by the end of 1948. These, plus repair programmes for war-damaged dwellings, the continued requisition of property (until 1948) and the provision of some 20 000 temporary huts, were emergency measures. With the exception of the establishment of a Housing Trust to supplement local authority activities in Northern Ireland (Murie and Birrell, 1971) the major innovations were in town planning, land use and new towns.

The crucial decisions taken by the Labour government in 1945 were to maintain the wartime controls on private building and to charge local authorities with carrying out the building programme. As Minister of Health Aneurin Bevan put it: 'if we are to plan we have to plan with plannable instruments, and the speculative builder, by his very nature is not a plannable instrument... we rest the full weight of the housing programme upon the local authorities, because their programmes can be planned' (quoted in Donnison, 1967, p. 164).

The monetary value of the exchequer subsidy was trebled and legislation triggered an unprecedented rate of construction of high-quality housing. However the focus of policy was different, as expressed by Bevan:

> Before the war the housing problems of the middle-classes were, roughly, solved. The higher income groups had their houses – the lower income groups had not.... We propose to start at the other end ... to solve, first, the housing difficulties of the lower income groups ... we propose to lay the main emphasis of our programme upon building houses to let ... we shall ask Local Authorities to be the main instruments for the housing programme. (*Hansard*, vol. 414, col. 1222, 1945–6)

This energetic approach meant that local authority completions (excluding prefabricated and other temporary dwellings) rose from 3364 in 1945 to 190 368 in 1948. This compared favourably with progress after 1919 and the previous high point at 121 653 in 1939. However it was not sustained and economic crisis soon reduced building activity and housing quality. The Housing Act of 1949 introduced grants for the improvement or conversion of dwellings in the public and private sectors (Table 2.3). It also dropped the term 'working-class housing' as the remit for local authority building programmes, although this restriction had already been disregarded for some years (Nevitt, 1968).

In 1951 the new Conservative government raised subsidies to encourage even greater production. But once the target of 300 000 houses had been reached in 1955 the subsidies were reduced and by the end of 1956 they had been removed on all general needs housing other than one-bedroom flats for the elderly. As in the prewar period subsidies were shifted from general needs housing to slum clearance which had restarted in 1954. They were also used to influence the type of dwelling constructed, with higher subsidies available for blocks of flats of more than three storeys.

Towards a residual approach

According to Malpass (2004), 1954 was a key turning point, marking the end of the exceptional approach adopted after 1939 and a return to the market approach to housing. The Conservatives considered that the extraordinary shortages occasioned by war had been remedied: 'a national sufficiency of housing existed and a return to economic rents would allow housing policy to be directed at real problems instead of a larger and artificial and spurious shortage occasioned by rent restrictions' (Howe and Jones, 1956 p. 28). While Bevan's aspiration for housing no longer applied at the national level and the framework of national policy was changed, local variations in policy were allowed to continue (Griffith, 1966).

Measures to increase rents in both the public and the private sector were introduced. In the case of the private sector, the 1957 Rent Act decontrolled all dwellings with a rateable value of more than £40 in London and more than £30 in the rest of England and Wales. Other dwellings were decontrolled when let to a new tenant. In the case of the public sector, the Housing Subsidies Act of 1956 enabled rents to be increased to realistic levels and greater emphasis was placed on differential rent schemes. By 1964 realistic rent policies had had a marked impact on local practice, with almost 40 per cent of housing authorities operating rent rebate schemes, compared with 5 per cent in 1949 (Parker, 1967).

The decontrol of private rents in the 1957 Rent Act was presented as a measure to remedy underoccupation, immobility, underrepair, underinvestment and an irrational rent structure. However it was based on very limited information about who private landlords were and how they would respond, the number of properties that would be decontrolled, and the pattern of housing demand. One unintended consequence was that 'the removal of

Table 2.3 *Principal housing legislation, 1945–77*

1946	*Housing (Financial and Miscellaneous Provisions) Act*: raised level of subsidies and rate fund contributions.
1949	*Housing Act*: removed statutory restriction that limited public housing to the working classes. Introduced improvement grants.
1952	*Housing Act*: raised subsidies.
1954	*Housing Repairs and Rents Act*: restarted slum clearance and encouraged private sector improvement.
1956	*Housing Subsidies Act*: reduced subsidies for general needs housing. Rate fund contributions made optional. Subsidy structure encouraged high-rise building.
1957	*Housing Act*: major consolidating Act.
1957	*Rent Act*: decontrolled rents at next change of tenancy.
1958	*Housing (Financial Provisions) Act*: consolidating Act for financial matters.
1959	*House Purchase and Housing Act*: extended improvement grant system. Encouraged local authority mortgage lending.
1961	*Housing Act*: reintroduced subsidy for general needs housing, but at two rates.
1964	*Housing Act*: extended improvement grants. Established the Housing Corporation.
1965	*Rent Act*: introduced 'fair rents'.
1967	*Housing Subsidies Act*: introduced a new subsidy system that was more generous to local authorities.
1968	*Rent Act*: a consolidating Act.
1969	*Housing Act*: raised level of improvement grants. Introduced 'general improvement areas'.
1971	*Housing Act*: increased improvement grants in assisted areas.
1972	*Housing Finance Act*: introduced fair rents for council tenants. Replaced all existing subsidies with a new deficit subsidy system. Housing Revenue Accounts now permitted to generate a surplus. Mandatory rent rebate scheme.
1974	*Housing Act*: introduced 'Housing Action Areas' and expanded the remit of the Housing Corporation.
1974	*Rent Act*: gave security of tenure to tenants in furnished dwellings.
1975	*Housing Rents and Subsidies Act*: fair rents abandoned in the council sector. Rebate scheme retained. New interim subsidy arrangements to replace 1972 Act provisions.
1977	*Housing (Homeless Persons) Act*: placed a duty on local housing authorities to provide accommodation for homeless households and priority needs groups.

Source: Malpass and Murie (1999).

rent controls which took place between 1957 and 1964 hastened the process of transfer to owner-occupation and did little to improve the conditions of rented housing' (Donnison, 1967, p. 237). This encouragement of owner-occupation was aided by tax relief, which increased in value with rising income, the abolition of Schedule A tax in 1962, the development of option mortgages, leasehold reform, improvement grants and movements in house prices.

Another key change in this period was the construction of high-rise council housing. These blocks later assumed highly negative connotations and contributed to the delegitimization of council housing (Dunleavy, 1981). Again the subsidy system was a key driver of this shift, with the introduction of higher subsidies for blocks of flats of five storeys or more. However more complex factors underlay the change, including political pressure on larger urban authorities to build within their boundaries. In the 1950s and 1960s a coalition of interests resisted major overspill activity, and the need to build more homes within urban authority boundaries promoted the construction of high-rise blocks. While this was not logical in terms of cost, it was seen as a technological shortcut and was backed by some professional groups and the national government (ibid.). The era of high-rise building was quite short-lived. Technical failures were exposed when a block flats in Ronan Point, East London, collapsed in May 1968. However other criticisms had already emerged: the savings in land were negligible and the costs excessive. Architects became more critical of high-rise blocks, particularly in terms of their use as family housing and their establishment in peripheral locations that lacked community facilities and places of employment. The construction of very high blocks declined after 1970, while that of blocks of less than five storeys increased. In terms of completions, flats accounted for 23 per cent of all local authority and new town dwellings between 1945 and 1960, 52 per cent in 1965 and over 50 per cent until 1973.

There were more general reductions in the quality of new local authority housing in this period. Between 1945 and 1951 council dwellings were built to a higher standard than had been recommended by the Dudley Committee in 1944. For example the average area of a three-bedroom house was 37 per cent greater than it had been in 1934–39. In 1951 the Labour government advocated reductions in 'circulation space', and subsequent policy reduced living space. Between 1949 and 1953 the average floor area of three-bedroom dwellings fell by 13 per cent. Thus dwellings built by local authorities in the 1950s were considerably smaller than those built in the 1940s. With the publication of the Parker Morris Report in 1961, average dwelling size began to increase again. However the reassessment of overall dwelling-space standards had construction cost implications, for example an 11 per cent increase for a five-bedroom, two-storey dwelling. By 1964 only 14 per cent of new council dwellings included all the Parker Morris standards and 39 per cent met the new floor-space standards (Merrett, 1979).

Things began to change again in the 1960s, a decade in which poverty was rediscovered, significant immigration occurred from the Caribbean and South Asia, grass roots campaigns by churches and other groups drew attention to homelessness, leading to the formation of Shelter, and many new housing associations were established (see Chapter 9). The 1961 Housing Act reintroduced a general needs subsidy, and council house construction began to increase. Housing was a major issue in the 1964 general election, which brought Labour to power for the first time in 13 years. The new government's objective was to increase local authority housing production and adopt the Parker Morris standards. Higher subsidies were made available under the 1967 Housing Subsidies Act, and the latter also included measures to modify the effects of the Rent Act of 1957 and deal with the exploitation of private tenants by rogue landlords, as personified by Peter Rachman (Milner Holland Report, 1965). The Rent Act of 1965 introduced 'regulated' and 'fair' rents but held back from municipalization of the sector.

For a brief period housing output expanded, exceeding 400 000 in both 1967 and 1968, but wider economic problems caused the government to cut the programme as part of the package of public expenditure reductions that followed the devaluation of the pound sterling in November 1967. Public-sector completions reduced sharply after 1968, reaching a low of 88 000 in 1973. But there was no reduction in support for home ownership. The expansion of the public programme had been to meet exceptional needs:

> it is born partly of a short-term necessity, partly of the conditions inherent in modern urban life. The expansion of building for owner-occupation on the other hand is normal: it reflects a long-term social advance which should gradually pervade every region. (MHLG 7–8 1965)

A white paper published in 1968, *Old Houses into New Homes*, marked the end of the period of mass construction. The emphasis on improvement rather than redevelopment was apparent in the 1969 Housing Act, which introduced 'General Improvement Areas', and the 1974 Housing Act, which added 'Housing Action Areas'. In these areas, systematic rehabilitation and environmental improvement were to be stimulated by increased grant aid. Although presented as a switch of resources, this policy actually involved a major reduction of public investment in housing (Merrett, 1979).

In 1972 the Conservative government's Housing Finance Act and Housing (Financial Provisions) (Scotland) Act reaffirmed the 'realistic rents' policy. It was thought that the main obstacle to achieving the aim of 'decent house for every family at a price within their means, a fairer choice between owning a home and renting one, and fairness between one citizen and another in giving and receiving help towards housing costs' (DoE 1971) was the current structure of housing finance, and especially of subsidies for public sector housing. If rents in the public and private sectors were allowed to rise to their 'natural' level (but not a level inflated by scarcity), better use of the housing stock would result.

The Housing Finance Acts would remove local authority discretion in setting rents and granting rebates. Local authorities were required to raise rents in stages, and in England and Wales council rents were to be linked to the 'fair rents' introduced for private tenancies by the Rent Act of 1965 – the estimated market rent that a dwelling would command if supply and demand were broadly in balance in the area. For the first time the rent to be paid by council tenants was not related to the cost of providing, managing and maintaining council houses. The fair rent principle was not applied in Scotland, where in general rents in the private sector were so low that linking council house rents to them would almost certainly have resulted in a reduction of rents and therefore in the rent income of local authorities. Thus the rents for Scottish council houses were to increase, phased in the same way as in England and Wales, but by sufficient amounts to bring local Housing Revenue Accounts into balance by 1975–76. Linked to the increase in rents, a mandatory national system of rent rebates for council tenants was introduced. The size of the rebates available to tenants took account of need, income, family size and composition. The legislation of 1972 completed the abandonment of the fixed-unit subsidies established in 1919.

The 1972 Act would have increased rents, reduced subsidies and placed welfare costs on tenants as a whole. However it did not remain in force long enough to have its intended impact. The Labour government that came into office in February 1974 introduced a rent freeze the following month and prevented further progress towards 'fair rents'. Then the Housing Rents and Subsidies Act of 1975 restored local authorities' power to fix reasonable rents. It retained the mandatory rent rebate scheme and used the subsidy level operating in 1975 as a base for subsidy calculation. In this way the new scheme retained the principle of a single unified subsidy that was related to the costs incurred. This system was a substitute for the fundamental reform of housing finance described by Anthony Crosland (secretary of state for the environment in 1974–76) as a 'dog's breakfast' (quoted in Harloe, 1978). The Act of 1975 was temporary and new proposals were promised. In 1977 the housing policy review (DoE, 1977; SDD, 1977) adopted a 'modifying' rather than a fundamental approach. Proposals for revision of the subsidy system were included in Housing Bills introduced in 1979 and formed the basis of the new subsidy scheme introduced when a Conservative government replaced Labour later that year.

The Labour government also introduced new arrangements for housing capital expenditure. In an attempt to control public expenditure at a time of high inflation and high and volatile interest rates, the government introduced cash limits to fix a maximum level of spending by each authority. These replaced the 'volume' targets, which had related to numbers of dwellings rather than levels of expenditure. A system of annual local authority 'bids' and central government 'allocations' had been introduced for improvement expenditure under the 1974 Housing Act. In 1976 the secretaries of state for Scotland, England and Wales extended this approach to all capital spending through similar Housing Investment Programmes (England and Wales) and Housing Plans (Scotland), beginning in 1977–78. These required all local authorities to prepare an annual programme for the next four years. There would be an annual capital allocation, and this would set the cash limit within which they could spend without being subject to detailed scrutiny by the centre. Although the system was presented as an increase in local autonomy and was generally welcomed as such, in practice it constituted an extension of central control and was used to bring about substantial cuts in investment.

The postwar period discussed in this section saw several important developments in housing. In the 20 years between the wars local authorities had built over 1.3 million dwellings, well under half the total built in the private sector, but in the 20 years after 1945 they built over 2.9 million, nearly a million more than the private sector. To this extent housing was part of the expanding welfare state and the decommodification that took place in the postwar period. From the 1950s it shared in the steady erosion of the welfare settlement presaging the aggressive privatization drive in the 1980s.

During the 1970s inflation, rising interest rates and new orthodoxies in public expenditure meant that financial instruments replaced production subsidies in the politics of housing. The subsidies on new council houses had been raised in 1967, and assistance to home owners through tax relief on mortgage interest had risen with the growing number of mortgagors, rising house prices and the movement of interest rates. Between 1967/68 and 1976/77 relief to mortgagors rose by 146 per cent in real terms, while subsidies in the public sector rose by 107 per cent (Lansley, 1979).

As governments in the 1960s and 1970s reduced and reoriented expenditure there was a steady centralization of policy and loss of local autonomy. At the same time, as home ownership expanded the institutions that managed that sector moved into sharper focus. The new governance of housing was less about central–local government relations and more about the part played by private-sector institutions, such as building societies, and the voluntary sector through housing associations.

At the end of the 1970s housing conditions reflected the enormous improvement afforts made in the previous decades (Table 2.4). Overcrowding

Table 2.4   *Households unsatisfactorily housed, England and Wales, 1951–76 (thousands)*

	1951	1961	1971	1976
Multi-person shared households	1442	582	380	275
Single-person shared households	430	448	440	375
Concealed households[1]	935	702	426	360
Overcrowded households[2]	664	415	226	150
Households in dwellings below standard[3]	7500	4700	2846	1650

Notes: 1. Married couples or one-parent families living as part of another household. 2. Living at a density of above 1.5 persons per room. 3. Unfit or lacking one or more basic amenities.
Sources: DoE (1977); Lansley (1979).

(more than 1.5 persons per room) had fallen from 18.6 per cent in 1931 to 2.9 per cent in 1971, not only as a result of changes in family size but also because of the marked improvement in space standards. The standard of new buildings in the public sector may have fluctuated but it was consistently better than in older housing stock and speculative developments. Lighting and ventilation had improved enormously, back-to-back building had ended and from 1936 all new houses were built with a fixed bath, washbasin and internal WC.

Conclusion

The history of housing policy until 1979 can be depicted as the modernization of housing tenure. Table 2.5 highlights the decline of the private rented sector through redevelopment and transfer to owner occupation. The public

Table 2.5   *Housing tenure in Britain, 1914–79 (percentage of all households)*

	Public rented	Owner-occupied	Private rented*
1914	< 1	10	89
1945	12	26	62
1951	18	29	53
1961	27	43	31
1971	30	50	20
1979	32	55	13

* Including housing associations.
Source: Adapted from Malpass and Murie (1999).

sector expanded from some 20 000 dwellings in 1914 to about six million in 1979, with the most rapid growth occurring in the period 1945–56.

Private renting had few advocates and the evidence (sometimes dramatic) of the failure of this tenure made it no one's favourite. Home ownership was increasingly promoted as natural and as bringing benefits to the family and society. For a considerable period – from before 1919 to the 1970s – it was possible to support the growth of home ownership without restricting the growth of council housing, and both expanded at the expense of private rented accommodation. By the 1970s there was much less scope for the private rented sector to be further squeezed and the politics of housing tenure entered a new phase. By then council housing, which had always been treated with suspicion by some (see Olechnowicz, 1997), had acquired negative connotations, particularly in the case of high-rise blocks.

Housing associations were promoted as a 'third arm' of housing policy from the 1960s onwards, and were increasingly seen as complementing local authority provision by catering for special needs and aiding area renewal. Their role was boosted by the introduction of a generous public subsidy regime under the 1974 Housing Act, and their annual output of new homes reached 40 000 across Britain between 1977 and 1979 (Malpass, 2000a). Nevertheless they still accounted for only 2 per cent of all dwellings in England and Scotland and 1 per cent in Wales by the time the Thatcher government was elected in 1979. The key historical role of local authorities had been to increase the supply of housing and enhance its quality. While this had not always benefited the poorest groups it was redistributive and provided high-quality housing at less than market prices. But by 1979 the political support for council housing was weaker than it had been for at least 60 years. Council housing was no longer a state of the art tenure catering principally for the affluent working class and the private rented sector was no longer the point of comparison for most households. The failings of council housing and the promises of home ownership exerted a stronger influence than in the past. Both were partly generated by policy, and the next phase of the modernization of housing and housing tenure was a policy platform for the Conservative government elected in 1979.

Chapter 3

Housing under the Conservatives, 1979–97

The successive Conservative governments between 1979 and 1997 brought about marked changes in housing policy and the provision of housing in the UK. These changes included the promotion of home ownership, privatization, deregulation and a generally antimunicipal approach. However there were also important continuities from earlier periods. The reduction of public expenditure on housing had commenced in 1976 and the concern to keep spending under control was already embedded in housing policy through the adoption by the previous Labour government of cash limits, Housing Plans (Scotland) and Housing Investment Programmes (England and Wales). No equivalent measures were taken to control housing expenditure that fell into other programmes (for example Housing Benefit expenditure accrued to social security expenditure) and there was a growth of tax relief associated with home ownership. Rather than develop a coherent, unified financial framework for the provision of housing the government continued to operate a partitioned housing finance system with very different arrangements for different tenures.

The period 1979–97 saw the end of the approach to housing that had typified the post-1945 period. Earlier changes had eroded the position of housing in the welfare state, but it was only after 1979 that the post-welfare-state role of housing was established. This involved an increased commitment to market provision and a move from a needs-based housing policy (directed at everyone with a housing need irrespective of income) to an affordability-based approach (directed at those whose incomes were too low to afford market housing).

During the latter years of the Conservative governments the tax advantages associated with home ownership came under significant attack. The Conservatives' ideological favouring of home ownership, which had characterized their electoral and political strategies in the earlier years, was modified. Deregulation of the private rented sector had not resulted in a marked increase in the housing supply or investment in this sector, and the Housing Benefit system had incurred considerable additional costs. At the same time a crisis in the owner-occupied sector following the boom period of 1986–89 raised questions about the sustainability of home ownership in a changing economic and labour market environment.

Eighteen years of active centralization and diminution of the importance of housing policy resulted in a fragmented housing system with
dramatic differences between tenures, between urban and rural areas, and
between estates and communities. Growing problems related to concentrated deprivation, marginalized council estates and affordability were
partly attributable to housing policy. By the end of the period the traditional approaches to housing policy were still out of favour but the use of
planning and urban policies as part of a more holistic approach was being
promoted.

The years of Conservative government brought a number of key changes.
On the one hand housing became a less important policy area for the
government, and new building by local authorities and new towns fell to
the lowest peacetime level since 1920. On the other hand the programme
of council house sales was the government's largest privatization venture
and the largest single source of capital receipts. This period also saw
continuous growth in home ownership and regulatory changes to facilitate
this (Table 3.1). There was deregulation of the private rented sector and
erosion of private tenants' rights. There were significant changes in the
nature, finance and role of housing associations. There was a real

Table 3.1   *Principal housing and related legislation, 1979–97*

1980	*Housing Act and Tenants' Rights, etc (Scotland) Act*: introduced 'Right to Buy', tenants' charter, new housing subsidy system and changes to rent Acts.
1980	*Local Government Planning and Land Act*: changes to local government finance (England and Wales).
1982	*Social Security and Housing Benefits Act*: established Housing Benefit system.
1984	*Housing and Building Control Act and Tenants' Rights etc. (Scotland) Amendment Act*: extended and tightened 'Right to Buy'. *Housing Defects Act*: obligation placed on local authorities in respect of sold defective dwellings.
1985	*Housing Act*: consolidating Act (England and Wales). *Housing Associations Act*: consolidating Act (England and Wales). *Landlord and Tenant Act*: consolidating Act (England and Wales).
1986	*Building Societies Act*: enabled building societies to own and invest in housing directly and to compete with other financial institutions. *Housing and Planning Act Housing (Scotland) Act*: increased 'Right to Buy' discounts (but Lords' amendment excluded dwellings suitable for the elderly). Facilitated block sales of estates. *Social Security Act*: modifications to the Housing Benefit scheme.
1987	*Housing (Scotland) Act*: *Landlord and Tenant Act*: consolidating Act.

Table 3.1   (*Continued*)

1988	*Housing Act*: deregulation of private renting. New financial arrangements for housing associations Tenants' Choice and Housing Action Trusts introduced (England).
1989	*Local Government and Housing Act*: new local authority rent and subsidy systems. Changes to urban renewal policy (England and Wales).
1990	*National Health Service and Community Care Act*: new arrangements for care in the community as alternative to institutional/residential care.
1992	*Local Government Act*: extended Compulsory Competitive Tendering to housing management, introduced performance measurement.
1993	*Leasehold Reform, Housing and Urban Development Act*: enabled leaseholders to acquire freehold interest in their property. Rent to mortgage scheme.
1996	*Housing Act*: new regulatory framework for registered social landlords. Amendments to Housing Benefit, tenants' rights and homelessness.
1996	*Housing Grants, Construction and Regeneration Act*: amendments to improvement and repair grant systems. Abolition of mandatory grants.

Source: Malpass and Murie (1999).

increase in rents in all sectors, and general subsidies that had benefited all council tenants were largely replaced by individual means-tested subsidies for all types of rented housing.

The evolution of Conservative housing policies

This section summarizes the trends in new housing construction and key housing legislation under the Conservative governments of the 1980s and 1990s. Housing policy in this period went through four phases. After the 1979 election the first phase began with vigorous implementation of policies that had been worked out in opposition in the late 1970s, focusing mainly on the promotion of home ownership. After 1986 the second phase involved the development of a rented housing strategy. After 1989 economic difficulties led to some unexpected problems in the housing sector and the third phase of policy, which focused on reviving the housing market. The final years of Conservative rule saw renewed attention to the rental sector, with stock transfers and the implementation of a regeneration policy following a housing white paper in 1995 and the Housing Act of 1996.

Figure 3.1 shows that private sector housing construction grew during the economic boom in the 1980s but reduced during the recession of the

Figure 3.1   *Number of dwellings built in England and Wales, 1979–96*

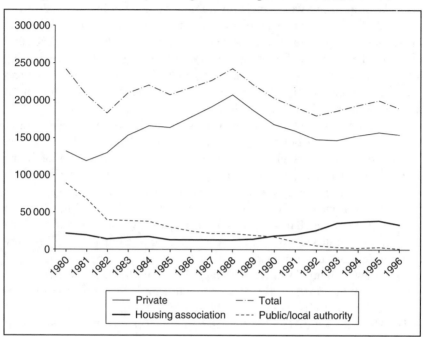

Source: Data from *Housing and Construction Statistics* (ODPM).

early 1990s. Over the period as a whole public housing construction fell to almost zero. Housing association output remained steady until the early 1990s, after which it increased but failed to compensate for the loss of public sector building.

The first phase: privatization, home ownership and deregulation

The Conservative manifesto of 1979 referred to housing under the heading 'Helping the family'. The importance attached to housing policy was apparent from the one and a half pages devoted to it in the manifesto – more than for social security, education, health and welfare, and the elderly and disabled (Conservative Party, 1979). The manifesto emphasized home ownership, the sale of council houses and reviving the private rented sector. While the primacy given to home ownership was not new, the specific policies designed to achieve it marked a break with previous policy and with local autonomy. The absence of reference to homelessness or policies for the council sector (other than the sale of council housing) was striking.

Housing was not an area of policy that would be developed in response to evidence of need but was principally about extending home ownership and the role of the market. This manifesto and subsequent ministerial statements largely ignored planning and projection of housing need and eschewed the language of housing shortage and crisis favoured by the housing lobby. They referred to 'what the country can afford', to underused resources (especially empty housing) and to the capacity of the private sector to meet needs and aspirations (Murie, 1985).

When the Conservative Party won the general election of 1979 it considered that its housing policies, and in particular its 'Right to Buy' scheme, had contributed to its electoral success. Hence the expansion of home ownership remained a key element of its policy and formed part of its approach to a property-owning democracy and popular capitalism in which home ownership was viewed as a means of broadening access to capital assets rather than simply as a housing policy. The transfer of assets through these policies proved to have a long-standing impact on UK society and politics, and underpinned the 'asset-based welfare' approach favoured by the New Labour government after 1997. For the Conservatives these policies had the further advantage of significantly boosting the government's capital receipts (Forrest and Murie, 1988).

The Housing Act of 1980 in England and the Tenants' Rights (Scotland) Act of 1980 introduced the right for public sector tenants to buy their homes, new tenancy arrangements for public and private tenants and new arrangements for the subsidization of council housing. The latter facilitated a reduction of the exchequer's general assistance subsidy. Consolidation of the rent rebate system into a new Housing Benefit system in 1982 formed the other part of a strategy to shift away from general 'bricks and mortar' subsidies towards individual subsidies based on household income.

After the 1983 general election there was a period of consolidation. Earlier measures were built upon: enhancing discounts available under the Right to Buy, dealing with the problems of people who had bought defective council houses, enabling block sales of council estates to private developers and other landlords, and modifying the Housing Benefit scheme. Measures related to financial deregulation and building societies were principally driven by considerations about the operation of the financial market, but the desire for private sector institutions and building societies to play a more active part in housing provision was also important. The Building Societies Act of 1986 enabled building societies to compete equally with the clearing banks in the personal finance sector and to offer unsecured loans and additional home-buying services, including estate agency services, conveyancing and insurance. This legislation led to major changes in mortgage lending in the UK. A number of the larger building societies converted into banks, and mergers and takeovers became common. For example during the early 1990s Abbey National converted to a bank and took over the National and Provincial Building Society; the Cheltenham and Gloucester Building Society was acquired by Lloyds Bank; and the Halifax and the Leeds Building Societies merged and subsequently became a bank. These institutional changes were accompanied by growth in competition and the development of a larger range of mortgage products.

The second phase: rental housing

By 1987 the narrow focus of first-phase policies was attracting widespread criticism, particularly in relation to housing finance and the failure to provide incentives for new building, repair and maintenance, and mobility within rented housing. This failure had also been the subject of a number of enquiries – for example one established by the Archbishop of Canterbury in 1985 and another chaired by the Duke of Edinburgh (National Federation of Housing Associations, 1986).

In response the government showed renewed concern about the finance and availability of rented housing. There were bold statements about the right to rent and for tenants to be able to choose different types of landlord, providing a potential means of breaking the municipal housing monopoly. While the chosen instruments for this strategy, 'Tenants' Choice' and Housing Action Trusts, had a very limited impact in practice, the aim of reducing municipal landlordism was substantially advanced by a strategy developed by local authorities themselves – the Large Scale Voluntary Transfer of council housing to housing associations (see Chapter 9).

New legislation and financial arrangements for housing associations treated them as part of the private sector in anticipation that access to private funds would facilitate an increased supply of rented housing. Using these bodies to spearhead the new rental strategy would also allow local authorities to be sidelined, and this was consistent with government's distaste for the municipal housing tradition. The other plank to the rented housing strategy, advanced by the Housing Act of 1988, was to revive private renting through the introduction of shorthold and assured shorthold tenancies (see Chapter 6).

These new institutional arrangements progressively took hold over the next 15 years. Local authorities became less important in providing new rented housing and determining future housing policy. They were recast as enablers rather than direct providers of housing, with a larger housing provision role being taken on by housing associations and private land-lords, who were able to charge higher rents while tenants could apply for rent subsidies through the Housing Benefit system (see Chapter 8).

The third phase: housing in recession

As this renewed focus on rental housing was developing the government was faced with a major crisis with its chosen policy priority: the promotion of home ownership. It was forced to make a rapid response to problems arising from economic recession and exacerbated by the deregulation of housing finance. The Building Societies Act of 1986 had led to lending on demand and competition for borrowers had resulted in loans for increasingly higher proportions of property value and much higher multiples of income than hitherto, with limited assessment of borrowers' job security and ability to make payments. Early notice by the Chancellor of the Exchequer of a change in taxation policy – abolishing the right of each of two people jointly buying a house to qualify for tax relief on interest payments on the first £30 000 of any loan – was the trigger for an unprecedented glut of new borrowing and resulted in the inflation of house prices in 1988. Many of the people who hurried to purchase a house in order to qualify for double tax relief in a three-month period in 1988 may have overextended themselves financially at a time of rapidly rising house prices and interest rates.

This tax-induced mini boom came at the end of a two-year period in which employment and incomes were rising and there had been an explosion of consumption, credit and house prices. The boom in house prices had commenced in 1986 and spread outwards from the overheated economy of the South-East. The booming market was also evident in the growth of private sector house building (from 180 000 in Britain in 1986 to 216 000 in 1988). Measured against total personal disposable income, mortgage debt rose steeply during the early to mid 1980s and began to level off in 1988.

This boom was unsustainable and contributed to the circumstances that caused unemployment to rise and an economic recession to develop. A home ownership crisis emerged after August 1988 and there was a sustained period of depressed housing market activity. The interest rate on new mortgages rose from around 9.5 per cent in 1988 to 15.4 per cent in February 1990 and remained at that level – the highest on record – until October 1990, when it fell to 14.5 per cent. The impact of these developments on individual home owners varied, but mortgage arrears and repossessions increased. Table 3.2 charts the impact on housing market activity. The number of transactions fell considerably after 1988 and this was followed by a fall in house prices and an increase in the number repossessions. The trend in mortgage arrears followed a similar pattern. This combination of factors was self-reinforcing. Extensive repossession depressed house prices, which made it financially unviable for people to sell and this depressed the number of transactions. Although the number of

Table 3.2   *Activity in the home ownership sector, 1986–98*

	Number of residential property transactions in England and Wales (thousands)	Average house prices in the UK (mix adjusted index: 1993 = 100)	Number of repossessions in the UK
1986	1600	61.8	24 090
1987	1744	72.1	26 390
1988	1990	90.6	18 510
1989	1467	109.5	15 810
1990	1283	108.1	43 890
1991	1225	106.6	75 540
1992	1032	102.6	68 540
1993	1114	100.0	58 540
1994	1168	102.5	49 190
1995	1047	103.2	49 410
1996	1122	106.9	42 560
1997	1296	116.9	32 770
1998	1220	129.7	33 820

Sources: Adapted from Malpass and Murie (1999), with data from Wilcox (1997, 2002).

repossessions began to fall after 1991 it remained at a historically high level throughout the period. House prices recovered only slowly after 1994 and did not exceed the 1989 level until 1997.

This led to the emergence of negative equity, in which the value of properties declined to the point where it was less than the outstanding mortgage. For people in this situation, selling the property would not clear the debt outstanding on it. In 1989 there were estimated to be 230 000 households in the UK with negative equity. This figure rose to 1 768 000 in 1992 and it remained at over 1 000 000 until 1996. The worst cases of negative equity were in the South of England, with Scotland and Northern Ireland largely escaping (Wilcox, 1993). In response lenders, local authorities and housing associations participated in mortgage rescue schemes. English housing authorities were allowed to use unspent capital receipts to increase market activity, and the Housing Corporation established a Housing Market Package, under which 27 selected housing associations had 100 days to purchase 18 000 houses on the open market or off the shelf from private developers in an attempt to revive the market (Malpass, 2000a). The whole episode constituted a dramatic, unplanned intervention in the operation of the home ownership market, but the costs of policy intervention for the government and lenders were very low and the immediate impact was limited (Foster, 1992; Ford and Wilcox, 1992; Forrest and Murie, 1994).

The final phase: 'our future homes'

In the general election of 1992 the Conservative Party's manifesto referred to housing in terms of the right to own and the Citizens' Charter. The main proposals were set out in a one-page statement that stressed support for the further expansion of home ownership and the encouragement of a strong private rented sector. There were proposals for a new 'rents to mortgages' scheme and 'commonhold' legislation, which would give residential leaseholders in blocks of flats the right to acquire the freehold of their block. There was a greater focus on housing need and social housing than hitherto, and the manifesto referred to increasing the supply of affordable housing, tackling homelessness and rough sleeping, and extending choice through the Tenants' Charter and Large-Scale Voluntary Transfers.

The tackling of homelessness and the problem of affordable housing followed steps taken in earlier years, including the 'Rough Sleepers Initiative', which had funded schemes to reduce the incidence of people sleeping on the streets. However because of the economic recession the government's first priority was to suppress public expenditure. Its focus shifted to social security expenditure, which had been growing rapidly, partly as a result of the earlier policies to encourage housing association provision and private renting and allowing Housing Benefit to take the strain of rising rents. Income support payments for mortgage costs had also increased significantly. The combined cost of rent rebates and rent allowances in Britain had increased from £3.4 billion in 1986/87 to over £11.4 billion in 1996/97. In that period rent rebates had risen from £2.4 billion to £5.6 billion and rent allowances from £996 million to £5.8 billion. In addition to these sums, income support associated with housing costs had increased from £351 million to £867 million. Thus while public housing expenditure had fallen, housing-related social security expenditure had increased by a substantial amount. What suited the Department of the Environment did not suit the Department of Social Security.

The government began to institute Housing Benefit reforms to provide tenants and landlords with incentives to economize on rents. Henceforth Housing Benefit would not in all cases cover 100 per cent of the rent charged but would take account of regional average rents. It also shifted its stance dramatically in relation to social security expenditure for home owners. It had previously allowed income support for mortgage interest to be paid directly to lenders; expenditure on this had increased from £286 million in 1988/89 to £1.2 billion in 1993/94. It now proposed that private insurance cover should be used to protect home owners, rather than income support. Despite the fact that building societies were unhappy with this arrangement, the changes were introduced in 1995.

An even greater policy change in this period was the reduction of Mortgage Interest Tax Relief (MIRAS). Despite assertions that the growth of home ownership remained an important goal there was a reassessment of the need for MIRAS to achieve this. The value of MIRAS had increased enormously with rising house prices and interest rates in the late 1980s, although the ceiling on the amount of mortgage qualifying for relief had been retained at the figure introduced in 1983 (£30 000) and in 1988 the government had ended double tax relief and linked the ceiling for tax relief to the dwelling rather than the person. In 1991 tax relief was limited to the basic rate of tax.

In 1993 the chancellor of the exchequer announced that mortgage interest tax relief would be removed in stages and the rate of tax relief would be reduced from 20 per cent to 15 per cent, with further reductions to be made at the rate of 5 per cent a year, as previously announced. However because of the extended depression in the housing market the chancellor came under pressure to modify this position, and in June 1994 he announced that Mortgage Interest Tax Relief would not be reduced below the 15 per cent rate during the life of the current parliament. Nevertheless the failure to raise the maximum figure for relief and falling interest rates eroded the amount of tax relief and reduced its most regressive aspects. At the same time house prices in many parts of the country had risen well above the £30 000 maximum eligible for relief. Mortgage interest tax relief was no longer important to affluent purchasers or to lenders, so its reduction did not arouse fierce opposition. Thus the environment was favourable for the further erosion of tax relief or its removal.

The final phase of the Conservatives' housing policies for England and Wales was set out in a June 1995 white paper, *Our Future Homes*, which emphasized choice, opportunity and responsibility. There would be continued attention to the promotion of home ownership, the revival of private renting and the transfer of public sector housing to other landlords. A key aim was to increase home ownership by 1.5 million over the next decade, with new provisions for housing association tenants to buy their own homes through a voluntary scheme. Housing Investment Trusts would be established to encourage financial institutions to invest in the private rented sector, which would also be assisted by further deregulation and the introduction of pre-tenancy determination of rents eligible for Housing Benefit.

Serious attention was given to encouraging local authorities in urban areas to transfer housing stock. It was recognized that such transfers would not be viable unless funds were made available to address the negative value of properties and the severe backlog of disrepair. The Estate Renewal Challenge Fund (ERCF) was established to provide dowry funding to enable estate-based transfers in some inner-city and deprived neighbourhoods (see Chapter 9). Encouragement for whole stock transfers was provided by a new governance option that allowed 'registered social landlords' (a new name introduced in the Housing Act of 1996 for all bodies regulated by the Housing Corporation) to increase the maximum proportion of local authority representatives on their boards from 20 per cent to 49 per cent. These bodies could also have up to 49 per cent tenant representation, but at least a third had to be independent persons to enable the companies to operate outside the public expenditure collar. Both of these mechanisms proved attractive to urban authorities that had previously eschewed transfers. Twenty-three local authorities took advantage of the ERCF to transfer 44 500 homes to 38 new landlords. Meanwhile Local Housing Companies with a governance structure of one third tenants, one third local authority representatives and one third independents became the norm for urban whole stock transfers.

Other measures in the white paper were aimed at reducing empty housing, transforming large, poor-quality public housing estates, creating mixed communities in the heart of cities, reforming renovation grant legislation and amending the duty on accommodation for homeless people. In a further threat to local authorities' direct landlord role, in 1996 housing management was added to the functions to which Compulsory Competitive Tendering applied (see Chapter 10). Finally, the whole approach to housing policy and renewal was linked to the agenda for urban policy and urban deprivation. A Single Regeneration Budget Challenge Fund was established to replace a large number of more specific programmes. Bids for funding from this source could include substantial housing elements but the agenda was shifting to a more broad based multidisciplinary approach (see the section on economic regeneration later in this chapter).

The Housing Act of 1996 introduced a new regulatory framework for registered social landlords, but it did not include the proposal in the 1995 white paper to enable private companies to compete with housing associations for grants. This controversial proposal, however, was eventually taken up by the Labour government in the Housing Act of 2004 (see Chapter 4).

The 1996 Act also introduced registration schemes for Houses in Multiple Occupation and made a number of detailed changes to landlord and tenant law, particularly in relation to assured tenancies and leasehold reform. It provided tenants with the right to acquire their housing association dwellings if these had been built with public funds. It established introductory tenancies for local authorities, gave councils new powers to tackle antisocial behaviour and gave the secretary of state the power to regulate local authority waiting lists and housing allocations. Finally, it amended the duty of local authorities to provide suitable accommodation to homeless people.

After 16 years in government the Conservative Party appeared to have come to terms with the need for a residual social rented sector. The white paper had referred to social rented housing as the most cost-effective way to provide long-term housing for people on low incomes. This was because providing a subsidy to social landlords to enable them to charge a below market rent was cheaper in the long term than paying Housing Benefit on market rents. It also reduced dependency on benefits and improved people's incentive to work, and therefore increased the prospect of their breaking out of benefit dependency. To this extent there was an adjustment of a long established policy position.

With the exception of the Housing Benefit measures the new legislation did not apply to Scotland. Even more significantly the Northern Ireland Office did not envisage a major change in the approach to housing policy there. It expressed confidence in the record and achievements of the Northern Ireland Housing Executive and rejected measures that might destabilize and undermine those achievements. However the executive's new development programme was transferred to housing associations after 1996 to reap the benefits of borrowing outside the public sector borrowing requirement (see Chapter 9).

The structure of the housing market

Table 3.3 shows how the structure of the housing market in the UK changed after 1970. During the period of Conservative government (1979–1997) the housing stock increased by almost three million dwellings, the owner-occupied sector expanded by 10 percentage points, and local authorities started the period housing almost one in three households and ended it housing less than one in five. Housing associations increased their market

Table 3.3   *Dwellings by tenure, UK, 1971–2001*

	Number of dwellings (thousands)	Owner-occupied (per cent)	Local authority (per cent)	Housing association (per cent)*	Private rented (per cent)
1971	19 426	50.4	30.7	–	18.9
1976	20 608	53.8	31.6	–	14.8
1981	21 586	56.4	30.4	2.2	11.0
1986	22 600	61.5	26.1	2.5	9.9
1991	23 710	66.0	21.4	3.1	9.5
1996	24 250	66.9	19.6	4.0	9.6
2001	25 456	69.4	14.5	6.5	9.7

* The figures for 1971 and 1976 are included in the private rented totals.
Source: UK housing statistics.

share, while the private rented sector continued to decline until 1991, with a small recovery in size thereafter.

These statistics obscure more complex changes. More than half of the growth of the owner-occupied sector was a direct result of the sale of public sector housing stock, especially through the 'Right to Buy' scheme. Thus the owner-occupied sector included properties that were not originally built for sale and were situated in locations not previously associated with home ownership. These were also older properties, and when they had been bought under the Right to Buy their purchasers were generally older first-time buyers who benefited from substantial discounts on their house purchase. In many cases former council properties formed a separate submarket, not fully absorbed into mainstream home ownership (Forrest *et al.*, 1995). The Right to Buy and stock transfers also altered the structure of the local authority sector. With very limited building of new local authority housing, the disproportionate sale of more attractive and better-quality stock left the authorities with a greater proportion of flats and non-traditional dwelling types.

The second significant change to the organization of housing in the UK was the Large-Scale Voluntary Transfer of council housing. These transfers were most extensive in England, although the sale of Scottish Homes housing stock and the transfer of a significant number of properties elsewhere in Scotland also merit attention. Between December 1988 and March 1997, 54 local authorities in England transferred around 250 000 dwellings. These transfers, as well as the changed financial environment for housing associations, contributed to the growth of the latter sector and this continued under later Labour governments (see Chapters 4 and 9).

Finally, the private rented sector was significantly deregulated. In 1988, 59 per cent of lettings in the private rented sector had been regulated but by 1997/98 this figure had fallen to 9 per cent (see Chapter 6). There were implications for both rents and tenants' rights. The Housing Benefit system only partly protected tenants against rising rents. There had always been rent caps, and these became more significant following changes in the mid 1990s.

This broad picture needs to be modified in relation to particular regions and localities. For example in 1997, 67.9 per cent of households in England owned their own homes, compared with 71.4 per cent in Wales, 70.3 per cent in Northern Ireland and 60.3 per cent in Scotland. The proportions of public sector tenants were 16.1 per cent, 16.2 per cent, 23 per cent and 27.8 per cent respectively.

Key indicators of housing changes in the period 1980–97 are presented in Table 3.4. There was a decline in the construction of new public sector dwellings from more than 88 000 in 1980 to just over 3000 in 1997. While housing association construction increased after 1990, total housing construction remained well below the 1980 level and contributed to the

Table 3.4   *Housing performance and expenditure, UK, 1980–97*

	1980	1985	1990	1997
New housing constructed:				
Public sector	88 590	30 422	17 877	1543
Housing associations	21 422	13 648	17 911	28 249
Private sector	131 974	163 395	166 798	160 910
All dwellings	241 986	207 465	202 586	190 702
	1980/81	*1985/86*	*1990/91*	*1997/98*
General government expenditure on housing				
£ billion (cash)	5.6	4.2	4.9	3.7
£ billion (2000/01 prices)	13.6	7.3	6.4	4.0
Share of housing in government expenditure (excluding Housing Benefit) (%)		4.0	3.1	1.5
Gross social housing investment in Britain (£ billion cash)	4026	4568	5743	4064
Gross social housing investment in Britain (£ billion, 2000/01 prices)	9790	8178	7655	4356
Mortgage interest tax relief (£million)	2188	4750	7700	2700
Average tax relief (£)	335	585	800	250
Net subsidies for local authority housing in Britain (£ million)	2130	916	1217	(–674)
Housing Benefit				
Rent rebates (number)	1330	3710	2944	2762
Rent rebates (average payment per person, £ per annum)	240	606	1030	1893
Rent allowances (number)	240	1150	1044	1829
Rent allowances (average payment per person, £ per annum)	199	619	1323	2818

Sources: Adapted from Malpass and Murie (1999), with data from Wilcox (1997, 2002).

subsequent housing shortage. General government expenditure on housing remained relatively stable in cash terms but a dramatic decline in expenditure is revealed when inflation is taken into account. Housing's share of government expenditure had fallen below 2 per cent by 1997; and in real terms social housing investment declined over the period. This is evident in relation to investment in new building, and acquisitions by local authorities had fallen to a negligible level by 1997/98. In spite of increasing evidence of a backlog of repairs to the council housing stock, Housing Revenue Account (HRA) stock renovation declined after 1985 and most dramatically after 1990. In real terms total gross investment in 1997/98 was only 45 per cent of the 1980 figure.

While these cuts in conventional housing expenditure and housing investment were taking place, mortgage interest tax relief rose to a peak in 1990 and both the number of and the average payment for Housing Benefit increased considerably. The average annual payment for private sector rent allowances had overtaken the average payment for rent rebates for public sector tenants. The changes in the financing of council housing meant that in the aggregate local authority housing in Britain had moved into surplus. In 1980, £2130 million was spent on subsidies to local authority housing, but by 1990 this had fallen to £1217 million. In 1995 and 1997/98 there was a surplus of £483 million and £674 million respectively. The general assistance subsidy had been eliminated and this figure should be offset against the cost of rent rebates. Rather than a cut in expenditure, what had been achieved was a reorientation from council housing towards home ownership and the private rented sector.

These issues are relevant to the balance of spending between investment and subsidy over a long period. In 1981 the government announced its commitment 'To reduce the overall level of housing subsidies over a period of years so as to enable a greater proportion of the resources available for public expenditure on housing to be devoted to capital rather than current expenditure' (Treasury, 1981). This was focused on subsidies to local authority Housing Revenue Accounts rather than subsidies in general. The rising council housing subsidy bill in the early and mid 1970s reflected a combination of factors, including rising investment levels and high interest rates. A new subsidy system for local authority housing, designed specifically to give the central government more control over the total subsidy bill, was introduced under the Housing Acts of 1980 in 1981/82. The different systems introduced for Scotland, England and Wales gave the central government unprecedented power to force up council rents and left local authorities with limited room to manoeuvre. Rents initially rose rapidly, but after the early 1980s the increases were more limited.

Under the Social Security and Housing Benefits Act of 1982 a new integrated Housing Benefit scheme replaced the separate schemes for rent rebates, rent allowances, rate rebates and the supplementary benefits associated with housing costs. The Act gave local authorities little more than the power they needed to operate the scheme, and details of the scheme were left to DHSS regulations. The new scheme was introduced partially in November 1982 and fully in April 1983 (November 1983 in Northern Ireland).

The problems experienced in implementing the new scheme were considerable and subsequent revisions resulted in an increasingly severe poverty trap for tenants in receipt of benefit. It has been suggested that making the local authorities responsible for the administration of Housing Benefit placed them in the front line in explaining and implementing the cuts and therefore constituted a distancing strategy by the central government. For the housing authorities, their income maintenance and means test role involved a significant change in relationships, especially with their own tenants.

The subsidy schemes established under the Housing Acts of 1980 operated alongside the Housing Benefit scheme until 1 April 1990. In England and Wales the rules governing subsidies for local authority housing were replaced on that date by a new scheme established by the Local Government and Housing Act of 1989. In Scotland the operation of the Housing Support Grant (HSG) involved similar elements, with ministerial judgements about management and maintenance costs, interest rates, rent losses, rent income, general fund contributions and other elements that determined the HSG. In practice the formula was used to reduce the HSG steadily.

One of the most striking features of the first phase of policy was the severity of the cuts in public spending. In 1980 the House of Commons Environment Committee noted that housing cutbacks accounted for 75 per cent or more of all public spending reductions. Although subsequent years saw an enormous flow of capital receipts, public expenditure on housing did not recover. Capital receipts from the Right to Buy scheme between 1979 and 1996 amounted to almost £27 billion. This enormous flow was not used to boost public expenditure on housing but rather enabled the government to fund a major part of a declining programme from receipts.

Consequently to view the pattern of public expenditure in terms of cuts is misleading. On top of capital expenditure cuts there was a transfer away from the public sector and direct investment and towards the support of owner-occupation. Latterly there was also an increase in expenditure on housing associations and Housing Benefit.

Territorial differences are important in this respect. In both Scotland and Wales, restrictions on the use of capital receipts were less than in England. Capital allocations in Scotland were made in two blocks (Housing Revenue Account and non-Housing Revenue Account) after making assumptions about the level of capital receipts. Apart from some negative allocations local authorities were able to make full use of receipts. In Wales 50 per cent of the receipts from council house sales and 30 per cent of other receipts were taken into account. The processes connected with capital programmes also differed, with Housing Strategy and Operational Programmes in Wales and Housing Plans in Scotland, both of which had different time scales and procedures than Housing Investment Programmes (HIPs) in England.

According to Wilcox (1993), Scotland and Wales maintained or even increased their public expenditure on housing investment in real terms after 1979/80 and the brunt of reduced housing investment was felt in England. In Northern Ireland public expenditure on housing was regarded as a high priority until the late 1980s, and for the Northern Ireland Housing Executive – the only public sector landlord in that part of the UK – the process of determining and allocating public expenditure involved direct and close consultation with a wide range of stakeholders and communities.

Finally, there were significant changes in expenditure in new towns. The postwar new town experiment had been terminated by 1985 and proposals to dispose of new town dwellings to the private or voluntary sector had become the major feature of housing policy in such towns. By 1990 new towns were obtaining more than twice as much in capital receipts than they were spending on housing.

Rented housing

The combination of public expenditure changes and the sale of public housing led to a steady decline in the size of the public housing sector. The private rented sector also declined, although there was a temporary expansion in the late 1980s and early 1990s when people who were unable to sell their homes turned to renting, and when the Business Expansion Scheme was extended in 1988 to cover new equity investment in companies that engaged in residential lettings. This provided investors with tax relief at their marginal rate for up to £40 000 a year for new shares in qualifying companies. Investors had to hold their shares for at least five years, after which they could be sold free of capital gains tax. Residential letting companies could raise up to £5 million in this way to acquire and let properties. After five years they were free to sell the units, the resulting capital gain being tax free. Between 1988/89 and 1993/94, 4527 business expansion schemes were established in the UK for housing. The total investment was almost £3 billion and 75 100 lettings were generated. Eighty per cent of the investment was in London and the South-East. The value of the income tax relief was in excess of £1 billion, or £16 450 per letting (Wilcox, 1997).

The availability of housing to rent was affected by the decline in the construction of new council dwellings, and construction by housing associations fell far short of compensating for this. The Right to Buy scheme also had a long-term impact on the supply of relets as purchased properties would not be available to council tenants in the future. In England lettings to new tenants fell from some 275 100 in 1980/81 to 247 000 in 1985/6 and 239 600 in 1990/91. However they did not continue to fall and fluctuated between 220 000 and 260 000 between 1989/90 and 1997/98. These figures reflect an increasing turnover (the ratio of new letting to dwelling stock) in the council stock: from 5 per cent per annum to 7 per cent per annum – an increase of 33 per cent. This and the changing profile of new tenants reflected the changing nature and role of council housing (Cole and Furbey, 1994).

Homelessness

The Conservatives had inherited the requirements of the Housing (Homeless Persons Act) of 1977, which placed a statutory duty on local authorities to provide advice and assistance to people who were threatened with or were experiencing homelessness, and in certain circumstances to secure housing for them. This meant that households that were not intentionally homeless and were deemed to be in priority need (the main categories of which were families with children, pregnant women, the elderly and the vulnerable) should be found accommodation by the investigating authority, or by an authority with which a stronger local connection existed.

As Table 3.5 shows, the number of homeless households in priority need rose – significally up to 1990, but declined thereafter in all parts of the UK except Scotland. Alongside this there was a rise in the number of homeless households living in temporary accommodation. Such accommodation, especially that in bed and breakfast hotels, was usually insecure, substandard, unsafe and expensive. In 1980, 1330 households in England were housed in bed and breakfast hotels and 4710 in some form of temporary accommodation. By 1991 these figures had risen to 12 150 and 68 630, but by 1997 they had fallen to 4520 and 54 930.

The two main criteria for acceptance as homeless were the breakdown of shared arrangements with relatives or friends or the breakdown of a relationship with a partner. Social and demographic trends were key elements in homelessness. Although there were flaws in the homelessness

Table 3.5   *Homeless households accepted as in priority need, 1980–97*

	1980	1985	1990	1997
England	62 920	93 980	145 800	107 380
Scotland	7976	11 972	15 813	17 400
Wales	5446	5371	9963	4640
UK	76 342	111 323	171 576	129 420

Source: Adapted from Malpass and Murie (1999).

legislation, the lack of additional resources to meet needs and the broad direction of housing policy from the mid 1970s were more important factors. Homeless people received a growing share of new allocations of council and housing association properties but the characteristics of those allocated housing as homeless people were very similar to those at the top of the general waiting lists. Homelessness legislation was wrongly portrayed as giving special priority to single parents and others and was increasingly associated with attacks on the structure of the welfare state.

These trends did not accord with Conservative policies and their impact on the demand for social housing was a cause of growing disquiet in the party, prompting a series of policy reviews. The first of these, in 1989, concluded that the law should remain unchanged, and new codes of guidance issued in relation to homelessness emphasized prevention and performance monitoring. In 1993 the housing minister, Sir George Young, announced another full-scale review of homelessness legislation. Government proposals published in 1994 were more restrictive than expected and claimed that homelessness had become a 'fast track' into social housing. Following this, and despite strong opposition to legislative change, Part VII of the 1996 Housing Act replaced the existing homelessness law and came into effect on 20 January 1997. The new legislation contained similar definitions of people in priority need but changed the entitlements of many people from abroad. It removed the duty to house homeless people if suitable accommodation, including private rented housing, was available in the area, limited the duty to provide accommodation to a two-year period and focused the main duty on the provision of advice and information to the homeless.

This new framework was closely linked to new legislation on the allocation of social housing. This required every authority to maintain a housing register, but only 'qualifying persons' were allowed to be placed on it, and excluded many people from aboard. Homeless people were allowed to join the register, but were no longer to be given 'reasonable preference' in the allocation of tenancies. The overall effect of these changes was that homeless people had less chance of obtaining long-term housing from local authorities and housing associations. Private landlords were expected to play a much larger role in housing homeless people. However this was often not a realistic option, given the high rents, restrictions on Housing Benefit and the reluctance of many landlords to house people with children or vulnerable persons.

Single homeless people were affected by a number of policy decisions in the 1980s. The 'hostels initiative' to improve the standard of temporary accommodation for single homeless people involved closing down very large traditional hostels, including the resettlement units run by the DHSS, and replacing them with a more diverse range of accommodation, mainly through housing associations. The reform of social security in the late

1980s involved the replacement of board and lodging allowances by income support and Housing Benefit. It also reduced the rate of income support for those aged under 25 and removed the entitlement for most of those aged less than 18. It is generally accepted that these measures contributed to the growth of single homelessness, and the government's recognition of this was apparent in the development of a series of initiatives relating to homelessness. In June 1990, £96 million was made available for the period 1990–93 to tackle the problem of people sleeping rough in central London by providing extra hostels and longer-term accommodation. Additional funds – £6 million in 1992/3 – were given in grants to organizations and projects that provided advice and assistance to single homeless people. The 'Rough Sleepers Initiative' was subsequently extended, both in and beyond London.

Tenants' charters and rights

The Tenants' Charter (introduced in the Housing Act of 1980), while not as radical as the proposals contained in the Labour government's Housing Bill of 1979 (especially in respect of tenants' involvement in management and of tenants' mobility), changed the conditions and rights associated with public sector tenancy. Tenancies were placed within a precise legal framework, with a fixed definition of security of tenure and procedures and grounds for obtaining possession. The right of succession for widows, widowers or members of the family who had been resident in the property, and rights to take lodgers or to sublet, to carry out improvements (subject to the landlord's permission), to apply for improvement grants and to consultation and the provision of information were specified. The wider public was given the right to information on the rules on and procedures for housing allocations and transfers, the right to information on consultation procedures and the right to check details they had provided when making an application for housing.

In 1987 a new phase of the discussion of tenants' rights commenced. The Conservative manifesto of 1987 introduced the idea of a 'Choice of Landlord' scheme under the heading 'Rights for Council Tenants'. The proposals sought to add the right of exit to those of voice. As the manifesto put it, 'If they are ever to enjoy the prospect of independence municipal monopoly must be replaced by choice in renting.'

The Housing Act of 1988 gave tenants the right to choose their landlord. Subsequent guidelines set out the criteria under which the government would consent to Tenants' Choice transfers. The Housing Corporation in England, Scottish Homes and Housing for Wales were made responsible for regulating prospective landlords and providing advice to tenants. The government's expectation that private landlords would be interested in taking part in Tenants' Choice proved unfounded, probably due to the regulatory requirements (Mullins, 1991). This left housing associations as the obvious agents, but many were unwilling to damage their relationship with local authorities by being seen as 'predators'. There were also difficulties with ballot procedures and the long-term effects of tenants' rights forfeited under the new landlord (Right to Buy, Tenants' Charter). Tenant's choice was repealed in England and Wales by the Housing Act of 1996; over a seven-year period it had resulted in the transfer of just 1470 homes in five schemes (Tulloch, 2000).

The Housing Act of 1988 also included provisions to set up Housing Action Trusts. Subject to tenants' views and parliamentary approval, the trusts would tackle the problem of run-down, predominantly public-sector housing by taking over responsibility for local authority housing in designated areas. They would be responsible for ensuring its repair and improvement, improving management, diversifying ownership and encouraging local enterprise and employment through cooperation with bodies concerned with economic development. The trusts would have a limited life, after which the housing would pass to other forms of ownership and management. The proposals to set up trusts in Lambeth, Southwark, Tower Hamlets, Leeds, Sandwell and Sunderland were either abandoned or delayed because of tenant consultation and ballots. After significant adjustment, trusts were set up in Hull, Waltham Forest, Liverpool, Birmingham, Brent and Tower Hamlets. Separate and very generous funds were earmarked for these projects, and partly because of this only one generation of trust was ever funded (Karn, 1993).

Under Section 129 of the Act, from April 1989 local authorities were able to seek the approval of the secretary of state for Cash Incentive Schemes to help tenants to obtain other accommodation. This would generate a supply of rented accommodation at much lower cost than new construction, an approach that featured prominently in the development of a homelessness initiative. A similar scheme for cash incentives to help tenants to become owner-occupiers was developed for housing associations (the Tenants' Incentive Scheme).

The idea of tenants' rights and a tenants' charter re-emerged in the context of the government's wider Citizen's Charter proposals. The new tenants' charter included in these proposal, would only apply to council tenants and it set out their rights in respect of security of tenure, exchanges and the freedom to take lodgers. Annual reports to tenants on key issues – including empty properties, rent levels and arrears, lettings, housing benefit administration, homelessness and management costs – were intended to increase accountability to tenants and improve the standard of services.

The 'right to manage', introduced under the Leasehold Reform, Housing and Urban Development Act of 1993, appeared less dramatic than Tenants' Choice and Housing Action Trusts but it was to have a much greater long-term impact. It enabled tenants' groups to set up organizations to provide a range of management and maintenance functions while retaining their council landlord, and it provided capacity-building funding for this purpose. Tenant Management Organizations (TMOs) encompassed two earlier forms of organization: tenant management cooperatives and estate management boards, both of which would have devolved budgets and would either employ staff directly or work with staff seconded by the local authority. TMOs were later described as 'one of the most important developments in tenant empowerment in recent years' (Cairncross *et al.*, 2002, p. 15). By 2002 TMOs were responsible for the management of over 84 000 homes in England.

The same legislation introduced an improved 'right to repair', enabling tenants to have urgent repairs done, and a 'right to compensation for improvements', under which tenants moving out of a dwelling could be compensated for improvements they had made. This legislation also aided the possibility of council house purchase through the 'rent to mortgage' scheme. With the Right to Buy continuing (but with removal of the rights to shared ownership and to a mortgage) the rights of council tenants were broader than ever before and more extensive than elsewhere in the rented sector. But resources were limited and the rights of applicants and new tenants of housing associations of were diminished by the new assured tenancies.

Planning for housing and regeneration

The underlying thinking of the government in this period was that the private sector, especially if it was not crowded out by the public sector, would provide most of the housing needed. In this context it was reasonable to look to the planning system to address any affordability problems that might emerge. Planning was seen principally as a mechanism to facilitate private development. Urban Development Corporations by-passed local planning authorities, and the repeal of the Community Land Act ended the comprehensive approach to land policy. There was a consistent trend towards reliance on public–private partnerships. At the same time rejection of the traditional way of providing affordable housing (councils and new towns) created the opportunity to use the planning system to fill the void.

In the period 1979–97 there were three phases of planning for housing: public provision, a transitional phase and new planning for affordable housing.

The public provision phase

Public provision dominated the postwar housing and planning policies of all governments until the early 1980s. Central and local governments identified targets for meeting housing needs, largely through public sector provision. Estimates of the required provision by new towns or local authorities were often based on local authority waiting lists but took into account household projections. In this phase there was a considerable separation between housing policy, which involved a programme of building to meet housing needs, and planning policy, which sought to control development, including residential development, but largely accommodated the building programmes established by local authorities and new towns.

The transitional phase

In the early 1980s the government switched its emphasis to the encouragement of owner-occupation and the restriction of local authority house building. As the latter declined it became clear that insufficient affordable new housing was being built to meet the increased housing demand brought about by the rise in the number of low-income households. The government therefore sought to encourage a variety of schemes for affordable homes. Building for sale, shared ownership, homesteading, improvement for sale and other approaches were all promoted as a way of overcoming the shortage caused by the reduction of council house construction. Meanwhile planning authorities sought ways of using the planning system to ensure that any development that did take place was targeted at meeting local needs. For example planning conditions that restricted new development to high-density and small-dwelling construction were used as means of indirectly targeting low-income purchasers. Legal agreements were also negotiated alongside planning consent to restrict the first and subsequent sale of dwellings to local purchasers.

As Whitehead and Crook (2000) note, this use of planning powers was not generally endorsed by the central government. When local authorities attempted to set out formal policies on local needs and structure their plans, these were vetoed by the secretary of state. Local authorities had to use their discretionary powers to bargain and negotiate with developers to provide affordable housing in the absence of a formal policy to this effect. Such negotiations became more regular in the latter part of the 1980s in rural areas, where the planning authorities would exceptionally grant planning permission for housing provided it met local needs even when situated outside 'village envelopes'. New settlements were also proposed especially in the South-East of England. In general, however, it was thought that this approach created problems since it undermined the authority of statutory plans. It was in this context that a more coherent and consistent policy began to be developed.

New planning for affordable housing

After 1992 local authorities in England were required to develop formal policies on affordable housing. Local planning authorities could include policies on affordable housing in their local plans and Unitary Development Plans (UDPs), but not in their structural plans. Planning policy could not directly address housing tenure but the term 'affordable housing' could be used in respect of low-cost market housing and social rented housing. Once a planning authority had provided evidence of the need for affordable housing and established an affordable housing policy, it could negotiate with developers in the case of sites above a minimum threshold. These negotiations might result in construction elsewhere, but the presumption was that there should be mixed provision on the site. (For details of this process see Bramley *et al.*, 2004.)

It was not evident that planning-led approaches could produce a sufficient supply of affordable housing where it was needed. A large proportion of local planning authorities adopted such policies but their contribution to the total provision of affordable housing was small. The exclusion of small sites limited the impact of the policy in rural areas and areas where the available development land consisted principally of small sites. It is estimated that affordable housing resulting from planning permissions ranged from 10 000 to 15 000 dwellings a year, but in most cases these were not net additions to the housing supply because they also used the Social Housing Grant provided by the local authority or the Housing Corporation – grants that would otherwise have been used for social housing elsewhere. Whitehead and Crook (2000) suggest that the policy worked better for greenfield sites and in the South of England than for brownfield and inner-city sites and in the North of England. Some developers were resistant to mixed-tenure developments as they believed that properties were less saleable in such developments or that prices would have to be reduced. Consequently they avoided negotiating such arrangements and preferred to provide low-cost homes in areas where they considered the demand was predominantly for low-priced housing.

Economic regeneration

The Estates Renewal Challenge Fund and attention to run-down and deprived urban housing estates reflected a wider agenda than was traditionally associated with housing policy. Stronger links were made between housing problems and social and economic change in certain areas. This made sense for housing policy since the residualization of council housing and the increasing concentration of lower-income groups in council housing made it clear that residents' problems would rarely be solved by housing intervention alone. From the early 1990s there was preference for holistic approaches to regeneration, joining up different levels of government, mixing public, private and voluntary sector inputs, and bringing together a range of resources to focus on problems with multiple origins. This approach to 'joined-up government' was to be developed much further under New Labour (see Chapter 4).

Leading the way was a 1994 review of urban policy (Robson *et al.*, 1994), which stated that areas of deprivation were acting as a drag on the economy, damaging its recovery and restricting its impact. Against this background there was renewed interest in economic regeneration in neighbourhoods with high levels of unemployment. As many of these neighbourhoods had a high proportion of council housing the role of housing in urban regeneration was reassessed. In England the review led to the establishment of new government offices in the regions and a Single Regeneration Budget (SRB), which included major former housing programmes (including 'Estate Action' and Housing Action Trusts), as the framework for regeneration.

The SRB marked a significant departure in policy and had a profound effect on housing. Housing was increasingly absorbed into broader strategies linked to employment, training, education and other factors required to achieve sustained recovery. Once the existing programmes had expired there would be fewer programmes focusing on housing alone. New approaches to regeneration also applied in other parts of the UK. Taken together they represented a significant shift in thinking, which was seen by some as heralding the 'end of housing policy'.

Conclusion

There is no disputing the extent of change to housing policy and the housing system that occurred during the 18 years of Conservative government. However it is too easy to attribute this change to 'Thatcherism'. As discussed throughout this book, there was a constant interplay between policy and other drivers of change, the results of which can be difficult to pin down to political ideology. There were continuities with earlier phases and the fiscal and public expenditure situations would have restricted the options for any government. There were also examples of events taking over from policy in setting the agenda – as in the crisis of home ownership in 1989 and the long recession that followed. But there were also core ideas that served to reduce the scale of public investment regardless of evidence of overall need, to reduce subsidies, to target assistance and to promote the role of the private sector.

The privatization programme was certainly unique. The levels of discount and financial support for the Right to Buy scheme were consistent not with global economic pressures but with an ideological stance. By 1997 some two million council houses had been transferred to owner-occupation. Similarly, under large-scale transfer there was a further shift away from local authority landlordism, with more than 50 local authorities transferring their total housing stock to housing associations by 1997. These developments contributed to a greater diversity in housing governance in the UK and determined the trajectory of change in the social rented sector during the subsequent period. Housing associations had been the preferred vehicles for the provision of new rented housing since the 1980s. However the new financial regime for housing associations resulted in higher rents and new housing association tenants had fewer rights. Over time the housing market structures, housing choices and the rights given to residents were increasingly complex and related not just to tenure but also to property type, length of residence, type of landlord and tenancy history.

Nevertheless many of the changes, including the residualization of council housing and the changing role and balance of tenures, were reinforced rather than initiated in this period. Many were the product of wider economic policies and of general movements in the economy rather than housing policy itself. For example inflation and interest rates affected housing subsidies and other expenditures and costs. House price inflation, economic recession and rising unemployment affected individual housing costs, mobility, maintenance and repair. These factors overwhelmed the formal housing policies set out by the government.

Some policies achieved less than expected. The relative failure of affordable and low-cost home-ownership initiatives (other than the Right to Buy) were attributable to cost factors as well as to local implementation (Forrest *et al.*, 1984). Private sector output reflected commercial judgments and opportunities for profit, as well as public policy. The failure of Tenants' Choice, the right to repair and the rent to mortgage schemes was related to consumer responses and regulation. By 1990 housing debates had begun to focus on problems with owner-occupation: marginal ownership, undermaintenance, affordability, selling in a depressed market, mortgage arrears, repossession and negative equity. By 1997 the government was talking about sustainable home ownership, the continuing need for social rented housing and regeneration. The interconnections between the housing situation, economic opportunity and local economic regeneration were recognized in urban policy. Planning debates on where to house the 4.4 million additional households forecast for the UK by the year 2010 involved re-engagement with the traditional housing policy concerns of supply and demand forecasting and planning the provision of housing in different tenures and different locations. The 1979 agenda was no longer sufficient, and indeed had not provided the conditions required for the market to flourish and for state intervention to be eliminated.

In public spending terms, by the end of the period housing had declined from a major to a minor capital programme. While expenditure on social security, education, health and social services grew in real terms, there was more public debate on real and threatened cuts in these services than there was on housing, which had been subject to much more marked cuts in total expenditure. Perhaps council housing had less public support than other areas of the welfare state, and the development of a dual tenure system may have divided or confused political opposition to cuts in public expenditure and privatization.

In terms of governance there was a clear move away from the central–local relations framework that had dominated earlier phases of housing policy. The shift from production subsidies to Housing Benefit high-lighted the lack of coordination between the policies and budgets of the Department of the Environment and the Department of Social Security. While the aim of reducing housing programme expenditure was met, there was an apparently unanticipated explosion of Housing Benefit expenditure. Stock transfer and the promotion of housing associations also resulted in more complex and varied patterns of housing supply in different parts of the UK, and competitive bidding resulted in a wide dispersion of stockholding by some housing associations that could not be efficiently managed. The development of community care policies called for, but did not always result in, better integration between housing and care providers and health services. This set an agenda that was to be worked out in subsequent periods, for example through 'Supporting People' initiatives (see Chapter 11) and the development of local multi-agency homelessness strategies (see Chapter 12). In all it is easier to portray the policy package as a contradictory, fragmented and incoherent series of initiatives and experiments built upon prejudices and poor information, rather than a coherent strategy for the development of cities and regions. Perhaps it was recognition of this that caused the adoption of more holistic regeneration strategies at the end of the period – albeit with insufficient resources and policy changes.

In the early years Conservative governments had based much of their housing policy on electoral calculations. Their view that council tenants were more likely to vote Labour and that home owners would be natural supporters of the Conservative Party had influenced their decisions.

In the longer term this assumption proved to be misplaced. Tenure alone was no longer a predictor of party allegiance, neighbourhood problems or other social issues. Furthermore the expansion of home ownership did not secure the Conservatives' place in government and it is unlikely that governments of the future will regard housing tenure in quite the same way.

Chapter 4

Housing under Labour, 1997–2004

When the 18 years of Conservative government ended in May 1997 there were expectations of change and hope that housing would move up the political agenda. However there was also fear that Labour's commitment to public investment had been weakened by the apparent popularity of the Right to Buy scheme and changes in tenure since 1979. There was uncertainty about the Labour Party's attitude towards further stock transfers; some municipal leaders anticipated a policy shift, but the leading housing spokesman in opposition, Nick Raynsford, had been a strong supporter of Local Housing Companies (see Chapter 9). In the event housing was not high on the policy agenda in the election campaign in 1997, although the Labour Party did announce its commitment to release £5 billion of accumulated capital receipts from the sale of council houses, despite claims that these had been taken into account in earlier public expenditure calculations.

A new housing policy?

Early signals

The first surprise after Labour took office was that the new minister for local government and housing would be Hilary Armstrong, who had little prior experience of housing issues. Although she was would be supported by Nick Raynsford, who was appointed as parliamentary under secretary of state and Minister for London and Construction, some commentators saw her appointment as an indication that housing was not a high priority for the government and that there would be substantial continuities with Conservative policy. More concretely, the chancellor committed himself to following the spending plans set out by the previous government. Therefore it seemed there would be a continuing reduction of housing expenditure.

However this was partly mitigated by a change in approach to capital receipts, £5 billion of which would be spent over a five-year period. Very little of this could be made available quickly enough to affect spending in 1997, but the benefits would be felt in subsequent years. The announcement in 1997 of the implementation of a housing investment programme for England the next year heralded the first increase in local authority housing investment for at least six years. While the general allocation fell in line with the previous government's planned reduction from £628 million to £540 million, it was more than offset by an extra £570 million from the capital receipts initiative. Whether this change of direction would be maintained depended on the new government's approach to future public expenditure. This was clarified in the chancellor's budget speech in July 1997.

In this speech it was announced that there would be a cross-departmental review of housing expenditure – reporting jointly to the Secretary of State for Social Security and the Deputy Prime Minister – to correct the disjuncture between housing policy and Housing Benefits under the Conservatives, as described in Chapter 3. Answers to parliamentary questions had indicated that the cost of shifting from consumer to producer subsidy would be very low and such a step would significantly reduce the impact of the poverty trap. However the possibility of a radical change to Housing Benefits was not realized at that time, partly because of the continuation of high rent policies.

Prior to the comprehensive spending review there were some policy changes. Two adjustments through secondary legislation would 'restore a proper safety net' for families and vulnerable people who were unintentionally homeless. Local authorities were required to ensure that any temporary accommodation used for the homeless would be available for at least two years, and to restore homeless households to the list of those who must be given reasonable priority when social housing was allocated. The intended replacement of Compulsory Competitive Tendering of local government services with 'Best Value' in respect of housing, and the resulting Best Value regime for housing associations and other voluntary bodies, signalled that the new government's public service management agenda would include the voluntary and community sector (see Chapters 7 and 9). In the July budget the Chancellor announced that mortgage interest tax relief would be reduced to 10 per cent from April and that stamp duty for more expensive houses would be increased. The government also intended to address the problems of cowboy builders and gazumping in England. The latter would involve a new approach to property sales that placed the onus on sellers to provide survey information on their property.

Housing Green Paper

In 2000 the government produced a Green Paper on housing (DETR, 2000), but this was more notable for continuity than for radical change. Continuity related to the Right to Buy, additional options for transfer of local authorities' stock and the convergence of social housing rents in different market areas to reflect market differentials (see Chapter 8). A proposal for housing for key workers in high-cost areas built on the Conservatives' affordability policy. There would be no reform of Housing Benefit, despite the continuing growth of housing costs. Most of the changes were related to homelessness and decent homes.

The Homelessness (Priority Need for Accommodation) (England) Order 2002 extended the priority categories to include young people aged 16–17 (with certain exceptions), young people under 21 formerly in care, and people deemed vulnerable as a result of having been in care, in the armed forces, in custody or having fled their homes because of violence or plausible threats of violence. Local authorities had to ensure that suitable accommodation was available for the homeless, and their duty to provide accommodation would continue until a permanent housing solution was found.

In relation to decent homes, a new standard was set and all social housing had to meet this by 2010. Stock transfer was accelerated by the decision to maintain the definition of public spending with the consequence that local authorities could only secure substantial new investment by transferring their housing stock. Treasury support for negative value transfers was negotiated, enabling large transfers to go ahead in Burnley, Coventry and Sunderland. However there were setbacks in this programme, including the decision of tenants in Sandwell and later Birmingham to refuse transfer. Funding for new partial transfers under the Estates Renewal Challenge Fund came to an end in 2000, although partial transfers to existing housing associations continued into the 2000s. The capital receipts initiative was not sufficient to deal with the backlog of investment. The green paper established new options to secure additional investment by setting up Arm's-Length Management Organizations (ALMOs), which would receive additional public subsidies, subject to the meeting of performance standards, and the Private Finance Initiative (PFI) would secure privately funded investment and management under 30-year contracts (DETR and DSS, 2000a).

As Figure 4.1 shows, the private sector continued to dominate new housing construction after the 1997 election – it accounted for over 80 per cent of all new building during this period. Public sector building in the UK had virtually ended with the transfer of the Northern Ireland Housing Executive's new-build programme to housing associations in 1996, and disappeared altogether after 1998. The decision to retain the Conservatives' public spending plans, despite the capital receipts initiative, meant that housing association output declined each year in 1997–2003.

Table 4.1 shows the key legislation and measures that affected housing under New Labour. It highlights a firming up of the direction of housing

Figure 4.1 *Number of dwellings built in England and Wales, 1997–2004*

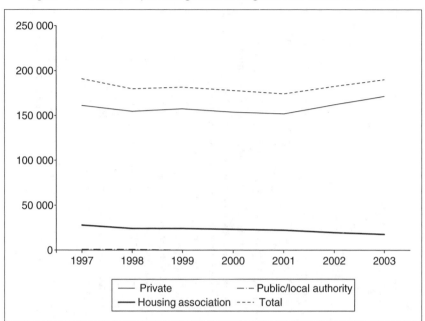

Source: Data from *Housing and Construction Statistics* (ODPM).

policy, a degree of difference among the housing policies in the UK jurisdictions following devolution, and the growing importance of broader factors such as antisocial behaviour and immigration policy in defining the roles and responsibilities of housing institutions.

Marsh (2004) identifies three related areas of reform that were pursued by the Labour administration following the 2000 green paper, based on an economic analysis of the social housing sector. The three areas were the promotion of choice, rent restructuring and Housing Benefit reform.

Promotion of choice

The Labour government's housing policy emphasized the twin themes of choice and responsibility (DETR, 2000). In the private sector this included the development of home sellers' packs to provide prospective purchasers with information on the properties in question to enable more informed choice. It also included modification of the repair and improvement grant regime to reduce dependency on these grants and replace them with loans and equity release. In the social rented sector this involved a continuing debate on choice of landlord but new initiatives were introduced to provide greater choice in relation to accommodation. Changes in

Table 4.1 *Principal housing legislation, related legislation and policy statements, 1997–2005*

1997	*Building Societies Act*: amended the Building Societies Act of 1986, defining the powers of control of the Commission, the accountability of societies to members and the investigation of complaints. *Town and Country Planning (Scotland) Act*: comprehensive Act setting out a development plan and a development control system for Scotland covering matters such as the compulsory purchase of land.
1998	*The Scotland Act*: devolved housing policy and legislative authority (among other matters) to the Scottish Parliament. However Housing Benefit, financial regulation and other key matters remained with the Westminster parliament. *Government of Wales Act*: National Assembly for Wales assumed responsibility for some housing policy matters. Tai Cymru abolished and its functions transferred to the secretary of state for Wales, but most legislation continued to cover England and Wales.
1999	*Local Government Act*: Replaced Compulsory Competitive Tendering with 'Best Value'. Scope of Best Value extended to voluntary sector, including housing associations. Role of Audit Commission extended, with the Housing Corporation providing appropriate advice and assistance. *Immigration and Asylum Act*: persons subject to immigration control excluded from tenancy or licence to occupy social housing throughout the UK. Secretary of state made responsible for arranging accommodation and support for asylum seekers. NASS to negotiate five-year contracts with housing providers.
2000	*Abolition of Feudal Tenure etc. (Scotland) Act*: abolished system in which land was held 'by a vassal' on perpetual tenure from 'a superior'. *Race Relations (Amendment) Act*: brought Housing Corporation, Scottish Homes and housing associations into the general statutory duty under Section 71 of the Race Relations Act of 1976 to eliminate discrimination and promote equality. *Warm Homes and Energy Conservation Act*: required a strategy for reducing fuel poverty in England and Wales. *Care Standards Act*: established National Care Standards Commission with authority to inspect care homes, including those operated by housing associations. *Housing Green Paper*: set direction for a number of housing reforms including option appraisals, 'Arm's-Length Management Organizations and Private Finance Initiative options to meet, the Decent Homes Standard, rent restructuring, Housing Benefit reform and Choice-Based Lettings.
2001	*Housing (Scotland) Act*: Major legislation covering homelessness and allocation of housing, Scottish secure tenancies, Right to Buy, tenant participation, regulation of social landlords, housing management, strategic housing functions and private sector grants.

2002   *Commonhold and Leasehold Reform Act*: established system of registration for commonhold, right to manage and collective management by tenants of flats. *Homelessness Act*: required local authorities to produce homelessness strategies. Amended priority needs groups to include 16–17 year olds. Repealed the 1996 Housing Act provisions that limited the period for which duty was owed to the homeless. Abolished the duty to maintain housing registers. *Regulatory Reform (Housing Assistance) England and Wales Order*: required local authorities to publish private sector renewal strategies. Repealed private sector grants and loans provisions, enabled local authorities to assist housing renewal directly or through third parties such as housing associations and private sector loan finance.

2003   *Sustainable Communities Plan*: gave higher profile to housing policy and responded to regional disparities. Led to the establishment of Regional Housing Boards, Regional Housing Strategies, additional investment in new homes in the South and the establishment of Housing Market Renewal Areas in parts of the Midlands and the North. *Anti-Social Behaviour Act*: required social landlords to have policies on antisocial behaviour, introduced new considerations in respect of possession proceedings on the conduct of tenants, parenting orders and antisocial behaviour orders. *Health and Social Care (Community Health and Standards) Act*: replaced National Care Standards Commission with Commission for Social Care Inspection. *Homelessness (Scotland) Act*: abolished priority need test and made new provisions for determining intentionality, local connection and suitability of accommodation. *Land Reform (Scotland) Act*: established 'community Right to Buy', which enabled community bodies to purchase land from landowners.

2004   *Public Audit (Wales) Act*: transferred responsibility for regulation and supervision of social housing in Wales to the Auditor General for Wales. *Housing Act*: major legislation on provisions for the enforcement of housing standards, the licensing of Houses in Multiple Occupation and selective licensing of other residential accommodation. Required home information packs to be produced by sellers when putting their properties on the market. New provisions in relation to Right to Buy (exceptions and discounts). Amended the Housing Act of 1996 to enable the Housing Corporation to allocate Social Housing Grants to private sector companies. *Anti-Social Behaviour etc (Scotland) Act*: local authorities required to develop antisocial behaviour strategies with chief constables; antisocial behaviour notices could also be served on landlords.

2005   *Sustainable Communities: Homes for All. ODPM Five Year Plan*: set out the government's housing priorities in the run-up to the general election. Placed strong emphasis on the promotion of home ownership. Introduced 'HomeBuy' equity stakes scheme for housing association tenants and further help for first-time buyers. Continued the themes of private finance for social housing and the promotion of choice through lettings and mobility schemes. Sought to reverse the growth in temporary accommodation.

Source: Data from HMSO UK legislation website.

the rent regime and Housing Benefits system were designed to give house-holds a greater incentive to optimize their standard of housing.

Considerable prominence was given in the green paper and subsequently to the introduction of choice-based lettings, drawing on the experience of the Netherlands. Choice-based lettings involved the replacement of the administrative matching of applicants to vacancies with published details of homes to let, from which applicants could select directly (see Chapter 10). Initially the government funded pilot schemes and built on changes that were already taking place, particularly in low-demand areas. But over time a more coercive approach was adopted, with targets set for all authorities to meet by 2010. Choice-based lettings avoided the unnecessary pressure of the 'take it or leave it' approach, in which applicants were expected to decide about a single housing offer without knowing what might be offered next or when, and in places such as Bradford this increased demand and strengthened tenants' commitment to the neighbourhoods and homes they had chosen. However the status and attractiveness of social housing in comparison with other tenures remained of fundamental importance. Unless the decent homes policy succeeded in improving the attractiveness of social renting the sector would continue to attract similar types of household with similar needs who would move on if their circumstances improved.

Rent restructuring and Housing Benefit reform

A more comprehensive application of the choice approach was evident in the government's policies on rent and Housing Benefit. The aim of these policies was to develop a more coherent framework for rents of social housing, with clearer links to local markets, to provide consumers with an incentive to choose between properties on the basis of price and quality, and to avoid disincentives to employment. These policies are discussed more fully in Chapter 8.

Concern about the lack of coherence in the rent structures of social housing had existed since at least the 1960s, when the issue had been raised in the context of prices and income policies (Marsh, 2004). Local govern-ment reform in 1974 had brought within a single organization landlords who had been setting rents at different levels using different principles, even within their own stock. While many landlords had subsequently revised their rent structures, differences had still been detectable in the rent structures used by some landlords in the mid 1990s. This lack of coherence had been thrown into sharper relief by the move from producer to consumer subsidies because the absolute size of differentials and anomalies had increased. The move to partial private finance in the housing associa-tion sector after 1989 had often accentuated rent differentials between the local authority and the local housing association sector.

Proposals for rent reform involved applying a consistent formula across social housing to take account of property values, property size and local earnings when calculating the target rents that social landlords were expected to move towards. Rent restructuring came into operation in April 2003. Local authorities were given 10 years and housing associations 15 years to progress from the current rents to the target rents. According to Walker and Marsh (2003) the formula did not make rent setting more transparent for tenants or align rents more closely with the housing qualities that tenants valued. Moreover there was no benchmark against which to assess whether rents were fairer after restructuring.

The stated objectives of the reform of Housing Benefit were to reduce barriers to work; ensure that people on low incomes could afford a decent home that met their needs; give tenants more choice; increase tenants' personal responsibility to pay their rent; provide a better, quicker service based on simpler, clearer rules; and to make fraud more difficult to commit. Housing Benefit was to be replaced by a flat-rate local housing allowance that would vary by locality according to local market rents and by household type. Prior to this being introduced the government launched local pilots. Early evidence suggests that the changes to the Housing Benefit scheme may not have the effects that the government intended, nor increase mobility and choice (see Chapter 8).

Both reforms were strongly influenced by economic assumptions about consumer behaviour rather than criticisms raised by tenants themselves, such as the complexity of the systems and administrative inefficiency in making payments. Changes in rent regimes, Housing Benefits and letting procedures for many households would simply add a further advantage or disadvantage and in most cases would not be sufficient to trigger a change in housing decision. Marsh (2004) questions the coherence of the reform package. While it is too early to predict how the various reforms will play out, there are good reasons to believe that they will not influence behaviour in the way intended or achieve the efficiencies expected, and they may have a perverse effect on the behaviour and experience of different groups, including vulnerable households, landlords and funders.

Alternatives to housing policy?

Despite the flurry of activity associated with the green and white papers on housing, many observers detected a lack of enthusiasm for a clear housing policy and a continuation of the practices of the Conservative period, which some had seen as the 'terminal decline of housing policy' (Bramley, 1997). The new government retained the generic approach to regeneration, which since the introduction of the Single Regeneration Budget by the Conservatives had tended to shift funding away from housing towards a more holistic policy approach to economic and community regeneration. However the new government was developing new approaches to regionalization, social exclusion and neighbourhoods and was looking beyond housing policy as traditionally conceived to tackle housing and neighbourhood problems (see Chapters 12 and 13).

In August 1997 Peter Mandelson (minister without portfolio) announced the establishment of a Social Exclusion Unit, whose initial remit was to tackle the problems of rough sleeping and substandard council estates. There was some concern that the emphasis on these estates meant that ministers thought that a policy of targeting the council housing sector and the worst parts of it would be an adequate response to housing and housing-related problems. The Social Exclusion Unit was also charged with reporting on neighbourhood problems (see Chapter 12). But the main initiatives in this phase – Education Action Zones, Health Action Zones, 'New Deal for Communities', 'Sure Start', 'Excellence in Cities' and Employment Zones – largely skirted around housing. A flavour of the thinking of the time is provided by the Social Exclusion Unit's report on neighbourhood problems:

> Over the last generation, this has become a more divided country...the poorest neighbourhoods have tended to become more rundown, more prone to crime, and more cut off from the labour market...They have become no go areas for some, and no exit zones for others...
>
> These neighbourhoods are not all the isolated high rise council estates of popular stereotype. Many are publicly owned, but others are privately rented or even owner occupied. Some are cut off on the edge of cities but others can be found close to wealthy suburbs and prosperous city centres. Some consist of very traditional housing designs that would sell for six figure sums elsewhere...
>
> Poor neighbourhoods are not a pure housing problem. They are not all the same kind of design, they don't all consist of rented or council housing, and they are not all in towns and cities. They aren't all 'estates', or 'worst', nor do the people who live there want them described that way. (Social Exclusion Unit, 1998b, pp. 9, 13)

An important new policy strand – a national strategy for neighbourhood renewal – followed in 2000 and similar strategies were developed for Scotland (Social Inclusion Partnerships and a Social Justice Strategy) and Wales ('People in Communities'). Despite the rhetoric of joined-up thinking the mainstream housing policy agenda set out in the green paper took little account of the spatial and social issues highlighted in the social exclusion agenda. The approaches to rents and subsidies, described above, seemed likely to increase segregation and took no account of differences among regional housing markets or patterns of demand. The housing and social exclusion agendas were built on the assumption that neighbourhood and estate problems were best addressed through small area (neighbourhood) approaches that concentrated on management and behaviour. The 'New Deal for Communities' explicitly ruled out spending on housing investment: better neighbourhood management involved better housing management and not capital investment in housing, except to achieve the Decent Homes Standard.

Another strand of policy grew out of the 1999 report by the Urban Task Force, which had been appointed by the deputy prime minister. It recommended an approach to Urban Renaissance that emphasized high-density development on brownfield sites with high standards of design and better transportation provision, and this influenced the thoughts contained in the urban white paper (DETR 2000) and changes in planning.

After 2003 the policies on choice, social exclusion and urban renaissance were set within a new regional governance framework in England that complemented some aspects of devolved governance introduced earlier in Scotland, Wales and Northern Ireland. Devolution had established the legitimacy of differences in the detail of housing policy in the various territories of the UK and in relation to housing policy and legislation. Hence there was greater recognition of the need for different responses to regional housing matters.

By 1997 the housing market had recovered from the long crisis that had begun in the early 1990s. Transactions and prices rose steadily and there was fear of overheating, especially in the South-East. The government expressed concern about gazumping and commissioned an investigation of the house purchasing process in England. The problems of repossession and negative equity received much less attention as they were diminishing. In the following years the boom in home ownership gathered momentum, despite the elimination of mortgage interest tax relief. While the improved employment rate and new housing market factors partly accounted for this, the failure of the stock market and its impact on pension funds had added to the attractiveness of home ownership. The growing buy to let market also contributed to housing demand and house price inflation.

As with previous booms this one was geographically uneven and was concentrated in the South-East of England, while in some subregions of the Midlands and the North there was growing evidence of market failure. The government saw this as reflecting neighbourhood and management failures, but research findings suggested that it was the consequence of changing demand and the working through of various market processes at the regional, subregional and local levels (Nevin *et al.*, 2001). This differentiation needed to be addressed strategically to avoid short-term local responses that would merely move it elsewhere, rather than resolve the problem. The government was faced by two lobbies representing the two facets of the housing problem in England – affordability in the South and the need for market renewal in parts of the North and the Midlands.

The return of housing policy

Over the next few years, and in direct response to the two lobbies mentioned above, there was a rediscovery of housing policy that was reminiscent of the rediscovery of poverty in the 1960s. This was signalled in 2003 by the publication of *Sustainable Communities: Building for the Future* by the Office of the Deputy Prime Minister (2003a). This document, which was commonly referred to as the Communities Plan, acknowledged the importance of regional and local housing market differentiation and the need to have different policies for spatially different markets.

The Sustainable Communities Plan

The Sustainable Communities Plan involved an assertion by the government of the need for a housing policy that would address different patterns of housing need, thus 'reversing the legacy of decades of neglect and under-investment' (Office of the Deputy Prime Minister, 2003a, p.3).

> A step change is essential to tackle the challenges of a rapidly changing population, the needs of the economy, serious housing shortages...and the impact of housing abandonment...

> We are determined to put an end to poor housing and bad landlords, to deliver more affordable housing, especially for key workers and young families, and to develop new sustainable communities....For more than 30 years this country lost its way. All governments failed to meet housing need. We built housing in a way that failed to put the needs of communities first. We did not invest for the long-term. We now have an opportunity to do things differently and to break from the past. (Ibid.)

The plan emphasized a sustainable approach to housing and planning by adopting long-term measures to stabilize communities and remove the need for periodic injections of funding into the same areas to address the same problems. It acknowledged the need to develop different policies in places with different markets, with a focus on the problems of growth and affordability in London and the South-East of England, and on the problem of low demand in the Midlands and the North. However the disparity in the size of the resources initially allocated for these two agendas highlighted the extent to which housing and planning policy was driven by the problems of the South-East. The intention was to respond to the problems occasioned by economic drivers in the South-East while doing nothing to damage the economic competitiveness of that region internationally.

The plan also involved significant institutional change, with the establishment of Regional Housing Boards (later to the merged with the planning boards – see below) to bring about sustainable communities without additional resources. They were expected to achieve this by:

- Recognizing that housing markets did not respect local authority boundaries and adjusting planning to reflect the fact that housing markets were subregional.
- Combining the separate local authority and housing association capital allocation mechanisms.
- Joining housing with other services (jobs, health services, schools, transportation) and with regional strategies for planning, economic development and transportation. This involved joining up with other services to fund particular opportunities to provide housing or respond to problems as and where they arose.

In England the Regional Housing Boards were appointed to be accountable to non-elected regional assemblies. This involved some devolution from national bodies. The Members included government regional offices and government agencies (English Partnerships and the Housing Corporation). However there was also a significant shift of power away from local authorities and other local institutions This promoted a reorganization of key interest groups on a regional basis. For example in the West Midlands it led to new regional housing networks to mobilize rural interests, black and minority ethnic communities and the voluntary and community sectors (West Midlands Voluntary and Community Housing Network, 2005). While local governments were represented, there was a significant diminution of control by elected members of individual authorities over new housing development in their areas. All capital expenditures were determined regionally through a single housing pot that combined the previously separate funding through the Office of the Deputy Prime Minister and the Housing Corporation. This raised the possibility that some local authorities and housing associations would have no capital programme at all, and the imposition of a single approach reduced the ability to argue exceptional cases.

In their first year of operation the Regional Housing Boards developed their first Regional Housing Strategies. This process was generally quite hurried since there was insufficient time for new research, but it did highlight some of the difficulties that would continue to be faced. The process was contested because it had shifted power away from local authorities towards to the small groups of appointed members of the Regional Housing Boards. This raised significant issues in respect of legitimacy and knowledge of the impact that policies would have in practice. Typically there were attempts to consult with and involve a large group of local authorities, housing associations and other stakeholders who were more used to operating at the district level. On the one hand this led to consultation fatigue, with numerous consultations being held about different elements of the strategy with different stakeholders. On the other it led to a sense of exclusion by stakeholders who had previously enjoyed considerable local power and saw regional and subregional agendas as a threat to their positions. Other stakeholders – including the voluntary sector, the private sector and perhaps particularly community groups and tenants groups – were now further from the centre of power and their influence was weakened. There was concern that the important knowledge about local and community matters that these groups could offer would be lost to the policy process (Chartered Institute of Housing, 2003).

Planning and housing: The Barker Review

The Labour government continued to develop the affordable housing framework inherited from the Conservatives (see Chapter 3). Bramley *et al.* (2004) provide a detailed account of this policy under Labour, and note that the policy was very slow to deliver additional affordable homes, partly because planning authorities did not always apply it rigorously. However they anticipated that the system would grow in importance in the future and that greater reliance would be placed on the planning system to deliver more affordable homes, noting the target of 50 per cent affordable homes set by the mayor of London for new developments across much of the city.

Almost as soon as the Regional Housing Boards had begun to develop their strategies, there was a significant change in their role and status. This was a result of measures to combine housing and planning policies in response to a review of issues affecting the housing supply in the UK, commissioned by the Treasury and the deputy prime minister from the economist Kate Barker. The weak responsiveness of the new-build housing market in the face of rising house prices had had several undesirable economic consequences:

- Rising house prices had driven up the 'affordability threshold' as incomes had failed to keep pace in many areas, leading to a high demand for public subsidies for affordable new homes.
- High-price areas had been unable to attract workers on ordinary salaries.
- The leakage of equity into consumer spending had made it difficult to control the money supply, which had implications for inflation and the setting of interest rates.

These factors had not only adversely affected economic growth but also, in the context of the government's plan to join the euro, prevented the clear convergence of the UK economy with those in the euro zone, thus hindering the achievement of a major macroeconomic and European policy objective.

An interim report in December 2003 identified the ways in which the housing supply was affecting economic and social well-being and estimated the scale and causes of the housing shortage. The final report was published on the day of the budget statement in March 2004. (Barker, 2004)

The report made 36 recommendations, including changes to the planning system, incentives for local authorities to speed up delivery, and better integration and strengthening of the available evidence. It recommended that the Regional Housing Boards and Regional Planning Bodies be merged into one body in each region, with responsibility for:

- Managing the regional housing market.
- Delivering the region's affordability target.
- Advising on funding allocations.
- Integrating housing, planning and other regional strategies.

The long-term stability of the housing market, with house price increases being held to a low and predetermined level, required a substantial increase in house building. The current levels of building were insufficient and an increase of between 70 000 and 120 000 housing units per annum was needed to improve affordability. However the report acknowledged that this could cause sustainability problems and have environmental consequences. It also made recommendations aimed at changing the way new house building, was delivered including national guidance on housing market affordability and the establishment of an independent regional planning executive to provide advice to the Regional Planning Body on how much and where housing was required to meet the market affordability target.

The report recommended that additional funds would be needed to provide additional social housing to meet future needs. Other proposals were for a 'planning-gain supplement' to capture some of the increase in development value for local communities, the establishment of a community infrastructure fund to help lower some of the barriers to development, and a provision for local authorities to keep council tax receipts from new housing developments to provide incentives to plan for growth and meet the transitional costs of development. The government welcomed the review in the Chancellor's budget speech, and indicated acceptance of its recommendations.

In general the report contained elements that would appeal to most stakeholders in housing, but much depended on the details that would emerge later in respect of the implementation and delivery of all the elements proposed. In particular there was concern about the nature of the new regional bodies, the proposed regional planning executive and the consistency of the proposals with the existing Regional Spatial Strategies.

Against this background, in March 2003 the government had asked the chair of the Housing Corporation, Baroness Dean, to head a home ownership task force to look at practical ideas to support home ownership, including helping tenants and others on modest incomes to buy a home whilst minimizing the loss to social housing (Home Ownership Taskforce, 2003). The government accepted the majority of the task force's recommendations, including the streamlining of existing products and the provision of more advice and information to individuals on sustainable home ownership.

The regionalization of housing policy

The new focus on affordability in the Sustainable Communities Plan and the Barker Report continued the process of delivering housing policy through the planning system (see Chapter 3), and combined housing and planning agendas into a regional framework. The first step in England was the development of Regional Housing Strategies, which were viewed as being equal to Regional Planning Guidance, and the Regional Economic Strategy. The assumption was that housing was as important as planning and economic strategies in determining what happened regionally and locally.

One view of these changes is that they represented a further stage in the depoliticization and professionalization of the making of housing policy. In this respect there was a difference both from the *laissez faire* local policy tradition of the 1950s and 1960s and from the more confrontational, centralization of policy that had occurred in the 1980s and 1990s and reduced the power of local authorities. Regionalization could be seen as a more subtle process that on the surface assimilated both local and central government, but in practice reduced local influence still further. This fits with the general critique of regionalism: that it tends to draw power up from below, rather than down from above. This could result in policies that are less transparent in origin and purpose to citizens or even local elected members, and mean that key decisions would be less subject to local influence.

Before arriving at a view of these issues there are other considerations to be taken into account. First, the accelerated process of stock transfer and the establishment of 'Arm's-Length Management Organizations' left only just over half of English local authorities with their own housing stock. This significantly weakened their capacity to develop and implement local housing strategies. While the orthodox housing policy literature has tended to stress the advantages of divorcing strategy from delivery, there is an equally persuasive body of strategic management literature that suggests that strategies are least likely to succeed when there has been little participation by those who will be involved in delivery; this is what Mintzberg (1994) calls the 'fallacy of detachment', particularly of strategy from operations. After housing transfers local housing authorities often have quite limited staff to develop their strategies and may have lost their best senior managers to housing associations in a process aptly described as 'intellectual asset striping'. In this context the renewal of strategic capacity at the regional and subregional levels could be seen as strengthening the housing policy framework.

Second, it is important to recognize that decisions about new investment at the regional, subregional and even national strategic levels are not the only factors that influence housing choice and opportunity. Housing management, allocation of properties, rent collection, rent arrears administration, repairs, maintenance and liaison with residents and communities remain at the local level. While the central government will continue to influence these activities through inspection, regulation and the provision of incentives and good practice advice, day-to-day relationships between landlords and tenants will still be determined at the local level, increasingly by housing associations but by other social landlords as well. Nevertheless for organizations that are involved in both the development and the management of housing, as in the case of the larger 'Investment Partner' housing associations (see Chapter 9), there are likely to be tensions between these activities and roles and a tendency for local management services to be subordinate to regional resource acquisition activities.

What emerges from this is an increasing division between community-based housing management agendas and strategic housing investment agendas. While the former in theory have become more community-based and responsive to residents, the latter are becoming more regional and even cross-regional as part of a grander spatial strategy tied to agendas for economic competitiveness and the long-term restructuring of housing and other markets. The optimistic view would be that this division is the best response to the different pressures that influence housing and planning policy and avoids the situation in which one is adequately addressed at the expense of the other. However bodies such as housing associations are left to manage the tensions involved from adapting to both the regional and the neighbourhood agendas and this is explored further in Chapter 9.

A new comprehensive housing policy?

Greater attention to housing policy was evident in the Housing Act of 2004. This replaced the housing fitness standard with a Housing Health and Safety Rating System and introduced new licensing schemes for private rented property. It also introduced a mandatory requirement to produce a home information pack before marketing a property in England and made changes to the Right to Buy scheme in order to curb abuses by property developers and tenants (see Chapter 5).

In early 2005, during the run-up to the general election, the next phase in the delivery of the Sustainable Communities Plan was set out in a five-year plan (Office of the Deputy Prime Minister, 2005). This combined continuation of the Sustainable Communities Plan's 'growth areas' (to meet the needs of the expanding population of the South of England) with a commitment to increase the public and private housing supply and extend the 'renewal areas' (introduced to address changing and low demand in the Midlands and the North) into other locations. It also continued the emphasis on housing for key workers decent homes and enhancement of the environment and neighbourhoods, and gave renewed attention to reducing the use of temporary accommodation for homeless households. In addition the recommendations of the Barker Report, the Home Ownership Taskforce and the Egan review were to be implemented. Egan (1998, 2004) had identified skills shortages in the construction sector and recommended a 'partnering' model for construction contracts, as well as improvements to processes, products, components and project implementation in construction.

Home ownership

The main focus of future policy was on increasing home ownership: 'the Government supports home ownership. People's homes have become more and more important to their sense of security and well-being' (Office of the Deputy Prime Minister, 2005, p. 32). Over 80 000 people currently renting privately or living with their families were to be helped into home ownership by 2010. A new first-time buyers initiative would help 15 000 first-time buyers, the key worker living scheme would help 30 000 key workers and over 35 000 people would be helped through existing schemes, including shared ownership and homebuy.

The new scheme for first-time buyers would use public land to keep down the cost of new homes, thereby shielding buyers from the land cost of their purchase. A new package for social tenants was entitled 'choice to own' – an interesting development from the Right to Buy – which would give social tenants a choice of routes into home ownership rather than relying solely on the Right to Buy. The Homebuy scheme would enable tenants in the social rented sector to buy a share in their home and purchase the property outright at a later date if the Right to Buy became less generous and the Rent to Mortgage scheme did not work. Thus Homebuy provided an alternative way of enabling people to accumulate a stake in the asset value of their homes. In areas where the market was rising and prices were high, this asset could become considerable, in contrast to its impact in lower-cost markets or where values were not appreciating.

In addition the government would explore options for tenants who wanted to move out of high-demand areas, such as providing interest-free loans linked to the value of the property they bought. There would be better information to help people to sustain home ownership. 'Key facts' for new mortgages would explain the costs of the mortgage, monthly repayments and the effect of interest increases on payments. There would be cooperation with the lending and insurance sectors to promote more flexible repayment arrangements and increase the availability of mortgage payment protection products. Home information packs would be introduced from January 2007 to raise awareness of repair and maintenance responsibilities, to help buyers make informed choices, to make buying and selling a home quicker, more reliable and more transparent, and to provide owners with information on the energy efficiency of their homes and help them manage their household budgets (Office of the Deputy Prime Minister, 2005, p. 37).

Commitment to the 'Decent Homes' Standard and expansion of the social rented sector would accompany the effort to increase home ownership. Social rented housing provision would continue and would be raised to a minimum (but not high) standard; it would change not on a planned basis in relation to need, but in relation to the uptake and sale of properties. So in parts of the country where uptake of the various home ownership schemes was particularly high, the availability of social rented housing would decline further.

Local authorities and housing associations that sold properties would be able to use the money raised under some of these schemes to reinvest in housing, and they would have the right to first refusal on the resale of some properties, but this did not necessarily mean that they would use the money or the right to purchase in a way that would maintain the social rented sector. As with the Right to Buy, the outcome of these policies would be an uneven pattern of tenure that was unrelated to need. Local political decisions about affordable housing provision, planning and development, the recycling of capital receipts, the repurchase of sold properties and other factors would result in a complex and fragmented pattern of housing tenure and access to housing. The nature and availability of local social housing would reflect an accrual of political decisions over time with little relationship to patterns of need.

Policies for rented housing

The government reaffirmed its intention to make all socially rented homes meet the Decent Home Standard by 2010, but it had a less ambitious target in the case of the private rented sector, where only 70 per cent of the homes of vulnerable households would have to meet the standard. According to Office of the Deputy Prime Minister (2005, p. 9), 'we are more than doubling investment in social housing from 1997 to £2 billion in 2007–8 and we will build an extra 10,000 homes a year by 2008 – a 50% increase compared to current rates'.

There was a need to increase the number of new homes beyond that provided for in existing plans, and under the Sustainable Communities'

Plan many would be situated in high-growth areas, including the already established Thames Gateway and three new areas: Milton Keynes/South Midlands, Stansted/Cambridge, and Ashford. A new programme was established to help fund the latter three, and the intention was to develop them in a way that would benefit various groups, including existing communities, within a sustainable community framework.

With regard to areas where demand was low, the government maintained its commitment to the nine housing market pathfinders and set aside additional resources for other areas where there was a need for investment in relation to low housing demand. The money would be distributed through Regional Housing Boards and the main beneficiaries would include the Tees Valley, West Yorkshire and West Cumbria. Regional Housing Boards were also expected to support programmes to tackle smaller areas of low demand, to work with English Partnerships and to devise a strategy to deal with housing in former coalmining areas.

Choice-based letting schemes were expected to achieve nationwide coverage by 2010 and a 'Move UK' scheme was announced to provide information on jobs and housing. Action was to be taken against rogue private landlords, the number of people housed in temporary accommodation would be reduced by half as part of a programme to address homelessness, there would be investment in housing-related support for elderly and disabled people, and accommodation would be provided for gypsies and travellers. The general approach to policy was also couched in terms of environmental sustainability and enhancing the environment, with the emphasis on brownfield sites and high-density building.

Despite the language of choice, when challenged ministers made it clear there would continue to be only three options for managing and improving council housing: transfers to housing associations, public finance initiatives or the establishments of Arm's-Length Management Organizations (Centre for Public Services, 2004; Office of the Deputy Prime Minister, 2004d). Audit Commission inspection was seen as pivotal to improving the quality of services and to efficient housing management and maintenance. Local authorities were expected to adopt a more strategic role in planning and building homes for communities. Despite the disempowering effects of regionalization, local authorities were still presented as having an extensive local remit and the democratic legitimacy to act to ensure that all aspects of the housing market in their area operated effectively. Strong leadership by local authorities was seen as key to the better planning and provision of homes for the whole community, engaging the community in plans for new development, building new social housing and addressing the problem of long-empty homes. The long-term erosion of their influence had clearly reduced local authorities' capacity to meet these expectations, but their planning and development control functions remained significant sources of influence.

Regional housing and planning bodies would be merged, as recommended by Barker, and a single body would be responsible for spatial and housing strategies. The regional assemblies (in their capacity as Regional Planning Bodies) would be responsible for housing and planning and would work in cooperation with Regional Development Agencies, Government Offices in the Regions, local authorities and others. Up to £40 million was to be made available between 2006/7 and 2007/8 to help five additional growth areas.

Other proposals to be taken forward were the reform of Housing Benefit (extending the trial in which benefits had been paid directly to households in the form of local housing allowances), the licensing of Houses in Multiple Occupation and the licensing of homes in some other circumstances, particularly in areas of lower housing demand. In this sense the management aspirations of the government extended to significant parts of the private rented sector as well as the social rented sector.

While these commitments to rented housing were significant they must be seen against the historically low level of social rented housing and the huge support for home ownership. By 2005 the government's approach was gaining considerable momentum. In contrast to the early years of the Labour government, there was now a clear direction to policy and an obvious intention to adopt a more comprehensive approach to overcome some of the fragmentation of policy and loss of governmental control. Unlike earlier comprehensive housing policies, this one was driven by the unqualified commitment to home ownership.

Conclusion

The actions taken by the Labour government since 1997 in respect of housing have been underpinned by continuity in policy. Continuation of the Right to Buy, new policies to promote home ownership, enthusiasm for stock transfer (as well as Arm's-Length Management Organizations and Private Finance Initiatives) reflected acceptance of a public expenditure and taxation orthodoxy and a commitment to home ownership that was as unqualified as that of the Conservatives. However it was less moderated by an enthusiasm for private landlordism. The policy environment further embedded a residual approach and the belief that the role of the state could be reduced and better targeted. However no policy regime is one dimensional or wholly coherent.

While the continuities in policy are clear, the Labour government embarked on innovations that its predecessor was unlikely to have considered. These included the minimum wage, working families tax credit, an overall approach to the management of the economy, the regionalization of government and the modernization of public services through Best Value and inspection regimes. It is unlikely that a Conservative government would have been so impressed by arguments about housing market renewal (see Chapter 13) or modernizing the planning system to address affordability concerns.

Local housing provision has shifted to a multiplicity of public and non-profit providers (some of which are far from local), driven from the centre and subject to audits, inspections and performance measurement (see Chapter 7). The centralization of policy, regionalization and the growth of non-elected bodies add further dimensions. The accountability of Regional Housing Boards, the Housing Corporation and housing associations is still generally unclear to most people, leading to accusations of a 'democratic deficit'.

Although housing policy has responded mainly to households seeking home ownership it would wrong to imply a total neglect of other needs. Rising affluence has been accompanied by growing inequality, rather than trickling down to benefit all sections of the population. Social exclusion has become more evident, and where and in what housing people live is a key contributor to inequality as well as a product of it. The government has given greater recognition to these issues than governments in the past, and high levels of employment and a minimum wage have been fundamental in addressing these issues. The emphasis in housing policy on decent homes, regeneration and renewal through stock transfer has addressed some of the problems of the worst housed. But it has failed to bring about a high-quality, decommodified rental sector. The policy is fundamentally residual: committed to raising the quality of the housing service but not to altering its residual status.

Chapter 5

Home Ownership in Transition

The earlier chapters of this book have discussed the dramatic shift in the structure of housing tenure in the UK over the last century. At the beginning of the twentieth century Britain was a nation of tenants, but now it is a nation of home owners. Throughout Europe there has been a decline of private landlordism and a fundamental change in the way in which the private sector responds to the demand for housing, but the changes have been more dramatic in Britain and Ireland than elsewhere.

Some explanations of these changes tend to be rather one-dimensional. For example Saunders (1990) has explained the shift purely in terms of demand, the preference for owner-occupation, 'ontological security', and underlying cultural or even biological preferences for the ownership of property. While demand factors are no doubt part of the story, the explanation of the growth of home ownership needs to be more broadly based. The undeniable preference for home ownership that emerged in the late twentieth century was less about an innate desire for ownership than about the comparative advantages associated with that tenure compared with others (Merrett, 1982). The private rented sector was second best in terms of quality, condition, management and maintenance to both home ownership and council housing, and therefore the latter two tenures increased during the twentieth century.

The advantages of home ownership are not restricted to better property type and condition but also include financial benefits: tax relief to support purchase and increases in the asset value of housing in many markets. These advantages have been greatest for those with higher incomes and higher taxes, but some advantages have extended down the income scale. However the explanation also involves supply-side considerations.

Much of the growth of home ownership in the twentieth century was fuelled by the opportunity to purchase properties from the private rented sector, and latterly from the local authority sector through the Right to Buy. In both these cases the growth of home ownership resulted from supply-side decisions by owners to sell their properties due to financial, political and other considerations. The lack of political support for the private rented sector, the impact of slum clearance, the impact of rent control and the poor reputation of the sector with consumers are also part of the explanation of the growing importance of home ownership.

Both demand and supply influences on the growth of home ownership were affected by policy interventions. This is apparent in the partitioned system of housing finance (Nevitt, 1966; Merrett, 1982; Hills, 1991) and the differential treatment of tenures in financial terms – the positive encouragement of home ownership through tax relief and other financial measures, and subsequently through the Right to Buy scheme and a range of other policies.

This chapter discusses some of the key and contested issues related to home ownership:

- It provides a brief account of the historical development of the tenure, and particularly the influence of policy in facilitating a major long-term shift from renting to owning.
- It considers the role of taxation policies in consolidating the advantages of home ownership during critical periods in the growth of the sector.
- It discusses the origins and operation of the Right to Buy scheme and the significance of this in transforming the home ownership sector.
- It discusses contemporary policy approaches to home ownership in relation to affordability and other policy issues in the twenty-first century.
- In conclusion reference is made to emerging divisions in home ownership.

Table 5.1 provides a profile of the sector in 2001. While this conceals internal differences it is clear that home owners were more likely to occupy houses than flats, to be over 45 and in full-time employment. Satisfaction with accommodation was very high. Comparisons with profiles of other tenures are provided in Figures 5.1 and 5.2.

From renting to owning

By 2001 just over 14 million dwellings were classified as owner-occupied, or about 69 per cent of all dwellings in the UK. The dominance of home ownership was most pronounced in England, and in certain regions. Outside major urban areas, home ownership reached 80 per cent or more with a small social rented sector and an even smaller private rented sector. These figures stand in stark contrast to those in much of the twentieth century.

In 1910 fewer than 10 per cent of dwellings were owner-occupied. Subsequently the proportion rose to 25 per cent in 1938, 42 per cent in 1960, 51 per cent in 1971 and 57 per cent in 1981. Home ownership was much higher in some parts of the country, for example in West Yorkshire and Tyneside, where the building society movement was better developed, and parts of North-West England and South Wales. Around four million dwellings were constructed in England and Wales between 1914 and 1938, and approximately half of these were built for owner-occupation. Both the

Table 5.1 *Profile of home ownership, England, 2001 (per cent)*

Dwelling types	
Houses	92
Detached houses	30
Semidetached houses	36
Terraced houses	26
Purpose-built flats	4
Converted flats	2
Built prior to-1919	21
Built 1945–64	21
Built since 1985	14
Household types	
Household head over 45	61
Household head 16–24	1
Household head 25–44	37
Single-person households	23
Childless couples	44
Single parents	3
Full-time employment	62
Retired	27
Unemployed/other inactive	5
percentage satisfied with accommodation	95

Source: Data from ONS *Survey of English Housing 2000/1*.

government and building societies promoted home ownership and provided substantial assistance in the form of building subsidies and loans, land registration procedures and mortgage and loan guarantee schemes. The 1923 Housing Act had provided direct subsidies to builders of modest homes and allowed local authorities to lend to them for the same purpose. Local authorities could also guarantee building society advances on small dwellings and offer their own mortgages. However the early growth of home ownership was dominated by larger properties with higher values.

The flight from renting was initially restricted to the middle class. Swenarton and Taylor (1985) suggest that only the elite of the working class could afford to buy their own homes at that stage, and then at the expense of self-sacrifice and thrift. The variation in rates of home owner-ship between and within towns was related to the performance of the local economy, occupational structure, the built form, the willingness of private landlords to sell their properties and the rate of new house building. In 1939 the rates of home ownership in 24 towns ranged from 14 per cent in Nottingham to 68 per cent in Plymouth (ibid.). A survey of British households carried out in 1947 (Gray, 1947) revealed that 22 per cent of households owned their dwellings and 4 per cent were in the process of buying them.

Figure 5.1   *Dwelling age and type by tenure, England, 2001(per cent)*

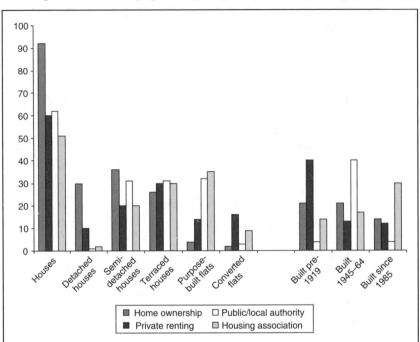

Source: Data from ONS *Survey of English Housing 2000/1*.

The rates ranged from 66 per cent for better-paid managerial and professional workers to 15 per cent for low-paid workers. Thus home ownership grew over the decades but varied according to locality and socio-economic group.

The age profile of home owners also changed. There were two principal groups. The first consisted mainly of newly forming or expanding households; these tended to be younger and bought new or second-hand properties on the open market. The second group comprised households that bought their properties as sitting tenants, either from a private landlord or from the local authority or housing association. These purchasers were more likely to be older and gained access to home ownership because of where they lived rather than because they had been actively seeking to purchase a house, but the properties in which they lived suited their requirements and resources. Initially home ownership was greatest amongst the younger age groups, but as they aged, older owners grew in proportion.

The expansion of home ownership has been facilitated by the activities of builders and developers, and decisions taken by private and public land-lords. Builders' decisions about what to build, where and when have been influenced by a range of financial and market considerations. Similarly

Figure 5.2 *Age, household type and employment by tenure, England, 2001(per cent)*

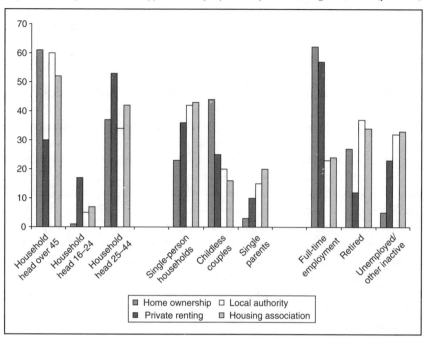

Source: Data from ONS *Survey of English Housing 2000/1*.

private landlords' decision to sell properties has reflected commercial and financial interests rather than tenants' wishes. Public landlords' decisions have also been affected by policies laid down by the central government. Thus tenants have responded to the opportunities and choices presented to them by landlords, rather than determining the choices available.

Over time the housing market has come to be dominated by second-hand transactions and home ownership is now much more mixed in terms of age, income, social class and ethnicity. While it would be wrong to argue that the structure of home ownership was ever uniform and consisted mainly of better-off members of the middle class, as this form of tenure has expanded it has become more fragmented and differentiated (Forrest *et al.*, 1990). The rights and meanings associated with home ownership have also changed over time. In the 1930s there were major disputes about the rights of home owners, and collusion between building societies and builders often operated to the disadvantage of home owners (ibid.). Even in later periods, limited access to credit from building societies and other sources, practices relating to red-lining and discrimination in providing loans to women, minority ethnic groups and certain occupational groups affected the development of the sector. The regulation of building societies and the practices they adopted meant that they often rationed loans rather than responded to demand.

The rise in home ownership was also associated with a continuous lack of political support for private landlordism and a progressive under-mining of public housing. The proportion of those who expressed a preference for home ownership rose from 66 per cent in 1967 to 81 per cent in 1999. The link between the growth of this tenure and the activities of building societies has been well established, but a wider industry associ-ated with the home ownership sector also developed. It is also evident that home ownership grew as a result of energetic sponsorship by the government. We have already referred to the 1923 Housing Act, and later in this chapter we shall consider the Right to Buy scheme. Some of the most important legislative measures were those that provided a clear and sound legal and financial basis for the development of home ownership. Politicians and the media increasingly referred to home ownership as the natural and most desirable form of tenure. More concretely, governments began to provide more generous subsidies and explicit incentives for homeownership: tax relief, the abolition of Schedule A tax, the develop-ment of option mortgage schemes, and greater cooperation with building societies, builders and developers to achieve the optimum growth of home ownership.

The role of taxation policies

Mortgage interest tax relief was a major driver of home ownership in the twentieth century and became very important in the last quarter of the century, when the proportion of households in the UK that owned their own homes grew from 53 per cent to 69 per cent (Wilcox, 2004). Its origins lay in the income tax system set up in 1803, which allowed borrowers to repay the interest on loans net of tax, and a special arrange-ment introduced in 1925–26, which removed the tax on building society loan interest and allowed borrowers to set interest charges against their income for tax purposes. This procedure was given legislative force in 1951. At that stage there was a balancing factor in the equation – Schedule A tax, or taxation on the imputed rental income from a dwelling – but in 1963 this was abolished and the balance of advantage shifted further in favour of home ownership. In 1974 a ceiling was set on mortgage interest tax relief and the maximum mortgage eligible for tax relief was £25 000; in 1983 this was raised to £30 000. However these levels were very high compared with the price of properties at those times. In effect the system enabled home owners to write off some of the costs of mortgage interest against tax. These were written off at the highest rate of tax that the purchaser paid, so high-income earners in the highest tax bracket benefited enormously from being a home owner rather than a tenant.

Initially tax relief was relatively unimportant because most people did not pay income tax. However as incomes rose and tax thresholds were lowered it became increasingly advantageous. The value of mortgage interest tax relief rose sharply after the 1960s, when house prices and interest rates increased, the number of home purchasers grew and tax thresholds and tax rates changed. Tax relief was regressive and provided no benefit to those who did not pay tax because their incomes were too low, including many elderly people. The value of tax relief was greater in areas with higher house prices – for example the South-East of England – than in lower-price areas. In spite of the ceiling on tax relief, the value of mortgage interest tax relief continued to increase until the 1990s, when pressure for its modification began to have an impact.

The scale of mortgage interest tax relief was reduced by the Conservatives, starting with the abolition of double relief for unmarried couples in 1988, and then limiting relief to the basic rate of tax in 1991. Its phased removal was announced in 1993 (see Chapter 3) and it was finally abolished by the Labour government in 2002, but there were ironies in this situation. By the time tax relief was removed a large proportion of the population had already benefited from it and the maximum mortgage eligible for the subsidy (£30 000) meant that its remaining significance in terms of overall housing costs was less for higher-income groups in high-price areas than for lower-income groups in lower-price areas.

The removal of mortgage interest tax relief did not mean that home ownership was no longer favoured by the government. Capital gains and inheritance tax arrangements still favoured home ownership, and the unequal treatment of different tenures continued to provide a relative advantage to home ownership. The promotion of home ownership is now less dependent on explicit subsidies than in the earlier phase, and is more strongly ingrained in the practices of what has become a nation of home owners and in the institutions associated with home ownership. Each new generation of households entering the housing market in the UK is likely to consist of more second-generation home owners, and the greater variety of products now on offer from banks, building societies, insurance companies, estate agents, builders and developers mean that home ownership has become increasingly normal, or even the natural form of tenure.

The sale of council houses

Earlier in this chapter we discussed how the transfer of properties from the private rented sector to owner-occupation supplemented new building in the growth of home ownership. In the final part of the twentieth century individual sales of public sector properties became another significant driver of home ownership. Sales to tenants became part of housing policy in the 1960s, increased in the 1970s and became a dominating influence in the 1980s with the introduction of the Right to Buy scheme.

The Right to Buy was introduced in 1980 in the first year of office of a newly elected Conservative government, which implemented its manifesto pledge to replace discretionary powers with a statutory scheme. Over the next 25 years over two million homes were sold to qualifying tenants at a substantial discount. After 1980 a number of changes were made to the scheme to increase take-up, for example the introduction of higher discounts and a differential, higher rate for flats.

Under the Right to Buy individual dwellings were sold on either a freehold or a leasehold basis to qualifying sitting tenants at a price determined by an independent valuation (based on the vacant possession market value and adjusted by a discount determined by length of tenancy and property type). This was essentially an administrative transaction determined by bureaucratic rules and underpinned by legislation. Subsequent transactions for the resale of properties were more market-based and depended on local patterns of supply and demand and the position that former council properties had in the local market (although discount claw-back rules were likely to inhibit sales in the first few years). However with leasehold properties (flats) there was a relationship between each new purchaser and the local authority or other landlord in terms of maintenance, repair and service obligations for common areas.

The emergence of the Right to Buy from earlier discretionary sales schemes to become a major element of the housing landscape has been extensively documented (for example Murie, 1975, 1989; Forrest and Murie, 1988; Jones and Murie, 1998). Table 5.3 summarizes the main phases of its evolution. When the scheme was introduced in 1980 it was regarded as a flagship policy by Margaret Thatcher's first administration and a symbol of the government's intention to roll back the state and privatize public services. However it is should be recognized that its origins lie deeper in the evolution of Conservative thinking on housing and that local authorities in England had already sold some 210 000 dwellings under discretionary policies. Had these policies continued there would still have been a substantial sale of council houses, especially in view of the strength of Conservative control of local government for a considerable period after 1979. The Right to Buy was not responsible for the wider package of policies that began to reshape the perceptions and realities of council housing and other tenures in the 1980s and 1990s. Thus the residualization of council housing was well under way before 1980 and it would have continued, especially if rents, Housing Benefit and capital investment had

Table 5.2 *Evolution of the Right to Buy scheme, 1970–2005*

	Character of policy	Key features	Number of homes sold
Pre-1980	Discretionary sales policy	Ministerial consent to sales required. In practice this involved setting out the general terms for consent in ministerial circulars, with changing requirements	210 000
1980–85	Right to Buy legislation	Statutory sales with very few exceptions and no local discretion	643 000
1986–96	Second wave	Increased discounts and more favourable market conditions	1 100 000
1997–2005	Third wave	Anxiety about restrictions on the Right to Buy, some reductions in maximum discounts and new legislation to address specific problems	700 000

remained largely the same. In this respect the Right to Buy can be seen as accelerating changes that were already occurring.

Discretionary sales

The precursor of the Right to Buy was the power given to local authorities – under legislation that went back to the origins of council housing – to dispose of council dwellings. This legislation was used between the wars and increasingly from the 1950s onwards (Murie, 1975). Local authorities had to obtain the permission of the relevant minister to dispose of dwellings but the minister, rather than scrutinizing each individual proposal, issued a general consent that indicated the terms under which such disposals should be carried out. Hence individual permission was not required for each disposal.

With regard to the way in which local authorities used this policy, it is clear that by the 1960s the local Conservative Party in a number of areas saw an electoral advantage in offering to sell council houses. This was particularly apparent in Birmingham and Greater London. Here and elsewhere the Conservative Party fought local elections with a promise to sell council houses. Substantial sales ensued, concentrated in a small number of authorities and with the consent of the responsible ministers in both Conservative and Labour governments. However it is evident that Labour ministers were nervous about increasing the sale of properties and by the late 1960s had begun to restrict sales, but not to prohibit them through the general consent. Equally some Conservative-controlled authorities were opposed to the sale of council houses, especially in high-price areas. To some Conservatives council housing was part of the proud record of local government provision for local citizens and there was strong opposition to disposal. One example is that of Guildford, where the council leader, Lady Anson, was also chair of the housing committee of the Conservative-controlled Association of District Councils. Although the divisions on this issue did not follow simple party or central–local government lines, they became more clearly drawn as enthusiasm for sales increased in the 1970s. The Heath government introduced a general consent to encourage tenants to buy and increased the discounts, with discounts of up to 30 per cent of the market value of properties being allowed. Against this background and the wider economic climate, sales increased dramatically in the early 1970s but soon began to decline because of the high interest rates and the economic problems that arose in the latter years of the Heath government.

In summary, discretionary sales established the basic mechanism for sales at market value, discounted according to length of tenancy. However discounts were limited to a maximum of 30 per cent. Most of the properties sold were houses with gardens and the purchasers were most likely to be more affluent tenants in later middle age. Not all local authorities engaged in sales and in the non-selling areas there was likely to be more pent-up demand than elsewhere. Studies conducted in this period in Birmingham analyzed the impact of the policy on different groups: existing tenants, future tenants, the local authority and the central government. It was concluded that there was an unambiguous benefit to those who purchased houses under discretionary schemes, but a loss to existing tenants who did not buy and to future tenants whose choice would be restricted (Niner, 1975; Murie, 1975). Figure 5.3 shows sales to date under the statutory Right to Buy scheme.

Pioneering the right to buy

When the Thatcher government came into power in 1979 it immediately adjusted the discretionary policy and introduced the same terms that would subsequently be incorporated into the Right to Buy scheme: a more generous system of discounts and the inclusion of almost all properties and tenants of at least three years' standing. With Conservatives in charge of the majority of local authorities, sales under the discretionary policy were wide spread and the numbers increased rapidly. By the time

Figure 5.3 *Right to Buy sales, Britain, 1980–2003*

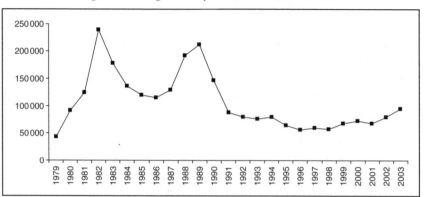

Source: Compiled from data in Wilcox (2004).

the Right to Buy was introduced in 1980 there had already been a surge in sales.

The government's commitment to the Right to Buy was unqualified. It was not impressed by evidence about winners and losers, or fears about the consequences of the Right to Buy in respect of the way in which council housing would evolve. It could see nothing but good coming out of the policy and robustly pursued local authorities that were deemed to be implementing the policy in a laggardly way. It harried underperformers and went as far as to use the default powers in legislation and to set up a commissioner to ensure that sales were carried out vigorously in the city of Norwich (Forrest and Murie, 1994).

During the pioneering phase of the Right to Buy, sales rose to a peak of over 200 000 dwellings in 1981. This generated windfall capital receipts on a much larger scale than had been anticipated because many tenants borrowed from private financial institutions rather than take out local authority mortgages, as under the discretionary scheme. Consequently the transfer of funding responsibility from the public to the private sector was more significant than expected and the benefits to the exchequer were much greater.

After the initial surge, sales began to fall away. This was not because of any obstruction by local government – the legislation was sufficiently tightly framed that local authorities could not significantly prevent or even delay the Right to Buy once the workload associated with the initial surge of applications had diminished. The decline was partly because pent-up demand had been met and partly due to economic factors, including rising unemployment and high interest rates.

The second wave

In this phase the government responded to the general decline in take-up and the much lower take-up in urban areas and by tenants of flats and maisonettes, and to a series of problems connected with the sale of defective dwellings.

In 1984 the discounts were increased. The maximum discount of 50 per cent on all properties was raised to 60 per cent for houses and 70 per cent for flats. The discount entitlements for tenants in houses rose from 32 per cent after a minimum of two years' tenancy to 60 per cent after 30 years. In flats they rose from 44 per cent after two years to 70 per cent after 15 years. These discount rates must be regarded as extravagant and, especially in the case of flats, consciously designed to persuade people to buy less desirable and perhaps less saleable properties by reducing prices so far below the market values.

The housing defects legislation of 1984 attempted to deal with the problem created by the sale of defective dwellings. It prioritized refurbishment of certain sold dwelling types that would otherwise not have been seen as the first targets for investment. To this extent the Right to Buy began to distort decisions about where to spend housing resources.

Take-up increased after 1984, partly because of the higher discounts but also due to improvements in the economy (falling unemployment, rising incomes) and awareness that the housing market and house prices were booming. Tenants who could see owner-occupiers benefiting from appreciating asset values became convinced of the advantages of joining that club.

As in the pioneering phase, the second wave was seen as a great success by the government and it again delivered in terms of public expenditure. However the capital receipts were not used to reinvest in housing but to assist the government's policies on taxation and public expenditure. The absence of any policy vision for rented housing and council housing in particular was apparent.

Further problems began to emerge in relation to the sale of flats and maisonettes. The government had given little thought to how leasehold properties would be managed and what kind of charges would be incurred after the sale had taken place. In a number of London boroughs, including the then housing minister's own constituency of Ealing, there were conflicts with home owners over arrangements for leasehold management and service charges that had not been fully explained at the time of sale. Some home owners who had bought because the prices were so low now found that the high service charges and the charges for major essential repairs were causing real financial difficulties. Others discovered that lenders would not contemplate further mortgages on certain types of property, particularly flats in blocks of more than five storeys, making these properties virtually unsaleable.

The boom in flat sales began to tail off, partly because of growing awareness of these issues but also because of further changes in the economy and the housing market at the end of the 1980s. The end of the housing boom was signalled by unprecedentedly high interest rates and falling sales and property prices. Tenants who bought at the peak of the boom were affected by these developments and prospective purchasers were put off. Although Right to Buy purchasers were less likely to end up with negative equity or mortgage arrears than purchasers in general (because they had bought at such generously discounted prices), they were nonetheless affected by some of these problems and generally experienced a considerable increase in mortgage payments and a reduction in the value and marketability of their properties.

The third wave

After the Labour government came to power in 1997 it initially did nothing to alter the Right to Buy. While in opposition the Labour Party had gradually moved from opposition to the scheme to acceptance of it, and interfering with it now was viewed as risky and unnecessary. However it did adopt stock transfer as a core policy, and over time this would reduce the number of tenants entitled to buy their dwellings as new tenants of transfer landlords had no Right to Buy. Nonetheless changes in the economy and housing market began to take effect, much as they had done in the first and second phases. Increased employment and affluence, greater confidence in the economy, lower interest rates and a booming housing market created an environment that was favourable to the Right to Buy. Sales increased, and no doubt the windfall benefits of this for the Treasury were welcomed.

While the scheme was supported, doubt was expressed about its value for money and some questioned whether the terms of sale were appropriate and the levels of discount excessively high. In England, following a period of consultation, it was decided that the maximum discount ceiling should be reduced and applied at a variable level in different regions from February 1999. The probable consequence of this was that although in theory there would still be a relationship between length of tenancy and the rate of discount, an increasing number of people would hit the discount ceiling before their full entitlement was reached.

Early news of the intended change and sometimes inaccurate publicity by organizations providing 'guidance' for purchasers triggered a rush to buy. This did not diminish everywhere when the new discount arrangements were implemented. One possible reason for this was that younger tenants realized that their discount entitlement would not increase with time, and this encouraged them to purchase immediately. By now many middle-aged tenants had already bought their dwellings, and a large proportion of the remaining tenants did not have a 30-year or even a 20-year tenancy on which entitlement could be calculated. Purchase was also attractive to younger tenants who expected house prices to rise in a booming market.

New problems emerged during this phase, including the activities of canvassers and others seeking to exploit the Right to Buy. There was a significant number of abuses, mainly in high-price areas such as London (Jones, 2004). There were also issues relating to the demolition or major restructuring of local authority estates where considerable purchases had been made. By this stage it was no longer feasible to remove the Right to Buy, not only politically and because of impact on the Treasury, but also because of claims under human rights legislation. The most that could be done would be to make the Right to Buy less generous, to make abuse less easy, and to address interaction with regeneration policies. The changes made to the scheme from 18 January 2005 included the following:

- The initial qualification period was extended from two years to five years for new tenancies.
- The discount repayment period was extended from three years to five years, with discretion not to require the repayment of the discount if doing so might cause hardship.
- The amount of discount to be repaid if a property was sold within five years would be a percentage of the market value at the time of resale, irrespective of the value of improvements made by the owner.
- If a landlord intended to demolish a property the Right to Buy could be suspended when an initial demolition notice was served by the landlord and ended when the final demolition notice had been served.
- Tenants who agreed during the discount period to sell their home to a third party at a later date should repay some or all of the discount, as though they had actually sold their home at the time of the agreement.
- Owners who wished to resell their home within 10 years of it having been sold under the Right to Buy should first offer it at market value to their former landlord or to another body prescribed by the secretary of state.
- Landlords should give their tenants information on the costs and responsibilities of home ownership.

Policy impacts

By the end of 2004 over two million properties had been sold in the UK under the Right to Buy scheme and its equivalent in Northern Ireland. It was the biggest privatization project ever carried out by UK governments, and it had sustained a flow of capital receipts over a period of 25 years.

However the scheme had fallen far short of the expectations of some of its promoters. More than half of all council tenants had chosen not to take advantage of it, and those who had, had not become confirmed Conservative voters or kept the scheme's initiators in power.

Most of the households that had exercised their Right to Buy had obtained some financial advantages. In some cases there had been short-term disadvantages if the market had turned against them immediately after purchase, but five or 10 years on, former tenants were owners of properties that had a much higher value than when they were purchased. When problems were experienced they were problems that affected all home owners, such as those arising from changes in employment, the breakdown of relationships, changes in health or ageing, which could lead to diffi-culties in retaining ownership, maintaining and repairing properties, or being able to move on. These problems were no more pronounced among Right to Buy purchasers than among home owners in general, and problems with the condition and repair of properties were generally less marked.

A significant number of Right to Buy purchasers were able to move on to different kinds of housing in different locations, and had more choice than they would have had if they had remained tenants. At the same time some owned properties whose value was too low to allow such a move, and if their incomes were also low they were better off remaining as council tenants as then they would be eligible for transfer to housing that was more appropriate for their circumstances. Nonetheless for most of those who exercised their Right to Buy there were significant and measurable benefits. Very few failed to benefit and the risk was no greater than among home owners in general.

However real problems arose from the impact of the scheme and other policies on the council housing sector. Those still living in it had less choice and poorer-quality housing. Less desirable flats and maisonettes were still available as their sale had lagged behind that of other properties, especially houses in the better estates and the most affluent neighbourhoods. Thus the Right to Buy had rewarded those who were already benefiting most from council housing, to the detriment of those in the worst properties or on the council waiting list.

If the question 'Did the policy achieve the government's aims?' is asked about the Right to Buy, the answer must be mixed. It did to the extent that governments increased the opportunities for home ownership amongst council tenants, but did not insofar as this was only partially achieved. The aims of government to privatize public assets, change patterns of ownership and secure a continuous stream of income that could be used to manage public finances, taxation and investment were achieved. At the same time they failed to anticipate some of the problems that emerged from the Right to Buy: disputes about defective properties and leaseholds, and abuses of various kinds. Nor is it evident that they anticipated the effect that the Right to Buy would have on the overall position of council housing.

In conclusion it is clear that the Right to Buy and related policies have had mixed consequences. On the one hand they have provided opportunities and advantages to a particular group of tenants whose assets, wealth and mobility options have changed, and they have boosted government finances. On the other hand they have left a legacy of devalorized devalued neighbourhoods, a highly stigmatized tenure and a pattern of fragmented ownership that has made estate and market renewal more difficult and costly. This will present a policy challenge for governments over the next 30 years and will require consistent public expenditure. Thus the Right to Buy has rescheduled governments' financial commitments by altering the pattern of income and expenditure, generating substantial capital receipts and achieving short-term windfall gains for governments in the 1980s, 1990s and the early years of the twenty-first century, but leaving an inheritance that will involve increased expenditure in the future years.

Affordable housing

In addition to tax benefits and the sale of council houses, there have been a variety of government programmes to promote wider access to home ownership. These programmes have generally focused on lowering the cost of home ownership to first-time purchasers or providing additional rungs on the home ownership ladder, and latterly on bridging the affordability gap. Low-cost home ownership has been defined as 'increasing the supply of and demand for existing and new homes for sale at low cost' (Booth and Crook, 1986). The question has often arisen as to whether such schemes actually increase the take-up of home ownership or simply add to the choices to available households that already have the means to enter owner-occupation.

Early schemes

Among the forebears of today's low-cost home ownership programmes were the homesteading scheme initiated by the Greater London Council in the 1970s, and the improvement for sale scheme initiated by Birmingham City Council in the same decade. There were also a number of local schemes for area improvement and renovation, including the provision of improvement grants. These schemes offered subsidies to shield purchasers from the full costs of improvement and purchase, or to reduce the extent to which costs were loaded in the early year. In the 1970s some local authorities introduced innovative schemes to expand the variety of home ownership in their districts. Building-for-sale schemes became popular, and some benefited from local authority land provided at cost price or under licence, enabling builders to produce new housing at a lower price than if they had had to purchase the land at the outset. The local authorities in Plymouth and Birmingham received considerable publicity for their schemes and this encouraged private sector builders to construct affordable homes for people on the local authority waiting list, with marketing extended beyond the waiting list when appropriate. In the same period Birmingham's equity sharing scheme was developed, a precursor of the later shared ownership schemes. Hence local authorities did not simply provide council housing for rent, although their involvement in urban renewal and new housing development was sometimes constrained by the legislative and financial framework within which they had to operate.

In this period local authorities were also major providers of mortgage finance, and while their mortgages did not fully meet the needs of people excluded from bank and building society mortgages they did effectively channel finance to some lower-income households. In Birmingham, local authority mortgage lending had an enormous impact on the development of home ownership among black and minority ethnic communities, and in inner city areas where slum clearance and improvement policies had led building societies and other lenders to restrict their lending in other parts of the city. In these areas home ownership was stimulated by local government measures including the sale of council houses prior to the introduction of the Right to Buy.

Conservative low-cost home ownership initiatives

Initiatives introduced by the Conservative government after 1980 consolidated the above approaches. There were seven elements to its overall programme:

- Selling council houses to sitting tenants.
- Selling local authority land to private builders with planning permission to build starter homes.
- Building starter homes on local authority land in partnership with private builders.
- Improving homes for sale.
- Selling unimproved homes for improvement by purchasers.
- Offering shared ownership as an alternative to outright purchase wherever possible.
- Using the new local authority mortgage guarantee power to facilitate downmarket lending by building societies.

The most important schemes were those that involved building for sale, and housing associations played an increasing part in this. Shared ownership had different dimensions, including a do-it-yourself shared ownership scheme that enabled people to share the ownership of properties that had not been earmarked for shared ownership sale. Other schemes included cash incentives to council tenants under the Housing Act of 1988. This Act allowed local authorities to provide grants to help tenants purchase a home in the private sector, which not only enabled people to move to private sector housing of their choice but also released housing in the local authority rented sector. The grants were particularly advantageous to people who did not wish to exercise their Right to Buy because their current property was insufficiently attractive, although it also meant that the property released might not be attractive to future tenants.

It is difficult to evaluate the overall impact of such a wide range of schemes, each with rather different features and take-up (but see, for example, Forrest *et al.* 1984). However in general the beneficiaries tended to be households that already had some degree of housing choice and had a similar profile to those entering the home ownership market in general. They did not have significantly lower incomes or different social and economic characteristics from other first-time buyers. Some of the schemes had limited effect, partly because the housing market had matured by the 1970s and 1980s. It no longer consisted exclusively of higher priced houses but also included unimproved, low-priced, inner-city terraced properties. Some of these were sold by private landlords to sitting tenants, others were sold when they became vacant, but in general they had a poor history of maintenance and repair and their value reflected their neglect over a considerable period of time.

Consequently the market was providing some less desirable options at lower prices without special schemes. This even applied in parts of London, where the process of gentrification was underway but had not developed sufficiently to remove the low-cost element. Newly built housing, even with subsidies for land purchase or construction, was unlikely to cost less than the cheapest terraced house, especially in cities in the Midlands and the North of England. The argument that the government should intervene to provide low-cost housing was therefore difficult to sustain – there was often no missing rung on the ladder and providing new low-cost housing could deplete the funds for renewing older housing stock. There was also some abuse of home ownership schemes, for example in Westminster empty council homes were sold for electoral vote-gaining purposes.

New Labour and low-cost home ownership

As discussed earlier, when the Labour government was elected in 1997 it maintained the Right to Buy scheme and this, together with the Right to Acquire and Voluntary Purchase Grants, continued to have the greatest impact on the growth of home ownership. Low-cost home ownership schemes were also continued. Bramley *et al.* (2002) identify two main types of scheme – shared ownership and homebuy – as well as flexible tenure, cash incentive schemes, shared ownership for the elderly, and grants for rent and ownership in Scotland.

Shared ownership was divided into conventional shared ownership and the more small-scale do-it-yourself shared ownership. In conventional shared ownership the supplier, usually a housing association, built a new housing unit and the purchaser part-owned and part-rented it from the supplier. In England and Wales the shared owner was a leaseholder of the housing association, which retained the freehold of the property. Usually the leaseholder had a 99-year lease and there was a possibility of increasing the share owned by the leaseholder by means of 'staircasing', buying further shares up to 100 per cent. Eligibility for conventional shared ownership varied, but schemes funded by the Housing Corporation were generally targeted at tenants of housing associations or local authorities, or those on waiting lists for such housing.

Homebuy was introduced in Wales in the early 1990s and in England in 1999. It involved the provision of an equity loan for the purchase of any property, so it was not directly linked to additions to the housing stock but rather provided access to existing housing. Under Homebuy, housing associations provided interest-free equity loans to cover part of the purchase cost. Purchasers took out a conventional loan to cover the part of the purchase cost they could afford and the equity loan covered the balance. Upon resale or staircasing, the housing association that had provided the equity loan was paid the relevant percentage of the current market value, and in periods of rising values received a return on its loan in the form of capital appreciation.

For both the shared ownership and the Homebuy schemes, housing associations benefited from a rising market, and from the mid 1990s this gave a better return on investment than other alternatives would have done. Consequently these schemes were very popular with housing associations and the Housing Corporation. The ability to recycle receipts, including recycled capital grants, meant that not only were there good returns on investment, but also these could be periodically reinvested in housing.

Bramley *et al.* (2002) draw attention to the limited scale of Low Cost Home Ownership (LCHO) compared with the Right to Buy scheme. In 1999 the total number of shared ownership units in England was 80 000 and there was a similar number under the Cash Incentive Scheme, compared with two million under the Right to Buy. Annual additions to the programme between 1998/99 and 2000/1 amounted to less than 4000, compared with the Right to Buy sales of more than 40 000. Homebuy was strongly targeted at London and the South of England, while there was a downward trend in the Midlands and the North. The research suggests that almost all LCHO purchasers in London would have been unable to afford to buy locally. In other regions the pattern was different; while in the South-East and South-West very few LCHO purchasers could have bought on the open market, the proportions were much higher in the North-East and North-West.

Bramley *et al.* (ibid.) also provide evidence of the types of household involved in LCHO. Almost one in two were without children and 85 per cent had one or more full-time workers; 71 per cent were in professional, inter-mediate clerical, junior managerial or skilled manual jobs, 17 per cent had previously been owner-occupiers (42 per cent in Wales, only 3 per cent in London) and 30 per cent were new to home ownership. The beneficiaries of the scheme expressed a high degree of satisfaction. They were not typical of people moving into the social rented sector and had more bargaining power in the housing market, but insufficient bargaining power in places where the supply of low-cost housing was limited – that is, London and the South.

This raises questions about the value of the schemes in markets where lower-price properties were available for sale. It appears that LCHO schemes had sometimes been adopted with little attention to market circumstances, and were intended to expand home ownership irrespective of local market impacts. There was strong support by the Housing Corporation for the schemes (Home Ownership Taskforce, 2003) and the benefits to housing association balance sheets in rising markets have already been noted. In this context it is important to note that 18 per cent of the properties bought under all types of scheme were flats, rising to 50 per cent in London. The usefulness of the schemes to provide what the CML referred to as 'a foot on the home ownership ladder' is open to question if the next rung was an extremely long way up and there were few choices in the housing market.

The Sustainable Communities Plan and the five-year plan for housing (Office of the Deputy Prime Minister, 2005) provided a stimulus to address the housing problems faced by key workers in high-costs areas. The aim was to add a further million to the number of home owners by 2010. The Starter Homes Initiative and its successor, the Key Worker Living Scheme, were both targeted at the housing markets in London and the South-East and East of England, where the high cost of housing was considered to be affecting employers' ability to recruit and retain staff. The Key Worker Living Scheme was targeted at nurses and other NHS staff, teachers, police officers, prison service and probation service staff, social workers, full-time junior fire fighters and other public sector employees. Equity loans of up to £50000 were available to the targeted groups, and loans of up to £100000 for elite teachers with the potential to rise to leading positions in the London education system. Shared ownership and an intermediate rented sector, with rents lying between those charged by social and private landlords, were also developed under the scheme, which was operated by 'zone agents': housing associations that marketed the schemes for key workers in individual areas. The intention was to secure some 30 000 homes for key workers over a three-year period, although not all of these would be newly built homes.

These initiatives provided an opportunity not just for entry to home ownership but also for existing owners to purchase larger houses. People in professional and other well-paid occupations could obtain good-quality homes in other regions, so if rented housing or small open market houses were all that were available to them in high-cost areas they would be unlikely to seek employment there. The consequence of this would be a leakage of key workers away from London and the South-East. In order to recruit and retain such workers it was therefore important not just to give them a foot on the ladder but also to assist them to progress towards the kind of housing to which they aspired. All of this made sense in the light of the uneven circumstances in the housing market and the shortages arising from that, but looked at from another perspective it added a new type of inequity to the system. State subsidies were being provided to well-paid key workers in some regions, while in other regions households with lower incomes were not offered comparable support.

After the 2005 election the re-elected Labour government continued to voice its intention to push home ownership to beyond 75 per cent. It began to negotiate a new form of shared ownership in which building societies and banks would work with the government to protect new home owners from some of the risk of future market decline as well as enabling first-time buyers to purchase dwellings in high-cost areas. The responses to this proposal were less positive than anticipated, with the press questioning the use of public subsidies in this way (*Daily Telegraph*, 24 May 2005), lenders seeking additional security and assured profits, Shelter (2005) arguing that the scheme would divert resources away from the homeless and fuel house price inflation, and commentators generally questioning its effectiveness unless the supply of housing was also increased.

Divisions in home ownership

The expansion of owner-occupation to become the dominant form of tenure in the UK does not mean that it can be treated as a single category. It has always embraced very different types of property in different markets ranging from dilapidated inner city terraced properties sold by neglectful private landlords, to flats in mansion blocks in central London sold off by their owners to generate a return, large detached houses with extensive gardens in rural areas, retirement homes in coastal resorts, and Right to Buy properties in large council estates. It includes leasehold and freehold properties, properties owned outright or with substantial mortgage debt, properties that have appreciated in value and are in high demand, and properties in low-demand areas where prices have remained static or at times fallen.

The extent of this heterogeneity renders it difficult to discuss affordability based on average house prices and average incomes. For example few people with an average income were able to afford to buy any type of property in large parts of the South-West and the South-East of England. Clearly some people have chosen to pay the very high prices for housing in these areas. They may have done so because they have high incomes or have decided to commit a high proportion of their income to housing in anticipation that the value of this asset will grow more rapidly than their income or alternative forms of investment. As affluence increases, additional increments of income may be disproportionately committed to housing than to other consumption expenditure. This may reflect views on the value of property as a store of wealth, especially in times when pension plans and the stock market are failing. Purchasers' willingness to pay a high price may also be because they see themselves as buying a very specific product, status and neighbourhood (for example a large detached house in a particular school catchment area). Moreover differentiation of the product may mean that there is increased differentiation in price in certain parts of the market, with housing becoming a positional good.

If this is the case these will be distinct submarkets within the overall housing market, such as a mass urban housing market, a high-status urban market, and a market on the urban–rural fringe, unaligned with particular places of work but related to considerations of commuting distance and affordability. Indeed there are enormous variations in price within small areas and between adjacent neighbourhoods. Some of these variations are to do with different types of dwellings lying in close proximity to one another. Others are to do with features of the neighbourhood environment, including local services, accessibility, reputation and other factors.

Attempts to summarize the accessibility of home ownership by crude affordability calculations at the district council level raise broader questions about the way in which we understand and describe housing situations. It is more appropriate to talk about home ownership in terms of different parts of the housing market, access to and the affordability of those parts. In some cases these may be defined in spatial or geographical terms, in others they may relate to dwelling type and size, neighbourhood characteristics or even whether they are former Right to Buy properties.

Similarly we need to refer to potential purchasers in very different ways. The conventional affordability calculations do not take account of different cohorts or demand groups, but use terms such as first-time buyer. They are disproportionately dependent on employment income as the key determinant of home ownership, when we know that people draw upon savings, borrow from friends and family, are willing to commit different proportions of income, especially in the short term, and manage their housing finances in different ways. Potential purchasers also include buy-to-let landlords, people looking for second homes, people who benefit from relocation packages or special support from their employer, and people who receive very substantial bonuses as part of their remuneration package.

All of the above mean that house prices in some parts of the market reflect very different circumstances than in other parts of the market. Discussions of housing market and affordability trends need to consider the range of products and niches in regional and local markets. This is already evident in policy debates on leasehold and commonhold property, low-demand neighbourhoods and home ownership in low-priced areas, and in policies on low-cost home ownership and the improvement and repair of older properties.

However it is possible to detect some moves towards homogeneity, for example in relation to institutions and financial mechanisms in different parts of the housing market. In the past there was evidence that at the lower end of the market there were different institutional structures in different markets. One response to the 'redlining' of certain areas by building societies in the 1960s and 1970s was the use of local authority mortgages, as described earlier; another was the development of different institutions by black and minority ethnic households people to facilitate purchase in certain areas (Sarre *et al.*, 1989). Karn *et al.* (1985) found that Asian house purchasers in Liverpool and Birmingham made very substantial use of informal loans rather than mortgages for house purchase in the late 1970s. More recent evidence suggests that this is less likely to be the case today. In 2004, lenders and interest rates at the bottom end of the housing market in Housing Market Renewal Areas appeared to be no different from those in booming markets in other parts of the country (Office of the Deputy Prime Minister, 2005). Moreover lenders had expanded their range of products to penetrate these markets, such as forms of finance that were compatible with Islamic Sharia law.

This takes us back full circle to debates on home ownership and the promotion and meaning of home ownership. Some commentators have emphasized the common class interest of home owners and contrasted this with the interests of tenants. Saunders (1990) refers to home ownership as a key 'consumption sector cleavage', representing a vertical division in society. In this perspective home owners have common interests irrespective of social class, and the consumption sector cleavage cross-cuts traditional conceptions of class and inequality. But home ownership now embraces enormous variations and inequality in circumstances. Home owners do not have a common interest with all other home owners, but the part of the housing sector they occupy may align with their interests in relation to work and other aspects of life. If in the past home ownership was a measure of social position, it has become less of a positional good in that sense. Instead parts of the housing sector have become associated with social position, a factor that has long been responded to by the marketing professions, which uses detailed profiles of owners in different postcode and census areas to market different lifestyle and positional goods.

Conclusions

Home ownership is now the dominant tenure in the UK. During the twentieth century owner-occupation gradually became the preferred tenure for all social groups, and the financial and organizational activities of the private sector were reoriented from the letting of properties to their sale. This was encouraged by successive governments and can therefore be thought of as state-sponsored: tax relief and the Right to Buy scheme are examples of subsidies designed to encourage the expansion of home ownership. As this form of tenure has grown it has also differentiated, and differences within the tenure should not be overlooked, including inequalities associated with where people buy.

Home ownership is also a significant constituent of household wealth and it has become the most important element in the wealth of most households in the UK. Thus home ownership is not just about use value but is increasingly about asset value and wealth accumulation. This asset value is not always realizable as the sale of a home is usually accompanied by the purchase of another property. However equity extraction has increased enormously over the past 25 years: Holmans (1991) charts a tenfold increase between 1981 and 1988, amounting to £16 billion a year. Household strategies to extract equity – such as trading down, for example by moving to a lower-price area or a smaller dwelling – have been supplemented by institutional support for remortgaging to release equity for home improvements and general household spending, and by new products that enable older home owners to enjoy their assets while they are able. These changes in home ownership will have an impact on the next generation in terms of inheritance and wealth transfer.

In recent years the government has given greater attention to asset ownership. It has begun to see this as a significant feature of home ownership and discussed ways of achieving equity shares through other processes or in other tenures. With this agenda housing policy is less about providing shelter or guiding housing consumption than about differences in the value of property and equity stakes, and the opportunities that are created through this. These opportunities relate in the short term to access to credit and opportunities for mobility, and in the longer term to the release of equity in older age, the opportunity to assist other members of the family or ultimately to pass on the asset to the next generation. In this respect housing policy has been increasingly linked to wider social policies on pensions and asset appreciation. Its relationship to the welfare state agenda has also changed from concern with the provision of shelter to concern with inequalities of wealth and equity stakes (see Groves and Murie, 2005).

Chapter 6

Deregulating the Private Rented Sector

Before the First World War the UK was a nation of private tenants. Since then private renting has undergone a dramatic and continuing decline. The reasons for this are a matter of considerable debate, with some writers emphasizing the positive support given to home ownership or the growth of council housing, and others emphasizing the low returns from private lettings compared with other types of investment. Most accounts, however, discuss the impact of rent controls. These were first introduced during the First World War, partially removed between the wars, reintroduced in 1939 and remained in operation until the 1980s. Some commentators (for example Maclennan, 1982; Black and Stafford, 1988) have adopted models of economic rationality to analyze landlord behaviour and explain the decline in private renting in terms of the constraints on profit imposed by rent control. Others have looked at the variety of rationales adopted by different types of landlord (Allen and MacDowell, 1989) and note that some landlords continued to let properties in spite of limited returns and rent control (Cullingworth, 1963). Empirical studies have also pointed to the high volume of lettings that were not subject to rent control (Greater London Council, 1984). Yet others have argued that rent control merely added to a process of decline that was already under way (Wilding, 1972).

This chapter first outlines the policy history of the private rented sector and the impact of deregulation. It then discusses the key contemporary features of this form of tenure in two English cities, and considers the extent of differentiation within the deregulated private rented sector, plus the importance of different niches, such as student housing.

Table 6.1 provides a profile of the sector in 2001 and can be compared with the profile of home ownership in Table 5.1 and Figures 5.1 and 5.2. Again there are substantial internal variations, but it is apparent that in that year the private rented sector included more older housing and more converted flats than other tenures and that private tenants were more likely to be younger, single and in full-time employment. Satisfaction with accommodation was high.

Table 6.1   *Profile of private renting, England, 2001 (per cent)*

Dwelling types	
Houses	60
Detached houses	10
Semidetached houses	20
Terraced houses	30
Purpose-built flats	14
Converted flats	16
Built prior to 1919	40
Built 1945–64	13
Built since 1985	12
Household types	
Household head over 45	30
Household head 16–24	17
Household head 25–44	53
Single-person households	36
Childless couples	25
Single parents	10
Full-time employment	57
Retired	12
Unemployed/other inactive	23
Percentage satisfied with accommodation	81

Source: Data from ONS *Survey of English Housing 2000/1*.

The policy history

In 1910 private landlords owned some 90 per cent of all dwellings. As Pooley (1992) notes, the market was highly differentiated, with a series of submarkets defined by quality, cost and location. The standard of housing available to different groups varied according to income and the supply of rented housing was controlled by a large number of individuals and agencies. Englander's (1983) account of private landlords emphasizes their political marginalization and their ineffectiveness in resisting demands for reform in the twentieth century. In the nineteenth century, interventions to improve public health standards had reduced the ability of private landlords to profit, and in the twentieth century the development of a more mature housing policy further eroded their position. The combination of interests antagonistic to landlords increased as awareness of housing problems developed, and as tenants and working-class organizations became increasingly involved in the housing debate.

The First World War is associated with two key measures in UK housing policy: the political commitment in 1919 to providing 'Homes fit for heroes to live in' and the introduction of rent control in 1915. However even before the war there was evidence that landlords were investing less heavily in the housing stock. With the arrival of new types of investment opportunity, including in North America, landlords began to shift their investments to other parts of the economy. Arguably the increasing isolation of the landlord class and the reduction of investment in housing would have led in due course to state intervention. However the precise form this intervention actually took and its timing were affected by the outbreak of war, circumstances during the war and subsequent events. Attention has focused on the rent strike in Clydeside during the war, when under the inflationary conditions brought about wartime production, especially the production of munitions and naval vessels, landlords saw an opportunity to profit and therefore raised their rents. Tenants refused to pay these rents and the threat of civil disturbance during wartime led the government to introduce rent controls.

The events in Clydeside took place after a long period in which landlords had been consistently charging unreasonable rents and adopting inflexible management policies, and this had generated discontent and solidarity among tenants and others. Therefore the strike marked the culmination of a long period of activity and was not solely in response to an isolated act of opportunism by landlords (Melling, 1989). This was an important factor in the subsequent decline of the sector. Landlords were increasingly stigmatized and were inclined to shift their investments to sectors of the economy with easier profits.

The intervention of the government through rent control in 1915 had a considerable effect on the next 50 years of housing policy. Once it was established that exploitative rents posed a threat of civil unrest, successive governments were reluctant to remove the rent controls and were resistant to expanding the role of private rented property in future housing policy. Although rent control was not removed at the end of the war, properties were decontrolled upon vacant possession and there was partial decontrol of more expensive properties between the wars. By the Second World War significant rent controls were still in place and a more comprehensive scheme of control was introduced as part of the emergency measures in 1939. The housing stock in the sector had declined considerably between the wars, partly as a result of governments' encouragement of alternative tenures – exchequer subsidies for council housing and tax advantages for home ownership – and partly as a result of slum clearance and improvement policies. This continued during the postwar reconstruction period, when first council housing and then building for owner-occupation led the way.

As the UK moved further away from the wartime emergency measures and the housing shortage continued, advocates of private renting began to argue for its revival, and for the removal of rent controls to achieve this. The relaxation of rent controls in the 1950s probably speeded its decline as it enabled landlords to sell properties at inflated prices upon vacant possession (Donnison, 1967). Moreover a high proportion of lettings were made outside the Rent Acts, and therefore were unaffected by the measures they contained (Greater London Council, 1984). Nevertheless the view that private renting was desirable persisted, bolstered by comparisons with other European countries that suggested the UK had an abnormally small private rented sector due to years of market distortion.

Deregulation in the 1980s and 1990s

After 1980 successive Conservative governments included private renting as a subsidiary part of their housing policies, although their primary focus was on home ownership. The Housing Act of 1980 introduced assured tenancy arrangements that were more favourable to landlords and reduced the scope of rent control and regulation. A second and more strident attempt at deregulation was contained in legislation in 1988 as part of the Conservatives' second phase policies, which were more focused on rented housing (see Chapter 3). The aim was to provide additional opportunities for new private investment in rented housing by extending the system of assured and shorthold tenancies. This would permit new lettings on terms that, it was felt, would attract more investment by institutions and encourage new lettings by smaller landlords (including the owners of many of the 550 000 private dwellings that stood empty) as well as making the provision of new rented housing a more attractive investment.

After the general election in 1987 the Secretary of State for the Environment and the Minister for Housing and Planning reiterated these themes. They stated that for new lettings independent landlords should be able to charge rents that were high enough to ensure that dwellings could be kept in decent repair, and would give a reasonable return on investment. According to Waldegrave while 'It is impossible to predict precisely the effect that these changes will have on the supply of accommodation... I am optimistic that we might get at least a quarter of a million additional lettings in the next 10 years; the total could be a lot higher' (William Waldegrave, Minister for Housing and Planning, Speech to the Institute of Housing, 19 June 1987).

In white papers legislative proposals were outlined for England, Wales and Scotland 'to put new life into the independent rented sector', so that 'The letting of private property will again become an economic proposition' (DoE, 1987, SDD, 1987). The white paper for England emphasized the role of the private sector in providing 'a variety of accommodation readily available in different places for short or long let so as to assist mobility, especially for job movers' (DoE, 1987, para 3.3). It stated that 'The first essential step to encourage new investment in this sector is to enable private landlords to charge rents on new lettings at a level that will give them a reasonable return' (DoE, 1987, para 3.4).

The white papers rejected the argument that the right way to revive the market was to abolish all controls on the ground that this would give insufficient protection to tenants. When entering a tenancy, the tenant should expect to pay the market rent for the property but should have reasonable security of tenure with some degree of statutory backing (SDD, 1987).

The government proposed to build on the assured tenancies that already existed in England and Wales, but not in Scotland, and to introduce short-hold tenancies in England and Wales and short tenancies in Scotland. All new lettings would be either on an assured tenancy basis, with rents freely negotiated between landlord and tenant and protected security of tenure, or on a shorthold/short tenancy basis, with no security beyond the period of the tenancy but the right to seek registration of an appropriate rent. The main distinction between the two forms of tenancy was that short-tenancy occupants could seek registration of their rent at any time – this would not be at the 'fair rent' level but the market level. The minimum length of a shorthold/short tenancy was reduced from one year to six months. Established safeguards were continued or improved for existing tenants and safeguards against harassment were introduced.

These changes were based on the assumption that the Housing Benefit system would provide help to those who needed it. However once rents were deregulated it would be necessary to ensure that landlords could not increase the rents of benefit recipients at the expense of the taxpayer. Local authorities' discretion to restrict benefits if rents were unreasonable had been strengthened in April 1988, and the new arrangements required rent officers to scrutinize the rents being met by Housing Benefit and, if a rent was deemed excessive, to restrict the subsidy to an appropriate market rent.

Expectations of the impact of deregulation

The Minister of Housing and Planning's view in 1987 that 250 000 new lettings would become available in the sector over the next 10 years reflected the government's expectations about the impact of deregulation. However evidence on demand and supply did not suggest that deregulation would revive the sector. The most authoritative studies of the economics of private renting in Britain (House of Commons Environment Committee, 1982; and Whitehead and Kleinman 1986), indicated that demand was low and the demand for easy access tenancies was declining rapidly. The sector did not strongly attract people who were seeking employment but did cater significantly for households that had experienced a change in circumstances, particularly divorce. About a third of tenants, mainly pensioners, had been in their accommodation for over 10 years, and there were also job-related sectors, for example for agricultural workers and members of the armed forces. There was also a high degree of dissatisfaction among private tenants and a strong inclination to change tenure, especially in the case of non-pensioner households. Whitehead and Kleinman (ibid.) concluded that although the private rented sector was providing a range of accommodation for different types of people, only elderly long-term tenants tended to prefer private renting. The preference for alternative accommodation did not take account of relative costs, and it did not imply that there was no demand – just that people would choose another form of tenure if they had a choice.

Most people whose earned incomes were sufficient to pay higher rents were better off as home owners. However there was a continuous demand for short-term renting by newly formed or mobile households, home owners in the process of moving and people whose circumstances had changed. Unless owner-occupation became less financially advantageous, the demand by these groups would continue to be met by frequent vacancies in the residual private rented sector and temporary lettings, with very few households being attracted to long-term private rented accommodation.

The implication was that the demand for private renting would continue to be divided into short-term demand and long-term demand by long-established tenants or tenants in receipt of Housing Benefit. Market rents were not high enough in all areas to persuade commercial landlords to enter and remain in the sector, and a House of Commons select committee concluded in 1982 that landlords whose main objective was long-term investment (companies and non-resident individual landlords) were likely to continue to reduce their investment in the sector.

Supply-side analyses generated similar conclusions: unless rents rose or terms and conditions became more favourable to landlords the supply would continue to decline. There might be some expansion in areas with low demand or as a result of increased pressure on the sector, but a significant proportion of landlords did not let wholly for economic reasons, so predicting changes in their actions was problematic. In other cases, for example in the London flat market, asset stripping was part of a strategy to restructure investments in order to obtain better returns (Hamnett, 1999). In general the difference between the value of vacant and tenanted property was large enough to prompt landlords to sell when tenants moved out.

An important empirical factor in deregulation at that time was the proportion of lettings already being made outside Rent Act protection. An influential survey (Greater London Council, 1984) found that in London 66 per cent of all tenancies were probably protected, but less than a third of lettings made after 1980 were in that category and only just over a third of tenants understood that they were protected. The conclusion of the select committee was that in certain areas, especially in inner London, lettings outside the Rent Acts formed a significant proportion of available accommodation. These findings demonstrate that the Rent Acts had not prevented landlords from letting.

Whether they let and what they let were affected by financial consider-ations. There were incentives to let in high-demand areas such as London, and properties with a relatively low sale value were most likely to be rented out, with income maximized through subdivision and the sharing of amen-ities by tenants. Another key factor was whether market rents provided a rate of return that was comparable to the returns from other types of investment. The calculation of expected rent, future capital gains and returns elsewhere depended on individual circumstances, but even if rent control was removed and all rents rose to the level of unregistered rents, this would still not generally provide the returns necessary to keep landlords' investment in the sector at its current level.

Where high rents were charged outside the Rent Acts, such lettings were the most buoyant part of the market but the returns were still not enough to halt the decline. Landlord strategies and tenant knowledge further constrained the operation of economic rationality. For example the level of unregistered rents might be constrained by landlords' desire not to provoke tenants into rent registration. However tenants were often ignorant of their rights under the Rent Acts, and some rents were higher than in the free market, including a premium to cover the risk that tenants would seek rent registration.

Whitehead and Kleinman (1986) concluded that the decline of private renting would continue unless rents rose significantly. This would only happen if people were prepared to pay far higher rents, but this was unlikely unless Housing Benefit also rose significantly or home ownership became a less attractive alternative. Households that were not eligible for Housing Benefit would probably find it more desirable and cheaper to buy.

Debates on market deregulation at that time paid relatively little atten-tion to institutional factors such as sources of finance and the types of organization that might bring about revival. There was an expectation that deregulation would encourage large financial institutions to invest in rented housing, but vehicles for this – such as Housing Investment Trusts – were not developed until much later. Financial institutions continued to be unconvinced of the viability of the sector and its long-term security, espe-cially in view of legislative and policy history. As a result institutional investment in rented dwellings was channelled into housing associations from 1988. Housing associations had greater credibility than private landlords, and lenders were able to draw comfort from robust regulation by the Housing Corporation (see Chapter 9).

Three other changes offered some prospect of the revival of private landlordism. First, under the arrangements announced in the 1988 budget in respect of the Business Expansion Scheme there would be tax relief for short-term investment in rented housing. Second, in England the Local Government Act enabled local authorities to give capital grants of between 50 per cent and 75 per cent (originally set at 30 per cent) to investors in new or refurbished private housing for rent. Third, in Scotland, Scottish Homes and the Scottish Special Housing Association could provide grants to private investors in rented housing.

Deregulated private renting

Table 6.2 provides details of the private rented sector under the combined influence of deregulation and Housing Benefit. It is important to recognize that deregulation occurred both through legislative change and because of the decline in the number of tenants with controlled and regulated tenancies. Table 6.2 shows the size of the active market sector that was accessible to would-be tenants. This excluded regulated tenancies and those defined through survey data as not accessible to the public. The size of the active market increased almost eightfold in the 15 years after 1988. Some of this

Table 6.2   *Number of private rented homes, England, 1988–2001 (percentages in brackets)*

	All tenancies	*Regulated*		*Not accessible to public*		*Unregulated active market**	
1988	1814	1071	(59)	508	(28)	235	(13)
1990	1787	590	(33)	482	(27)	715	(40)
1993/94	2132	371	(17)	379	(18)	1382	(65)
1994/95	2197	311	(14)	431	(20)	1381	(63)
1995/96	2254	272	(12)	427	(19)	1555	(69)
1996/97	2280	242	(11)	416	(18)	1622	(71)
1997/98	2255	205	(9)	349	(15)	1701	(75)
1998/99	2247	188	(8)	387	(17)	1672	(74)
1999/2000	2305	154	(7)	444	(19)	1707	(74)
2000/1	2186	122	(6)	382	(17)	1682	(77)
2001/2	2129	117	(5)	308	(14)	1705	(80)
2002/3	2221	127	(6)	354	(16)	1741	(78)
2003/4	2350	138	(6)	347	(15)	1864	(79)

* Assured, assured shorthold, resident landlord and other.
Source: Data from ONS *Survey of English Housing 2004*.

growth was due to student and executive lettings, but some was in accommodation that directly competed with social rented housing and was available to households in receipt of Housing Benefit. The condition of the private rented stock and the problems faced in securing improvement of the worst properties are discussed in Chapter 13.

The impact of the removal of rent control was a contested topic before, during and after the Conservative government implemented measures to put new lettings outside rent control through the new forms of tenancy introduced in 1980 and 1988. This was partly because these measures were introduced alongside other contingent changes, such as the introduction of Housing Benefit and Business Expansion Schemes. There were also many changes that were beyond the government's control, such as demographic change and movements in the wider economy and housing market, and these may have had an equally important impact.

The Housing Act of 1980 marked the final phase of the deregulation of private renting. It introduced assured and shorthold tenancies, and all new tenancies after that date fell into one of these two categories. However after 1987 the distinction between the two types of tenancy was removed. In effect no new tenancies in the private rented sector were subject to any form of direct rent control and the ability of landlords to remove tenants was strengthened. The balance of advantage was shifted from tenant to landlord, and only tenants who had previously been in the system had additional rights.

The available statistics (Table 6.2) suggest only a modest growth, despite active encouragement of new investment in 1988–94 through the Business Expansion Scheme and the growth of Housing Benefit payments. A number of explanations can be offered for this phenomenon. It is argued that major financial institutions were not confident that rent control would not be reintroduced at a later stage and their time horizons for investment did not make the private rented sector an attractive investment proposition. The Business Expansion Scheme was time limited and only encouraged short-term investment and subsequent sale (Crook *et al.*, 1991, 1995). Privatization and the transfer of council housing stock also meant that there were major opportunities for building societies and banks to invest in rented property through housing associations that were regulated and properly managed. This reduced risk meant that it was unnecessary for these investors to consider untried, speculative and new enterprises.

The demographics of the private rented sector were such that the rate of tenancy termination due to death or people moving into institutional care was particularly high in this period. Because of this the sector would have declined further following vacant possession even if regulation had continued to exist. The fact that the housing stock did not decline and even rose a little reflects substantial growth in the active part of the market.

Another factor in this growth was the house price slump of 1989–93, during which time many home owners were unable or unwilling to sell their properties. Those who moved to other areas for employment or other reasons often rented out their own properties and became tenants themselves in their areas of employment.

The above discussions leave us with almost as confused a picture as that which prevailed before deregulation. Did rent control and regulation affect the size of the sector or not? It is impossible to separate the impact of deregulation from that of a variety of other factors occurring at the same time. In particular, changes in the social rented sector associated with privatization, the encouragement of housing associations and the boom and slump in the owner-occupied sector between the mid 1980s and mid 1990s confuse the picture.

In the remainder of this chapter the shifting nature of the deregulated private rented sector is illustrated by the findings of research in two English cities: Liverpool and Birmingham (Groves, 2004; Groves *et al.*, 2001). The evidence shows there were different influences on the sector and the growth of distinct niches. The patterns of private renting in these cities were clearly affected by local economic and housing market factors and were different from those in higher-demand areas such as the South-East of England and London. This illustrates the importance of exploring housing policy within a local or regional context rather than trying to address the impact of deregulation in the abstract.

Liverpool: long-term change and the impact of student housing

According to the population census, 33 per cent of dwellings in Liverpool in 1971 were privately rented (67 203, including approximately 500 housing association properties). The private rented sector roughly matched the size of the council sector (71 757) and the owner-occupied sector (65 952). By 1981 the number of properties in the council sector and the owner-occupied sector had risen to 78 381 and 80 024 respectively, and the housing association stock had risen to 13 443 (7 per cent of the total stock). In contrast the private rented sector had declined by some 57 per cent to 28 857 properties (14 per cent of the total). The decline in the relative size of the private rented sector was greater outside the inner city than within it – 26 per cent of properties in the inner-city area were privately rented in 1981 (City of Liverpool, 1986; Groves *et al.*, 2001).

The decline of the sector in the 1970s was mainly driven by slum clearance and sales to owner-occupiers and housing associations; there was very little new building for private rental. In 1971 the majority of pre-1919 dwellings lacked exclusive use of basic amenities. Just over a third were in clearance areas. Between 1971 and 1981 more than 22 000 properties were demolished or closed in Liverpool. The bulk of these were located in the inner city and in the private rented sector. By 1981 the clearance programme was largely complete and had been replaced by improvement programmes in Housing Action Areas and General Improvement Areas. The Housing Action Area programme began in 1976 and intially involved 4400 dwellings; subsequent phases would involve over 36 000 dwellings. Both the clearance and the renewal programme concentrated on the worst properties first – the majority of which were in the private rented sector – and the number of dwellings that lacked amenities declined from 63 500 in 1971 to 7700 in 1985. Many of these properties were acquired by housing associations as part of the area improvement programme.

By 1985 demolitions and privatization had contributed to the decline of the council sector (to 68 069 properties, or 34 per cent of the total) and the growth of home ownership (to 93 642, 47 per cent of the total). The private rented sector had declined by a further 30 per cent to 20 101 (10 per cent of the housing stock) while the number of housing association dwellings had risen to 17 956 (9 per cent). The decline of the private rented sector was due not only to slum clearance but also to the sale of some of the best properties to owner-occupiers. The stock that remained was concentrated in the inner city. One consequence of clearance and sale was that the holdings of individual landlords were smaller and located in mixed tenure areas rather than in areas dominated by particular landlords.

Three other factors had an important impact on the sector, the second two of which resulted in growth rather than decline:

- A further decline was caused by the death of longstanding, ageing tenants who had security of tenure in controlled tenancies.
- The introduction of the Housing Benefit system in 1981 had a more positive impact. The new system enabled young single people in particular to rent accommodation in their own right. This expanded demand in the sector.
- Third, a student housing market developed. Backed by the Housing Benefit system, students created a demand for shared housing in some parts of the city. Landlords began to switch their properties into this market and a number of new landlords entered the sector. Student tenancies were attractive to landlords because there were fewer problems with security of tenure and regaining possession.

At the same time as the general decline was taking place the government was taking steps to revive the private rented sector in England. While deregulation was the key measure to encourage revival, other elements of the government's approach to housing served as reinforcements. The extension of Housing Benefit to private tenancies meant that more people could afford to rent. Housing Benefit initially operated in a way that was advantageous to landlords, who in certain circumstances could obtain the rent payments direct from the local authority and therefore the risk of letting to low-income and benefit-dependent households declined. In Liverpool some new landlords entered the market specifically to provide housing for people on Housing Benefit. In the early and mid 1980s a rise in the number of single young people who wanted and could afford separate housing encouraged growth in this market. High unemployment and economic problems may also have encouraged growth.

Student housing

The rise in student numbers was marked in Liverpool in the 1980s. As in other cities, students were increasingly opting to live in the community rather than in halls of residence, the supply of which was failing to keep pace with rising student numbers. In 1988 the government announced its intention to double the number of students in higher education by the year 2000. The number of students attending higher educational institutions in Liverpool grew from around 19 000 in 1986/87 to over 41 000 in 2000/1 (Liverpool Student Homes, 2000). The student population rose to some 10 per cent of the population of the city and student demand for accommodation increased by over 100 per cent over a period of 15 years. The most rapid growth took place during the first half of the 1990s. Meanwhile university and college accommodation marginally declined. A number of local housing associations also provided accommodation for students. Allowing for double counting and assuming that 10 per cent of full-time students were living at home or did not require accommodation for other reasons, the figures suggest that the demand for student accommodation in the private rented sector grew by up to 8000 bed spaces, or a rise of 50 per cent over the decade (Groves *et al.*, 2001).

In the early 1990s most of the private accommodation rented by students was in shared houses and flats built prior to 1919 in the older areas of the city. The financial circumstances of students became increasingly stringent with their exclusion from Housing Benefit in 1991, downward pressure on student grants, the introduction of means testing and later the introduction of student loans. One way in which students could save money was to minimize transport costs by living closer to college, and after 1992 there was a dramatic fall in the proportion of students living in peripheral locations and the east of the city.

Another important development in the 1990s was substantial provision of newly built and converted halls of residence by housing associations and private developers. This accommodation was provided independently of the universities and was intended to cater for the rapid expansion of student numbers during the early 1990s. Some schemes were grant aided through City Challenge funding, ranging from some fairly basic hostel accommodation to new purpose-built properties. The latter constituted a substantial rise in standards compared with pre-1919 rented housing, and most also had a locational advantage.

With the improvement in the local housing market after 1995 and the implementation of the city council's 'city centre living' strategy the building of new halls of residence in central locations continued, despite the fact that the growth of student numbers had slowed substantially. The later buildings were larger and constructed to higher specifications, most notably with *en suite* showers and WCs, plus individual internet connections. There were also plans to provide shops, fast-food restaurants and pub facilities. The growth of private sector hall provision from 1995/96 almost matched the increase in student numbers over the same period.

Further decline and increasing differentiation in the 1990s

The factors that contributed to the growth in demand for private rented housing in the late 1980s were not sustained. In particular the government became concerned about escalating Housing Benefit expenditure, and therefore Housing Benefit for students was discontinued in 1991 and the regulations on local reference rents and the rents that could be reclaimed by benefit were significantly tightened. In Liverpool, landlords serving the Housing Benefit market could no longer charge high rents unless their tenants were able to supplement their Housing Benefit with money from other sources. Following changes in the Housing Benefit entitlements for young single people, demand by this group declined and provision became economically marginal. This led to oversupply in parts of the private rented sector, and especially in the case of accommodation oriented towards Housing Benefit. Oversupply was exacerbated by new market entrants in this period, including home owners who were unable to sell in the depressed housing market and therefore became 'reluctant' landlords, speculative purchasers who bought properties at the very bottom of the market at a very low price and sought returns from rental income alone, and new student accommodation in the purpose-built halls discussed above.

The consequence of all of this was that by the late 1990s landlords were letting to whomever they could. Because of the oversupply there might have been an incentive to improve properties in order to attract custom, but without improvement grants the cost of improvement would have been greater than could be recovered through rents. Many of the private rented properties improved under the General Improvement Area and Housing Action Area programmes needed replacement windows and central heating and were in a poor state of repair. A further effect of oversupply and declining condition was that the local reference rents, which determined the rent level eligible for Housing Benefit, declined in some parts of the market. If the only people seeking accommodation were those on Housing Benefit the decline in the reference rents meant that landlords had two options: accept reduced rents or try to attract tenants who could pay the difference. The poor condition of properties was partly a consequence of landlords' views of tenants and the rents that could be charged in a housing-benefit dependent market. Landlords expected tenants to move on quickly and consequently they did little about redecoration or recarpeting.

The structure of the Liverpool rental sector

The private rented sector in Liverpool, as in other cities, remains in transition. There is a growing split between the new primary market, located largely in the city centre and serving clearly defined niches, and the secondary market, operating in mixed-tenure, inner-city areas with a wider range of older properties. The differences between these two markets are becoming more pronounced in terms of location, dwelling type, quality, condition, price, financing, market and customer profile. It might be argued that this reflects the formation of a new, post-regulation private rented sector. If this is the case then the process of transition is creating a sustainable primary market but an unsustainable secondary market.

Alongside the student housing niche discussed earlier has been the emergence of a primary market for executive rentals, mainly conversions and new buildings in prestige city centre locations such as Albert Dock. The key drivers of this are investors responding to the requirements of higher-income groups and companies for high-quality, short- and medium-term accommodation near the city centre. Uncertainty about the returns from private pension schemes is likely to sustain this investment-led demand.

Meanwhile the secondary market includes properties that have been in the private rented sector for a considerable time, plus some recent additions resulting from problems in the home ownership market. It is situated in the traditional areas of renting, but is more dispersed than previously and has moved away from its traditional market role to house predominantly households with a periodic or long-term dependency on Housing Benefit. This market is associated with younger people, low-income households and high turnover. The overlap with the student market has decreased with its decline in quality and the rehousing of students in new dwellings. Areas of the city that housed students in the 1980s and 1990s are now more likely to house benefit-dependent households. Even in areas that still have a mixture of student and other clientele it is probable that there will be a decline in student demand over the next decade. This is likely to lead to a further reduction of quality and demand.

The Liverpool case illustrates the importance of exploring change in the private rented sector within a local market context as it reveals a complexity that is not apparent from aggregate modelling of the impact of deregulation. The relative importance of different drivers of change has varied considerably over time. National changes to Housing Benefit have been at least as important as deregulation in demand and investment decisions. Landlords have demonstrated an ability to switch between different niche markets (students, professional clientele, benefit claimants and, most recently, refugees and asylum seekers) as circumstances in the wider market have changed. Private investment in purpose-built student accommodation and, to a lesser extent, new city centre investment properties let at high rents to executives and professionals are examples of local changes since deregulation. While it could be argued that these have been encouraged by the removal of rent regulation and reduced tenancy rights, they cannot be explained without reference to a much wider set of policy and market factors, such as increased student numbers, city centre regeneration and changes to Housing Benefit policy that have caused new investors to avoid the Housing Benefit market.

Birmingham: immigration and differentiation

In Birmingham the history of urban renewal and local policy implementation differs from that in Liverpool, as does the location and nature of the private rented sector. There are also different dynamics underlying the operation of the private rented market in areas with a high proportion of landlords from the black and minority ethnic communities. Landlords' decisions about disposal and letting are influenced by different factors. The local authority has been active in working with private landlords and seeking to influence their activities, as well as carrying out enforcement measures in relation to Houses in Multiple Occupation. The development of the sector has therefore been affected by local policies and practices, and by local as well as national policy developments. The government's interest in licensing and other activities that affect the private rented sector, together with the changes introduced in the Regulatory Reform Order of 2003, will affect the future development of the sector.

In recent years Birmingham has felt the impact of demand by asylum seekers and refugees, and of government policies on the provision of housing for these groups. Parts of the city are characterized by low house prices and an oversupply of accommodation for rent, and it is in these areas that asylum seekers and refugees have been housed. This is partly because the Home Office (the government department with responsibility for housing asylum seekers and refugees) adopted a policy of contracting private landlords to make provision for a period of five years. The length and terms of these contracts made them attractive to landlords and helped to reshape the pattern of provision. As the contracts were renegotiated and in some cases terminated after the initial five years the sector was reshaped again (Groves, 2004). There was also a significant impact from the housing choice of refugees with leave to remain, who often sought independent rented accommodation in the same areas, thereby sustaining the private rental demand.

Alongside this the development of city centre apartments – encouraged by Birmingham's city living strategy – has produced a new niche investment market. While some of the investment in this market is by larger institutional investors it has also attracted smaller buy-to-let investors. The development of the buy-to-let market in the city centre and elsewhere has also been instrumental in reshaping the private rented sector. New financial products have been designed for this type of investment, whose attractiveness is associated with low interest rates, rapid asset appreciation and poor returns on other investments, including pension products. Investing in houses to let has become increasingly attractive to established home owners with spare resources.

Conclusions

In the 1980s the private rented sector declined to the point where it provided less than 10 per cent of all housing in the UK – a dramatic change from 60 years earlier. Recent years have seen some reversal of this trend. By 2003/4 the sector was providing some 430 000 more properties than in 1988, but it would be simplistic to view this as a consequence of the deregulation measures introduced in the 1980s. The regulated or controlled part of the sector would have declined anyway as people with controlled tenancies moved on.

Local studies make it clear that deregulation has combined with other factors that affect demand and investor behaviour to bring about change. The deregulated tenure has become increasingly flexible and this has enabled landlords to enter a range of market niches, such as the Housing Benefit market, student housing, city centre buy-to-let, and accommodation for asylum seekers and refugees. This has played out in different ways in different areas, with Liverpool highlighting the effects of long-term demographic decline and the significant local impact of the expansion of higher education. In Birmingham and Liverpool, city centre regeneration has spawned an executive rental market, and the government's policy of dispersing asylum seekers has opened up a new accommodation market and affected the location choice of settled refugees.

A more complex and differentiated market has developed in most places. Increased flexibility and separation into niches, the development of primary and secondary markets and the problems associated with the secondary market are features of markets in transition. All these developments have been influenced by deregulation but other influences have also been important. The size and nature of the private rented sector depend on the wider structure of the market and the extent of demand for other tenures. Oversupply and the separation of markets in Liverpool occurred because of weaknesses in the inner city housing market and not some intrinsic aspect of private renting. One important question emerging from this is the extent to which the development of the secondary private rented market is both a consequence of market weakness and a cause of it. It is unlikely that the market itself will remedy oversupply, which arises because of market problems and the lack of options for owners.

Conventional approaches that analyze rates of return and treat private renting as a single category take no account of important fault lines and differences in behaviour between the primary and secondary markets. Research that puts the private rented sector in its market context is more likely to produce an understanding of change. Positive views of deregulation and the expansion of private renting should not result in neglect of the problems associated with transition and market change. Nor is it appropriate to view the actions of landlords who stay in or enter a market in which there is oversupply as irrational. Problems in the secondary market call for active intervention if they are not to negate strategies for neighbourhood renewal and housing choice. More selective regulation of the secondary sector, policies to encourage better management and maintenance (including those related to eligibility for Housing Benefit) and reshaping the market through housing renewal programmes are essential. With or without new policy interventions it is clear that the private rented sector in the UK, freed from regulation, has a distinctive role compared with that of its counterparts elsewhere in Europe. The legacy of regulation and embedded institutional arrangements have shaped the sector. This suggests that the future of the latter will be path dependent rather than naturally converging towards models that apply elsewhere in Europe.

Chapter 7

Transforming the Governance, Management and Regulation of Social Housing

Having outlined the key changes in private sector housing in Chapters 5 and 6 we now turn to the transformation of social housing from the 1970s. This transformation reflected, or in some cases prefigured, wider changes to the delivery of public services in the UK. This chapter focuses on the governance, management and regulatory reforms that underpinned this transformation, and shows how new ideas on public sector reform, such as 'new public management' and 'modernization', influenced social housing. It goes on to look at the changing regulatory framework for social housing. The following two chapters explore these changes further by outlining the financial mechanisms used and the impact the reforms had on the non-profit sector as it took on a broader delivery role.

Governance relationships and ideas

Today, policy is coordinated and implemented through fragmented networks of service providers – an approach that is often referred to as governance. In addition to the central government and local authorities, these networks encompass a variety of funding and regulatory bodies: The Housing Corporation, The Audit Commission, Regional Housing Boards, other public bodies and private funders. There is also an increasingly diverse range of delivery agencies, including housing associations, other types of non-profit landlord, local partnership bodies of various forms, and profit distributing bodies such as Private Finance Initiative (PFI) contractors. To these might be added the plethora of representative (The National Housing Federation and the Local Government Association), professional (The Chartered Institute of Housing) and advocacy bodies (Shelter and, TPAS Disability Alliance) that influence not only housing policy and its implementation but also the beliefs and practices of people working in housing organizations. The governance of the housing system is coordinated through relationships within and between these institutions.

In this changing context the scope of governance, management and regulation includes the interplay between organizations, their internal systems and practices and their external environment. Internal issues include strategies, structures, systems, styles and shared beliefs. Key features of the external environment include flows of resources from and regulatory controls by the government, collaborative and competitive relationships with other organizations, and wider systems of beliefs and assumptions that affect the ways in which organizations work together.

Ideas on the reform of public services embedded in 'new public management', 'managerialism' and 'modernization' have had a strong influence on the ways in which housing policy has been shaped and delivered over the last 30 years. One recent stream of thinking has emphasized the need to move policy making away from specialist government departments and the associated networks of delivery agencies: the education sector, the health sector, the housing sector and so on. 'Joined-up' policy has become something of a mantra and the application of common management paradigms to different public services has reduced the extent to which housing policy can be discussed in isolation.

An associated stream of thinking has emphasized the need for customer-focused services and to move away from producer definitions of the scope, purpose and model of service delivery (see Chapter 10 for the application of this to social housing management). This thinking has prompted attempts to shift the control of some state services from professionals to managers, leading to struggles by professionals to maintain control. Le Grande (2003) portrays these struggles by depicting providers as knights or knaves and consumers as pawns or queens. Governments have tended to treat service providers as though they were self-interested knaves rather than publicly spirited knights, and have sought to empower consumers by shifting their role from that of passive pawns to demanding queens.

Perhaps this change has been less pronounced in housing, where professionalization has been less complete than in, say, education or health. But there has been a discernible shift of power away from housing profession also. For example in the recruitment process now used by many social landlords there is less emphasis on housing-specific qualifications and more on general competences and aptitudes. There has been a strong rhetoric of user empowerment, for example through the tenant management organizations that have sprung up since the introduction of 'the right to manage' in 1993 (Cairncross *et al.*, 2002), and greater emphasis on user involvement in stock transfers through the 'community gateway model' (Confederation of Co-operative Housing, 2001).

This chapter begins with a brief review of new public management, managerialism and modernization. It then considers the impact of management reforms in social housing, the role of local authorities and the part played by regulation and audit in the governance of housing.

New public management, managerialism and modernization

This section reviews two main types of management reform in the housing sector and their links to broader reform programmes in the public services:

- The gradual replacement of the public administration model with the concepts of new public management and managerialism.
- The emergence of modernization under New Labour with the development of 'Best Value' and joined-up government, with emphasis on more inclusive organizations and strategies.

From public administration to new public management

One response to the concept of new public management might be to question the relevance of the descriptor 'public'. Surely management is management, and to state that public management is different from private sector management is to create an unnecessary distinction. This question did not arise for most of the twentieth century since running public services was deemed to be public administration, a quite separate discipline from commercial management. Hughes (1998, p. 22) describes public administration as 'a professional occupation, one which would be most efficiently carried out by a distinct merit-based public service'. The characteristics of public service and the need for a distinct management approach have been elaborated by Stewart and Ranson (1988, p. 13): 'the public domain has its own purposes. It expresses collective purpose in society. That sets the conditions and tasks for management.'

From the late 1980s such views formed the basis of the public service orientation, but they were challenged by the arrival of new public management (NPM), which transformed public administration into management and brought private sector management assumptions and practices into the public services. Sometimes, however, the distinctiveness of the public domain was acknowledged and assumptions and practices were adapted accordingly.

The introduction of NPM ideas was associated with the political ideology of the new right in the 1980s and 1990s, underpinned by public choice theory and market-oriented economics. Public choice theory (Niskanen, 1971) was particularly influential with the new right. This highlights the tendency for publicly funded bureaucracies to be expansionist as a result of the dominance of producer interests and the absence of effective performance measures. Public bodies are depicted as exploiting their monopoly power to maximize budgets unless they are broken up into smaller units operating under market-type arrangements to facilitate greater consumer choice. As Newman (2000) notes, NPM was seen as providing solutions to the perceived problems of monopoly producer power, large units and limited consumer choice.

> The 'New Public Management' was a term used to describe a series of reforms which reshaped the relationships between public and private sectors, professionals and managers, and central and local government. Citizens and clients were recast as consumers, and public service organisations were recast in the image of the business world. (Ibid., p. 45)

Managerialism

Clarke and Newman (1997) argue that the NPM reforms introduced in the UK by Conservative governments installed 'managerialism' as the basis of a new organizational settlement. This shifted power from professionals to managers in what they describe as 'the managerial state'. Managerialism emphasized the general application of management models derived from the private sector and highlighted the importance of efficiency and performance over more qualitative aspects of public services. Newman (2000, p. 58) later defined managerialism as 'a discourse which sets out the necessity of change; a set of tools to drive up performance; and a means through which an organisation can transform itself to deliver a modernised notion of public purpose to a modern conception of "the people"'.

Different variants of managerialism applied at different times, some based on rational notions of scientific management, others on importing business ideas to drive efficiency. However the important feature of managerialization was the increasing ability of governments to impose these theories and tools on public services by strengthening the role of management over other interest groups, such as professionals, trade unions and local councillors. This also provided business opportunities for consultancies engaged in knowledge transfer from the private to the public sector.

Key features of new public management

What features of NPM distinguished it from both public administration and commercial management? Typologies of NPM abound and there is some variation in the elements emphasized by different writers. While Walsh (1995) places particular emphasis on marketization, outsourcing and the management of contracts, Clarke and Newman (1997) track the growth of managerialism and Hood (1995) identifies a number of distinct but related elements, including disaggregation, competition, private sector management, economy, hands-on top management, performance measurement and the measurement of outputs.

An overview of the different variants of NPM is provided by Ferlie *et al.* (1996), who have drawn on research on change in the health sector to identify four main approaches: 'the efficiency drive', 'downsizing and decentralization', 'in search of excellence' and the 'public service orientation'.

The earliest to appear was the efficiency drive in the early 1980s. This stressed the need for public services to emulate private sector efficiencies by means of tighter financial control, stronger management, more auditing and benchmarking, and shifting the balance of power from professionals and trade unions to managers, and to a lesser extent consumers, through new incentives and governance structures. This approach was picked up in an influential Audit Commission (1986) report, which diagnosed a 'crisis' in the management of council housing in the mid 1980s. It has remained influential in its emphasis on cost reduction and meeting business plan assumptions. The efficiency drive led to the establishment of performance management systems, for example to increase the proportion of rents collected and minimize the number of empty properties. Some writers have argued that this emphasis was at the expense of more supportive aspects of management such as advice and support (for example Davis, 2003). A key driver of the more commercial ethos was the introduction of private finance for housing associations in the late 1980s, bringing with it a change 'from comfort to competition' (Walker, 1998, p. 71) and a focusing of organizational attention on the bottom line.

The second variant, downsizing and decentralization (Ferlie *et al.*, 1996), involved more fundamental structural changes: replacing large hierarchies with smaller units, separating the purchase of services from their provision by means of contract management, and emphasizing flexibility and variety rather than standardized products. These changes could be observed in the housing sector from the early 1980s in the form of decentralization, estate-based management programmes and the shift from local authorities to housing associations as providers. This reflected the broader shifts to post-Fordist modes of production and from hierarchies to networks. These measures had a greater impact on the shape of public services than did efficiency drives. The move from hierarchy to network and market was particularly marked in the case of social housing, where: 'local service delivery depends upon the successful formulation and operation of interorganisational networks, and the policy implementation process presents itself as a complex interorganisational, rather than a simple linear process' (Reid, 1995, p. 147).

The third variant of NPM is labelled by Ferlie *et al.* (1996) as 'in search of excellence' after the title of an influential book by American business gurus Peters and Waterman (1982). This was a people-centred approach that built on the work of the human relations school of management, which had been developed in the 1920s and 1930s in reaction against the mechanical approach associated with Frederic Taylor and symbolized by time and motion studies. From the late 1980s this approach influenced public management through the concepts of 'learning organizations', 'strong cultures', 'empowering staff' and reshaping organizational cultures to achieve excellence.

Within the concept of excellence there is a big divide between top-down emphasis on rebranding, reshaping and imposing strong cultures and bottom-up emphasis on empowerment, learning and deep-seated behaviours and beliefs. Evidence of both can be seen in recent changes in the housing sector. Bottom-up change has been driven by continuous improvement practices and interdepartmental 'Best Value' review groups (often including tenant and board members), and there is growing interest in the potential of 'double loop' models of organizational learning, which encourage the challenging of organizational norms rather than simply implementing directives (Reid and Hickman, 2002). However the top-down influences are probably stronger, with attention to symbols of 'strong culture', such as mission statements, corporate logos, communication strategies, human resource functions and organizational development activities designed to deliver the corporate vision (Mullins and Riseborough, 2000).

The fourth variant is the only one to focus explicitly on a public service orientation. Ferlie *et al.* (1996) see this approach as an attempt to confer legitimacy on the 'new-style public sector', symbolizing a break from 'the pathological aspects of the past' (ibid., p. 14) by borrowing and adapting private sector management practices while remaining true to the identity and purpose of the public domain. Key elements of the approach include a focus on service quality (alongside cost), greater attention to citizens rather than simply customers, the development of local accountability and an emphasis on societal learning and values. Walker (1998) regards these as least evident in the housing association sector in the late 1990s. It is interesting to consider whether the Labour government's modernization agenda has led to renewal of the public service orientation. Stock-transfer housing associations constitute an excellent arena in which to observe tensions between the new and old public services, since these organizations have a strong local authority heritage (inheriting both staff and assets from the municipal sector) but a very different governance model and strong business drivers to meet long-term financial targets, and are regarded as part of the private sector for borrowing purposes (Mullins *et al.*, 1995).

Modernization

In 1997 the association of NPM with the new right raised interesting questions when a Labour government was elected in the UK for the first time in 18 years. Would NPM be displaced by a new set of management principles and ideology? This question was explored by a number of writers but notably by Newman (2000, 2001), who studied Labour's early agenda for modernizing government and identified some continuities and changes from earlier NPM approaches.

Modernization was one of the longest lived buzz-words of the Labour government, embodying notions of common sense, the need for change, freshness and popular appeal, all of which were viewed as defining features of the Blair administration. It also had the advantage of looseness and flexibility, which enabled it to be applied to a range of contexts. These included local government, industrial disputes (e.g. fire service) and internal politics within the Labour Party, where the modernizers were seen as having ensured electoral success by distancing themselves from 'old Labour'. But what was its particular content in relation to public service management and how did it differ from NPM?

According to Newman (2001) there were considerable continuities with NPM in that managerialism remained the central tool for public service reform. Producer dominance and monopoly power still needed to be checked and accountability to funders, consumers and other stakeholders promoted. Public service problems were still seen as soluble through the application of appropriate private sector expertise. Since Newman's account the emphasis on organizational efficiency, performance and measurement has increased even further. During the Labour government's second term, increases in public funding for selected services were conditional on outcome-focused Public Service Agreements (PSAs) and the stress on 'delivery' became overwhelming in the face of public scepticism about the impact of reforms.

However modernization also embraced some changes of approach, including a shift from efficiency and process to effectiveness and outcome and an apparently more open-minded judgement of the merits of markets in achieving public goals. There was greater emphasis on consultation and social inclusion (going well beyond the consumerist recipes of NPM), on 'joined-up' government and on balancing the forces of collaboration and competition. Coinciding with modernization was growing attention to regionalism. This was to affect the governance and management of housing during the second term of the Labour government, when devolved assemblies were established in Scotland and Wales alongside the new Northern Ireland Assembly (implementing the Belfast agreement but suspended for an extended period in the early 2000s), and Regional Housing Boards (later housing and planning boards) were established in England.

Best Value

One of the key early changes was the development of the 'Best Value' regime to replace Compulsory Competitive Tendering (CCT), under which local authorities had been required to tender for specified services. Woods (2000, p. 140) describes Best Value as 'a core part of a new discourse of modernisation which places increased emphasis on partnership, community consultation and service improvement, without necessarily requiring service providers to compete in the market place'.

Research on the implementation of Best Value in the housing association sector (Mullins, 1999a; Walker *et al.*, 2000) confirmed the shift of emphasis from CCT, particularly in relation to involving users and front line staff in service reviews and in the growth of partnership working and partnering, for example by involving private repairs contractors in service reviews. The redefinition of competition from a process requirement to consider outsourcing options to an outcome orientation for more competitive services was an interesting example. Earlier lessons from CCT were relearned as housing associations discovered that outsourcing would only lead to service improvement if they understood their existing service and cost structure, had a good knowledge of the potential contractor market and had good contract management skills (Mullins, 2002).

Alternatively Best Value can be seen as strengthening the grip of earlier NPM reforms, particularly as the reach of Best Value extended to voluntary sector bodies that had not been directly affected by CCT, such as housing associations. Best Value provided a conduit for many aspects of the managerialist agenda, for example the concept of 'continuous improvement', to be embedded in social housing organizations. By 1999 housing associations were already using a range of managerial tools, such as external accreditation (Investors in People, ISO 9000 and Business Excellence), organizational development techniques (values and mission statements, staff and board development programmes and social audits) and corporate review activities (business process engineering, activity-based costing, risk management and business and operational plans). Many larger housing associations were well versed in NPM and there was a clear desire for this to spread across the sector. Guidance produced by the National Housing Federation (Taylor, 2000) aimed to speed the adoption of these tools, although there was concern among smaller associations that some would be expensive to implement and of limited value. As one survey respondent put it 'everything that this questionnaire implies is an expensive, cumbersome approach... and if it saves any money at all it will be a great surprise' (Mullins, 1999a, p. 11).

Joined-up and inclusive organizations and strategies?

Two of the most influential themes introduced under modernization were joined-up government and social inclusion. These two themes helped to redefine the public service orientation, filling some of the missing ground identified in 1998 by Walker. Initiatives introduced by new government units such as the Social Exclusion Unit and the Neighbourhood Renewal Unit had a considerable impact on the organization of housing services, promoting social inclusion through better coordination. One key change was a greater focus on poorer neighbourhoods, which became the target for the 'New Deal for Communities', an ambitious £2 billion programme to transform 39 of England's most deprived neighbourhoods within 10 years. In some neighbourhoods joined-up working was enhanced by stock swaps to reduce the number of housing associations and develop more effective communication with residents (Sharples, 2002). The neighbourhood focus was further exemplified by the development of multitenure neighbourhood management (see Chapter 12) and the branding of housing associations as 'In Business for Neighbourhoods' (see Chapter 9).

However the implementation of an inclusive approach to neighbourhood renewal has been a fraught process. While evaluation of the New Deal for Communities Programme will necessarily be a long-term task, evidence of tensions was provided in 2002 when the Urban Affairs Select Committee investigated delays, underspend and high turnover of executive staff and board members, and in 2004 when the National Audit Office published a further critical review. There was a conflict between top down managerialism and the aspiration for greater inclusion of residents in decision making, as illustrated by the following quote from Matt Weaver, the resigning chair of one New Deal for Communities scheme:

> It's supposed to be a community initiative but it's actually driven from the top...It's very controlled and there's an awful lot of monitoring. If you run it like that, it stifles the whole thing. You are not allowing the community to spend the money in their way, rather than a forced way. (*Observer*, 7 July 2002)

Another illustration of the impact of joined-up government and social inclusion is the duty placed on local housing authorities to develop and publish homelessness strategies in 2003. They were expected to develop these strategies on a partnership basis and to involve the voluntary sector, social service authorities and the health sector through Primary Care Trusts and police and criminal justice agencies such as the probation service and NACRO. Research indicated an absence of prior links with health and social service authorities in many areas, which made the joining up process a very considerable task (Shelter, 2003). Local strategic partnerships provided a key point of engagement with related local networks, such as health and care partnerships, drug and alcohol action teams, community safety partnerships and early years partnerships.

These examples illustrate the tensions between the new policy themes under modernization and core facets of the earlier NPM agenda. The fragmentation of public services into functional business units had created a policy landscape in which joined-up approaches were difficult to implement. The transfer of risk and the assumption of financial responsibility by decentralized management units had encouraged each agency to defend its own budget rather than pooling resources with others. The implementation of joined-up policies therefore required new incentive structures – such as joint partnership bidding for resources and joint management of delivery – that cut across the business unit autonomy of the earlier NPM era. Similarly the emphasis on including local communities and 'hard to reach' groups in decision making was often difficult to marry with a delivery-orientated agenda in which public investment was expected to be translated into measurable outcomes with minimum delay.

Impacts of management reform on social housing

To assess the impact of NPM and modernization reforms on the governance and management of social housing in the UK we shall first review the general research evidence and then then look at specific impacts in relation to organizational behaviour and institutional structure. Table 7.1 lists some of the elements of NPM and modernization and their impact on the housing sector.

Impact of housing legislation

The earlier impact of NPM on social housing in the UK was studied by Boyne and Walker (1999), who assessed the influence of the three main prescriptions of public choice theory – promoting competition, providing information on performance, and reducing organizational size – on 12 pieces of housing legislation between 1980 and 1996. Twenty-nine reforms were contained in the legislation and all but three of these were consistent with at least one of the three prescriptions, 13 reflected two of them and four (Tenants' Choice, Housing Action Trusts, Compulsory Competitive Tendering and Local Housing Companies) embodied all three. Only three reforms contradicted the three principles: the reorganization of local government into larger management units, increased regulatory powers, and a reduction in choice for homeless

Table 7.1 *Impact of new public management and modernization on social housing*

Feature	Key elements	Impact on housing
Breaking up monopolies	Privatization. Fragmentation	Right to Buy. New development by housing associations. Stock transfers
Reducing organizational scale	Break-up/decentralization of services. Size limits might also be imposed	Size limits to stock transfers (in place until 2003), but competitive housing associations encouraged to grow organically and through merger. Scale of operation of larger associations considerably increased
Introducing competitive markets	Changing incentive structures. Introducing new competitors (private and non-profit sectors). Internal markets (purchaser–provider split)	Private finance, emphasis on business plan and balance sheet. Housing association sector: competitive bidding CCT, PFI. Emphasis on local authority enabling role and outsourcing options (LSVT, CCT, Best Value)
Empowering consumers	Introducing opportunities to opt out. Market research. Shopping incentives	Tenants' Choice. Tenant management organisations, community gateway. Consumerist tenant involvement rent restructuring and Housing Benefit reform
Managerialism	Growth in managerial power, centralization of decisions. Delayering and downsizing. Adoption of private sector management ideas	Housing association management structures. Group structures. Strategic–operational management split. Best Value a conduit for Investors in People, business excellence and so on
Performance measurement	Emphasis on cost. Economy and efficiency measures. Benchmarking. Regulation and audit	Resource accounting. Dominance of rent collection and void management. Huge growth under Best Value. Inspection, Public Service Agreements 'regulatory web'

Table 7.1 (*Continued*)

Feature	Key elements	Impact on housing
Public service orientation	Values and ethos. Service quality. User involvement. Local accountability	Housing association rebranding. Best Value. Tenant compacts, option Appraisals. Local housing companies
Transforming organizational cultures	Staff empowerment. Learning organizations. Leadership. Strong cultures. Double-loop learning Joined-up government.	Investors in people. Best Value service reviews. Management development training. Business excellence, rebranding. Continuous improvement.
Modernization	Social inclusion. Strengthening civil society. Regional agenda. Regional strategies	Linking housing to local strategic partnerships and community plans. Strategy for neighbourhood renewal. Emphasis on community involvement and hard-to-reach groups. Devolution (Scottish Assembly, National Assembly for Wales, Northern Ireland Assembly). Regional Development Agencies, regional chambers, Regional Housing Boards and strategies

Sources: Boyne and Walker (1999); Hood (1995); Ferlie *et al.* (1996); Mullins and Riseborough (1997, 2000, 2001); Walker (1998, 2001).

people (under the Housing Act of 1996). There was stronger evidence of cost reduction and efficiency than of equity, leading Boyne and Walker (ibid., p. 2259) to conclude that 'resources in social rented housing may be better targeted on households in greatest need, but the standard of service provision that these households receive has deteriorated. It can be argued that this is, to some extent, the result of reforms that reflect public choice principles.'

Walker (2001) later conducted a more comprehensive assessment of the impact of social housing reforms using the framework developed by Hood including the seven factors: disaggregation, competition, private sector practices, economy, hands-on top management, performance standards and output measures. Adoption was high for all seven dimensions and the reforms were more far reaching in housing associations than among local authorities. The latter were less likely to have adopted private sector management styles or hands-on top management, and somewhat less likely to have disaggregated, or adopted performance standards.

As found by Boyne and Walker (1999) in their earlier study, quantitative impacts were difficult to identify but there was qualitative evidence of organizational and cultural change in stock-transfer and other types of housing association. Growing market pressure on these organizations had caused them to refocus on core business (rents, lettings and repairs) at the expense of the welfare of tenants and the regeneration of their homes. There was also tighter financial management, a growing emphasis on business skills and asset management, and a tendency for mergers and group structures, thereby undermining the putative size advantages of disaggregation. The apparent contradiction of emphasizing diversification at the same time as retrenching into core business is explained by the tension between an entrepreneurial drive to find new income streams on the one hand and regulatory pressures to avoid risk on the other. Perhaps questioning the ability of housing associations to adapt to the shift from NMP to modernization, Walker (2001, p. 693) considers it 'unlikely that they will develop as welfare or people-based organisations that commentators and politicians desire'.

Impact on organizational behaviour

Further evidence of the impact of NPM and modernization on the organizational culture and structure of housing associations is provided by longitudinal research by Mullins and Riseborough (1997, 2000, 2001) and Mullins (2004a) on the responses of a panel of housing association executives to changes in their external environment since the election of the Labour government in 1997. It was found that in many respects organizational behaviour now resembled that of a private sector business, with a strong focus on positioning, business planning and asset management, organizational strategies aimed at growth through merger, geographical expansion and diversification, innovation in customer services and the replacement of a voluntary sector identity with a social entrepreneurial one.

The research also indicated that social purposes and ethos had made a difference to these organizations. This was reflected in growing responsiveness to service users (see Chapter 10) and rejection of business opportunities that were inconsistent with the values and ethos. The importance of government funding and regulation was another distinctive feature of the environment driving these organizations. The rent reforms introduced in the late 1990s (see Chapter 8) had had a fundamental impact on organizational strategies by limiting the extent to which income could be managed, both through limits to annual increases and restructuring to reflect market differentials. In many senses housing associations now appeared to be regulated social businesses, with regulation playing a larger role than public choice prescriptions would suggest was necessary once the forces of competition and markets had been unleashed.

Impact on the institutional structure of UK social housing

Perhaps the most enduring impact of the reforms has been on institutional structure. While the reforms played out in slightly different ways in each jurisdiction and region, there was a general tendency for governance based on hierarchy to be supplemented by markets and networks. At the national level, government departments were broken up and services were provided by executive agencies, non-departmental bodies and external contractors. At the local level, fragmentation involved the separation of commissioning and service provision, the removal of services from local authority control and outsourcing to non-profit and private sector organizations through contracts or service agreements.

Modernization sought to overcome this fragmentation by encouraging partnership working, an area-based focus and user and citizen involvement. Coordination was enhanced by local strategic partnerships, community strategies and a plethora of substrategies. This appeared to be restoring some control at the local authority level. However by the early 2000s the focus was shifting to the regional and subregional levels and new institutions were developed that appeared to sideline local authorities and reduce local coordination. Regional Housing Boards and regional housing strategies paved the way for the shift of social housing investment allocations to the regional level from 2004/6 onwards.

These reforms have not replaced hierarchy (see the discussion of hierarchy and regulation later in this chapter) but led to a more complex governance of housing in which three modes of coordination coexist. Housing associations engage in competitive, market-type relationships at the same time as participating in more collaborative partnerships and networks. Nevertheless, government policies remain key drivers of organizational behaviour. Regulation imposes hierarchical control on the day-to-day activities of providers, and despite periodic attempts to reduce the regulatory burden, a notable feature of reform of the housing sector has been the tendency for regulation to increase.

At the organizational level, continuities between NPM and modernization demands are apparent. There is growing emphasis on positioning and strategy and organizations are less dependent on single sources of funding or areas of activity. They have developed sophisticated repertoires of behaviour that enable them to compete, collaborate or conform, depending on the context. Some housing organizations have been quite successful in shaping the context in which they operate by influencing policy and taking alternative approaches, rather than simply complying with the government's expectations (Mullins and Riseborough, 2001).

NPM prescriptions have been increasingly challenged in respect of the scale of operations and product specificity of housing organizations. Disaggregation was expected to generate benefits by breaking up unresponsive monopolies and freeing managers to focus on the core business. The expectation that smaller, single-purpose housing organizations would develop as a result of stock transfer and the Right to Buy scheme has not been realized. Housing associations have tended to pursue growth-orientated strategies as a result of competition-related factors such as the need to reduce unit management costs and borrowing margins while remaining active in housing development. Mergers and group formation have produced significant changes in the size of housing associations, and there are now strong policy drivers to rationalize the sector and reduce the number of providers in each neighbourhood.

The impact of these changes has been uneven across the UK. This partly reflects variations in institutional heritage and sociopolitical context, and the opportunity provided by devolution for divergent and locally relevant policies to be introduced. Thus housing associations in Scotland tend to be smaller and more community based than in England (see Chapter 9).

Changing role of local authorities

Discussions of the reform of social housing management tend to focus on housing associations, whose role has been transformed by the modernization process. Walker (2001) suggests that this is partly because the reforms have had less impact on local authorities, but it is important to acknowledge that there have been profound changes for local authorities too. The most direct impact has been on their housing provision role. Once the dominant providers of rented housing in the UK, this function began to be stripped away from them in the early 1980s, with new social housing being developed by housing associations. Whole stock transfers to housing associations began in 1988, and after 1997 the option of stock retention became increasingly difficult to sustain. Authorities that had been inspected by the Audit Commission and received a two-star rating were able to set up 'Arm's-Length Management Organizations' (ALMOs), which were eligible for public funds to meet the Decent Homes Standard but operated under local authority control (see Chapter 9). This model introduced a strong separation between local authorities' strategic role, which remained with them, and their operational roles, which had to be transferred to separately governed ALMOs. One view is that only authorities that had been awarded two stars could be trusted to continue as landlords, while for all others the transfer of assets to a housing association or long-term management to a Private Finance Initiative (PFI) contractor was the only option. By 2005 there were 20 ALMOs in receipt of funding and a further 29 had been accepted to join the programme (Office of the Deputy Prime Minister's website).

There were also considerable changes to local authorities' wider strategic role and the resources available to effect this role. While early stock-transfer authorities had tended to reduce their strategic housing functions (Mullins, 1998), from the late 1990s there was increased emphasis on ensuring that certain housing needs were met, such as accommodation for the homeless. This resulted in a number of authorities re-internalizing outsourced functions such as homelessness assessment, housing register maintenance and housing advice (Office of the Deputy Prime Minister, 2004b). The Audit Commission (2002) highlighted the important housing-related functions of local authorities (for example planning, Housing Benefits and private sector policies) and began to stimulate attention to them through inspections of the strategic housing role. For a time local authorities played a key part in determining the priorities for social housing investment in their areas, in cooperation with preferred housing associations. However this was considerably diminished by the establishment of the Regional Housing Boards and the strategies described earlier, by Investment Partnering, which awarded 70 lead associations 80 per cent of the national Housing Corporation programme (see Chapter 9), and by a move away from allocating grants to individual local authority areas.

Finally, it should be recognized that local authorities and housing associations have both been subject to a similar range of management concepts and models, including customer focus, Best Value, continuous improvement and efficiency drives. Local authority governance was reformed in the 1990s, with small cabinets of leading members and scrutiny committees replacing large service committees. Meanwhile external controls were strengthened by the Audit Commission's Comprehensive Performance Assessment system. In these respects it is not possible to assess the impact of NPM and modernization simply by contrasting housing associations with local authorities.

Regulation and audit

One of the key changes in the governance and management of social housing over the past 25 years or so has been the growth of regulation and audit. Power's (1997, p. 1) depiction of the 'audit society', in which 'people are constantly checking up on each other', is an increasingly appropriate image. The relationship between regulation and management reform is a curious and sometimes contradictory one. On the one hand the purpose of the public choice reforms was to expose public services to market influences and reduce the extent of state intervention. On the other hand these reforms were generally implemented through regulatory directives and new types of regulation to achieve public purposes. These purposes were broadened under the modernization agenda to include accountability for public funds, the protection of consumers, the provision of comfort to private funders by reducing risk and the pursuit of wider public policy aims, such as equal opportunities, environmental protection and consumer involvement.

Who regulates social landlords?

Hood *et al.* (1998) have identified 'regulation inside government' as a key element of the realignment of UK public services. According to Clarke *et al.* (2000), this was a process of separating the public from public services, constructing 'auditable organizations' and moving from compliance to competition. Labour's modernization programme continued this process by increasing the degree of independent evaluation and audit to ensure standards that would meet the public interest, by promoting 'evidence-based practice' and by seeking continuous improvement. This constituted 'a distinctive approach to the need to process risk' (Power, 1997, p. 123).

In housing the most visible symbol of the stepping up of the regulatory state was the establishment of the Audit Commission's housing inspectorate, which was set up under Section 10 of the Local Government Act of 1999 to inspect local authority housing services. In 2001 a separate inspection function was established in the Housing Corporation for housing associations. After a year of operation this function was transferred to the housing inspectorate. However inspection was just one element of the regulatory framework for housing associations, which also included self-regulation, regulation and financial audit by the Housing Corporation and accountability to several other regulatory bodies. Social housing regulation can be depicted as incorporating two main sets of influences: hierarchical influences, through which government exerted hands-off control over public services, and network influences, partly associated with resource diversity, whereby housing service organizations were subject to multiple sources of direction. The latter can best be portrayed as a regulatory web.

Hierarchical influences

Modernization replaced hierarchies within organizations with sets of hierarchical relations between organizations, with the government now controlling a more diverse set of delivery agencies (Figure 7.1). Clarke *et al.*

Figure 7.1   *Hierachical influences on regulation*

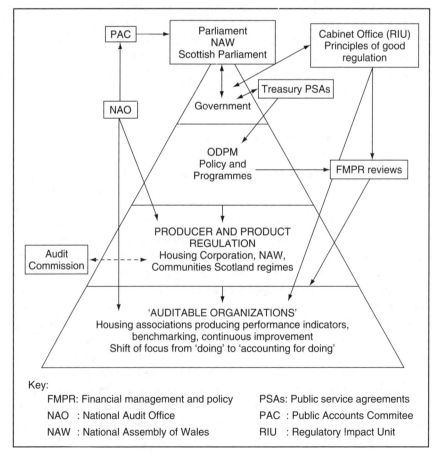

Key:

FMPR: Financial management and policy	PSAs: Public service agreements
NAO : National Audit Office	PAC : Public Accounts Commitee
NAW : National Assembly of Wales	RIU : Regulatory Impact Unit

(2000) view this process as part of a contest to impose the technical authority and organizational independence of audit bodies over the professional authority of specific service provision domains. Audit expanded as a generic process that claimed authority irrespective of the service or product in question. Hughes *et al.* (1996) note that such contests produced different outcomes depending on the extent of professional authority enjoyed by the practitioners in each domain.

While professionalization in social housing was fairly limited (Walker, 1998), professional authority was supported by strong policy networks that included the regulator (the Housing Corporation), a trade body (The National Housing Federation) and a professional body (The Chartered Institute of Housing). For some time these networks facilitated a consensus on many areas of practice (Mullins, 1997) and had the effect of excluding external competitors such as profit-distributing companies from the field. This supports the notion of regulatory capture (Stigler, 1971). However after the 1997 election there was an increase in regulatory influences from outside the housing field.

Hierarchical control of public services was strengthened under New Labour through the establishment of Public Service Agreements (PSAs) by the Treasury. PSAs created auditable organizations based on the premise that it was possible to specify, monitor and evaluate the output of each spending programme. PSAs measured outputs purchased by taxpayers and held to account government departments, executive agencies and ultimately service delivery agencies such as housing associations. A central element of the Office of the Deputy Prime Minister's PSA was the Decent Homes Standard, based on the 2000 Green Paper's commitment to 'offer everyone the opportunity of a decent home and so promote social cohesion, well-being and self-dependence' DETR and DSS (2000 p. 1). Later the housing minister Sally Keeble stated that 'the public expenditure settlement in 2000 sets us well on the way to meeting the Housing Green paper commitment to bring all social housing up to a decent standard by 2010, enabling a one-third reduction by 31 March 2004 in the number of households living in non-decent social housing' (DTLR news release November 2001).

This led to increased evaluation and monitoring at every level (Figure 7.1). This meant more work for watchdog agencies such as the National Audit Office and the Audit Commission, whose housing purview had previously been largely confined to central and local government but now embraced housing associations. 'Value for money' studies conducted jointly by the Audit Commission and the Housing Corporation began in 1995, and subsequently a number of reports were published on topics such as internal audit and housing group structures (Audit Commission, 1999, 2001). The National Audit Office, an agency with 750 staff dedicated to 'helping the nation to spend wisely', became interested in non-profit housing as the sector grew. This interest increased after a lengthy investigation of a major fraud and the Housing Corporation's oversight of this (National Audit Office, 2000). In 2002 the National Audit Office's remit was extended to include the Housing Corporation and access to individual associations' accounts (*Guardian*, 14 March 2002, p.11). The chairman of the Public Accounts Committee commented that 'the rights of audit and inspection over public spending had not kept pace with the way in which public services were delivered...[these changes reflect] the principle that all public spending, by whatever vehicle should be subject to parliamentary scrutiny' (Edward Leigh, MP, reported in *Guardian*, 14 March 2002, p. 11). Influential studies of the management of financial risk by housing associations (National Audit Office, 2001) and value of the stock transfer programme (National Audit Office, 2003) followed.

A 'better regulation task force' and a Regulatory Impact Unit were set up to advise the Labour government on ways to improve the effectiveness and credibility of its regulations and to ensure that regulation was necessary, fair, affordable, simple to understand and administer and did not pose unnecessary burdens. Regulatory impact assessments were used to identify the costs and benefits of proposed regulations, who would be affected and possible alternative, non-regulatory approaches.

The Housing Corporation was subject to regular five-yearly reviews (and *ad hoc* reviews such as the 2004 end-to-end efficiency review) by its sponsoring department, the Office of the Deputy Prime Minister. These reviews investigated adherence to principles such as transparency, accountability, proportionality, consistency and targeting. The 2000 review resulted in the Housing Corporation adopting a more outcome-focused approach in its regulatory code (Housing Corporation, 2002a).

Devolution led to a realignment of the regulatory hierarchies in Scotland and Wales, where the new assemblies had oversight of housing associations through the committee systems of the National Assembly for Wales and the Scottish Parliament. A significant development in both jurisdictions was the emergence of single regulatory bodies for local authorities and housing associations. In Wales the regulatory function became part of the duties of the National Assembly, while in Scotland the chief executive of Communities Scotland reported directly to the Scottish Parliament (Walker *et al.*, 2003). Audit Scotland was made responsible for the types of function undertaken by the Audit Commission in England and Wales. In the case of Northern Ireland, it had been anticipated that the Northern Ireland Housing Executive would become the regulator of housing associations while retaining its landlord role. However the Northern Ireland Assembly rejected this and a new Department of Social Development took over the funding and regulation role previously undertaken by the Department of Environment (Mullins, Rhodes and Williamson, 2001).

At the base of the regulation hierarchy were the service delivery agencies, which had been re-invented as auditable organizations. According to Clarke *et al.* (2000) this involved the production of auditable information on their activities, an emphasis on the specification of outputs and outcomes and a shift of focus and resources from 'doing' to 'accounting for doing'. This in turn imposed compliance costs on audited organizations (Hood *et al.*, 1998), which must be added to the costs incurred by the auditors themselves if we are to gain a comprehensive picture of the costs of this approach.

The regulatory web

An alternative view of regulation uses the image of a web to highlight the impact of multiple activities and associated forms of regulation on housing associations (Figure 7.2). The regulatory state was a crowded state. There

Figure 7.2　*The regulatory web*

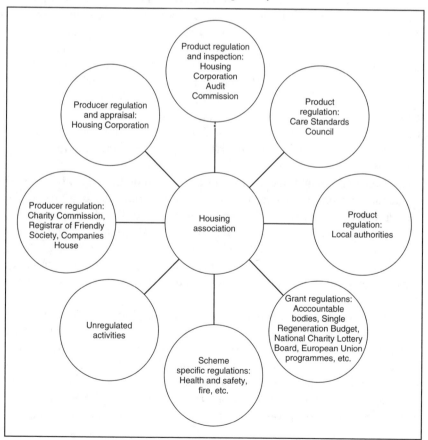

was a clear tension between the attempt to specify and monitor the achievement of service-specific outcomes and more holistic outcomes that required 'joined-up government'. Alongside the hierarchy of regulators described above, there were numerous service-specific regulators, of which the Housing Inspectorate was one. These regimes were of direct relevance to housing associations, that were involved in activities other than housing services.

Many housing associations had always been involved, and in the 1990s some increased their involvement in activities outside the 'product regulation' remit of the Housing Corporation (Newcombe, 1998; Mullins *et al.*, 2001). However, new definitions developed by the Housing Corporation following consultation on how it should 'regulate diversity' captured a fairly high proportion of most associations' activities (Housing Corporation, 1999a, 1999b). Housing association activities included community regeneration, employment and training schemes, care and support services, the provision of key worker accommodation and private rented housing. Such activities brought housing associations into a web of regulatory relationships that included the National Care Standards Commission (later absorbed into the Health Inspectorate). Local authorities were often responsible for funding arrangements such as the Single Regeneration Budget, 'Supporting People' contracts, the National Charity Lotteries Board and European Union programmes. The report on the 2000 review of the Housing Corporation noted that 'it is helpful to distinguish between the Corporation's oversight of an Registered Social Landlord's (RSL's) business viability (producer regulation) and its oversight of the quality of services which the RSL provides (product regulation)...the impact of diversification on the Corporation's ability to scrutinize risk is not yet fully understood' (DETR, 2001d, p. 7).

Research on housing associations in the Midlands (Mullins *et al.*, 2001) found that housing association managers considered their activities to be overregulated, with overlapping and sometimes conflicting requirements, for example between health and safety issues on the one hand and service quality on the other. There was a view that the regulatory regime could be simplified and responsibilities focused, but the associations themselves were not generally developing strategies to deal with the regulatory burden in a systematic way.

Some associations questioned the need for the Housing Corporation to play a 'producer regulation' role when this was already being played by their primary regulators (the Charity Commission, the Registrar of Friendly Societies or Companies House), albeit generally very passively. From this perspective the producer regulation role might have been more appropriate prior to the 1996 Housing Act, when the Housing Corporation had also been responsible for promoting the interests of housing associations.

This role was seen as redundant in the context of the regulated competition model that underlay that legislation (Mullins, 1997). There was general agreement that the Housing Corporation's producer regulation role was not being routinely informed through liaison with other regulators.

Housing associations that provided residential and nursing homes were subject to the most extensive regulation and inspectors had considerable power to intervene to protect service users. Community investment and regeneration activities were generally subject to looser forms of regulation, based on the requirements of specific funding regimes. This usually involved regular monitoring against agreed performance indicators, sometimes with external evaluation of the outputs and outcomes of programmes. The regulatory web was wider than social care and community investment and included relationships with private funders who imposed further audit requirements, and these were sometimes more demanding than those imposed by the Housing Corporation. The monitoring of business plans and funding covenants may be viewed as a key element in the transformation of housing associations into auditable organizations over the past 15 years. Other regulatory relationships have tended to arise at the project level (fire regulations, health and safety, environmental health and so on) rather than at the strategic level.

There have been many attempts to tidy up this regulatory web by central government organizations such as the Regulatory Impact Unit and the Performance and Innovation Unit, and by improved liaison between regulators, for example the Best Value Inspection Forum brought together the Audit Commission's main inspectorates. Nevertheless the image of a web of regulation provides a useful complement to that of hierarchy (Figure 7.1) by conveying the multiple sources of authority and the divergent approaches of the various regulators, despite the emphasis on joined-up government.

Understanding regulation

Regulation can be understood as 'an exercise among groups and between groups and the state' (Francis, 1993 p. 8). This suggests that there is a constant process of adjustment as the different groups affected attempt to change or subvert regulatory objectives while the state continuously attempts to rebalance these interests. Table 7.2 summarizes some of the ways in which the regulatory regime for housing associations in England has affected the various interests involved. The second column outlines the influence enjoyed by different stakeholders in the performance standards regime operated by the Housing Corporation between 1997 and 2002, while the third column 3 shows the changes that have taken place under the new regulatory code adopted by the Housing Corporation in 2002. Overall there has been a reduction of the influence of housing associations,

Table 7.2 *Interest representation in the regulation of housing associations, 1997–2005*

Interests	Performance standards regime 1997	Regulatory code regime 2002
Larger housing associations	Protection from external competition and having a say in framing the standards more than outweighed the regulatory burden	Protection from external competition gradually reduced, culminating in the 2004 Housing Act, which provided for grants to be paid to the private sector. Influence also diminished as general regulatory bodies gained ground at the expense of housing-specific regulation
Smaller housing associations	The regulatory burden fell principally on smaller associations, which gained little protection from external competition. Smaller associations could be quite influential in policy networks (e.g., the National Housing Federation and their values were reflected in the overall sector values)	Some benefits for small associations from proportionate approach to regulation (the RASA regime) and the option of deregistration. But compliance costs were still significant and the move from a producer to a consumer focus was more difficult for small associations such as Black and minority ethnic associations
Consumers	Performance standards provided for tenant involvement. However there was little involvement in the regulatory process itself. Tenants' complaints were dealt with by separate agency. The tenant guarantee lay outside the main regulatory system	The regulatory code allocated a more central role to 'championing a tenant focus in the housing association sector'. The inspection system placed the consumer 'closer to the sector's work'. But Housing Association Tenants Ombudsman Service (HATOS) and the tenant's guarantee remained separate from the regulatory system. Tenants' role ring-fenced to focus on services rather than strategy

The taxpayer: public funds	Probity, value for money for the taxpayer and making funding conditional on the meeting of minimum standards were key elements of the performance standards (and all previous regimes). Strong emphasis on the meeting of acceptable performance standards. Few parallels to the price regulation practices in much economic regulation, such as for privatized utilities	These considerations remained a key element of the regulatory code. The influence of the Treasury was increased through Public Service Agreements and a direct role for the National Audit Office and the Audit Commission. The new focus on 'moving to a fairer and more understandable rent structure' introduced a new dimension to public interest regulation. Restructuring provided more consistency with local authority landlords
Private funders	Private finance led to increasingly sophisticated of financial monitoring, requirements for business plans and the adoption of PLC accounts. However lenders were expected to take their own decisions as this underlay the concept of transfer of risk for borrowing outside the Public Sector Borrowing Requirement	Increased sophistication of financial appraisal to match the more complex funding packages and instruments. Specialist unit to evaluate stock transfer business plans. Controls on diversification partly intended to address lenders' concern about risk. Lead regulators to take wider view of managing business risk and individual associations' regulatory plans. Lenders to continue to take comfort from the regulatory system

a growing consumer emphasis and a significant increase in intervention on behalf of the taxpayer. The position of larger housing associations, which were arguably the main beneficiaries of the performance standards regime, has been challenged by the introduction of private developers and the more generic nature of regulatory influences. The interests of private funders remain an important but largely implicit influence on the regime. The following sections discuss these changes with reference to the concepts of regulatory burden, regulatory capture and regulated competition. This supports the view that generic regulation has gained ground over professional networks and housing associations have become more subject to hierarchical controls from outside the housing domain.

Regulatory burden

Regulatory burden describes the costs imposed on regulated bodies. There has been a concern to address the issue of regulatory burden in line with the principles of good regulation (such as proportionality and regulatory impact assessment) that have cascaded down from the Cabinet Office. Smaller housing associations have had their burden reduced by a shorter annual regulatory return form and the option of deregistration. However the overall effect of the regime change has been to increase the number of regulatory staff and the oversight of housing associations by the Housing Corporation and others, for example due to the expanded remit of the National Audit Office and the new requirement for monitoring Public Service Agreements. One way in which the regulatory burden might be reduced is through 'earned autonomy', whereby high-performance organizations are given greater freedom. This approach has been adopted through the designation of beacon councils and by allowing arm's-length management organizations with two-star housing inspections to acquire additional capital funds.

Regulatory capture

The concept of regulatory capture (Stigler, 1971) was first applied to housing association regulation in the mid 1990s to describe certain aspects of the relationship between some housing associations and the regime (Mullins, 1997). In its submission to the Commission on the Future of the Voluntary Sector, the National Federation of Housing Associations (1995, p. 1) argued that 'housing associations are fairly intensively regulated, and (generally) have welcomed the framework that exists'. Regulatory capture involved the development of a regime that was favourable to the interests of housing associations and excluded competitors, and was developed with the participation of associations themselves through well-established policy networks and their representative body. These networks involved regular contact and frequent staff moves between the regulator and the regulated (including between senior positions). A common understanding and distinctive discourse developed within these networks and differentiated the social housing product from that provided by private landlords. This was illustrated by the reaction of private landlords to the approval criteria developed by the Housing Corporation for landlords under Tenants' Choice (see Chapter 3) Private landlords were put off by aspects of the Tenants' Guarantee – such as equal opportunities and tenant participation – that did not feature among their own practices at the time. As a result the few housing associations that were interested in Tenants' Choice did not face serious competition from private landlords.

However since 1997 there has been some rebalancing of interests away from producers and towards consumers, with the concept of 'the public as consumers' gaining considerable ground. Hierarchical elements of the regulatory framework have also been strengthened, thereby increasing the influence of parliament, national assemblies and independent auditors, partly at expense of the influence of the housing policy community. Most of the reforms empowered larger associations that were better equipped to manage the regulatory burden, and their reported comments on the draft regulatory code (Housing Corporation, 2002b) suggested that they were well able to accommodate themselves to the new regime. However the extent of regulatory capture was diminished by wider regulatory influences, particularly from the Treasury, the National Audit Office and the Audit Commission, which were less subject to professional sector influences. A further shift away from capture towards regulated competition was heralded by the Housing Act of 1996 and culminated in a provision in the Housing Act of 2004 to fund private developers. This shift is discussed in the next section.

Regulated competition

A move away from regulatory capture and towards regulated competition was signalled by consultation papers issued prior to the 1996 Housing Act, but it did not occur at that time. Unlike those for the health and education sectors, the New Labour reform package for housing associations did not initially subject existing providers to direct competition from private sector providers. However after 1997 the relationship between the Housing Corporation and housing associations began to change. The Corporation no longer had responsibility for promoting the work of associations and it shifted its focus from the producer to the consumer. This was evident in the regulatory approach to rent restructuring (see Chapter 8), which was not significantly modified despite the difficulties faced by certain landlords.

The 2000 green paper (DETR and DSS, 2000a) heralded increased private sector involvement – through the Private Finance Initiative – in social housing, housing management and maintenance. Although the pilot programme took some time to get off the ground, extension of the programme was announced in 2003. Another step towards regulated competition was evident in the Sustainable Communities Plan of 2003, which announced the development of social and affordable housing in growth areas such as the South-East of England. Cost-effectiveness and timely delivery were to be enhanced by new procurement methods, modern methods of construction and the provision of grants to a small number of efficient performers. The involvement of private housing developers would start with a pilot scheme that would be implemented as soon as legislation allowed (see Chapter 9). The Housing Act of 2004 encouraged the market entry of private developers as it rendered them eligible for the Social Housing Grant. Associated proposals were developed for 'streamlined regulation' through pilot programme agreements that embraced the principle of earned autonomy.

Conclusion

Housing policy has been influenced by new public management and modernization. The most significant impact has been on the institutional framework within which policies are developed and implemented. One consequence of institutional change was the breaking up of hierarchies in the form of monopoly providers of housing services at the local level. This led to market and network forms of coordination, with the former being stimulated by new public management and the latter encouraged by the Labour government's modernization project through partnership, social inclusion and joined-up governance. The introduction of these ideas was accompanied by the concepts of 'targeting', 'doing more with less' and being 'lean and mean', and had a clear adaptive purpose.

Nonetheless hierarchical influences remained strong as there was increased external control in the form of audits and inspections. The degree of 'capture' of these regulatory forms by the housing policy community was reduced by reforms that led to more generic regulation and high-level accountability, and by the gradual introduction of new forms of competition. This suggests that the outcome of the contest between professional interests and generic regulatory interests was similar in housing to that in other service areas (Clarke *et al.*, 2000). The renewed focus on delivery in Labour's second term of office resulted in the re-establishment of hierarchy through regulation. Public Service Agreements provided the framework to link the provision of Treasury finance to evidence of delivery.

While the implementation of new public management and modernization explain much of the reform of social housing, some distinctive features remain. Until very recently the disaggregation process had not resulted in a mixed economy of welfare that was as extensive as in other areas of the welfare state. The home ownership market remained privileged, and while private renting was facilitated by Housing Benefit, social housing essentially remained the preserve of the non-profit sector. Tenure restructuring took the form of transfers to the non-profit sector rather than full privatization, and the private sector was not eligible for state subsidies for the construction of social housing. However this began to change in the Labour's second term of office, when the Private Finance Initiative was expanded to include the management and maintenance of council housing, providing an alternative to stock transfer for authorities that were striving to meet the Decent Homes Standard. Later private developers were invited to take part in new housing development under the Sustainable Communities Plan, a programme that is expected to expand rapidly when the 2006–8 Social Housing Grant is allocated.

The reform process has played out in different ways in different parts of the UK. For example Europe's largest housing bureaucracy, the Northern Ireland Housing Executive, has survived and has not been subject to significant stock transfers despite losing responsibility for the development of new social housing. Meanwhile distinctive governance practices have continued to characterize the housing association sector in Scotland, where the community-led model has retained its significance. There has recently, been greater support for the mutual model in stock transfer in England and Wales, but take-up has been quite low to date.

Chapter 8

Social Housing Finance: Policies and Problems

A fundamental premise of economics is that individuals and organizations will respond to changes in price in a broadly predictable way. If the price of a particular product increases, consumers will tend to consume less of that product while profit-seeking producers will be encouraged to supply more of it. Conversely if the price falls, consumers will tend to consume more of it but producers will generally wish to supply less. A policy implication of this is that if the government wishes to encourage the consumption of a product it can attempt to lower the price to consumers while not discouraging its continued supply by producers. The provision of appropriate subsidies to consumers, producers or both can potentially achieve this.

This principle underlies the highly complex system of housing finance in the UK. For almost 90 years successive governments have offered incentives and disincentives to consumers and producers in significant parts of the housing system to affect their behaviour and choices, primarily by influencing house prices and costs. This chapter identifies the main ways in which governments have tried to do this, and the broad effects their actions have had on housing provision. The focus is on principles, outcomes and policy change, rather than on the details of the financial system. First, however, we shall explore the factors that govern the choice between producer or consumer subsidies.

Consumer and producer subsidies: the principles

The purpose of housing subsidies is to encourage or enable consumers to purchase more or better housing than they would otherwise be able to purchase. Since subsidies are not intended primarily to benefit the producers of housing, it could be argued that they should be paid in such a way they that they primarily benefit consumers. The form in which subsidies should be provided has been widely debated in the literature (see for example Galster, 1997; Yates and Whitehead, 1998), but in essence there are three ways of subsidizing consumers.

First, consumers can be given money or additional income through a tax credit to enable them to secure better housing. Many consumers might prefer subsidies in this form, and certainly many economists argue that consumers would prefer it. However an obvious problem for the provider of the subsidy – usually the taxpayer – is that the recipients may prefer to spend some or all of the additional money on goods other than housing. Since the aim of the subsidy is to improve recipients' housing circumstances rather than their general welfare, this may not be acceptable to the provider.

Second, the subsidy can be paid to consumers in such a way that they can only spend it on housing, for example in the form of a voucher. Consumers can then determine their housing consumption in the light of the prices/rents of housing provided by the market and their subsidy-enhanced incomes. This approach has been used in the United States (see for example Steuerle *et al.*, 2000). However, where the supply of housing is not very sensitive to price the additional purchasing power of subsidy recipients might result in higher rents and prices rather than access to better housing. In the UK after the two World Wars, supply-side constraints on new housing ruled out direct consumer subsidies. Market supply might have adjusted in time but the need for new and better housing, and the potentially serious social and political consequences of it not being provided (Merrett, 1979), meant that leaving the supply of housing to the market was not an option.

The third way of providing housing subsidies is by subsidizing producers. The idea is that by reducing the cost to producers of providing housing, more housing at lower rents can be made available. Hence the subsidy is passed on to consumers 'in kind', through direct housing provision rather than cash or vouchers (Kelman, 1986). However some form of control or regulation of producers is required to ensure that the subsidy is not absorbed into higher operating costs or profits, with no benefit to consumers. The regulatory problem of controlling private profit-making producers' production, pricing, letting and management decisions is substantial.

As a result, until 2004 (see Chapter 7) UK governments took the option of confining producer subsidies to not-for-profit landlords; that is, from 1919 to local authorities and from the 1970s to housing associations. There are theoretical grounds for arguing that the absence of a profit-making objective for subsidized, not-for-profit housing providers could encourage the diversion of resources into managerial perks or activities that are at odds with the primary objective of providing social housing (Duizendstraal and Nentjes, 1994; Nentjes and Schopp, 2000). This may make them less efficient than unsubsidized private producers operating in a competitive market. Nevertheless these organizations have the explicit objective of providing higher quality at lower prices than the market could supply and are potentially less costly to monitor and control. Unlike private sector suppliers, local authorities do not have the option of failing to ensure that such housing is available.

Hence for much of the history of UK social housing, producer subsidies have been the main incentive employed by governments to encourage provision. However the form that the subsidies have taken in the local authority and housing association sectors has differed, and over the last twenty years the significance of producer subsidies has declined.

Producer subsidies for council housing

The origins of local authority housing in 1919 and its uneven growth over the next 60 years were discussed in Chapter 2. Prior to 1980 subsidies were paid to local authorities to reduce the cost of the long-term loans they had taken out to finance approved housing construction. The value of these subsidies and the period over which they were paid was determined by the Act under which the dwellings were built. Since 1935 all the housing subsidies to which a local authority has been entitled under the various Acts has been grouped into a single payment and paid into the authority's Housing Revenue Account (HRA). An authority's HRA records the income from all the council housing they have provided – rents, local tax subsidies and national subsidies – and the expenditure on that housing – loan repayments, management and maintenance.

HRAs are required to balance each year. This means that rents have traditionally been set to make up the difference between expenditure and income from subsidies and local tax contributions. The combination of central and local subsidies and the requirement to balance the HRA has enabled authorities to charge lower rents than would be charged for similar housing in the private rented sector. Hence households that have been allocated a local authority dwelling can for a given rent consume more housing – in the sense of larger or better-quality dwellings – than they would have been able to do in the absence of the subsidies.

The central government has manipulated the subsidy system to achieve particular goals. For example, with the housing shortage that prevailed after each of the World Wars, subsidies were paid to increase the total amount of housing. In 1930 and again in the mid 1950s, subsidies were paid to clear slum housing, primarily in the private rented sector, and replace it with council housing. The 1956 Housing Subsidies Act encouraged authorities to save on land and increase housing density by giving more subsidies for flats in high-rise blocks. The overall impact of government subsidies on local authorities' willingness to build was dramatic. For example after the increase of subsidies under the 1924 Housing (Financial

Provisions) Act, council house completions more than doubled between 1924/25 and 1925/26 (Holmans, 1987).

The low rents charged by local authorities for comparatively high-quality dwellings increased the demand for council homes. By 1980 almost a third of British households lived in council housing, subsidized to a greater or lesser degree by taxpayers. This apparent success of the housing subsidy scheme began to be questioned in the 1960s. The cost to the Exchequer of financing council housing was substantial, and there were significant variations in the rents charged for similar dwellings by different local authorities. These variations reflected differences between their past and current building programmes (and hence their differing subsidy entitlements) and the different management and maintenance costs arising from this. The variations were summarized by one contemporary source as the result of 'historic accidents which...determined the composition of each local authority's housing stock' (HMSO, 1971, para. 6). Local authorities also varied in their use of discretionary local tax contributions and were free to vary the rents of individual dwellings within their HRA.

The high demand for council housing at the time reflected differences in rents and housing quality in the private sector. Rents in the council sector did not take account of the market value of the dwellings since local authorities were not required to set rents in relation to local markets. From an economics perspective, the failure of rents to reflect the value of the services provided led to distorted household choices between sectors and between dwellings within the sectors. This became a problem when the government wanted to encourage tenants to choose alternative landlords – housing associations, which set rents on a different basis.

In 1980 the Conservative government began to reduce the size of the social rented sector and made fundamental changes to the way in which the sector was subsidized. We shall consider the latter in the next section.

The decline of producer subsidies for council housing

The government's Right to Buy scheme was so important to its housing policy that, as Malpass (1990) notes, almost no attention was paid to council rents and subsidies during the passage of the 1980 Housing Act through parliament. The Act retained the freedom of local authorities to determine the rents of individual dwellings but returned to the principle of 'deficit funding' for determining exchequer subsidies. Under this system, which had been introduced in 1972 and withdrawn in 1975, the government subsidies paid to authorities were calculated as the amounts required by the authorities to balance their HRAs – that is, to make up the difference between their expenditure and rent income. The minimum sum that an authority could receive as a result of this calculation was zero, but the increases in expenditure and rent income used in the subsidy calculation each year were not the actual increases the authority might face but rather the increases determined by the minister. Since the minister assumed that income (from rents) was increasing faster than expenditure, most authorities experienced an annual fall in subsidy entitlement.

Local authorities did not have to follow these determinations when managing their housing expenditure and rent income but their HRAs still had to balance. Consequently they were faced with the choice of following the determinations or introducing a combination of expenditure reductions, rent increases and local tax transfers to the HRA. Since one way of reducing expenditure and finding extra income for the HRA was to encourage tenants to purchase their homes, this accorded with government policy. Furthermore the sharp rent increases that authorities found it necessary to impose were an added incentive for tenants to consider purchasing their dwelling, given the discounts available under the Right to Buy scheme.

Average rents almost tripled during the period 1980–90, and the impact of this on local authorities' housing subsidies was almost as dramatic. The proportion of income that English and Welsh authorities received from the central government in subsidies averaged 31 per cent in 1980/81, but by 1988/89 it had fallen to 5 per cent. However the average amount received in HRA income from the government in Housing Benefit payments for council tenants (discussed further below) rose from 8 per cent to 33 per cent over the same period. These figures clearly demonstrate a change from producer subsidies for council housing to a system of personal subsidies for council tenants over these ten years in question.

From the central government's perspective the decline in subsidies was problematic, in that towards the end of the 1980s the great majority of authorities no longer received a subsidy and therefore had no need to conform to the government's expectations for rent and expenditure increases, upon which the subsidy calculation was based. Hence the government introduced the 1989 Local Government and Housing Act to reassert financial control over local authorities' housing operations. The details of this legislation have been extensively discussed in the literature (for example Hills, 1992; Gibb *et al.*, 1999) and have been summarized by Walker and Marsh (1995, pp. 3–4). The Act retained the 'deficit' funding system and prevented transfers between the HRA and local tax (general rate) funds.

The major provision in the Act combined the two previous subsidies to the HRA: the housing subsidy and the Housing Benefit subsidy. Since every local authority had some tenants who received Housing Benefit, all local authorities were brought back into the subsidy calculation. If an authority was deemed to be in deficit, then the subsidy required to make up this deficit was added to the authority's Housing Benefit subsidy entitlement and paid as a single subsidy. However if the authority was judged to have a surplus in its HRA it received its Housing Benefit subsidy minus that surplus. Tenants entitled to benefit would still pay a reduced rent or no rent at all, but the authority would only receive from the government an amount net of the assessed HRA surplus.

An authority faced with a Housing Benefit subsidy entitlement below that required to make up the difference between what tenants actually paid in rent and the actual rents set for council dwellings still had to balance its HRA. The only options open to the authority were to reduce expenditure or increase rents. Since tenants in receipt of Housing Benefit were protected against such increases, only those who did not receive benefits actually paid a larger rent. Consequently tenants who were paying full rent were part funding, through higher rent payments, the entitlements of tenants who were in receipt of Housing Benefit.

The impact of this subsidy system was such that between 1990 and 1994 rents rose by 52 per cent. By 1995/96 all metropolitan and shire districts and outer London boroughs were deemed to be in notional surplus (Walker and Marsh, 1997) and the central government was no longer providing general financial support for local authority housing (Wilcox, 1995).

Producer subsidies for housing associations

The recent history of housing associations is inextricably linked to the degree of funding provided by successive governments (Malpass, 2000a; Mullins, 2000). The same principle that has applied to the funding of council housing – that subsidies will affect individual and organizational behaviour in broadly predictable ways – has also been evident in the funding of housing associations since the early 1970s. The type and level of funding for associations introduced in 1974 provided a major stimulus to the growth of the sector, which has continued to expand over the last 30 years.

The 1974 Housing Act established a generous public subsidy scheme that was to last until 1989 (Hills, 1992; Cope, 1999; Gibb *et al.*, 1999). Under this Act the rents of approved developments were determined by the rent officer but allowances for managing and maintaining the properties were deducted, leaving a net annual income from the development. This sum determined the annual amount available to repay a fixed-interest 'residual' loan from the Housing Corporation or local authority over 30 years (refurbished housing) or 60 years (new housing). The difference between this loan and the capital costs of the scheme were met by a one-off grant from the Housing Corporation. This was first known as the Housing Association Grant (HAG) and then the Social Housing Grant (SHG).

Notwithstanding the limits placed on the capital costs of schemes that were eligible for the HAG and the 'excessive systems of scheme scrutiny' (Cope, 1999, p. 113) to which the schemes were subject at each stage of the development process, the HAG was a generous form of funding. HAG rates averaged 85 per cent of allowable costs during the 1980s and could rise to 100 per cent if there was insufficient net rental income to finance a residual loan. Additional HAG funds could be claimed if major repairs arose during the life of the scheme. Associations were also eligible for an annual Revenue Deficit Grant if rental income was insufficient to meet expenditure on management, maintenance and loan repayments.

The impact of these subsidies was significant in two ways. First, given that access to the scheme required registration with the Housing Corporation, there was a rush to register. In 2000, over 55 per cent of registered general needs associations in England had first registered with the Housing Corporation in 1975–76, and Malpass (2000b) estimates that of the 500 largest registered associations in 1996, two thirds had been formed since the mid 1960s. Second, the subsidies gave associations an enhanced role in the provision of new social housing. Data provided by Hills (1992, Table 3.5) indicates that in an age of public expenditure cuts, real (gross) capital spending by English housing associations fell by almost a half between 1976/77 and 1988/89, from £1.3 billion to £0.7 billion. However the permitted and actual spending of local authorities and new towns on new housing construction over the same period fell by about 88 per cent. In 1986/87 and 1988/89 real capital spending on new construction by associations exceeded that of local authorities, although by 1991 housing associations still owned only 12 per cent of the social housing stock.

Nevertheless, in a period of growing concern about public expenditure and value for money, this funding regime came under scrutiny. The government argued that the system of financing associations did little to encourage efficiency in new housing provision (Department of the Environment, 1987). The relative efficiency of housing associations as providers of social housing was then, as now, a matter of some dispute (see Walker and Murie, 2004). Associations were protected from cost overruns and revenue shortfalls, leaving these risks firmly with the taxpayer. As a result there was little incentive for associations to monitor and control costs efficiently. Moreover there was a need to maximize the output of housing from a given amount of public investment.

The government's solution to these perceived problems was a 'mixed funding' regime. Introduced in 1989, this involved fixing at the outset the percentage of the capital costs of a scheme that could be met from the HAG, and therefore associations were made responsible for bearing (or preventing) cost overruns. The fixed percentage varied according to the type of scheme and the area in which the development was to take place. Competitive bidding between associations rewarded schemes that would produce the most housing for the amount bid. This encouraged associations to bid below the fixed grant rate to increase their chance of success. Thus the average grant rate fell from 75 per cent in 1989/90 to 56 per cent in 1998/99 (Cope, 1999). Associations were also given the freedom to set rents on new and relet property at levels that reflected their new financial and continuing social responsibilities.

This combination of lower grant rates, competitive bidding and the need to satisfy the financial market's criteria for viability was intended to increase the efficiency of associations' operations by shifting a significant proportion of the risk of investment to the associations and their lenders. The difference between the grant awarded and the costs of development had to be met by the association, either from its own resources or by borrowing from the private sector. Obtaining private finance subjected associations to the discipline of the capital market. Private lenders would only be prepared to invest in schemes that were financially viable and undertaken by associations with sufficient managerial capacity and experience to minimize the risk to the lender. The government did not guarantee loans in the event of an association defaulting and schemes thus funded were not eligible for a Revenue Deficit Grant.

In the early years of the new funding scheme lenders were 'understandably cautious, reflecting a new market and limited competition' (Williams, 2003, p. 11). Whitehead (1999) ascribes this caution to the fact that the activities of housing associations were not well understood by lenders and the latter had very little experience of investing in rented housing, given the small scale of the private rented sector in the UK. Interest rates were relatively high in this period, and considerably higher than for lower-risk lending to local authorities (see ibid. for details). In the main the interest rates charged were, variable so that they could reflect market changes, and the loans were often short term, giving lenders the chance to withdraw and associations the opportunity to refinance in the light of their growing experience in a developing market.

These factors help to explain the relatively slow start to private lending, which amounted to about £300 million in 1989/90 and a little more than that in 1990/91. However by the middle of the 1990s associations were borrowing over £1.6 billion per annum and there had been no instances of an association defaulting on its loans. Thus Saw *et al.* (1996, p. 1) could justifiably claim that the 'introduction of private finance into housing associations has been a spectacular success'.

While the demand for private finance can be partly explained by the lower grant rates, a clear influence on borrowing was associations' participation in the Large-Scale Voluntary Transfer (LSVT) programme (see Chapter 9). LSVT was significant from a financial point of view because the purchase of local authority properties was not accompanied by public subsidies for the purchasing associations. Rather the funds for the purchase of stock and its subsequent improvement had to be raised by the associations from the private market.

Between 1988/89 and 2001/2, 104 authorities transferred over half a million dwellings at a combined purchase price of £4.9 billion (current prices). As there was a need for further borrowing to make improvements to the stock, the total loan was almost double that needed to finance the transfer itself – £9.2 billion. The value of funding committed to the social housing sector in England at the end of March 2002 was £26 billion (Housing Corporation and National Housing Federation, 2003a). According to Williams (2003) the majority of private finance (around 60 per cent) was taken up by traditional non-LSVT associations. However LSVT associations were expected to take up the majority of funding in 2004/5 to 2005/6 (Housing Corporation and National Housing Federation, 2003).

While the demand for private finance has clearly been a result of the changing grant regime and the LSVT initiative, the willingness of private lenders to meet that demand can be explained by the following. First, lenders bear only part of the cost but have first call on the value of the asset. This has 'built in' a safety margin between the value of the asset and the size of the loan.

Second, in the event of default lenders can, with the secretary of state's permission, require empty properties to be sold at their open market value rather than their 'existing use value as social housing', the basis upon which stock is valued at transfer. Whitehead (2003) argues that this is an implicit subsidy to LSVT associations and their lenders, who are investing in an asset valued at a lower price than it would command in the market.

Third, in the event of associations getting into loan repayment difficulties, their freedom to determine their own rents on new and relet properties initially gave them the ability to increase their revenues to meet their liabilities. However this option has since been constrained by the Housing Corporation's 'rent influencing' regime and rent restructuring (discussed below).

Fourth, the rental income stream is effectively underwritten by Housing Benefit as around two thirds of housing association tenants receive this benefit (Wilcox, 2002). As will be discussed below, Housing Benefit fully compensates recipients for rent increases if their circumstances do not change. Since many associations require tenants' benefit entitlements to be paid direct to themselves the difficulties and costs of rent collection are obviated.

Finally, the regulation of the sector by the Housing Corporation further reduces the risk to lenders as the financial viability of associations is regularly assessed by the regulator. The financial health of housing associations has always been a regulatory concern but the Regulatory Code (Housing Corporation, 2002d) provides additional safeguards. Associations must produce audited accounts, external auditors' reports, an assurance statement on internal financial controls, and detailed financial returns (Housing Corporation, 2002b). The Corporation can also demand copies of documents the associations use for their own business purposes and their own internal use. The information thus gained enables the regulator to draw up a regulatory plan and a report on each association's financial viability. In so doing the Housing Corporation 'will have regard to the financial risks facing the sector as a whole. We will publish information periodically on the financial profile of the sector and specific risks to associations' viability' (Housing Corporation, 2002c, para. 17).

The security that these considerations provide for lenders has been reflected in lower interest rates, particularly those charged to larger associations with more assets against which loans can be secured. By 2001/2 interest rates were similar to those charged by organizations lending to manufacturing firms (Saw *et al.*, 1996).

The liberalization of housing associations' funding and rent setting arrangements has had two significant effects. First, average rents in the sector have risen significantly, reflecting associations' desire to build up surplus funds for future development and major repairs, and the higher costs brought about by the replacement of grants by commercial loans.

Second, there has been a significant change in the activities of housing associations (see Chapter 9). There has been a trend for the larger housing associations in particular to diversify their activities away from solely social housing provision and to become, for example, providers of nursing homes and accommodation for key workers. According to Mullins (1999b) the two main reasons for this diversification are associations' desire to cross-subsidize their social renting activities, given the costs of private finance and the Housing Corporation's attempts to limit rent increases, and to expand their role in other social programmes, drawing on public funds other than Social Housing Grant.

This diversification has been one reason for the creation of group structures and subsidiaries that enable associations to separate out their various activities for the purposes of management, governance and finance. By April 2000 three quarters of the social housing stock held by associations that owned at least 250 dwellings was in some form of group structure (Audit Commission and Housing Corporation, 2001). The formation of subsidiaries and group structures offers potential economies, for example in terms of central management services and procurement, and in service delivery more generally, although the evidence of this is not strong (Walker and Murie, 2004).

However diversification also introduces new elements of risk to organizational viability and to the core social housing activity of associations, and thus to their funders. Peter Williams, deputy director general of the Council of Mortgage Lenders, commented that associations may 'over-reach themselves and put at risk therefore all the public and private borrowing that they have undertaken' (quoted in *Housing Today*, 4 May 2000, p. 3). In its role as regulator the Housing Corporation clearly has a part to play here, both as the taxpayer's representative and – because private lenders cannot be directly represented on housing association boards – as the representative of private lenders. The Housing Corporation also places restrictions on the non-core activities of housing associations (Housing Corporation, 1999a, 1999b)

The private finance regime has generally been successful in funding LSVTs and encouraging a larger number of new housing completions each year than at the time of the regime's introduction in 1989 (Wilcox, 2002). However this achievement has relied partly on the ability to raise rents and on the income guaranteed by Housing Benefit. Both of these advantages have been weakened, as will be discussed in the following sections.

Rents and restructuring: harmonizing the local authority and housing association sectors?

From the central government's perspective the problem of rents in the social sector can be summarized as 'incoherence' (Wilcox, 1997) within and between sectors due to the significant degree of autonomy that local authorities and, since 1989, housing associations have had in rent setting. The move away from fair rents and the need to raise private finance caused housing association rents to increase rapidly in the early 1990s. By 2000, on average housing association rents were 30 per cent below private sector unfurnished rents, compared with around 40 per cent in 1991, and were 30 per cent higher than local authority rents in England in 2001, compared with 20 per cent a decade earlier (Wilcox, 2002).

Local authorities' freedom to set rents while receiving government subsidies has a long history. For much of the last century the only statutory requirements were that local authorities should 'charge "reasonable" rents,... review rents "from time to time", and... make such changes "as circumstances may require"' (Cullingworth, 1979, p. 49). By 1998/99 the method used by just over half of English local authorities to set the rent of individual dwellings was some form of points system (Walker and Marsh, 2000), although this method has been less popular in Scotland

(Moore *et al.*, 2003). Under this system, housing characteristics that individual local authorities decide should be of significance in determining rents – for example the number of bedrooms or the presence of a garden – are allocated a specific number of points. The value of each point is broadly determined by dividing the total sum that an authority needs to raise from rents to balance its Housing Revenue Account by the total number of points allocated to the stock to yield a 'price per point'. The rent of a particular dwelling is the number of points allocated to the dwelling multiplied by this price.

In principle, points systems and methods based on a more explicit measure of the value of a dwelling have much to recommend them as they are transparent and arguably rational, in contrast to *ad hoc* approaches to determining rent. However the variety of ways in which these and other rent-setting methods are applied in practice by individual local authorities means that there is little similarity between the rents charged for otherwise identical dwellings by, say, two adjacent authorities in the same area using the same rent-setting method and operating under similar financial constraints.

Both the rent-setting methods employed and the practice of pooling rents, which potentially weakens the relation between the rent set for a dwelling and its current value and/or cost of provision, have led to relatively narrow differentials in the rents of properties in an authority's stock. By 1998/99 the average rent for local authority one-bedroomed dwellings in England was 78 per cent that of three-bedroomed dwellings (Walker and Marsh, 2000). In Scotland in 2000/01 this ratio was very similar, at around 83 per cent (Moore *et al.*, 2003).

Housing associations, like local authorities, have had a relatively high degree of autonomy in rent setting since 1989 and have engaged in some rent pooling, thus potentially decoupling from property values or costs of operation the rent set for a property and for the rent set for one property relative to another. There is also variation in rent setting among associations, given the coexistence of the pre- and post-1989 regimes and rent-setting arrangements that reflect the specific financial arrangements of each association (ibid.) The overall effect on rent differentials in the housing association sector has been very similar to that in the local authority sector. In 2000/01 the average rent for a one-bedroom property as a percentage of the rent for a three-bedroom property in Scotland was 77 per cent (ibid.) and it varied from 71 per cent in London to 87 per cent in the West Midlands (Wilcox, 2001), thus covering a similar range to the local authority figures quoted above.

From a policy perspective the different rent levels (average rents) obtaining in the local authority and housing association sectors and the relatively narrow differentials in the rents set for different properties within the two sectors have been seen as a problem. Current policy encourages tenants to choose housing association rather than local authority dwellings. However the higher rents charged by the former are likely to dissuade current and potential social sector tenants from so doing.

Moreover if the rents for larger or better-quality dwellings in the two sectors are not significantly differentiated from those for smaller or lower-quality dwellings in the two sectors, then tenants will have less incentive to choose the latter rather than the former. Thus tenants who do not need the large dwellings they currently occupy – perhaps due to a reduction of household size – and tenants who would otherwise opt for lower-quality dwellings have no financial incentive to do so. There are large numbers of households with at least one spare bedroom in the social rented sectors (Barelli, 1992) and rent differentials are not a major reason for households moving from larger to smaller properties (Barelli and Pawson, 2001; Pawson and Sinclair, 2003).

Walker and Marsh (2003) argue that the narrow rent differentials and their effects on tenants' occupation and location decisions has become an urgent problem for the government for two reasons. First, some of the dwellings in certain areas have high turnover and vacancy rates – the problem of 'low demand' (see for example Bramley and Pawson, 2002). It might be suggested that fewer tenants will choose to live or remain in such areas if the rents do not differentiate between areas and properties in an appropriate manner. Second, the Housing Benefit system gives little incentive to recipients to make choices in the light of such rent relativities. Kemp (1998, 2000a, 2000b) and Hills (2001) argue that reforms to the Housing Benefit system will not affect tenants' choices in the social rented sector if rent structures are not also reformed. Thus reforming rent setting in order to provide a 'shopping incentive' is seen as a precondition for Housing Benefit reform.

The government's response to these concerns has been to introduce a rent restructuring policy for social housing in England. This policy has four main objectives (DETR and DSS, 2000c). The first is to make rents fairer and less confusing to tenants. This is to be achieved by applying a consistent formula to determine the rent for individual dwellings in both the local authority and the housing association sector. This is also intended to achieve the second objective: to reduce 'unjustifiable' differences in the rents set by local authorities and housing associations by removing any anomalies and differences in rents that do not reflect the size, quality and location of properties. Local rents for similar properties in the two sectors should converge as a result. The third and fourth objectives are to encourage better management of the social housing stock and to provide a closer link between rents and the qualities that tenants value in properties. These should be met by having rents that send appropriate price signals to social landlords as investors and managers of the properties, and to tenants as consumers. The choices of the latter will thus be influenced by rents being set on a more rational basis.

The formula chosen by the government to set the rents of individual dwellings includes property values, number of bedrooms and an adjustment to reflect affordability. It is argued that property values provide a good indication of the relative attractiveness to tenants of the size, condition and location of properties (DETR, 2000). The measure of property values used is the market value of the dwelling relative to the national average value of dwellings in the sector (local authority or housing association) in which the dwelling is located. The number of bedrooms a property contains is intended to generate a set of rent differentials between different sizes of property. Affordability is addressed by including in the formula a measure of the average manual earnings in the county in which the dwelling is located relative to the national average. This measure, as Walker and Marsh (2003) have observed, is rarely considered in the quite extensive literature on this issue (see for example Whitehead, 1991; Chaplin *et al.*, 1994).

Landlords have up to ten years from the date of the introduction of rent restructuring (2002/3) in which to implement it fully. Thus the rents that landlords are expected to meet – or at least to within a range of 5 per cent – will obtain in 2011/12. The annual rate of progress towards the target rents is for individual landlords to decide. However rent changes are constrained by a mechanism under which rent increases for individual dwellings in any one year in both sectors are limited to 0.5 per cent above the increase in the retail price index plus £2 per week, and rent reductions, where required, are limited to 0.5 per cent above the increase in the retail price index minus £2 per week. As an additional safeguard against affordability problems the government has set maximum rent levels for properties of different size.

While it is too early to evaluate the effects of rent restructuring in the two sectors, a number of studies have thrown light on whether the policy is likely to achieve its objectives. Research conducted prior to implementation by Walker *et al* (2002; see also Walker and Marsh, 2003) suggests that the average rents in the two sectors at the local level, and the rents set for similar dwellings, will in general tend to converge over the ten-year period, a finding that has been replicated in a study of social housing in rural areas by Walker (2004) and confirmed by a more recent review of the impact of the policy (Office of the Deputy Prime Minister, 2004a). Since the more equal rent levels will arguably result from the removal of unjustifiable differences in the rents of similar properties in the two sectors, the second policy objective is also likely to be achieved.

Thus housing association and local authority tenants occupying similar properties should eventually be paying similar rents. While this accords with the notion of fairness, Walker *et al.* (2002) suggest that average changes in restructured rents may not always be a reasonable guide to the impact of restructuring on individual properties. Similarly, according to the Office of the Deputy Prime Minister (2004a, para 2.8) 'a relatively modest change in the overall average rent conceals some significant changes in individual rents'. If households experience rent changes over time that are very different from those of many of their fellow tenants, they will have a very different perception of the degree fairness that the restructuring policy has achieved.

Establishing a more rational set of rent differentials between properties in the social housing sector could lead to better management by landlords, particularly if the new rent structure provides a closer link between the rent charged and the qualities that tenants value in properties. Tenants' responses to the price signals generated by restructured rents will help to guide their landlords' investment and stock management policies. Unfortunately, the initial effects of restructuring on the rent differentials between different properties in each sector appear to be contrary to expectations in this regard. Walker *et al.* (2002) and the Office of the Deputy Prime Minister (2004a) have found that, depending on how they are measured, the rent differentials of many social landlords have actually narrowed compared with those set prior to restructuring.

Social landlords previously based their decisions about rent levels and rent structures on their financial commitments. However the restructuring formula does not make any allowance for the amount of revenue that individual landlords need to raise in order to meet those commitments, and this could result in the accrual of large deficits. This problem is less of a concern for local authorities as the restructuring regime is accompanied by an amendment to the subsidy system. This in effect compensates authorities that are unable to balance their HRA as a result of restructuring by 'taxing', through reduced subsidies, authorities that generate HRA surpluses as a result of restructuring. This might explain why there has been relatively little objection to the policy by local authorities or their representative organizations, despite the loss of their traditional power to set rents (Marsh and Walker, forthcoming).

The situation for housing associations is very different. Many associations are required to reduce their (real) rents over the restructuring period (Walker *et al.*, 2002; Office of the Deputy Prime Minister, 2004a Walker, 2004). HACAS Chapman Hendy and KPMG (2000) have examined the effects of restructuring on 40 associations deemed likely to be exposed to financial risk as a result of rent restructuring. They found that even if corrective strategies were employed by the associations in order to remain viable under rent restructuring, only ten would be marginally viable and two would be unviable if they had to restructure their rents within the ten-year period. There is particular concern about the viability of black and Ethnic Minority associations because their stock is overrepresented in areas where property values are relatively low (HACAS Chapman Hendy, 2002; National Housing Federation, 2002). Unsurprisingly, therefore, Williams (2003) has identified rent restructuring as potentially threatening the private financing of housing association development.

The corrective strategy being considered by some housing associations when Walker *et al.* (2002) and Walker (2004) were conducting their studies was to reduce or postpone investment in new development or major repair programmes, a response that was at variance with the government's goals of expanding the role of housing associations in social housing provision and meeting the 'Decent Homes Standard' by 2010. The Housing Corporation has introduced 'extensions' for associations whose financial viability would be threatened or whose existing guarantees to tenants or lenders would be abrogated if they implemented the policy as required. These extensions are primarily intended to allow associations to restructure more slowly or at a future date, for example when loan conditions can be renegotiated or guarantees to tenants have expired. Even so most associations are required to charge new tenants rents that reflect the restructuring specifications and are expected to prepare plans for implementation. In this sense the extensions do not exempt associations from the policy imperative.

Clearly the impact of the policy on many associations is quite significant and may require major financial restructuring in the light of the changed revenue flows that restructuring implies. The longer-term effects of the policy, and particularly the effects on investment decisions and tenants' choice within and between sectors in the light of the changing rent structures, have yet to be felt. It is clear, however, that influencing housing choice through restructured rents based on the idea of market-like pricing is a central part of the government's policy towards social housing. This is also evident in the proposed changes to Housing Benefit, which are discussed in the next section.

Housing Benefit: problems and proposals

Housing Benefit assists eligible households in the social and private rented sectors to pay their rent. Although administered by the local authorities it is a national benefit that is almost wholly determined, like other aspects of the social security system, by highly prescriptive national rules on eligibility and payment. Housing Benefit is means tested and the amount to which any household is entitled depends on the results of the means test and on the rent set. As Gibb *et al.* (1999) point out, Housing Benefit is an *ex post* benefit – that is, it is determined, all other things being equal, by the rent that is charged for a claimant's property, not by a prior decision about the amount of assistance to which a particular household is entitled in the light of their personal and financial circumstances. It is thus a rebate on the rent paid rather than a fixed allowance determined irrespective of the rent actually paid.

The rent payment that is relevant for Housing Benefit purposes in all rented sectors is net of certain service charges that may be included in the rent, such as a charge for heating. The rationale here is that Housing Benefit is intended to assist solely with the cost of rent, not other elements of household expenditure. As the rent levels in the local authority and housing association sectors have been kept relatively low and the government has helped to determine, directly and indirectly, the rent levels in the two sectors, these levels are accepted as appropriate for Housing Benefit purposes.

In the case of the private rented sector a different set of arrangements apply. Benefit claimants in this sector have their rents referred to independent local rent officers who apply three tests to the dwelling in question: whether the rent is too high relative to that for similar dwellings in the area; whether the property is overly large relative to the household's needs; and whether it is the right size and commands an appropriate rent for its quality but the rent is too high to expect the taxpayer to fund it (Department for Work and Pensions, 2003). The rent officer sets a local reference rent, which is a broad average or mid-point rent for the type and size of property in the area. For single claimants under 25 years of age the equivalent to the local reference rent is the single room rent, reflecting the tendency of younger people to share accommodation. The 'claim-related' rent that is used for Housing Benefit is either the local reference/single room rent for an appropriately sized property or the eligible rent, whichever is the lower.

The reason for this approach is that the liberalization of the private rented sector from most forms of rent control in the late 1980s has caused rents to rise to market levels, and above those levels in areas where rented housing is in short supply. An open-ended commitment by the local authority to pay these rents in part or full would allow claimants to move up-market in terms of the size, quality or location of their dwelling and to collude with their landlord by agreeing to unreasonably high rents. The restriction that is applied to funding rents above the reference points is intended to mitigate these problems.

The means test to which Housing Benefit claimants are subject is the same in all rented sectors. It takes account of the claimant's age and working status and includes a set of standard deductions for the financial contribution that any non-dependent members of the household are assumed to make towards household expenses. The resulting sum is known as the 'applicable amount'. This can be expressed as:

$$HB = R - \alpha(Y - AA)$$

where HB is Housing Benefit entitlement, R is the claim-related rent or eligible rent for Housing Benefit purposes, Y is the claimant's assessed income, AA is the applicable amount and α is a taper.

If the claimant's income, including assumed income from any savings above a particular threshold, is less than or equal to the applicable amount $(Y \leq AA)$ or the claimant receives income support, Housing Benefit entitlement is equal to the eligible rent since $\alpha(Y - AA) = 0$. It the claimant's income exceeds the applicable amount $(Y > AA)$ the Housing Benefit entitlement is reduced by an amount equal to the taper, α, which is currently set at 0.65. Hence if claimants' incomes rise above the applicable amount by £1, their benefit entitlement falls by £0.65, an effective marginal tax rate of 65 per cent. On the other hand, if their rent rises by £1 and all other factors in the formula remain the same, their benefit entitlement rises by £1.

The current Housing Benefit system insulates claimants from rent changes but penalizes them significantly if their incomes rise. Hence there is little incentive to shop around for a lower rent or to find work. In the social rented sectors Housing Benefit is normally paid directly to the landlord. This is somewhat less common in the private rented sector, but a recent study suggests that payment is made directly to landlords in 40–80 per cent of cases (Department for Work and Pensions, 2004). This means that a significant proportion of claimants have to take no responsibility for making rent payments, which could further reduce their interest in the amount of rent being charged.

Unsurprisingly, as Gibb *et al.* (1999, p. 197) observe, 'a lengthy hit list of reforms' has been proposed to deal with these problems, to minimize the disincentive to work and to influence claimants' choice of housing (Kemp, 1992, 2000a). In 2002 the government announced a 'radical agenda' for the reform of Housing Benefit (Department for Work and Pensions, 2002a). Initially the reforms would apply solely to the private rented sector and nine 'pathfinder' authorities. The means test arrangements would continue, but there would be a change to the way in which Housing Benefit was determined and delivered. Rent officer determinations of the eligible rent would be replaced by a flat rate 'Local Housing Allowance' (LHA), under which a claimant's entitlement would broadly reflect the mid point rent in the area for a property of a size deemed sufficient for the household in question. The calculation of the LHA for different sized properties would be very similar to that employed to set the local reference rent and single room rent in non-pathfinder areas. The main difference would be that the amount would be fixed for each household and would not vary according to the property occupied. Hence while some households might find that the LHA was less than the rent they actually paid, for others it would exceed their current rent, a situation that could not arise under the previous arrangements. In addition, under the LHA arrangements in most cases the allowance would be paid directly to claimants.

The government argued that these new arrangements would improve tenants' choice of accommodation since the LHAs would be publicized and claimants would know their (maximum) LHA entitlement (Department for Work and Pensions, 2002a). There would be no need for claimants (and Housing Benefit administrators) to apply to the rent officer for the rent to be determined. Paying the allowance to claimants and allowing them to retain any excess meant they could choose whether to spend the excess on better accommodation or move to a property with a lower rent and keep the difference.

It was anticipated that there would be changes in landlords' behaviour in respect of rent setting and who they chose to house, depending on the situation in the local market. Much would depend on Housing Benefit administrators' decision as to which claimants, an anticipated minority, should not receive the allowance directly. The impact on fraud and landlord–tenant collusion might also be significant as there would be little incentive for landlords who focused only on the Housing Benefit market to set rents higher than the LHA.

The secretary of state for work and pensions announced in October 2002, prior to the start of the evaluation of the system, that it was the government's 'intention to roll out the reforms nationally' in the private rented sector (Smith, 2002 para. 19). Significantly, he added that the government 'wished to develop ways of bringing in the social housing sector' (ibid.) While the principle of extending the Housing Benefit reforms to the social rented sectors is arguably sound, the impact of doing so is likely to be much greater.

The number of households in the social rented sector is almost double that in the private sector, as is the proportion of tenants who receive Housing Benefit (Kemp, 2000b). Thus more households would be affected and the capacity of Housing Benefit administrators to deliver could be severely tested. While the proportion of private sector tenants with bank accounts or other vehicles for transferring the LHA is relatively high, this is less likely to be the case with local authority tenants, where direct payment to the landlord has been the norm. Early experience by the pathfinder authorities suggests that local authorities will have to devote significant resources to ensuring that LHA claimants have some means of receiving their allowance (Department for Work and Pensions, 2004). Moreover at an early stage in the LHA evaluation, landlords were anticipating 'an increase in management costs as a result of having to collect rent from tenants' (ibid., p. 12). This is likely to be worse in the social rented sectors, where direct payments to tenants could increase both the cost of collection for landlords and the risk of non-payment. This will affect housing associations in particular by threatening their revenue stream and thereby potentially reducing their attractiveness to private lenders. In adding 'an element of uncertainty regarding social sector landlords' future rental incomes' (Williams 2003 p6), the reforms may materially affect lenders' views of the attractiveness of continuing to lend on relatively favourable terms.

Taken together the rent restructuring initiative and the Housing Benefit reform experiment are intended to increase the use of price signals in the social rented sector and eventually enable tenants to respond directly to those signals. Whether social sector tenants will be willing and able to exercise choice in high-demand areas remains to be seen. If they respond to price differentials in the way intended, those who value and can afford better and/or larger properties will secure them, and those who do not value or cannot afford them will move to lower-quality and/or smaller dwellings. This may replicate 'efficient private market patterns', but at the risk of greater social exclusion and segregation. It also runs contrary to the view that social housing should meet the needs of those for whom market-like solutions are inappropriate. Walker and Marsh (2003, p. 2044) conclude that:

> If [these policies] were located more clearly in the context of broader policies on social inclusion or anti-poverty and labour market strategies, then it suggests that a pricing strategy based on willingness to pay needs to be treated circumspectly. That is not to say that the policy should not be pursued, but that it should be pursued with clearer knowledge of its implications.

Chapter 9

Incorporating the Non-Profit Sector

By 2010 most social housing in the UK will be provided and managed by independent, non-profit landlords rather than local authorities. This chapter explores the changing role of non-profit, non-state landlords using the generic term 'housing associations', although a variety of other organizational forms have developed at various times in different parts of the UK, including housing societies, trusts, companies and cooperatives.

Housing associations have been described as independent, non-profit-distributing organizations governed by voluntary boards to provide mainly rented housing at below market rents. This simple definition captures the essential features that have enabled registration with the regulatory bodies: the Housing Corporation, Communities Scotland, the Department of Social Development in Northern Ireland and the National Assembly in Wales. Registration was important until recently since only registered associations (legally termed 'registered social landlords' in England) qualified for a public subsidy to develop social rented housing.

There has always been considerable variation in the form and function of housing associations. Each of the main descriptors used above has been subject to change over time. For example housing associations have often combined housing provision with other roles – such as social care, community development and regeneration – and are increasingly providing market rent housing and home ownership options alongside their social rented housing. Non-profit distribution was not a characteristic of Victorian model dwelling companies and early twentieth-century housing societies, which often paid loan stock holders a dividend, the term 'philanthropy at 5 per cent' being used to describe the acceptance of lower than commercial rates of return and reflecting the social purposes of early investors. Registration with regulatory bodies is a comparatively recent feature, dating back to the 1974 Housing Act in England, and there are still unregistered housing associations that use other sources of funding. Changes to form and function continue. For example in 2003 English housing associations were given the right to pay their board members, thereby ending the tradition of voluntary boards. The Housing Act of 2004 enabled the Housing

Corporation to pay Social Housing Grants direct to private bodies, thereby eroding the advantage conferred by non-profit status. So of the descriptors set out in the definition above we are left with 'independent', and independence has been a contested issue for many of the non-profit bodies that provide public services.

This chapter describes the development of the housing association sector in the UK and considers state, market and 'third sector' influences on its growth through periods of independent funding, state funding and private finance. Particular attention is paid to stock transfer from local authorities from the late 1980s. The sector has evolved in different ways in different parts of the UK, and we shall explore the role played by housing associations in Northern Ireland and the impact of devolution on associations in Scotland and Wales. The final section reviews recent restructuring in England.

Origins and growth of the non-profit sector

The involvement of non-profit organizations in the provision of public services has been a major trend in many welfare states. In the UK the adoption of new public management ideas by successive Conservative governments led to the development of a 'mixed economy of welfare', in which non-profit and private profit-distributing companies increasingly operated alongside or in place of the state sector to provide a wide array of services, ranging from homes for the elderly to refuse collection. Enthusiasm for mixed modes of delivery has also been a key element of recent Labour governments' modernization agenda (see Chapter 7). In this context the housing sector has been one of the most successful examples of harnessing non-profit organizations and private finance for public purposes. While there have been more critical interpretations (Randolph, 1993; Walker, 1999), the National Housing Federation (the trade body for English housing associations) and the Housing Corporation (the industry regulator) have missed few opportunities to highlight the advantages of the non-profit sector in harnessing private finance, avoiding the potential hazards associated with private profit and outperforming (underresourced) state providers.

By the start of the twenty-first century the non-profit housing sector had been remarkably successful in gradually displacing the public sector as the provider of affordable rented homes while at the same time fending off competition from the private sector. Even the registration and regulatory system could be seen as operating in the interests of larger housing associations, which had sufficient resources to manage the burden of regulatory compliance and were thereby shielded from market entry by private sector competitors (see Chapter 7). While private landlords had accounted for a growing share of housing-benefit funded homes for low-income households from the early 1990s, proposals for the direct funding of private developers to produce social rented homes, as considered by the Conservatives for inclusion in the 1996 Housing Act, had been successfully quashed.

However during the Labour government's second term of office the focus on delivery and efficiency promised an even more mixed economy. The main options available to local authorities to meet the ambitious targets for decent homes by 2010 included the opportunity for high-performance authorities (as assessed by the Audit Commission) to set up Arm's-Length Management Organizations (ALMOs) to secure additional public funding for stock investment. Opportunities were also provided for the private sector to expand its role through 30-year Private Finance Initiative (PFI) contracts, under which local authorities retained ownership of their housing stock but contracted out management functions and improvement works to meet the Decent Homes Standard. However the transfer of housing stock to the non-profit sector continued to be an important means of securing funding outside the PSBR.

Most significantly, and despite considerable resistance, the Housing Act of 2004 made it possible to pay Social Housing Grants direct to developers by adding a new section to the Housing Act of 1996, which defined the Housing Corporation's funding powers. This was intended to 'drive efficiency, encourage innovation and widen the pool of potential types of provider of social housing' (Housing Corporation, 2004a). A £200 million pilot programme was launched in early 2005, with applications invited from both housing associations and unregistered bodies in order to boost output to meet the housing targets laid down in the Sustainable Communities Plan. Over 50 per cent of funding was earmarked for growth areas of London and the South-East of England. The pilot programme attracted 60 bids that totalled £1.7 billion, more than eight times the available funding. Twenty two were single bids from developers, the remainder were from housing associations and consortia, which no doubt encouraged the Housing Corporation to adjust its assumptions about the mix of providers in the 2006–8 programme (Housing Corporation website, 25 May, 2005). The long-term impact of this blurring of the boundary between the non-profit and private sectors will be interesting to observe.

Historical roots

The origin of social housing is commonly traced back to Victorian philanthropy but it could be claimed that it started even earlier, with medieval almshouses and 'bedehouses' catering for 'the poor of the parish' from the thirteenth century onwards (Tickell, 1996; Cope, 1999; Malpass, 2000a). Some of the constitutional structures of modern housing associations are also historically embedded, for example the industrial and provident society model, with boards elected by shareholding members, can be traced back to the 'front-line' societies set up in the 1920s and 1930s to provide an alternative model to Victorian housing trusts. Similarly the decision by some housing societies in the 1930s to abandon both the distribution of surpluses to shareholders and the payment of dividends on loan stock was important in establishing the strict rules that precluded the distribution of profits in the modern era. The following quotation describes this decision by one Birmingham-based association:

> It has been increasingly felt that it is becoming more and more difficult to describe the work of the society as a commercial venture since the adequate housing of the lowest paid workers is a work of social import-ance from which it is not possible or desirable to expect more than a very modest return on capital. (COPEC Housing Society, 1939 Annual Report, quoted in Gulliver, 2000, p. 142)

However the romantic notion of a direct connection between present-day housing associations and medieval almshouses, nineteenth-century trusts and model dwellings societies has effectively been debunked (Malpass, 2000b), since the majority of leading housing associations were set up after 1960 and comparatively few are remnants of earlier eras of philanthropy. It is therefore more plausible to relate the development of non-profit housing to the different eras of the housing welfare state (see Chapters 2–4), with new waves of associations emerging in response to different sets of circumstances and existing associations either transforming themselves or becoming more marginal to new developments.

Table 9.1 lists some of the main influences on the development of the sector in each era, illustrating the interplay between state policies and various forms of social action under changing welfare regimes (Esping-Andersen, 1990). After enjoying a brief period as the main providers of, albeit totally inadequate, housing for the working classes in the liberal era of the late nineteenth century, the voluntary sector was crowded out by local authorities, which became the main providers under the social democratic housing welfare regime of the mid twentieth century. Later, when the welfare state was restructured to a neoliberal recipe in the last quarter of the century, housing associations took on an increasingly mainstream role.

The summary in the table hides more subtle events, including the survival of some organizations from one era to the next, the continued formation of new associations, mainly as a result of voluntary initiatives, and the cham-pioning of housing association activity by antipoverty social movements in the latter part of the social democratic period as a way of challenging and

Table 9.1 *Brief history of English housing associations*

Period	Key drivers	Organizational responses
Preindustrial: rural poverty Nineteenth century: industrialization and urbanization; slums and poor sanitation	Poor Law, charitable foundations Philanthropy, enlightened capitalism	Almshouses Endowed housing trusts; model dwellings companies ('5 per cent philanthropy')
1900–1920s: emerging state responsibility for urban and housing conditions	Philanthropic solutions contested, municipalist solutions gain force; public utility societies (PUSs) able to raise public loans up to two thirds of the value of property purchase costs; alternative cooperative and employer models developed	Trusts and model dwellings continue; workers housing, copartnership and garden city experiments; municipal housing gains ascendancy
1930s: slum improvement and clearance policies; regional development interventions	Moyne Committee gives municipal authorities key role in slum clearance; PUSs retain subsidiary role; Church-based social action and charitable donations remain important	Complementary role in reconditioning slum properties pioneered by PUSs (e.g. Church-based grouping, COPEC in Birmingham); major regional associations formed; National Federation of Housing Societies (NFHS) founded (75 associations joined, mainly new organizations)
1940s and 1950s: postwar reconstruction; labour government supports welfare state; later the conservatives continue the housing 'numbers game'	Pre-eminence of municipal authorities confirmed; large-volume building required; housing associations recognized as 'not private sector'	Little state support but large number of new specialist associations formed (e.g. for older people, self-build and workers); 639 associations belong to the NFHS by 1959

1960s: rediscovery of poverty and homelessness; state initiatives promote new tenure forms through housing associations; 1967 and 1969 Housing Acts pave the way for expanded housing association role	Social reform: Churches active in forming new associations; Shelter formed and also promoted housing associations. State policies: Housing Corporation founded to promote cost rent and co-ownership. Low-cost loans to convert older homes (1967); funding increased and general improvement areas established	Value-based, urban rehabilitation not-for-profit organizations emerge; cost rent and co-ownership societies formed with more commercial ethos and management; large increase in number of associations – NFHS membership rises to 1949 by 1969; new housing associations founded for area improvement (e.g. Circle 33, Liverpool Housing Trust, Leeds Federated)
1974: Housing Act introduces generous public subsidy regime for associations	Public sector era for housing associations; Housing Corporation funding and regulatory regime incorporates existing and creates new associations	Associations sacrifice independence for state subsidies; differences between associations reduced and their role is to complement that of municipal authorities (limited general needs housing role)
1979: 'new right' government starts to 'roll back the state'	End of growth of municipal housing; some associations experiment with private finance to stretch their public subsidies, but public sector era for associations continues to 1988	Associations begin to take on more mainstream roles; new associations formed to meet special needs (e.g. rural communities, Black and minority ethnic communities)
1988 Housing Act; private finance and mainstream role for associations, which were designated (with private landlords) as the 'independent rented sector'; enabling role for municipal authorities	Major financial institutions lend to associations; business culture introduced into associations; Housing Corporation/municipal authorities fund public element of new schemes	Strong associations grow rapidly; competition for development subsidies increases; mergers and few new associations keeps numbers fairly static while stock rapidly expands

Table 9.1 (Continued)

Period and causes of housing initiatives	Key drivers	Organizational responses
1990s: privatization and mixed economy of welfare; 1996 Act fails to allow private sector to compete but relabels associations and other not-for-profit, organizations as registered social landlords	Funding for housing capital declines after 1992/23; transfer of municipal stock becomes a major source of growth; National Housing Federation succeeds in branding stock transfers and traditional associations as not-for-profit, thereby excluding private competition.	Large new associations formed through stock transfers from the municipal sector; associations now account for one in four social rented homes; new organizational forms begin to emerge: Local Housing Companies and group structures
1997: New Labour government elected; corporatist partnership develops between state and larger housing groups	Growing emphasis on delivery and efficiency; housing agenda broadened to incorporate regeneration and social care; Investment Partnering and grants for private developers changes investment landscape	Strong pressure for mergers, groups and alliances; associations involved in wide range of partnerships; Some associations diversify, e.g. to become 'social investment agencies' or to provide social care services; group parents play internal regulation role; 80 'lead investment partners' selected for 2004–6; development consortia and alliances emerge; new relationships with developers emerge

Sources: Adapted from figure 1 in Mullins (2000) (in *Voluntas*, vol. 11, no. 3, pp. 259–61, © The International Society for Third Sector Research and the Johns Hopkins University 2000) with additional data from Mullins and Riseborough (2000); Malpass (1998, 2000b); Mullins (2004a) and Housing Corporation (2004b).

improving state provision. An example of the latter took place in the 1960s, when Shelter – the newly formed homelessness campaign – worked with the Churches to establish a new generation of associations while pressing for improvements in state provision.

In the last quarter of the century the role of housing associations expanded as a result of their incorporation into state programmes and their engagement with both the state and the private sector. Following the establishment of the Housing Corporation in 1964, early experiments with co-ownership and cost rent housing were followed in the late 1960s by funding for urban renewal work (Housing Corporation, 2004b). However the provision of state funding did not take place on a significant scale until the passage of the 1974 Housing Act, after which it provided an important stimulus for the subsequent move of housing associations to a mainstream role. In the 1970s and 1980s expansion was largely into areas that complemented rather than competed with local authority provision, such as urban renewal activities, sheltered housing and housing for special needs groups. The fortuitous combination in the early 1970s of social action on homelessness and poor urban housing conditions and the first significant state funding for housing associations, on the one hand, with a switch in housing priorities from clearance and 'mass housing' solutions on the other was important in bringing about their expanded role. As Kendall (2003, p. 156) notes:

> English housing associations were in the right place at the right time to build up relatively attractive property portfolios and benefit from central state largesse. They became involved in policy in this field to a significant degree at just the moment when mass housing models were being rejected.

The extent to which the non-profit sector would eventually challenge and even displace state provision was not anticipated prior to the introduction of private finance and the first local authority stock transfer, as the following quotation attests:

> It would be a mistake to think that Britain's housing problems could be solved by dropping them on the shoulders of the housing association movement. The movement is not equipped or designed to provide compre-hensive coverage for all those needing rental accommodation. What it has done is to develop expertise in providing housing for particular groups and in particular areas. Its experience has given useful lessons to the more traditional sectors of the welfare state. (Hills, 1989, p. 265)

The 1988 Housing Act introduced a mixed funding model for housing associations, allowing them to borrow on the private market without affecting the government's Public Sector Borrowing Requirement. Over the next 15 years, 373 000 new homes were built by housing associations across the UK, 285 000 of them in England. However as Figure 9.1 illustrates,

Figure 9.1   *Number of housing association properties constructed, 1950–2003*

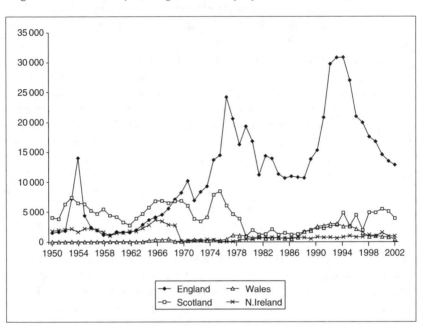

Source: Data from *Housing and Construction Statistics* (ODPM).

the impact of private finance on output should not be overstated as the pattern was similar to that which occurred after the introduction of public subsidies in 1974, with rapid growth peaking a few years later and output thereafter declining at an almost equal rate. Furthermore the impact was strongest in England and Wales, where output was generally above that achieved in the public funding era, whereas in Scotland a higher output had been achieved in the 1970s and in Northern Ireland the pattern was distorted by the transfer of all housing stock from the Northern Ireland Housing Trust to the Northern Ireland Housing Executive in 1972.

Nevertheless if the output of new homes is added to stock transferred from local authorities, the UK housing association sector expanded from 556 000 homes in 1986 to 1.8 million in 2005, with the English sector expanding from 475 000 to 1.6 million over the same period (Wilcox, 2004). The balance sheet of English housing associations became an increasingly important consideration for housing policy, with assets valued at £59 billion (Housing Corporation and National Housing Federation, 2003b) and borrowing in excess of £30 billion by 2004 (Housing Corporation, 2004b). Thus a combination of public policy decisions and private investment transformed the scale of the housing association sector and made it into a player that was difficult to ignore in the production and management of affordable housing and the regeneration of communities.

State, market or third sector?

A recurrent theme in discussions of housing associations is their hybrid status between the state and the market. While the history outlined above shows the importance of state support in the growth of housing associations, recent growth has been facilitated by their status as private bodies that are able to borrow 'off balance sheet'. Housing associations often highlight their social purposes, voluntary governance and non-profit distribution, all of which may be seen as key characteristics of de Tocqueville's concept of a 'third sector' operating alongside economic exchange and the activities of government (Wuthnow, 1991). This sector may include charities, non-governmental organizations, the 'social economy' and civil society.

Housing associations can be difficult to locate in this way; they are chameleon-like in their ability to present themselves as the private sector for funding purposes, the voluntary sector when community partnerships are required and the public sector when accountability is at stake. Figure 9.2 plots the changing location of UK housing associations between the three sectors based on funding sources and risk. At point A associations were part of the public sector. At that time the Housing Act 1974 provided almost 100 per cent state funding and bore virtually all the risk. After 1988 they moved towards the private sector (point B) following the introduction

Figure 9.2   *The locating of housing associations between the three sectors*

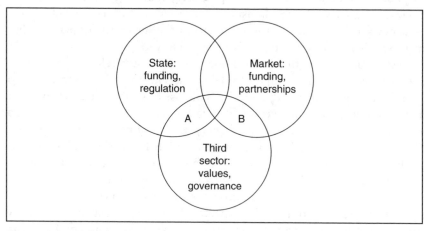

Source: Adapted by kind permission of Open University Press/McGraw-Hill Publishing company from Mullins (1998) drawing on Wuthnow (1991).

of private funding for a proportion of development costs and the transfer of risk from taxpayers. Meanwhile they continued to be part of a third sector; enjoying a degree of independence from the government and not being governed by profit distribution motives. The next section takes a closer look at some of the state, market and third sector characteristics of housing associations.

State influences

> [M]ost associations were set up in response to government policies of one sort or another, and pre-existing organisations have been changed or sent off into new directions by changes in policy. (Malpass, 2000a, p. 266)

At certain times and for certain purposes housing associations have been regarded as part of the public sector, in terms not just of funding but also of accountability and governance. In the mid 1990s housing associations were at the centre of the criticism that 'local public spending bodies' were dispensing large sums of public money at the local level but were no longer accountable to the local electorate in the same way as local authorities (Nolan Committee, 1996). For some commentators at the time, housing associations symbolized the 'democratic deficit', whereby public services were moving away from democratic control (Davis and Spencer, 1995).

More recently there has been new pressure to define housing associations as public bodies, subject to requirements laid down by the Equality Commission in Northern Ireland and the Human Rights Act of 1999 throughout the UK. European directives later defined housing associations as public bodies for procurement purposes, requiring them to advertise contracts publicly. As the housing association sector has expanded the tendency for the government to try to steer or influence their operation has increased. This is evident in government publications such as the 'PSA Plus review' of delivery of the decent homes target, which refers to the 'many agents Government relies upon to deliver decent homes', to 'incentives to help drive delivery forward' and to 'a staircase of support, persuasion, soft levers, hard levers and intervention that can be used to minimise and respond to delivery risks' (Office of the Deputy Prime Minister, 2003b, p. 10). However associations have sought to avoid being designated purely as public bodies, fearing that this would impose an even greater regulatory burden and threaten their right to borrow off balance sheet.

There is evidence that associations are strongly influenced by the state at both the central and local levels, principally through funding and regulatory mechanisms (see Chapter 7) but also through governance and staffing arrangements. Some commentators suggest that this means housing associations are state-controlled bodies, and one reason for moving housing from local authorities to housing associations was that the latter could be more effectively controlled by the state.

We have already highlighted the importance of public funding for housing development by housing associations. Research involving key decision makers in England and Northern Ireland (Mullins and Riseborough, 2000; Mullins, Rhodes and Williamson, 2003) has revealed the growing importance of public policy and public funding – particularly the funding of Housing Benefit, 'Supporting People' and regeneration – as key influences on housing associations.

Stock transfer associations

The influence of public policy on the sector increased considerably after 1988, when the first large-scale transfer of local authority housing to a newly established housing association was conducted by Chiltern District Council in Buckinghamshire. There had been earlier transfers of tenanted housing in individual estates and neighbourhoods – notably in Glasgow in the mid 1980s and the establishment of around 50 community-based housing associations across Scotland in the same period (M. Taylor, 2000), in a few English authorities (for example the transfer of Cantril Farm estate in Knowsley in 1983) and two partial transfers in Wales (Malpass and Mullins, 2002) – but it was whole authority transfer that was to have the greatest impact on the size and shape of the housing association sector.

As Table 9.1 shows, between 1988 and 2005 the volume of stock transferred by English local authorities was substantially greater than elsewhere in the UK – nearly 900 000 homes, compared with fewer than 200 000 in Scotland and 10 000 in Wales. By 2005, over 200 stock transfers had been completed by 155 English authorities and only 50 per cent of English local authorities retained ownership of their housing stock (ODPM website). From the mid 1990s transfers accounted for more council stock depletion than sales under the Right to Buy scheme and were a more important source of growth of the housing association sector than new construction. From 1988 onwards whole-stock transfer was the dominant factor in the formation of new housing associations. There were also smaller-scale transfers, mainly of run-down estates to existing and new associations. These transfers were partly publicly subsidized, by the Estates Renewal Challenge Fund, which supported 39 estate-based transfers of 44 000 homes in England between 1999 and 2000 (Pawson *et al.*, 2004). As the volume of transfers in England rose towards the end of the 1990s there was a geographical shift from more rural and suburban areas towards urban areas, and from the South to the North. These shifts led to an increased emphasis on tackling run-down housing and promoting social inclusion and community regeneration, shaping the purposes and culture of a new generation of landlords (Pawson, 2004).

The impact of stock transfer on the composition of the housing association sector in England was particularly significant, with over 50 per cent of the largest stock-holding associations in 2004 having their origins in the stock transfer process. The entry of these large-scale landlords presented particular challenges to the key institutions in the housing association sector. For the Housing Corporation there was the challenge of registering and regulating a significant number of new associations with high debt to asset ratios and relatively inexperienced board members and senior managers. For the National Housing Federation there was the challenge of maintaining a unified, non-profit housing sector by balancing the interests of traditional and stock transfer associations. Both these challenges have been addressed fairly successfully. While some transfer landlords have experienced Housing Corporation intervention and supervision and lessons have had to be learned, most transfers have not caused major regulatory problems. The National Housing Federation has successfully absorbed the new members, who are well represented in its committees and activities, such as peer mentoring for the chairs of newly established transfer associations.

Stock transfer associations are distinctive in that they were born from local authority housing departments and in response to public policy drivers. In both respects they could be seen as subject to strong state influences. The history of the transfer policy can be described as increasing incorporation into the state's housing policy during the four phases shown in Table 9.3. Even in the early phase, 'voluntary' transfer decisions by individual authorities were structured by government policies that constrained local authority finance, promoted the Right to Buy and threatened involuntary transfer

Table 9.2   *Local authority stock transfers, England, Scotland and Wales, 1988–2005*

	Whole stock		Partial transfers	
	Number of local authorities	*Dwellings transferred*	*Number of local authorities*	*Dwellings transferred*
England	155	876 346	23	81 000
Scotland	4	105 000	19	19 000
Wales	1	6 400	3	1 000
Total	160	987 746	45	101 000

Sources: England – ODPM stock transfer table, ODPM website; Scotland – Communities Scotland transfer dataset; Wales – Mullins and Pawson (forthcoming).

Table 9.3 *Evolution of stock transfer, England, 1988–2005*

	Character of policy	Key features	Completed transfers	Percentage of ballots lost	Homes transferred
1988–92	Voluntary	Individual authority initiatives (variety of motivations) Department of the Environment approval subject to positive ballot and compliance Learning by all players (many non-players) Mainly rural/suburban local authorities with good condition stock; new housing associations set up	18 (W) 18 (T)	43	 94 317
1993–96	National programme	Transfer replaces Tenants' Choice and Housing Action Trusts as the government's main demunicipalization measure Annual bids, limits to approvals, size limits to avoid monopolies Levy to be paid from receipts; Housing Benefit impacts Levy outweighed by Public Sector Borrowing Requirement benefits Slight broadening of take-up	26 (W) 12 (P) 38 (T)	34	129 140
1996–99	Broadening of take-up	Spread to urban areas and Labour-controlled local authorities New models include Local Housing Companies and estate transfers to existing housing associations; new focus on regeneration Incentives: governance models, funding for negative value transfers (from the Estate Renewal Challenge Fund), levy holiday Coercion: all local authorities required to consider transfer option, affecting resources	21 (W) 34 (P) 55 (T)	16	154 587

Table 9.3 (*Continued*)

	Character of policy	Key features	Completed transfers	Percentage of ballots lost	Homes transferred
2000–5	National Policy delivery	Decent Homes Standard (Public-Service-Agreement led); new public money in return for private funding to/deliver decent homes	60 (W)	17	
		Transfer as delivery mechanism for the Treasury	27 (P)		
		Transfer one of three options (transfer, private finance initiative, arm's-length management organization)			
		All local authorities to undertake option appraisals by 2005 (tenants to be involved)			
		Coercion and incentives strengthened; tighter monitoring			
		Large-scale urban transfers; group structures; increased involvement of existing housing associations; regeneration focus strengthened; community mutual model emerges; relaxation of transfer package size rules	87 (T)		498 302
Total					876 346

Notes: W = whole stock transfer, P = partial transfer. Partial transfers include split transfers to two landlords and estate transfers (for example under the ERCF scheme). T= totals of W+P.

Sources: ODPM website; Mullins *et al.* (1995); Malpass and Mullins (2002); Pawson (2004); Pawson *et al.* (2004).

under 'Tenants' Choice' and Housing Action Trusts (introduced under the 1988 Housing Act). In the next phase, from 1992 transfer approvals were subject to an annual government programme and growing regulation and prescription, for example of the permissible size of new landlord organizations.

After 1996 considerably stronger carrots and sticks were used to extend the process from rural authorities and suburban areas to inner urban areas, and to encourage participation by Labour-controlled authorities. The carrots included funding for estate-based transfers and new governance regulations that allowed increased local authority and tenant representation on boards. The sticks included a requirement for local housing strategies to include the transfer option, an approach that was intensified in the fourth phase by the Labour government, as it sought to harness private borrowing to tackle the local authority repairs backlog. In the latter phase all stock-holding housing authorities were required, in consultation with their tenants, to appraise the options available to them for bringing their stock into line with the Decent Homes Standard by 2010. Transfer was one of just three available options to meet this standard.

The intensification of state control in the fourth phase was evidenced by the government's growing focus on housing associations as 'delivery agents' for its policies (see Chapter 7). The Decent Homes Standard was applied retrospectively to assess the success of the stock transfer programme. The government imposed a more extensive monitoring system for all new transfers taking place after 2001. The National Audit Office called for even tighter control over the transfer valuation model to ensure that 'cost neutrality' applied, and more controversially to 'influence the use by Registered Social Landlords of additional surpluses arising' (National Audit Office, 2003, p. 7)

The increasingly closer alignment of transfer landlords' aims to central government objectives fundamentally questioned the status of the sector. Tighter regulation was criticized by housing associations as stifling innovation and reducing the rationale for transferring stock to the independent sector. A key question was whether the government had chosen the independent non-profit sector because of its intrinsic merits or simply because it was not local authority and borrowing was off balance sheet. Even if the policy choice was not based on the former there was still a danger that tighter control would hamper innovation and damage performance.

Public sector influence on organizational culture might be expected to have been particularly strong in stock transfer housing associations, given their roots in local authority housing departments. Under European Transfer of Undertakings Employment (TUPE) protection legislation, most former housing department staff transferred to the new landlord and it would therefore be surprising if there had not been some continuation of public sector practices. Public sector influence on governance was also more evident than in traditional associations. From 1996 transfer landlords were able to allocate up to 50 per cent of board seats to councillors or other 'local authority persons' – most opted for 33 per cent.

However research by Pawson and Fancy (2003) suggests that most transfer organizations made an effort to instil a culture that was distinct from that of the local authority. Name changes were one manifestation of this, with a number of stock transfer associations initially being named after their founding authority but later asserting their independent status by choosing a new, less constraining name (Mullins, 1996). Other measures taken by some early transfer associations were geographical expansion from the 'home authority' area and restructuring as groups, with the original local landlord relegated to subsidiary status to make room for other locally based or functional subsidiaries. Each of the latter was accountable to the parent board, on which there were generally fewer local authority represent-atives. A panel study in December 2003 (Mullins, 2004a) found that stock transfer chief executives placed greater emphasis than their colleagues in traditional associations on housing associations being seen as distinct from the public sector. If this was the case we might expect the state characteristics of these associations to diminish over time.

Market influences

> The Government's preference for housing associations over local authority delivered social housing over this period was essentially for two reasons: to get housing off the Government's balance sheet and to avoid what was seen as poor housing management by local authorities. (Maltby, 2003, p. 32)

Maltby (ibid.), writing for the influential think-tank IPPR, highlighted the preference by government for bodies other than local authorities. But does a non-local authority identity imply a private or market identity? Randolph (1993) persuasively argues that after 1988 there was a 'reprivatization' of housing associations. The pressure of private borrowing led to a variety of changes to the culture and organizational practices of housing associations, with increased attention to the financial and performance targets laid down in business plans and reduced attention to softer targets. Karn and Sheridan (1994) draw attention to the impact of cost pressures on design and space standards, while Walker (1998) charts the adoption of a variety of new public management methods by associations as they moved from the comfort of low-risk public funding to competition and risk management. The associations in Walker's case study showed little congruence with the public-service orientated model (see Chapter 7). In the 1990s competition for development funding changed the nature of associations, generating a 'superleague' of larger associations with different cultures and drivers from smaller community-based associations. This tendency was strengthened by the adoption of 'Investment Partnering' in 2004 (Zitron, 2004).

Davis (2003) draws attention to the impact of these changes on associations' handling of domestic violence. In three of the associations in her study the priority now given to maximizing rental income and minimizing staff and overhead costs had reduced the provision of less tangible services such as advice and support to vulnerable applicants and tenants. According to the vice-chair of a Black and minority ethnic association, 'It's become much more of a business. The pressures on the organisation have changed immensely. It's lost its community base' (quoted in ibid., p. 67).

However, when asked to consider a number of external influences on strategy, housing association executives in England and Northern Ireland have consistently rated responding to regulation as more important than complying with private lenders' requirements (Mullins and Riseborough, 2000; Mullins, Rhodes and Williamson, 2003). It is therefore important not to exaggerate the impact of market influences on organizational behaviour and to keep in mind the following question: how differently would these organizations behave if they were driven solely by profit? It may be easier to answer this in the future as government increasingly uses the profit-distributing sector to deliver public services such as housing (e.g. through PFI and grants for developers).

Third sector influences

Housing associations appear to meet the criteria used to define third sector bodies in cross-national comparisons (Salamon and Anheier, 1997). They are:

- Organized (that is, institutionalized to some extent).
- Private (institutionally separate from the government).
- Non-profit distributing (not returning profits to their owners or directors).
- Self-governing (equipped to control their own activities).
- Voluntary (involving some meaningful degree of voluntary participation).

One of the main debates arising from this definition concerns the extent to which associations can be said to be voluntary and self-governing. At one level these conditions are fully met and underlie the constitutional status of associations and the assumptions of the regulatory system. Cope (1999, p. 91) argues that 'voluntarism and independence are two of the most important and valued features of the sector that are considered fundamental to its governance'.

Many housing associations were established as small voluntary bodies, often to meet very specific needs, and some embraced the cooperative principle of self-help. Indeed the vast majority of the 2000 associations currently registered with the Housing Corporation are primarily voluntary in the sense that they employ very few staff and are run by voluntary committees, although they account for a low proportion of the housing stock managed by the sector. A good example is the Black and minority ethnic housing association sector, which was established in the 1970s to meet the needs of communities that, as a result of poverty and discrimination, had poor access to decent housing. This movement was successful in gaining state support from the mid 1980s, when a series of Housing Corporation programmes provided revenue support and capital funding for 63 such associations in England (Harrison, 1991, 1995).

However, despite being feted in the 1990s as a leading example of positive action in Europe and growing to manage in excess of 25 000 homes by 2003, Black and minority ethnic housing associations had considerable difficulty retaining their community accountability and achieving financial viability. Harrison and Phillips (2003, p. 9) observe that they 'played crucial roles in giving minority ethnic participants a voice...[and] provided valuable role models within minority communities...[but] although firmly established on the policy arena...[they] have remained individually vulnerable to distinct pressures related to their funding opportunities, stock acquisition, limited assets, size and periods of growth'.

Increasingly these associations merged or joined groups headed by stronger, white-led associations in the context of the Housing Corporation's BME housing policy that emphasized the needs of 90 per cent of Black and minority ethnic tenants who were not tenants of Black and minority ethnic associations (Housing Corporation, 1998). An indication of the changing opportunities for voluntary action in the sector is provided by refugee community organizations, which play similar roles in some new migrant communities to those previously played by Black and minority ethnic associations in earlier migrant communities. However in contrast to the situation the 1970s and 1980s there is little state interest in facilitating self-help programmes and the best way forward is seen as being through partnerships with statutory and stronger voluntary organizations (HACT, 2004).

Malpass (2000a, p. 272) concludes his comprehensive history of the sector by stating that:

> Voluntary housing has been changed, virtually out of recognition, transformed to a point where the voluntary element is of symbolic relevance only...the larger associations are in practice controlled by the Housing Corporation and can scarcely make a move of real significance without first gaining the approval of the regional office.

However, despite the increasing scale and professional dominance of the sector and its retreat from voluntarism there is evidence that housing associations enjoy a degree of independence and are able to play a part in shaping their policy environment. As Lowe (2004, p. 59) puts it, 'powerful associations are not simply driven by government policy but are able to choose what they become involved in'.

Corporate governance

Voluntary governance is a long-standing feature of the housing association sector in the UK. The virtues of voluntary governance have frequently been extolled, as illustrated by the following statement by the chief executive of a large Northern Ireland association:

> I like to stress the voluntary nature of the organisation because although we are a large social business today, we still have at our core a voluntary board that receives no payment. They provide a unique service to the community that should not be underestimated. (Quoted in Mullins, Rhodes and Williamson, 2003, p. 95)

For regulatory purposes boards are deemed to be 'in control' of their organizations and are responsible for employing senior staff, formally agreeing or approving key strategic decisions, performance reports and financial statements. Housing association boards tend to be quite large, with 15 or more members being common in stock transfer associations, and slightly fewer in traditional associations. Board members tend to be older and male, and increasingly come from managerial and professional backgrounds. Representation of Black and Ethnic Minority groups is broadly in line with their representation in the population as a whole (Cairncross and Pearl, 2003). The National Housing Federation code of governance was revised in 2004 to recommend smaller boards with a maximum of 12 members and a maximum length of service of nine years (National Housing Federation, 2004a).

However voluntarism has been subject to change over time with profit distribution to shareholders and loan stockholders common before the 1920s. The option of paying board members was allowed in England in 2003 following a protracted debate. There was also a growing tendency for paid senior executive directors to become full members of the boards of larger associations. Interviews with leaders of English housing associations in the late 1990s revealed that having a voluntary label was becoming less important than having a social purpose or being independent. Declining importance was attached to shareholding membership and the election of boards. Fewer volunteers were involved in shaping strategic decisions, with significant input from executive staff in the shaping and implementation of organizational strategies (Mullins and Riseborough, 2000). Many larger associations had begun to use terms other than 'voluntary' to define themselves, with terms such as 'non-profit', 'social enterprise' and 'independent' gaining currency.

Follow-up research in 2003–4 (Mullins, 2004a) found a continuation of these trends, particularly in larger associations that were seeking more businesslike and streamlined governance arrangements. Questions relating to voluntary governance and voluntary sector identity produced some of the most polarized views, with some smaller and community-based associations apparently determined to resist the trend initiated by some larger associations to move away from voluntary governance and identity. There were changes to the expectations and motivation of voluntary board members. According to the chief executive of an association that was not planning to pay the board members but had undertaken significant restructuring to form a larger association, 'The level of knowledge members need to have has dramatically increased and I can see it getting more so. There are some critical times ahead for our Board – I would imagine that some members will decide it is not for them' (quoted in Mullins, 2004a).

Independent social purposes

What evidence is there to support the claim that housing associations are institutionally separate from the government? Chapter 7 reviewed the debate on the diversification of housing associations into new activities in the late 1990s and discussed the regulatory responses to this. The shift from being dependent upon housing policy and grants for housing development to responding to a variety of public policies and having a range of funding sources (including private finance and non-housing public funds) can be seen as significant factors in the independence of housing associations. Broader activities have given associations additional sources of income and this has reduced their dependence on a monopoly funder and regulator. The concept 'resource dependency' (Aldrich, 1976) refers to the way in which agencies that are dependent on a single source of funds can be easily controlled, and in this sense can be viewed as 'contractors of the state'. Resource diversity, even if this simply involves taking public funds from a range of pots, theoretically gives housing associations a greater degree of strategic choice and more independence.

Another source of independence enjoyed by some associations is their ability to draw on accumulated reserves and funds from private sources, such as charitable donations. Sometimes a clear link exists between charitable endowments and charitable purposes, as in the case of a well-endowed housing trust that has claimed not to be driven by the public policies of the day, but rather by its organizational mission: 'We are making the move towards being even less reactive to what the Housing Corporation or

Government says...we are determined to develop as a charitable body' (quoted in Mullins, 1997, p. 61).

This sense of independence can lead to associations being prepared to challenge governments at the central and local levels. Research on lettings has found that some of the older charitable trusts have challenged local authority policies for nominating new tenants from council housing register when these have conflicted with their own policies set out in deeds of trust. One such trust, which is committed to housing people in low-paid employment, has challenged local authority nominations made without reference to income or employment status (Pawson and Mullins, 2003).

The best evidence of the independence of the housing association sector is provided by the ways in which it engages with the government to shape and define policy programmes rather than simply responding to directives. Mullins and Riseborough (2001) have found a range of 'policy shaping' activities in which housing associations have individually and collectively sought to influence the government. Examples include associations repositioning themselves as 'social investment agencies' in order to influence the policy agenda, the shaping of the 'Best Value' regime through housing association pilots, and attempts by associations that work with older people to reshape their funding and policy environment. Institutional capacity, built up over time, has enabled the sector to influence the programmes it is expected to deliver. Welfare regime changes are to some extent driven by institutional capacity, which is itself the product of earlier phases of regime development, supporting the notion of path-dependency (Esping Andersen, 1990).

Do values matter?

The final aspect of third-sector identity, which can be very difficult to pin down, concerns the values that drive organizational behaviour. Clearly values are not a unique feature of the third sector and it is common for profit-distributing organizations to define their values (including corporate social responsibility or 'ethical capitalism') and to communicate these to consumers and staff through mission, vision and values statements. The term 'double bottom line' is sometimes used to distinguish the third sector from the profit-distributing sector, where there is only one bottom line. Often non-profit organizations have quite explicit social purposes that reflect the motivations of their founders, and these may be institutionalized in charitable objects and deeds of trust. Common aims include the relief of poverty, the promotion of equality, the meeting of housing needs and the promotion of social inclusion. Many of the housing associations set up in the 1970s have maintained their original purpose as their founder-directors have continued to impose their values on the growing organizations.

Housing association boards are often seen as the 'guardian of values' or the 'golden thread' that links present activities to historical purposes. Tension can arise when strategic initiatives by executive staff, such as merger or geographical expansion, are seen by board members as contrary to the association's mission.

A study of 22 housing associations in the Republic of Ireland and Northern Ireland (Mullins, Rhodes and Williamson, 2003) identified four main ways in which housing associations were using their third sector status to construct distinctive identities based on social purposes. First, they were shaping their identities to build trust, for example by establishing a reputation for probity, a high degree of care and cost-effectiveness. Second, some associations were using their non-profit status as a marketing advantage. This was particularly evident in fields such as social care, where they faced private sector competition. Differential tax treatment of charities provided a concrete example of financial advantage secured as a result of organizational status. Third, many associations were developing niche roles by drawing on their knowledge and understanding of and relationship with the geographical communities or client groups with which they operated. This form of specialization was particularly important for small and medium-sized associations that could not compete with larger players in terms of the cost of general housing services. Fourth, and of particular significance in Northern Ireland, was the conscious playing down of community origins or identity (for example through a name change) to avoid the perception that they worked only with people from one community and might have difficulty complying with legislation on equality.

Attention to the positive shaping of values has also been important in England, where the National Housing Federation engaged branding consultants in a major exercise to encapsulate the values of the sector and to change people's perceptions of housing associations and what they did. Launched at the 2003 National Housing Federation Conference after two years of preparation, the slogan 'In Business for Neighbourhoods' was supported by a new visual identity, case studies of innovative neighbourhood initiatives and support for organizational development to encapsulate the values of the sector (National Housing Federation, 2003) in four key propositions (set out below). These propositions emphasize the common ground between different types of association supported the emerging social business identity, in contrast with the older identity of voluntarism:

- We are In Business for Neighbourhoods.
- We put our energy into creating places where people want to live.
- We invest in a range of services as well as homes.
- We are independent social businesses working with local people and partner organizations to deliver results.

High levels of adoption were achieved amongst member associations, with 75 per cent of the sector's stock being owned and managed by the adopters one year later. The National Housing Federation (2004b) saw the first year as the start of a long-term transformation of the sector, focusing on customers, neighbourhoods and excellence. Leadership support and peer reviews were used to promote organizational change, and 'InBiz' awards were used to encourage and publicize improvements. Strong emphasis was placed on relationships with key stakeholders and on actively influencing the policy environment (for example regulation and inspection). An independent consultant has gauged how perceptions of the sector had changed after the first year:

> Gripes about glossy relaunches matter but can be marginalized so long as substantial and positive change is both happening and is being seen to happen. The threat is not external as much as internal. Will the Federation and its members see the process through with a continuing sense of enthusiasm and drive? (Neal Lawson, LLM Communications, quoted in National Housing Federation, 2004b, p. 12)

Housing associations in Northern Ireland – voluntary action and state steering

The Northern Ireland housing association sector exemplifies many of the issues described above in relation to history and state, market and third sector influences (see Mullins, Rhodes and Williamson, 2003, for a fuller account). Philanthropic activity in the nineteenth century included housing and welfare work by the Belfast Charitable Society and almshouses such as the one developed by Alderman Gill in Carrickfergus. There were also early housing experiments by Quaker industrialists in Lisburn (County Antrim) and Bessbrook (County Armagh) well before the development of state attention to housing needs.

As in mainland UK, between the wars the majority of social housing development was undertaken by local authorities, but there were some activities by the non-profit sector after the Second World War. The most important of these was the establishment of the Northern Ireland Housing Trust (NIHT) in 1945 (Murie and Birrell, 1971). This was modelled on the Scottish Special Housing Association and was authorized to build housing in areas where local authority provision was inadequate. It was a public body rather than a voluntary housing association, although it had similarities to the voluntary housing sector on the mainland, such as the adoption of the Octavia Hill system of housing management and the dominance of women housing managers (Heenan, 2001). Over a 26-year period the

NIHT produced nearly 50 000 homes. These, together with the entire local authority stock, were then transferred to the Northern Ireland Housing Executive (NIHE), which became the UK's largest public landlord.

Prior to 1975 and alongside this state-fostered activity there was a number of more voluntary initiatives, some of which drew on private sector models. For example in 1946 a Belfast builder, Thomas McGrath, set up a housing society, Ulster Garden Villages, financed by loan stock issues and borrowed funds from banks and building societies. This society built some 1500 dwellings but went into receivership in 1952. The society was rescued in the 1970s and today is a well-endowed charity (McCreary, 1999). In the 1960s new housing associations were set up in Derry and Dungannon to address the underprovision of housing for Catholic communities. These associations initially used charitable donations and private funds to build houses for sale, the income from which was used for further development. Credit unions and savings schemes were set up to enable purchasers to afford deposits and mortgages.

While over 50 voluntary associations (including 24 Abbeyfield Societies) had been active in Northern Ireland in the postwar period it was, as in mainland UK, it was the provision of public funding from the mid 1970s that stimulated the growth of the housing association sector. Some of the founders of this movement had been involved in the earlier initiatives described above, others came from the political scene or the civil rights movement. A conference in 1974 brought together these voluntary actors with the relevant government department (Department of Environment, Belfast). Links were made with English housing associations and Shelter. A voluntary housing steering committee was formed to press for a similar public funding scheme to that introduced under the 1974 Housing Act (McLachlan, 1997).

The Housing NI Order of 1976 introduced public funding, and funding and regulatory powers were allocated to the Department of Environment (now the Department of Social Development). The importance of state steering of the sector is indicated by the registration of 45 new associations over the next few years (only a handful of the previously established associations opted for registration) and their focus on five priorities laid down in a Department of Environment circular (sheltered housing, community-based renewal, single people, special needs and equity sharing). The contemporary housing association sector was effectively constructed in a five-year period, few new associations have registered since 1990, and the key personnel base has been remarkably stable.

After 1996 the introduction of private funding and the transfer of new development activity from the NIHE brought a period of more rapid growth for the sector: the housing association stock of rented homes increased by 6000, or 40 per cent, in just five years and £155 million of private finance was raised. This period saw the intensification of public sector influence on the sector as well as a return of private sector influence.

Public sector influence was strengthened in response to the more significant role played by associations in social housing supply; for example a new common selection scheme required closer collaboration with the NIHE on lettings. Although associations were forced to consider changes to their product mix as they had generally been steered into special needs niches, many of the new opportunities arising from the transfer of the NIHE programme were for general needs housing. Greater regulatory pressure was placed on the sector after 1996, including the addition of 'Best Value' requirements to the regulations already imposed by the Department of Social Development, and treatment of the associations as public bodies accountable to the Northern Ireland Audit Office, the Equality Commission and the Northern Ireland Ombudsman. This increased regulatory burden was particularly felt by smaller associations, some of which were reported to be considering merger with larger associations, although merger activity was much lower than in England.

Private sector influence was most obvious in the use by associations of reserves and private borrowing to top up the public subsidies for new development. Additional pressure was brought about by the decision to put some of the transferred NIHE schemes onto a competitive basis, with associations that would require the lowest grant funds receiving the contract. This accentuated the divide between the larger associations, which became social businesses, and the majority of associations, which remained in the voluntary housing mould. Some of the larger associations diversified into health and social care, and all of these associations considered expansion into the Republic of Ireland in the late 1990s. The implications for the future structure of the sector were becoming clear by 2003: 'Predictions were for a further polarisation of the sector with larger associations growing market share through mergers and diversification while smaller and some specialist associations were exposed to decline and potential take-over' (Mullins, Rhodes and Williamson, 2003, p. 149).

A distinctive feature of the Northern Ireland housing association sector (compared with many English housing associations) in this period was the continuing emphasis on voluntary identity. A prominent statement of the dilemmas faced by value-driven organizations located between state and market was made by the chair of the Northern Ireland Federation of Housing Associations:

[We] Housing associations need to revisit our historical origins and to rediscover our original founding purpose if our future is not to become one of simply being agents for the delivery of official programmes. The prospect of becoming large multi-million pound companies may appeal to some but it should not be at the expense of our voluntary sector distinctiveness. (NIFHA, 1989)

Stronger links were made with the wider third sector in Northern Ireland, and the Northern Ireland Council for Voluntary Action (NICVA, 2000, p. 15) depicted housing associations as 'a striking example of the potential of social economy organisations to operate in the space between the public and private sectors, maximising and using opportunities and resources drawn from both to support local regeneration'.

By 2004, 39 registered associations and six unregistered associations were managing around 30 000 homes. The challenges of taking on the new development role had generally been successfully embraced, despite some difficulty with meeting targets, and £229 million of private funding had been acquired. New challenges were provided by the implementation of the Housing (NI) Order of 2003, which increased associations' accountability (to the Commissioner for Complaints and the Northern Ireland Equalities Commission) and extended the Decent Homes Standard to Northern Ireland, and by the possible extension of the Right to Buy scheme to housing associations (NIFHA, 2004).

The impact of devolution on housing associations in the UK

Housing associations exhibit territorial variations across the UK. The distinctive history of the Northern Ireland sector was described in the previous section. In the other parts of the UK the sector was accountable to a single funding and regulatory body, the Housing Corporation, from 1964 until the passage of the 1988 Housing Act, after which new bodies, Tai Cymru and Scottish Homes, took over responsibility for housing associations in Wales and Scotland. Ten years later the establishment of the Scottish Parliament and the National Assembly for Wales provided a further source of difference to the interaction between state policies and these third sector bodies. Research conducted three years after devolution revealed some of the differences that were emerging, as well as differences that had existed between the three jurisdictions before the changes to institutions and accountabilities (Walker *et al.*, 2003).

Prior to devolution the housing association sectors in the three jurisdictions had expanded at a similar pace (doubling their share of all housing stock between 1991 and 2001) but from different baselines. Housing associations in Scotland now manage a similar share of the national housing stock to their English counterparts (Table 9.4), but the size of associations in terms of their stock holding is very different, with the sector being dominated by

Table 9.4 *Size and share of the housing association sector, England, Scotland and Wales, 1991–2001*

	Housing stock provided by associations				Size of associations in 2001 (number of dwellings managed)		
	1991		2001				
	Thousands	Per cent	Thousands	Per cent	< 20,000	3000–20 000	1000–3000
England	608	3.1	1388	6.6	5	146	133
Scotland	57	3.1	145	6.2	–	5	49
Wales	29	2.4	55	4.3	–	7	14

Source: Walker *et al.* (2003). Reproduced by permission from *Housing Studies* (http://www.tandf.co.uk).

smaller, often locally based landlords. In Wales the sector is smaller in scale than in the other two jurisdictions – with just seven associations managing more than 3000 homes – but close to that in England in terms of structure.

Part of the reason for the differences in structure lies in the registration practices adopted by Tai Cymru and Scottish Homes following their separation from the Housing Corporation in 1988. Scottish Homes encouraged the registration of smaller landlords, notably the community-based associations that were dominant in the west of the country (although they managed only 19 per cent of the housing association stock), whereas in England and Wales, with the exception of the Black and Ethnic Minority and rural housing associations registered in the 1970s and 1990s, new registrations were mainly large stock-transfer associations. An important associated difference was the greater adoption of community governance models (Clapham and Kintrea, 1994, 2000) and tenant representation on boards in Scotland: 92 per cent of Scottish associations had tenants on their management committees (Scott *et al.*, 2001).

Some distinctive regulatory approaches were developed prior to devolution, such as the 'pattern book' guidance on new development developed by Tai Cymru for associations in Wales. In England and Scotland there were significant transfers of stock from public sector landlords. Nonetheless housing associations in England, Scotland and Wales worked to broadly similar policies, with common mechanisms to set, monitor and secure compliance, reflecting their common institutional history prior to 1988.

After devolution there was some convergence, with policies in all three jurisdictions promoting housing associations as the main providers of social housing in the future and a broadening of the housing agenda to include community regeneration. For example the Scottish Parliament introduced a New Housing Partnership initiative to encourage local authorities to explore the feasibility of whole stock transfers and to promote community ownership of housing. Enormous effort was made by Glasgow City Council to transfer its homes in two stages, first to the Glasgow Housing Association in 2003 and in the longer term to locally based associations (Gibb, 2003). The Welsh Assembly also encouraged transfer but with less success, with only Bridgend transferring all its stock to the Valleys to Coast Housing Association during the first few years of the policy. There was also some convergence towards the Scottish model in terms of governance and accountability structures and tenant involvement. More tenants were appointed to boards in England and there was greater interest in facilitating tenant control (Charity Commission and Housing Corporation, 2002), and 'community gateway' models were adopted for English and Welsh transfers (Confederation of Co-operative Housing, 2001). However the impact of these models was minimal, and by 2005 there had been just two English community gateway transfers and no Welsh community mutual transfers.

With regard to divergence, institutional arrangements for policy making and regulation began to diverge after the abolition of QUANGOs. In both Wales and Scotland a single funder and regulator for local authorities and housing associations was established, with accountability to the government. This contrasted with the slower pace of integrating the housing association and local authority regimes in England. The regulatory and investment functions of the Housing Corporation were preserved and a new single inspection regime was administered by the Audit Commission from 2004. Regional Housing Boards were made responsible for a single regional housing pot from 2005. Communities Scotland remained an executive agency with a high profile in the funding and regulation of housing associations, similar to that of its predecessor body. In Wales, by contrast, the National Assembly did not have the same profile as Tai Cymru once had with housing associations.

One area that has been strengthened since devolution is the regulatory barrier to English housing associations operating in the other jurisdictions. English associations that wish to operate in Scotland must work through locally governed partner organizations registered with Scottish Homes rather than operating directly or through local subsidiaries. Similar registration conditions prevent English-based associations from operating in Wales. Arguably these provisions have protected local associations from incursion or possible takeover by larger and financially stronger associations and prevented the formation of UK-wide housing groups. Nevertheless several associations use a federal structure to include partner organizations in each of the UK jurisdictions. Some of the largest English associations have established close relationships with Scottish-based partners. Two newly founded associations operating in the Republic of Ireland are the product of partnerships with English associations, and several Northern Ireland associations have established partner bodies with local committees to operate in the Republic of Ireland. To date there have been no reports of UK housing associations expanding into other parts of the European Union, although considerable exchanges of knowledge and experience take place through policy networks such as the European Liaison Committee for Social Housing (CECODHAS (www.cecodhas.org)), most famously involving the transfer of the idea of choice-based lettings from the Netherlands to the UK (see Chapter 10).

Sector restructuring in England

We end this chapter with an account of some recent trends in England, where the tensions between the public, private and third sector characteristics of housing associations have played out to the greatest extent. Many English associations have adopted a very active approach to strategic positioning, organizational growth and specialization (see Mullins and Riseborough, 2000) in response to a rapidly changing environment. Government has promoted efficiency, emphasized policy and supported delivery and progressive transfer of all social housing to the non-profit sector. Sector rebranding sought to reinvigorate housing associations and to offer the government and other stakeholders greater efficiency, focus on neighbourhoods, customers and promotion of excellence (National Housing Federation, 2004b). This strategic positioning became increasingly important with the introduction of Social Housing Grant for private developers (Housing Corporation, 2004a), which exposed associations to competition in some of their areas of activity.

Key dimensions of restructuring

By 2004 the structure of the English housing association sector had become extremely complex. There were still around 2000 registered housing associations, including a large number of small associations with fewer than 250 homes and few employees. The position held by small community-orientated associations is indicated by the Black and Ethnic Minority housing sector, which after 20 years of development accounted for just 1.5 per cent of housing association activity (Harrison and Phillips, 2003). Meanwhile the proportion of stock owned by the largest associations had increased significantly as a result of organic growth, the merger of existing associations and the large size of newly registered stock transfer associations. Each year from the late 1970s around 1 per cent of associations had been wound up (or 'transferred their engagements'). New associations were still being registered, but since the early 1990s these had mostly been stock transfer associations or new groups and subsidiaries formed by the restructuring of existing associations. These new registrations had further increased the average size of housing associations.

Stock transfers were adding to the sector at the rate of about 100 000 dwellings a year and by 2004 accounted for around 50 per cent of the housing association stock. While stock transfer associations had been successfully integrated into the sector and operated within the same regulatory and governance framework as traditional associations, they had certain differentiating characteristics, notably a geographical focus and distinctive governance arrangements. In the early years they had concentrated on delivering promises made to tenants at ballot, but over time some of the early transfer associations had expanded their development activities to a much wider geographical area, thanks to a favourable development environment in the early 1990s. Some had integrated with traditional associations through merger or the establishment of group structures. However new transfer associations remained a discrete part of the sector and faced distinct challenges and organizational changes (Pawson and Fancy, 2003).

A related feature of this growing complexity was the formation of group structures, with a registered housing association parent and a set of subsidiary organizations accountable to the parent, only some of which were registered housing associations. The majority of larger associations were part of group structures, and over two thirds of the sector's housing stock was managed by associations accountable to group parents (Marshall, 2003). The popularity of group structures as a vehicle for growth was partly explained by their potential to preserve a degree of independence for organizations that joined the group while offering savings through economies of scale (for example in relation to central services and borrowing margins), and the opportunity to ring-fence non-housing activities in special purpose subsidiaries (Audit Commission, 2001).

For associations that sought partners, groups were often preferred to mergers since they allowed for the continued involvement of key executives and board members. Groups also appeared to provide a way of preserving some local accountability through locally based subsidiaries with places on boards for local service users and communities. However by 2003, some groups were consolidating and simplifying their structures to reduce costs and bureaucracy. This was in part a response to concerns about the costs of complex governance and partly to clarification by the Housing Corporation (2004c) that subsidiary housing associations cannot avoid control by parents, and thus scope for real independence is limited. The future course of sector restructuring will partly depend on the balance between the drivers of group formation (federalism) and those of group consolidation (control). This will further increase the tension between scale and accountability (Mullins, 2004b).

Alongside the restructuring of the sector these were persistent calls for rationalization of the ownership of the stock within neighbourhoods. The introduction of competition into the allocation of development funding had led to a wide geographic distribution of the stock of some large landlords and increased the number of associations working in individual authorities and neighbourhoods. Rationalization efforts to overcome these problems tended to be locally led, particularly in low-demand neighbourhoods where associations were encouraged to 'lead, influence, follow or exit'. A leading example of rationalization in Liverpool involved the establishment of a new neighbourhood management organization that took on both the management of stock from a number of social landlords and broader neighbourhood services such as street cleaning under contract from the local authority (Sharples, 2002). Larger-scale rationalization through stock swaps between housing associations across several areas was more difficult to achieve due to legal and valuation hurdles.

Another related change was the diversification of some associations into broader social businesses. This tendency (discussed in Chapter 7) led to a polarized debate, with some arguing that housing associations should focus on their core business of developing and managing rented homes, while others maintained that housing associations had always been about more than just homes and that the current agenda demanded a wider neighbourhood and community focus. In practice the extent of the non-housing activities of most associations remained below the thresholds for non-housing activities set out in the revised regulatory guidance (Housing Corporation, 1999b). Concern tended to dissipate after the turn of the century but revived following changes to development funding.

In 2004 the Housing Corporation launched its 'Investment Partnering' policy by allocating 80 per cent of the two-year programme for 2004–6 to just 70 investment partners (mostly leading consortia with several partner associations), with the remaining 20 per cent going to 200 associations. There was an overall reduction of 40 in the number of associations that received funding compared with the previous funding round (Zitron, 2004). Associations that had been involved in development in the past but were not selected as partners were therefore forced to review their strategies. Two outcomes seemed likely: increased membership of development consortia, and a focus by non-development associations on housing management and non-housing activities. While Investment Partnering provided a sharp stimulus for such realignment, it also reinforced the competition that had been in operation since the introduction of private finance and competitive bids (see Chapter 8).

Conclusion: changing relations with the state, market and civil society

Recent changes in the housing association sector could be interpreted as expansion of a corporatist model of relations in which the state shares authority with certain interest groups (Middlemas, 1979; Houlihan, 1988). Larger housing associations have effectively been incorporated into the machinery of government, and as a consequence enjoy considerable influence over the ways in which programmes are delivered. Investment Partnering could be seen as an example of corporatism in action, with a 'club' of preferred partners to whom resources and trust are dispensed in return for performance and delivery. A further example is provided by the development of group structures: it can be argued that by encouraging poorly performing (or non-conforming) associations to join groups the Housing Corporation has been transferring aspects of its regulatory role to group parents, which have therefore become accountable for the performance of the subsidiary associations. As Lowe (2004, p. 59) comments 'The argument that these organisations are essentially agents of central government is much less plausible in this highly networked universe. These are powerful players that are not simply reacting to government directives but increasingly able to shape them.'

Both Investment Partnering and group structures involve increased efficiency but independence at a price. Arguably the fate of non-partner associations will be determined by their ability to construct viable business strategies that build on their strengths in housing management or other specialist services and exploit their connections with neighbourhoods and communities. In this regard the emphasis on the development of housing associations as independent social businesses could be particularly important.

While group structure is now the dominant organizational model in the sector, not everyone is convinced that this arrangement gives sufficient priority to local accountability. For example the Audit Commission (2001) has highlighted the low transparency of group parents to tenants and communities. Greater centralization of control within groups will only strengthen this concern. Alternative models of independent social business emphasizing federal relations within groups and looser coalitions between housing associations and partners such as social enterprises could be seen as an overlapping but alternative vision of the future for the housing association sector. Features of this model might include a greater emphasis on accountability to tenants and communities and an emphasis on partnership and shared aims, rather than control and accountability to group parents.

Some housing associations are seeking to build looser coalitions of social enterprises in which the association is a partner to a range of independent community businesses rather than the parent of a controlled group. The community gateway scheme for stock transfer is seeking to inject account-ability into a process that can often appear inflexible, making a mockery of the formal requirement for tenants to be at the heart of associations' operations. Two-stage transfers such as that being implemented in Glasgow may provide an alternative trade-off between the imperatives of scale and accountability to those being worked out in most of the English social housing sector. However at the time of writing it seems unlikely that this more federal vision of the sector will displace the tendency towards scale, control and corporatism, which is placing control of the sector into ever fewer hands.

Chapter 10

Choice and Control: Social Housing Management and Access to Social Housing

The nature and content of housing management have been widely debated, with key differences in the emphasis placed on property and people and the relative importance attached to efficiency, effectiveness and equality (Pearl, 1997). Property-related functions include repairs and maintenance, rent collection and void control (keeping properties occupied). People-related functions are more variable but usually include managing access and lettings, conferring rights and responsibilities (tenancy management) and managing arrears (Bines *et al.*, 1993). While the above functions are also common in private property management, wider definitions of housing management are often adopted in social housing that may include tenant involvement, community development, debt counselling, the prevention of racial harassment and antisocial behaviour, and employment and training schemes (Pearl, 1997).

The first part of this chapter explores the origins and development of approaches to managing what is now called social housing. Housing management developed in a distinctive way in the UK, reflecting influences of Victorian philanthropy and competing models that emerged in the voluntary housing sector at that time, the subsequent growth of larger-scale organizational structures in the council sector and the more recent fragmentation and residualization of social housing. Balance between choice and control has been an important theme throughout the history of social housing. The second part of the chapter explores the influence of citizenship and consumerism on current practices. The discussion draws on two case studies. The first is of the involvement of 'hard to reach groups' in collective decisions on stock investment as authorities work towards meeting the Decent Homes Standard, and the second is of the introduction of individual choice through choice-based lettings.

212

Origins and development of housing management

Housing management preceded council housing and was associated with a philanthropic tradition of social reform. From the 1840s onwards the management of model dwellings and charitable trusts was often put in the hands of ex-service personnel with a business-like approach to property management (White, 1980; Englander, 1983). However greater attention is usually given to the work of Octavia Hill, who adopted a casework approach to managing properties and reaching out to poor tenants in Marylebone from the 1860s onwards (Clapham, 1997; Malpass, 2000a). Hill's activities had a strong moral component, for example she sought to control tenants' behaviour in respect of budgeting and rent payment. According to Brion (1995, p. 11):

> From the beginning, in managing properties Octavia Hill put into practice a careful attention to the landlords' duties, such as repairs, together with a personal relationship with the tenants and an expectation that in the long run the tenants would behave in a way which was responsible both to their neighbours and to the landlord.

Although Hill was reluctant to set up formal organizations, her thinking affected the new housing trusts and societies that were emerging at the time and strongly influenced the introduction of professional training. Hill's system of people-based management, which combined elements of social work, reciprocity, improvement of the 'deserving poor' and sound business principles (Malpass, 2000a), subsequently influenced the activities of the Association of Women House Property Managers, formed in 1916, and the Society of Women Housing Estate Managers (SWHEM), formed in 1932 (Ravetz, 2001). This tradition was picked up by many of the housing trusts established in the late Victorian era and by housing societies established in the early twentieth century. A Conference of Christian Churches on Christian Politics Economics and Citizenship (COPEC) held in 1924 led the formation of five new housing societies one of which COPEC Birmingham was founded in 1925. The first General Manager of COPEC, Margaret Fenter, was a member of the SWHEM and had trained under a pupil of Octavia Hill at St Pancras Housing Association in London. She in turn trained women as housing managers in her own organization and was a strong advocate of Hill's principles as she indicates in her 1930 Annual Report:

> The value of having trained women workers cannot be too strongly emphasised. The fact that there is such a satisfactory high percentage of rents paid, in spite of the present hard times, and that there is such a good feeling between tenants and COPEC show conclusively that good business management and friendliness can be most successfully combined. (COPEC Annual Report, 1930, quoted in Gulliver, 2000, p. 18)

Hill's ideas had always been implemented alongside more businesslike property management methods and when council housing became the main form of provision her influence diminished. According to Ravetz (2001), militating against the wholesale adoption of the Octavia Hill system by the new council landlords were the fact that local authority departmental structures tended to split responsibility for housing between treasurers, surveyors, engineers and works departments, the establishment in 1931 of the predominantly male Institute of Housing, which pursued a different professional agenda from the SWHEM, the recruitment of housing managers from the declining private rented sector, and scale:

> The [Hill] method was expressly designed to work on a small scale – the optimum size of an estate for a manager was supposed to be not more than 300 units. Given that within a few years some estates grew to 2000 dwellings or more, it is easy to see why the Hill method would have been thought impossibly impractical. (Ibid., p. 112).

Hill's principles were later viewed as paternalistic and inappropriate to the ethos of the welfare state, particularly after the Second World War. Spicker (1985) argues that in this period the more intrusive practices were akin to social control and had become incompatible with the promotion of housing rights. Nevertheless elements of Hill's ideas can be detected in later approaches to housing management, such as the estate-based management advocated by the Priority Estates Project (Power, 1987).

The new approach to large-scale council housing management has been characterized by Malpass and Murie (1999) as the contractual approach, but it might be more generally described as the bureaucratic approach as it involved a move towards bureaucratic forms of authority and the application of rationality, as described by Weber (1947). In the late 1970s the City University Housing Research Group (Legg *et al.*, 1981) made one of the most important attempts to codify and inform housing management practice through better specification of the service, enhanced information, target setting and monitoring. This approach became particularly well developed in relation to housing allocation, where elaborate points systems were used to demonstrate that housing needs were met in an even handed and objective way and opportunities for officer discretion were minimized (Smith and Mallinson, 1996). This accorded with a hierarchical model of service delivery (see Chapter 7) that emphasized bureaucratic rules, codified procedures and minimized discretion to ensure fairness.

During the last quarter of the twentieth century increased attention was paid to performance management in the social housing sector. A series of external evaluations of effectiveness were carried out and increasingly sophisticated attempts to codify good practice and to benchmark and compare performance were developed. Local authority housing management was expected to be more competitive and new public management methods were used to encourage authorities to consider externalizing their services (Walker, 2001). Critiques of local authority housing management by the Audit Commission (1986) and others (for example Henney, 1985) supported the reforming Conservative government's wish to impose external competition on municipal landlords.

A succession of policies to reduce the part played by local authorities in the direct management of housing included the Right to Buy scheme, the externalization of housing management and finally the wholesale transfer of assets. 'Tenants' Choice', Housing Action Trusts and the 'right to manage' initially had only a limited impact on the council sector as a whole (Malpass and Means, 1993), but from 1988 large-scale transfers by local authorities began to gather pace (see Chapter 9). In 1996 Compulsory Competitive Tendering (CCT) was extended to housing management. The quest for efficient management of public resources continued under the Labour government after 1997 with the introduction of 'Best Value' and public service agreements (see Chapter 7).

These developments strengthened the contractual approach and the emphasis on service specification, service costing and performance measurement was maintained. As Franklin (2000, p. 910) puts it:

> The dictates of CCT and Best Value have demanded both rationalisation and standardisation, thus reducing the scope for flexibility and local responsiveness. Furthermore the need to specify, measure and monitor performance more rigorously, whilst it may have improved efficiency and effectiveness in those aspects of the service which are easily quantifiable, militates against the soft of welfare side of housing management.

Housing management from 1997

Three new developments became prominent after the Labour government took office in 1997. First, the growing vulnerability and disadvantage of tenants combined with the government's communitarian agenda to increase the social welfare and social control aspects of housing management. Second, the falling away of demand for social housing in some areas and the government's emphasis on consumerism and choice forced social landlords to adopt more customer-focused practices (see the next section). Third, the emphasis on business planning and asset management established by the Conservatives was strengthened, but was modified by new practices such as relational contracting.

The interplay between social control and social welfare remained central to housing management. The government responded to concern about crime and antisocial behaviour by requiring landlords to participate in local crime prevention partnerships and drug and substance misuse partnerships, as well as focusing their management activities on controlling antisocial behaviour. An area manager interviewed by Franklin summed up the attitude towards these measures: 'Over the last 12–18 months we're becoming more like a social police force, in as much as we're being the one who's being told to deal with the disruptive elements on our estates, when in reality that job really does rest with the police' (ibid., p. 922).

Renewed emphasis on social welfare was stimulated by the 'housing plus' agenda in the 1990s. This encouraged a more proactive stance by social landlords in tackling social exclusion (Clapham and Evans, 1998). There was renewed emphasis on locally based management, community involvement and user choice. Some of Franklin's (2000) interviewees saw this as stretching the boundaries of housing management to embrace social work and community development. However, many of the practices were not new and had long been part of housing management (Gulliver, 2000).

One response to the tension between social control and social welfare activities was to separate them through the specialization of housing staff. 'Supporting People' (see Chapter 11) was used to employ 'floating support' staff to help vulnerable tenants throughout the housing stock to retain their tenancies, while 'Best Value' required specialist staff to facilitate tenant and community involvement. Meanwhile the control of rent arrears became an increasingly specialized activity, with debts above a certain threshold and former tenants' arrears being handled by specialist teams or outsourced to debt collection agencies. Rather than stretching the duties and competences of generic housing managers the challenge was now to hold together the competing logics of these specialist functions.

Business planning and asset management were the favoured methods of coordinating the housing management goals. The asset management approach was based on the question: 'what are the costs and benefits of owning this piece of land or property?' (Housing Corporation, 2003b). This required landlords to value their assets, understand local markets and demand, and to make strategic decisions on investment and disinvestment on the basis of business risk. Stock-transfer housing associations led this trend, reflecting their long-term loan finance and the need to ensure that rental income was sufficient to cover costs and pay back the loan over a 25–30 year period (Mullins *et al.*, 1995). Regulation by the Housing Corporation hastened its spread across the housing association sector (Housing Corporation, 2003b). For local authorities the introduction of resource accounting and business planning required asset management strategies. The latter encompassed housing investment to meet the Decent Homes Standard and investment in neighbourhoods and communities to protect rental income by sustaining the demand for housing.

Outsourcing continued to be important under Labour, but the emphasis was now on achieving Best Value and more competitive services. The contractual approach advanced under CCT was modified to a more relational approach based on trust, discretion and the flexibility to tackle problems that were unforeseen when contracts were drafted. This reflected learning from private sector contractual arrangements, and was given a strong impetus in the housing sector by attempts to modernize the construction industry following the publication of reports by Sir John Egan and the construction task force; (Egan 1998, 2004, Confederation of Construction Clients, 2003).

The changing tenant profile

The above account of historical approaches to housing management focused on supply-side influences such as management philosophy. However the changing customer base of the sector has been just as important for the revision of practices. Council housing was initially occupied by the 'stable working class' with regular incomes rather than by the poorest households. Its base later broadened, and by 1979 a third of all households were council tenants, including some households in higher income groups. Then 30 years of 'residualization' left social housing with increasingly poor and socially marginalized tenants. This significant development reflected a change in the demand for social housing, increased uptake of other-forms of tenure and changes to allocation policies for social housing.

The impact of improved housing opportunities in other sectors is often neglected when considering the tenant profile of social housing. For most of the twentieth century the long-term decline of the private rented sector was a key factor in increasing the number of people with little choice but to apply for council housing, and slum clearance later played a direct part in changing the new tenant profile. Later in the century the expansion of home ownership and the tax advantages of this form of tenure were instrumental in reducing the pool of new applicants for council homes to those with little prospect of home ownership. Over time the combined effects of the contracting private rented sector and the expanding owner-occupied sector resulted in very different patterns of consumption of social housing than had been the case in earlier periods. Industrial changes significantly reduced the long-term, full-time employment opportunities in skilled and unskilled manual trades that had previously been the main livelihood of entrants to council housing. This led to a cohort effect, whereby existing council tenants from a wide range of income groups were moving into retirement, while new entrants to the sector were much less likely to be in full-time stable employment than earlier cohorts.

Table 10.1 provides a snapshot of the two social housing sectors in 2001 in terms of property type, property age and household characteristics. This profile can be compared with those of the other main forms of tenure in Figures 5.1 and 5.2. Further data on economic status by tenure is provided in Table 12.2.

A much lower percentage of social housing tenants were in full-time employment than were home owners and private renters The two social housing sectors also had the highest proportion of retired people (A further analysis of the economic status of social housing tenants is conducted in Chapter 12.) The housing association sector had the highest percentage of single persons and single-parent households of any tenure. In terms of property age and type, housing associations had a higher proportion of newer homes and flats, while local authority housing still consisted predominantly of houses built in the two decades after the Second World War, despite the selective sale of housing stock. Tenants' satisfaction with

Table 10.1   *Profile of social renting, England, 2001 (per cent)*

	Local authority	Housing association
Dwelling types		
Houses	62	51
Detached houses	1	2
Semidetached houses	31	20
Terraced houses	31	30
Purpose-built flats	32	35
Converted flats	3	9
Built pre-1919	4	14
Built 1945–64	40	17
Built since 1985	4	30
Household types		
Household head over 45	60	52
Household head 16–24	5	7
Household head 25–44	34	42
Single-person households	42	43
Childless couples	20	16
Single parents	15	20
Full-time employment	23	24
Retired	37	34
Unemployed/other inactive	32	33
Percentage satisfied with accommodation	80	80

Source: Data from Live Tables, ODPM website (http://www.odpm.gov.uk).

their accommodation was similar in the two sectors but significantly below that of home owners.

Approaches to lettings

There have been significant shifts in approaches to letting, as the following examples indicate. In 1960 Margaret Fenter looked back on 33 years as general manager of COPEC in Birmingham: 'When choosing tenants, the main considerations were whether the family would fit the house, whether they would be likely to get on with the neighbours, pay the rent with reasonable regularity and have a sufficient standard of cleanliness' (Fenter, 1960, p. 16). There were similar assumptions in the council sector in the late 1960s, when the Cullingworth Report commented that 'the underlying philosophy seemed to be that council tenancies were to be given only to those who deserved them and that the most deserving should get the best houses. Thus unmarried mothers, cohabitees, "dirty" families and "transients" tended to be grouped together' (Cullingworth, 1969, pp. 32–3).

Studies showing the extent of the disadvantage experienced by Black and minority ethnic households, single parents and other 'vulnerable groups' (Henderson and Karn, 1985; Phillips, 1986; Smith, 1989a), and especially the Commission for Racial Equality's (1984) investigation of Hackney, had a huge effect on allocation policy and practice over the next 25 years. These studies drew attention to the discretion exercised by (mainly white) housing allocation staff in the tenant selection process, which often involved the inaccurate prejudgement and stereotyping of applicants (Henderson and Karn, 1987). There were calls for the allocation procedures to be carefully specified, widely publicized to applicants, meticulously followed and open to public scrutiny. According to Smith and Mallinson (1996, p. 343) these prescriptions were widely taken up by social landlords:

> Since discretion has been defined as a problem related to subjectivity and flexibility, the recommended (and generally adopted) solution has been to formalise and objectify the system...most local authorities, and many other housing management bodies, now use professionally designed measurable criteria in order to recognise housing need; they have created several housing queues which deal with different types of housing requirement; and they operate computerised lettings lists to help ensure that the stock is let in priority order and offers are matched to needs.

In the 1990s there was a major rethink of the rational bureaucratic approach as landlords struggled with the challenges of residualization and needs-based rationing. Page (1993) argued that mechanistic application of the needs-based approach to lettings contributed to the stigmatization of neighbourhoods and their residents. In the late 1990s Butler (1998, p. 9) summed up the emerging consensus that was to support the shift to choice-based lettings 'increasingly restrictive' eligibility requirements imposed by social landlords during the 1990s 'may have the effect of marginalising those excluded, further removing them from contact with services and schools and moving them into insecure, possibly unsuitable housing'. This, Butler argued, would 'contribute to the process of social exclusion.'

All of these factors changed the customer base of social housing and therefore the approach to consumer choice, as discussed in the next section.

Consumerism and choice

The expansion of consumer choice has been a frequently stated aim of public service reforms in the UK over the past 25 years. Part of the rationale has been provided by public choice theory (Niskanen, 1971), which sees public service organizations as inefficient, producer-driven monopolies that are prone to empire building. In the early years the idea of consumer choice was seen as potentially popular with public service users who were becoming accustomed to exercising choice in other markets. Thus many of the Conservative reforms of the 1980s and 1990s contained the word choice: 'tenant's choice', 'more choice in social rented Housing' and so on. The reforms included the opening up of local authority provision to competition from other providers. However direct service users still had little real choice whereas government funding bodies were able to choose between providers (Mullins, 1998). The reforms often led to the creation of quasimarkets (Le Grande and Bartlett, 1993).

The reforms of housing management in the 1980s and 1990s imported management models and assumptions from the private sector under the heading 'new public management' (see Chapter 7). One of the key ideas imported from business was that of 'sticking close to the customer', which was held up by Peters and Waterman (1982) as contributing to corporate success in the United States. The message was that excellent companies built their competitive advantage by finding out what their customers wanted and adapted their business in order to provide it. Cairncross *et al.* (1997) have shown how publications by the National Consumer Council (1986) and the Local Government Training Board (1987) encouraged the adoption of a 'consumerist model' in housing that challenged paternalist housing management practices. Instead of relying only on political and professional judgements, consumerist housing management involved listening to consumers and obtaining their views, particularly through the use of market research, and by 1990 more than 50 per cent of local housing authorities had undertaken a tenant satisfaction survey (Bines *et al.*, 1993).

Supporting the case for consumer choice in public services John Stewart (1988, p. 1) argued that 'Too often in the past local authorities have provided services to the public. The authority has known what the public needs, so it does not have to pay any attention to what they want.' There was greater scope for individual choice than most local authorities recognized, and that this could involve choosing the provider of services as well as having a say in their content, accessibility and cost. But the scope for extending choice was limited by the purpose of some services, for example if they were related to enforcement or when a service was rationed and delivered according to need. The ability of housing services to respond to consumers was further constrained by the housing stock, a long-term fixed asset that could not easily be changed without the complete redevelopment of homes and neighbourhoods. Stock modernization alone was insufficient to tackle broader problems of neighbourhood stigma and outmoded layout and design. Perhaps the greatest constraint to user choice in social housing was the progressive sale of the best-quality homes and failure to invest adequately in either new homes or enhancement of the remaining stock.

The relationship between consumerism and citizenship in housing management policy is difficult to unravel, particularly as the terms have been used in different ways at different times, most notably in government policy statements. Consumerist policies are generally seen as more narrowly based and in some respects antithetical to the principles of citizenship upon which public welfare services were founded (Marsh, 1998).

The concept of citizenship as a system of rights and obligations provided an important underpinning for the development of universal services by the welfare state. Marshall's (1950) depiction of citizenship as a hierarchy of rights in which the establishment of civil and then political rights paved the way for the development of social rights underpinned the reforms carried out by the postwar Labour government. These included the development of universal public services such as housing, and local authorities built over 80 per cent of all new homes between 1945 and 1951. The model developed during this era has been described by Cairncross *et al.* (1997, p. 27) as the 'traditional model', '*built on the ideas of representative democracy and professionalism*', in which consumers' views were mediated by elected councillors in the course of their policy and casework duties.

These authors use the term 'citizenship model' to describe later approaches that went beyond market-type relations with individual consumers to embrace the collective case for service provision. Services based on citizenship were concerned with the interests of all citizens in the provision of decent public services, rather than just those individuals who were direct service users at any point in time. In the case of tenant involvement the citizenship agenda included community development and tenant empowerment, better housing management and the extension of choice.

The election of a Labour government in 1997 was expected to lead to renewed emphasis on citizenship and a move beyond the consumerism that had been the common currency during the preceding 18 years of Conservative government. Chapter 7 outlined some of the ways in which New Labour's modernization agenda can be depicted as different from the new public management agenda it inherited. Three key differences during Labour's first term of office, as identified by Newman (2001), are of direct relevance to housing management and tenant involvement:

- The emphasis on joined-up government and partnership working, exemplified by the work of the Social Exclusion Unit, had a direct impact on housing bodies' ways of working. For example the duty of housing authorities to publish homelessness strategies in 2003 required cooperative working with social service authorities, primary health care teams, the Probation Service and many other local voluntary and statutory agencies.
- The emphasis on democratic innovation and public participation created new opportunities for community involvement in policy and increased the importance of the citizenship model. This was particularly the case in relation to neighbourhood regeneration, for example through the National Strategy for Neighbourhood Renewal (Cabinet Office, 2001).
- The emphasis on remaking civil society and building community capacity required social landlords to place greater emphasis on empowerment and provide opportunities for communities to take the lead, for example by means of new models of stock transfer such as the community gateway model, with a higher degree of tenant control (Confederation of Co-operative Housing, 2001).

Best value and consumerism

Consumer involvement in housing management was given fresh impetus by the 'Best Value' regime, which replaced Compulsory Competitive Tendering (CCT). While the requirement to improve existing services and competitiveness contained some of the emphases of CCT, there was innovation in the involvement of tenants and staff in service reviews and in benchmarking services with those of other providers. This consumerist focus was reinforced by the introduction of housing inspection (see Chapter 7). Inspection focused on services that were of most direct interest to tenants and placed a strong emphasis on tenants' views of these services, as revealed by tenant surveys, formal meetings, home visits, focus groups and interviews with tenant board members. A key factor in assessing performance was the extent to which feedback from tenants and other service users had been used to improve services. An added tenant perspective was provided by including 'tenant inspectors' in each inspection team (Housing Corporation, 2002c).

Individual and collective choices

Housing management initiatives have been driven by both the consumerist and citizenship agendas and have sometimes incorporated both individual and collective choices. The range of approaches is summarized by Reid and Hickman (2002, p. 915): 'Government policy in recent years has cast the service user as an individual citizen, as a customer with some basic entitlement rights which can be asserted on an individual basis, and as a consumer whose consumption preferences are simultaneously individual and collective in nature.'

Table 10.2 maps the main examples discussed in this chapter. However it should be recognized that these developments have taken place at the same time as increasing social control and it would be misleading to see them as the only or even the most important drivers of change in housing management. The table separates initiatives into those aimed at the individual and those which are collective in nature. While many of the more rhetorical uses of the concept of choice refer to the individual level (Mullins, 1998), practical examples have tended to be more at the collective level. For the most part policies to promote tenant involvement in housing can be seen as examples of collective choice since much of the emphasis has been on supporting tenant associations and forums and in some cases responding to collective action organized by tenants' groups. Prominent examples include tenant participation in decisions on stock transfer, where the majority vote determines the outcome for all tenants, including those who vote against or do not vote at all.

Table 10.2   *Selected examples of consumerist and citizenship initiatives in housing management*

	Consumerist	*Citizenship*
Individual	• Right to Buy scheme (1980) • Housing association tenants' ombudsman • Choice-based lettings*	• Tenants' Charter (1980)
Collective	• Tenant satisfaction surveys • Reports to tenants • Tenants' Charter • Stock transfer ballots (1988) • 'Best Value' review groups with tenant membership • Option appraisals (2002) for 'hard to reach' groups*	• Citizens' juries • Tenant management organizations • Tenant compacts • Community Gateway model for stock transfer

* See the case studies later in this chapter.

Tenant involvement

Tenant involvement in social housing has had both bottom-up and top-down drivers. Locally based campaigns, rent strikes, tenants' associations and federations, and national tenant organizations and support arrangements have had an enduring bottom-up influence (Cooper and Hawtin, 1988). A less widespread but nevertheless important influence has been self-help through housing cooperatives, most recently promoted as mutual ownership models for stock transfers in England and Wales (Confederation of Co-operative Housing, 2001).

Top-down drivers have included statutory duties on local authorities to consult tenants (the Housing Act of 1980), to report on their performance to tenants (the Local Government and Housing Act of 1989) and to deliver Best Value and tenant participation compacts. Further impetus has been provided by the requirement for tenant ballots to be conducted before council stock can be transferred to housing associations, and by the regulation of housing associations (Housing Corporation, 2002a). Funding has been available for capacity building to facilitate involvement (Section 16 of the Local Government Act of 1988 for local authority tenants, Housing Corporation community training and enabling grants for housing association tenants).

Programmes to improve public sector housing and regenerate neighbourhoods have often placed an emphasis on tenant and resident involvement, notably the priority estates programme, estate action, Tenants' Choice, stock transfer, the Estates Renewal Challenge Fund, the Single Regeneration Budget and the national strategy for neighbourhood renewal. These programmes have spawned a variety of organizational forms, including estate management boards, tenant management organizations, community-based housing associations, local housing companies, community mutuals and neighbourhood management organizations, with varying methods of involvement and representation.

Many attempts have been made to classify involvement and empowerment, but Arnstein's (1969) ladder of participation, upon which Figure 10.1 is based, remains an enduring reference point. There are different views on whether this ladder represents a progression, with information provision on the lowest rung and community control as the ultimate aim, or a menu of possibilities from which users should select the one that best suits their needs (Riseborough, 1998). From a consumerist position an important question is whether the aim is a greater degree of involvement or a better service, particularly given that satisfied customers may be less motivated to become involved. From a citizenship perspective there may be greater emphasis on involvement *per se* and links with social inclusion, capacity building and social capital (Cooper and Hawtin, 1998).

During the Labour government's second term of office there was renewed emphasis on the earlier Conservative policy of replacing state provision

Figure 10.1   *The spectrum of resident participation and control*

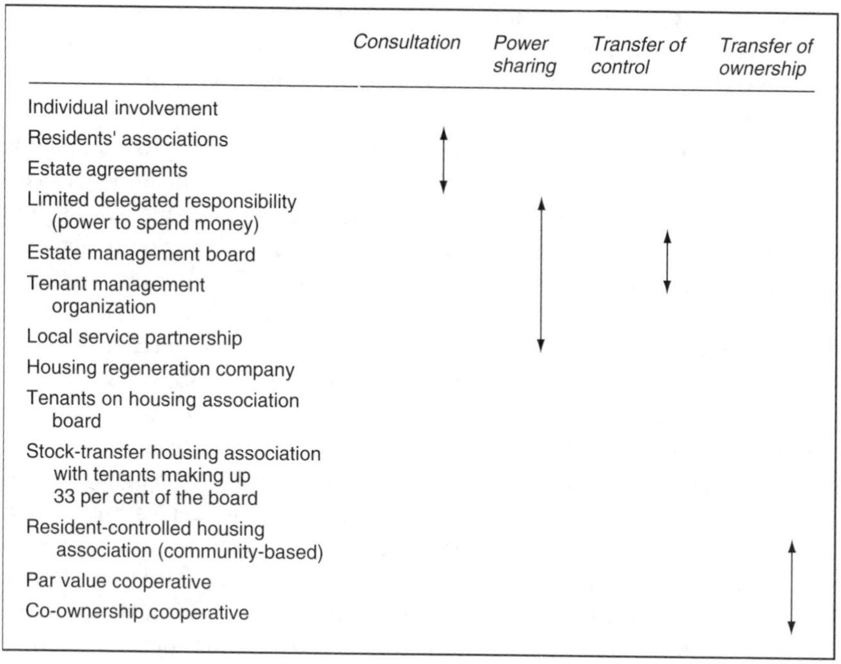

	Consultation	Power sharing	Transfer of control	Transfer of ownership
Individual involvement				
Residents' associations				
Estate agreements				
Limited delegated responsibility (power to spend money)				
Estate management board				
Tenant management organization				
Local service partnership				
Housing regeneration company				
Tenants on housing association board				
Stock-transfer housing association with tenants making up 33 per cent of the board				
Resident-controlled housing association (community-based)				
Par value cooperative				
Co-ownership cooperative				

Source: Mullins (2003) adapted from Housing Corporation (2000). Reproduced by kind permission of Key Haven Press and Housing Corporation.

with private and voluntary sector alternatives. Like the Conservatives before, the Labour government found 'choice' a useful talisman for policy documents such as the green paper *Quality and Choice: A Decent Home For All* (DETR and DSS, 2000a). After the election the government had made the reform of public services its key priority. The Office of Public Services Reform (OPSR) was set up to help realize this aim. In October 2001 Prime Minister Tony Blair stated that:

> The key to reform is re-designing the system round the user – the patient, the pupil, the passenger, the victim of crime... The point, very simply, is this: the user comes first; if the service they are offered is failing, they should be able to change provider; and if partnership with other sectors can improve a service, the public sector should be able to do it. (www.number10.gov.uk/output/Page1632.asp)

The housing green paper (DETR and DSS, 2000a) proposed continued stock transfers and a new private finance initiative model, with 30-year contracts being awarded to private sector providers to manage, maintain and improve council housing, but it was the policy on choice-based lettings that was seen as the trail-blazing measure to promote choice. Perhaps this was because externalization was less novel in housing than in other areas of the public service, such as health and education. Choice-based lettings was a relatively unusual example of a consumerist initiative with continued public service provision (by local authorities and housing associations) that enhanced the exercise of individual choice by making constraints on supply and bargaining power more transparent.

Another example of the re-emphasis of consumerism was provided by the Housing Corporation's (2002c, 2003b) review of its involvement policy. This had replaced two existing policies – making consumers count' (1998) and 'communities in control' (2000) – with a single policy that was more outcome focused and left the detail to each association. The Corporation concluded that 'involving residents makes good business sense. Housing associations need to make sure that services are responsive, efficient and effective, meeting the needs of their customers' (Housing Corporation, 2003b, p. 9).

Things seemed to have come full circle from the 1980s, when housing management had first picked up consumerist practices from the private sector. Underpinning the policy change was a reshaping of tenant involvement to provide opportunities to comment on services received rather than being involved in strategic decision making and governance. In reviewing its policy the Housing Corporation commissioned the Office of Public Management (2002) to review private sector practice and in their review reported their finding that 'the private sector tends not to involve consumers in issues of strategic decision making' (Housing Corporation, 2002d, p. 5). Moreover the National Consumer Council (2001, p. 5) questioned 'the extent to which consumers wish to be directly involved particularly in higher level areas such as strategy and governance'. Thus the focus of tenant involvement shifted away from formal governance activities, allowing associations to streamline their decision making, and potentially to exclude tenants from the highest levels of governance (Mullins and Riseborough, 2000; Audit Commission, 2001).

The potential for social landlords to make greater use of tenant involvement to inform business strategy is highlighted by Reid and Hickman (2002) who make explicit links between research on tenant involvement activities and the business literature on organizational learning. Not only can effective tenant involvement provide opportunities for tenants to influence decisions, but it can also provide opportunities for more effective organizational adaptation and change.

Consumerist and citizenship philosophies are likely to continue to be intertwined and to involve both individual and collective choices. The next two sections draw on case studies to illustrate how these ideas have worked out in practice, first in relation to the involvement of 'hard to reach groups' in stock investment decisions as local authorities worked towards meeting the Decent Homes Standard, and then in relation to the introduction of choice-based lettings.

Involving hard to reach groups

This case study is based on research conducted for the Office of the Deputy Prime Minister (Mullins *et al.*, 2004) to identify ways in which social landlords could involve Black and minority ethnic (BME) tenants in investment decisions that would affect their homes and neighbourhoods. The requirement for all stock-holding authorities to undertake an option appraisal by 2005 to decide how to meet the Decent Homes Standard by 2010 also carried a requirement to involve tenants and to engage 'hard to reach groups' (Office of the Deputy Prime Minister, 2003d)

There were many reasons for the government's attention to broadening involvement in stock investment decisions. Concern about transfer ballot defeats and criticisms of the absence of real choice for residents (summarized later by the Centre for Public Services, 2004) may have resulted in an emphasis on options and resident consultation in order to improve legitimacy. The early stock transfer programme had tended to bypass areas with significant black and ethnic minority populations, but after 1996, and particularly after publication of the 2000 green paper (DETR and DSS, 2000a) on tackling the investment backlog, the investment process was extended to localities with much greater ethnic diversity. Added to this were the emphasis of the modernization agenda on democratic renewal and public participation (Newman, 2001), the requirement under 'Best Value' for meaningful tenant involvement, and the proactive approach to involvement in transfers stimulated by the Community Housing Task Force, set up in May 2001 to support local authorities working on decent homes options, and the demand for 'good practice'.

The stock options

From 2000 innovations were made to each of the three options to meet the Decent Homes Standard: transfers, Arm's-Length Management Organizations (ALMOs) and Private Finance Initiatives (PFIs). There was also stricter prescription of the way in which option appraisals should be carried out (Office of the Deputy Prime Minister, 2003d). There should be resident involvement at both ends of the continuum described earlier: engagement in governance and decision making at the top end, and information provision at the bottom. This would require a strategy to facilitate information provision, discussion and feedback for all residents and a tenant empowerment strategy to enable certain residents to play a central role in decision making: 'The first stage of the option appraisal should involve developing capacity to engage in the process' (Community Housing Task Force, 2003a, p. 5).

Supplementary guidance reinforced this: 'The tenant empowerment strategy needs to make sure that tenants are at the heart of decision making, the communication and consultation strategy needs to make sure that all tenants and other stakeholders have the opportunity to contribute their views' (Community Housing Task Force, 2003b, p. 1).

High-level involvement (empowerment)

Each stock investment option provided an opportunity for high-level involvement by a small number of residents through membership of governance and consultative bodies. In the case of stock transfers and ALMOs, typically a third of the governing body consisted of residents, while PFI contracts were tendered and managed by resident-led steering groups, which demanded a high degree of commitment. In one case study (Mullins *et al.*, 2004) the steering group had been meeting fortnightly for four years before the PFI contract even started to operate. The community gateway model for stock transfer (Confederation of Co-operative Housing, 2001) also included high-level involvement. Some observers expressed doubt about how representative the relatively small number of active tenants were and it was suggested that targets should be set in respect of BME representation on governing bodies.

Surveys of authorities on the stock transfer, ALMO and PFI programmes (Niner and Rowlands, 2003) found that there had been some success in establishing ethnically representative governing bodies. Eighty per cent of the surveyed authorities that had completed transfers in 1988–2001 in areas where BME people accounted for more than 3 per cent of the population had at least one BME board member, and the combined boards of these transfer landlords had 18 per cent BME membership. Of the three possible routes to board membership these BME members were more likely to have been recruited through the tenant and local authority constituencies than through the independent route, where BME representatives might have been more easily 'headhunted'. However in many authorities the formal tenant consultative and governance bodies were predominantly white, despite the diversity of the tenant population. For example nearly two thirds of the authorities that took part in the 2001–3 transfer programme had no BME shadow board members. In areas where new migrant groups had joined long-standing BME communities it became apparent that boards could never be truly representative but should attempt to reflect the diversity of their communities.

Successful tenant involvement tended to be associated with new approaches to engagement, often using informal networks alongside more formal structures. One PFI scheme was developed in an area where the formal representative bodies (tenant and resident associations, tenant liaison committees and community forums) had failed to adapt to the growing ethnic diversity of the area. In this case the residents' steering group was a new institution, and innovative means were used to recruit tenant and leaseholder members. Door knocking, 'fun days' and 'headhunting' proved effective in attracting members and achieving greater tenant participation in the steering group than in other forums in the same geographical area. Networks were being built between the steering group and the wider voluntary sector, including BME community groups, to ensure that it continued to be open to new members (Mullins *et al.*, 2004).

Low-level involvement (communication and consultation)

The main means of overcoming barriers to the involvement of hard to reach groups was the communication and consultation strategy. This involved the difficult task of ensuring that the majority of residents were aware of the investment options being negotiated and had the opportunity to express their views.

Formal methods of involvement were used by most social landlords, who produced newsletters, held meetings, conducted surveys and established focus groups to secure feedback. These formal methods generally failed to engage hard to reach people who were unlikely to attend meetings, respond to written communications or have links with existing groups. There was little incentive for many people, particularly the young, to engage with processes that they saw as irrelevant to their own concerns. Sometimes there was a quite narrow technocratic focus on housing investment issues and a failure to attend to the more immediate concerns of residents, such as crime and antisocial behaviour or day-to-day repairs (Community Housing Task Force, 2003a).

The research found that informal methods had a greater potential to overcome the mistrust that had plagued attempts to engage BME people and other residents in plans to improve homes and communities. But these only worked when certain conditions were met. Successful authorities employed staff who reflected the communities they served, staff and tenant representatives used their own networks to make contact with hard to reach tenants, and these networks were extended to include places and organizations frequented by hard to reach tenants. These included supermarkets, specialist ethnic food shops, barbers, faith groups, schools, nurseries and community organizations (Mullins *et al.*, 2004).

The findings of the research were considered to be applicable to other public services with a similar imperative to involve communities in decision making in a wide-ranging and representative way, despite the low propensity for public participation at all levels, not least in the case of excluded communities in poor neighbourhoods.

Choice-based lettings

Our second case study concerns the adoption of a new approach to the allocation of social housing: choice-based lettings. This replaced the administrative matching of applicants and vacancies with advertisements of homes to let, from which applicants could directly select. According to its proponents, the empowerment of home seekers inherent in the choice-based approach represented a decisive break with the deeply entrenched paternalist tradition in this area of housing practice (Brown *et al.*, 2000). Unlike most of the consumerist reforms discussed earlier in this chapter, choice-based lettings made a direct link between use of the word choice in public policy pronouncements and the circumstances of individual consumers of social housing.

The housing green paper (DETR and DSS, 2000a) actively encouraged these changes and a £13 million fund for pilot schemes was set up. One in four local authorities in England bid to take part in the schemes and, one in three were successful. Twenty-seven pilots, involving 43 local authorities, were funded in England for the 2001–3 period. Most of these involved the wholesale adoption of an advertising system, although some planned to develop a more limited approach, for example for specific areas. A subsequent evaluation found that most of the pilots had made good progress. Housing applicants had increased in number and were generally positive about the greater transparency and more active participation required of them. The provision of support to vulnerable applicants was the greatest weakness and few pilots had drawn in private landlords. Nonetheless the pilots had demonstrated that choice-based lettings could work in both high- and low-demand areas (Marsh *et al.*, 2004).

Mullins and Pawson (2005) have used complexity theory to explain the nature and timing of the shift from bureaucratic rationing to choice-based lettings. Complexity theory is concerned with the ways in which competing sets of forces influence overall system behaviour and how their influence changes over time (Haynes, 2003). It has been widely used in the natural and social sciences and management studies to understand non-linear change (Morgan, 1998). The adoption of choice-based lettings policy after a prolonged period of bureaucratic rationing is a good example of a non-linear change influenced by strong sets of competing forces (Mullins and Pawson, 2005).

Figure 10.2 utilizes a complex systems framework to answer two questions: why was social housing allocation immune for so long to new public management's prescription for consumer choice, and what caused the rapid change in the early 2000s?

The left-hand column under the Figure 10.2 explores the 'attractor pattern' that underlay bureaucratic rationing of social housing for more than 20 years, despite the presence of alternative attractors such as new public management. Four main factors supported this pattern. First, a social housing tenancy was seen as a 'prize of citizenship', embodying the right to decent housing at an affordable rent, and this required judgements about entitlement and eligibility to be demonstrably fair. Second, for most of the postwar era the supply of social housing was insufficient to meet the housing need associated with low incomes and poor conditions in the private sector. Third, the needs-based rationing approach was strengthened by a points system. Fourth, there was concern about the distributional impact of allocation systems and the potential for discrimination. These factors constituted very powerful forces maintaining bureaucratic rationing.

The bureaucratic rationing that resulted became sufficiently embedded to withstand the ideas of new public management (see Chapter 7) and consumer choice. Thus while the adoption of new public management resulted in new funding and organizational arrangements for the delivery of social housing, bureaucratic rationing was reinforced by the introduction of common housing registers and common allocation policies for a range of housing providers (Mullins and Niner, 1996).

The middle column (Figure 10.2) shows how this consensus was eventually destabilized. The most important trigger was the growing diversity of housing market conditions across the country. The low demand for social housing in some areas forced landlords to adopt an approach that was more sensitive to consumers' needs, although they maintained their formal needs-based policy. Meanwhile supply shortages in other areas called for a very different approach to letting and helped made it difficult to apply rationing across the board. Changing consumer expectations and a stepping up of the emphasis on consumer choice in New Labour's modernization project pushed these destabilizing influences even further.

The right-hand column shows how a new attractor pattern became established by the identification and promulgation of an alternative model based on Dutch social housing practice (Kuulberg, 1997, 2002). The key roles of government in relation to change were exhortation and the provision of financial incentives. Later these were reinforced by the setting of a target for 25 per cent of housing authorities to have a choice-based lettings scheme in operation by 2005 (later increased to 100 per cent by 2010). Over a short period of time there was a rapid change in the consensus as lessons were spread from the pilot schemes through promotional activities.

Figure 10.2 *Using complexity theory to depict shift from rationing to choice based lettings*

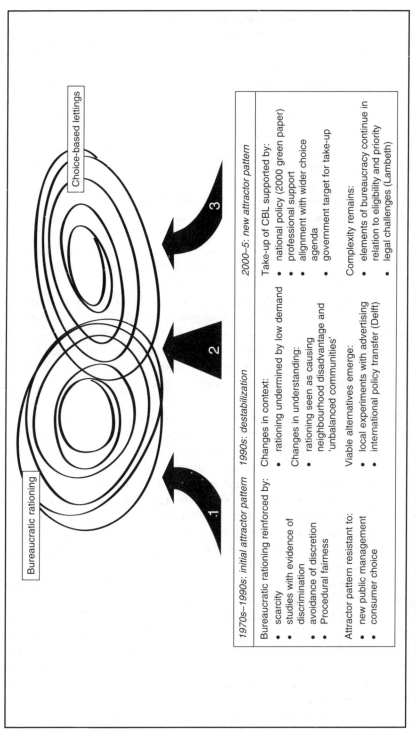

Complexity theory also highlights the continued competition between attractor patterns and the contingent nature of change. The absence of regulations on the form to be taken by choice-based lettings schemes (with the exception of case law) and differences in the prevailing conditions in different markets led to considerable variations in the impact on providers and consumers. Bureaucratic influences continued to operate alongside the new customer choice approach, with limits to choice resulting from statutory duties to secure accommodation for homeless people and others with high-priority needs, and restrictions on access in relation to antisocial behaviour and rent arrears. Legal challenges were also important, for example by challenging the ability of housing applicants to choose to bid for properties deemed to be too small for their household needs. The excessive simplification of applicant ranking policies was also challenged in the courts, and according to Marsh *et al.* (2004) some pilot schemes were adapted to take account of emerging case law. Complexity theory could also be used to explore the interaction between lettings schemes and other elements of complex urban systems to influence the role, social composition and trajectory of neighbourhoods. This would be useful in interpreting evidence, as it begins to emerge, of the wider impact and outcomes of choice-based lettings schemes.

Conclusion

This chapter has explored the origins of housing management and some of its contemporary dimensions. It has traced the impact of ideas such as universalism, citizenship, consumerism and social control and shown how these have interacted with socioeconomic and demographic changes to shape housing management practices. In recent years there has been an explicit emphasis on consumer choice, although the underlying policies have often been more associated with social control.

The examples discussed in two previous sections provide different perspectives on how ideas of citizenship and choice operate in practice. In the first case the discourse of modernization set an ambitious requirement for landlords to involve hard to reach citizens in decision making. Here implementation was sometimes undermined by a gap between formal opportunities for involvement that failed to connect with community networks of hard to reach groups. The representation of more powerful members of hard to reach communities in formal governance bodies sometimes replaced community reach as an objective. The second example illustrated the ways in which contemporary ideas such as choice could be hindered by strongly embedded control principles such as bureaucratic rationing to promote fairness and deal with scarcity. The example of choice-based lettings shows how change to established practice can be brought about as much by social and demographic influences as by policy drivers.

Our understanding of changing housing management practice therefore needs to be based on an analysis of the prevailing external context and customer base for social housing as well as a review of key policy and management ideas. Concepts such as new public management can be helpful in tracing trajectories of change across sectors, however it is important to take account of contingent factors such as local markets and sector-based influences that might lead to difference.

Chapter 11

Housing, Social Care and Supporting People

Housing policy can no longer be treated as separate from policies on health and social care. This chapter explores connections between these policies and links them to discussions of social exclusion in the UK. Health care has always been at the centre of the welfare state while housing has tended to be on the edge. Joined-up approaches designed to address the needs of vulnerable groups and tackle the roots of poor health, poverty, crime and social exclusion have led to the greater integration of policies for health care, social care, housing and community support. 'Supporting People', implemented in 2003, is a prominent example of this move and has had wide-ranging effects on statutory and voluntary support for vulnerable groups.

The chapter begins by relating changes in social welfare policies to some of the principal themes of public policy reform under recent Labour governments. Key social welfare changes have included care in the community and the development of primary care services, and there have been debates about paying for care and support. The next section reviews some of the institutional changes that have taken place as a consequence of policy change. This paves the way for our discussion of 'Supporting People' and a case study of its impact on services for older people.

Changes in social welfare policies

Earlier chapters in this book have discussed some of the key changes in public policy under successive Labour governments, involving joined-up approaches, consumerism and choice, inspection and regulation, and regionalization. Social welfare policies have been at the forefront of these changes and the interaction between health care, housing and social care has been a target for modernization. The government has emphasized cross-cutting themes rather than traditional services, including social inclusion, the modernization of welfare, the regeneration of communities and the creation of a healthier and fairer society. These themes have drawn central and local government, the health service, voluntary agencies and others into new types of strategic relationship. Table 11.1 shows the extent to

235

Table 11.1 *Housing, care and support: principal policies and legislation, 1997–2004*

1997	*Housing and Community Care – Establishing a Strategic Framework* (DTLR and Department of Health). *Making Partnerships Work in Community Care* (DTLR and Department of Health). *Better services for vulnerable people* (Department of Health).
1998	*Supporting People: A New Policy and Funding. Framework for Support Services* (Department of Social Security). *Modernising Social Services* (Department of Health white paper). *New Ambitions for our Country: A New Contract for Welfare* (Department of Social Security green paper). *Scotland Act. Government for Wales Act. Northern Ireland Act.*
1999	*Health Act. Modern Partnerships for People. Better Care, Higher Standards – the Long Term Care* Chapter (Department of Health and DTLR). Local Government Act. Part 1: Best Value. *Best Value for Registered Social Landlords* (Housing Corporation).
2000	Local Government Act. *Quality and Choice: A Decent Home for All* (DTLR and Department of Health green paper). *Best Value in Housing Framework* (DTLR). *Framework for Performance Assessment* (Housing Corporation). *Guidance on Joint Investment Plans* (Department of Health and NHS Executive). Care Standards Act. *Report from the Royal Commission on the Future of Long Term Care. With Respect to Old Age* (HMSO). *The NHS Plan, A Plan for Investment, a Plan for Reform* (Department of Health).
2001	*Fairer Charging Policies for Home Care and other Non-Residential Social Services* (Department of Health). *Introduction of the Promoting Independence Grant* (Department of Health). *Intermediate Care* (Department of Health Circular). *The Way Forward for Housing* (DTLR housing policy statement). *Addressing the Housing Needs of Black and Minority Ethnic People* (DTLR). *Best Value in Housing, Care and Support* (DTLR and Department of Health). *Quality and Choice for Older People's Housing. A Strategic Framework* (Department of Health and DTLR). *Supporting People: Policy into Practice* (DTLR). *Supporting People: The Administrative Guidance* (DTLR). *National Service Framework for Older People's Services* (Department of Health). *Building Capacity and Partnerships in Care* (Department of Health).
2003	*Developing Older People's Strategies: Linking Housing to Health, Social Care and other Local Strategies* (Office of the Deputy Prime Minister and Department of Health).
2004	*Choosing Health – Making Healthy Choices Easier* (Department of Health white paper).
2005	*Independence, Well Being and Choice – Our Vision for the Future of Social Care for Adults in England* (Department of Health green paper).

Source: Data from HMSO UK legislation website.

which joint policy making has become a central feature of social welfare, social care, health and housing.

The impact of these reforms is illustrated by the strategic frameworks that were required at the local level. First, the Health Act of 1999 required local health authorities to work with local authorities and other partners to draw up and implement health improvement plans, which are now incorporated into Local Delivery Plans (LDPs). Second, the Local Government Act of 2000 (Section 1a) introduced an overarching framework, 'community strategies', to link a wide range of local strategies, including the LDPs. This provided the opportunity for much more integrated work by a range of partners to identify and reduce health inequalities.

Another common feature of modernization was the use of regulatory incentives and penalties to influence the behaviour of these partnerships and ensure the delivery of results. As discussed in Chapter 7, Public Service Agreements (PSAs) were developed by the Treasury to link extra investment to delivery by setting outcome targets such as the Decent Homes Standard. PSAs were also developed to reduce hospitalization and residential care by funding new intermediate care provision and better discharge arrangements. Some housing organizations formed partnerships with health care and social care bodies to establish hospital discharge schemes and to provide aids and adaptations that enabled people to manage at home, thereby reducing hospital stays and residential care. These arrangements were subsequently incorporated into PSAs by many local strategic partnerships in order to meet national targets. For example the Comprehensive Performance Assessment for 2005 (Key Lines of Enquiry for Corporate Assessment, used by English local authorities to structure and present their annual performance and Best Value plans) includes sections on action to encourage and promote older people's wellbeing.

Regionalization and its impact on housing and planning has been outlined in Chapter 4. This too involved a considerable degree of joined-up government, with bodies such as local authorities, the Housing Corporation, housing associations, the Countryside Agency and English Partnerships being expected to develop regional strategies. One consequence of the rapid production of the first regional housing strategies in 2003 was that there was often too little information on the need for specialist housing and housing-related support services. In the second phase of strategy development, published in 2005, there was more time for research and some Regional Housing Boards commissioned linked regional Supporting People strategies and homelessness strategies, as well as securing cooperation by the health and social care sector, for example in undertaking health impact assessments of housing strategies (West Midlands Regional Assembly, 2005).

Regional (shadow) assemblies were established to oversee key regional strategies, and despite the 'no' vote in the first referendum on regional government in the North-East in 2004, regional governance continued to expand. Government Offices for the Regions (GORs) managed and administered evolving regional plans and worked closely with Regional Development Agencies. In the latest wave of health structure changes in 2002, which introduced strategic health authorities, provision was made for new regional directors of health, who would be located in the GORs.

Devolution to the Scottish Parliament and the Welsh and Northern Ireland Assemblies (see Chapter 1) also affected the functions and responsibilities of health and social care bodies and housing organizations. The Northern Ireland Housing Executive (NIHE), which carried out many strategic housing functions, became responsible for housing and support policy, including 'Supporting People'. In the absence of an appropriate local government structure the NIHE established regional arrangements with health boards and other partners and stakeholders to administer Supporting People. In Scotland these functions were overseen by the Scottish Assembly and devolved to local government.

We now turn to some of the key changes in specific areas of social welfare policy with a bearing on housing and support.

Care in the community

Care in the community was introduced in 1989 and marked a major shift in social welfare. As a consequence of this policy, today very few people enter long-stay care and health institutions. Some institutions remain but their services tend to be delivered in domestic-style settings. Service users have greater influence and choice over the regime and the treatments they receive.

The growth of home ownership and the general increase in wealth brought about changes in lifestyle and expectations. For example there was a growing market amongst older people for the purchase of retirement housing and services that would enable them to live independently (see Royal Commission, 2001; Joseph Rowntree Foundation, 2004).

Care in the community was launched with high expectations but was insufficiently funded. By the mid 1990s lack of funds and increased demand led to services being rationed. This left people, particularly older people who needed help with domestic tasks and some personal care, facing the loss of services. The introduction of charges for care based on levels of income and capital (including capital from the sale of their homes for people in residential care) was strongly criticized (evidence presented to the Royal Commission, 2001).

Community care assessment was introduced to ensure that people who needed help were able to secure a range of services. However delays occurred in many authorities and assessments failed to include housing and housing options (see Heywood *et al.*, 2002). Social and health care services failed to work together, and although housing was included to some extent in community care strategies, local housing authorities and housing associations were frequently left without adequate support and care arrangements for vulnerable people (Audit Commission, 1998).

In 1998 the Labour government introduced a white paper called *Modernising Social Services* (Department of Health, 1998). This set out a vision for reducing welfare dependency and controlling welfare expenditure, and set the tone for future community care policy and complemented local government and NHS modernization plans. It described failures in social care, referred to inconsistencies and inefficiency in services throughout England and the need to change the culture (primarily in social services departments) to promote independence amongst service users. Next came the *Better Care, Higher Standards – the Long Term Care Charter* (Department of Health and DTLR, 1999), which required local authorities and health authorities to publish annual charters on services such as finding people somewhere to live and helping people to retain their independence.

A number of government inquiries were established, including the Royal Commission on the Future of Long Term Care. The Commission's report, published in 2001, included a recommendation that had divided the Commission members: that long-term care as well as nursing and health care should be free and paid for out of general taxation. The government responded by agreeing that health care should be free for the individual but that social care would remain subject to means testing. The Scottish Assembly, however, voted to accept both recommendations (Scottish Executive, 2001), one of the most important examples of policy divergence since devolution.

Primary care

The Health Act of 1999 broadened the scope of health policy. The government was essentially looking for ways to shift the balance of public funding from the acute end of the health service to the primary level in order to prevent unnecessary hospital admissions and thereby reduce costs. In 2000, a number of changes were announced in the NHS plan, including the establishment of Primary Care Trusts (PCTs) in England to take over many health authority functions related to primary care and prevention. They were expected to join with social service departments to provide flexible local social care and health services, and to tackle health inequalities.

More changes followed, including expanded rehabilitation ('re-enablement') preventative services and services for people who had left hospital. In 2002

PCTs appointed intermediate care coordinators to improve accommodation, rehabilitation and care options for people. There was also a proposal to make the provision of equipment, aids and housing adaptations the joint responsibility of hospitals and social services (Department of Health, 2001). Joint community equipment stores and arrangements now exist in most areas of England and Wales. In 2002 the Department of Health established a 'change agent team housing and learning improvement network' and an intermediate care network. These were intended to improve health and social care staff's knowledge of housing options, including help with the cost of adaptations and moving, so that they could better inform patients and relatives. These initiatives have become part of ongoing projects to bring knowledge, networks and professionals together.

Performance and regulation

Service standards now apply to social housing, health, social care and support. Inspection and regulation have also increased. In line with the white paper on *Modernising Social Services* (Department of Health, 1998) a performance assessment framework was introduced in 1999. It incorporated a range of performance indicators for social service departments. Subsequently the Care Standards Act of 2000 introduced regulation, inspection and standards for domiciliary care services and brought more providers within scope of inspection (e.g. supported housing and registered care provider, hostels and independent living schemes). The National Care Standards Commission (NCSC) was set up in 2002 to regulate and inspect provisions under the Act, measured against national standards. In 2004 the NCSC was incorporated into the Commission for Social Care Inspection.

Finance for support services

While support is not the same as care, support services are an essential part of the arrangements to enable people to live in the community. By the 1990s it was clear that the cost of community support services had increased as a result of the community care reforms. There was concern about the amount of public money being spent (for example on Housing Benefit and special needs management allowances) and about the adequacy of some services to support vulnerable people. However the view in policy circles was that supported housing and support services were best left alone until they could be reviewed comprehensively. Events in 1996 and 1997 meant the review could not be put off any longer.

In May 1996 the Conservative government proposed minor Housing Benefit changes. During the subsequent consultation period the proposal was opposed by housing organizations and charities on the ground that even a minor change would affect people living in supported housing because the funding arrangements were fragile. The government withdrew the proposal and set up an interdepartmental review of social security arrangements for supported housing. However a number of local authorities were already refusing to pay Housing Benefit for supported housing service charges on the ground that services were not covered by the regulations. A High Court judgement by Mr Justice Laws on 23 July 1997 upheld the local authorities' decision, so the interdepartmental review team had no choice but to recommend changes in funding. A year later the government announced its intention to introduce a new system (Department of Social Security, 1998b).

Institutional change and impacts

Institutions that had previously been taken for granted were radically changed in the 1990s and early 2000s. The NHS was dramatically restructured with the demise of district health authorities and their gradual replacement by hospital trusts. Regional health authorities were slimmed down from 14 to eight and became regional department of health offices. General practitioners were invited to become fund holders, which enabled them to purchase services for their patients and provide more community-based services in-house. In common with other public services, business-like behaviour was encouraged.

Local government was also restructured, with fewer authorities and rearrangement into two-tier and unitary authorities. Local government services such as housing and social services were often integrated to form community services or health and housing directorates. Under Compulsory Competitive Tendering (CCT) there was a purchaser–provider split (Walsh, 1991; Bailey, 1995), and after 1993 social service departments were required to purchase a prescribed percentage of community care and residential care services from the independent (private or voluntary sector) market.

The process of institutional reform began with a Conservative drive to break up public services and continued under Labour with a mixed economy of public and private investment (Heywood *et al.*, 2001). Although the incoming Labour government abolished CCT it continued to rationalize funding, restructure services and encourage public–private partnerships. It also introduced the Private Finance Initiative, which was used to develop new hospitals.

The impact of these institutional changes on services was often slow. In the case of the community care reforms, it was not until 1993 that funds for the care element of services were transferred from hospitals and health authorities to social service departments. Arblaster *et al.* (1996) suggest that the joint planning, investment and commissioning arrangements did not have a major impact on how people experienced services until the second half of the 1990s. According to Fletcher *et al.* (1999) the pace of change in relation to joint planning for very sheltered housing was also slow.

Service planning and commissioning

An important aspect of the institutional changes was the government's objective to make planning more integrated, long term and thematic rather than functional, and there was enthusiasm for a 'whole systems approach' (Office of the Deputy Prime Minister and Department of Health, 2003). Again implementation was gradual. Most local authorities developed partnership groups to achieve planned targets, however service planning across departments and agencies was not always fully integrated. Social care planning arrangements (including joint health and care responsibilities) revolved around local development plans, whereas planning for social housing continued to be covered by housing investment programmes and the Housing Corporation's approved development programme (the two programmes were later combined and made the responsibility of the Regional Housing Boards).

Later, national service frameworks (NSFs) and legislation on joint health and social care planning led to a new commissioning environment. NSFs set overall standards for service commissioning and included housing targets; for example the NSF for older people included measures to reduce the number of falls in the home. Commissioning generally involved estimating the need for services, working out whether the supply could meet this need, making adjustments to existing services and identifying new suppliers to fill service gaps. Commissioning of this kind was used in joint arrangements for housing-based social care, such as very sheltered accommodation or extra care provision as part of a long-term strategy to shift the balance of services away from residential care.

Partners in commissioning often included members of a local strategic partnership, social services, at least one primary care trust and a number of voluntary organizations. Other partners were often brought in to provide services that lay at the heart of the community care reforms. Such services often involved radical change. For example in the late 1990s Sunderland City Council withdrew the resources for housing-based warden services and secured resources from health and social care funds to provide care and support for a wide range of vulnerable people. Liverpool City Council developed an integrated older people's strategy (ibid.) which commissioned community-based services (Riseborough and Fletcher, 2004).

Accommodation types

Throughout the 1980s and 1990s there was considerable debate on the need for improved accommodation standards in registered residential homes and better design standards for ordinary housing and specialist supported housing. Subsequently the Care Standards Act of 2000 set standards for residential care accommodation and design, while the extension of Part M of the building regulations to domestic properties in 1999 (part T in Scotland) and design standards set by the Housing Corporation in 1998 set new standards for accessibility into and within new domestic dwellings, drawing on 'lifetime homes' research (see Carroll *et al.*, 1999).

Interest in new residential care and housing models grew amongst social care and health commissioners from the late 1990s for two principal reasons: commissioners wanted to modernize and upgrade services, often in anticipation of the Care Standards Act, and to promote independent living; and it was financially advantageous to shift accommodation costs from social services or health budgets to Housing Benefit (Fletcher *et al.*, 1999; Joseph Rowntree Foundation, 2004).

Recent changes

Over time joint planning became more sophisticated, although institutional barriers remained. Primary Care Trusts (PCTs) became key partners in most community-based housing and care services, but housing organizations were not usually represented on PCT Boards. PCTs were not coterminous with local authorities; there could be one or several PCTs in a unitary authority and six or more in a two-tier authority. When providers were excluded from key strategic decisions they responded by setting up their own umbrella groups to influence PCT, and other strategy makers. For example a regional provider group was established in the West Midlands to have a say in plans for social care, health and Supporting People.

Regulation and inspection sometimes conflicted with policies to promote self-care, self-determination and flexibility. The National Care Standards Commission (NCSC) and its inspection regime focused on protecting vulnerable people and ensuring that the national standards on care and accommodation were met. This led to an emphasis on minimizing risk that was sometimes at odds with policies to promote personal choice for service users, such as Supporting People and direct payments to service users (introduced under the Community Care Act (Direct Payments) Act of 1996). In 2001–2 the consequent tensions threatened to undermine the development of very sheltered (extra care) and independent living accommodation, so the NCSC regulations were later amended to enable progress to be made.

Theory and practice

The implementation of community care reforms involved a continuing struggle between theory and practice. Often this simply involved inadequate funding or the failure to make sufficient linkages between services. The links between community care and regeneration policies were particularly poor, and the needs of vulnerable people living in neighbourhoods that were being regenerated were frequently neglected (Riseborough and Srbjlanin, 2000; Heywood *et al.*, 2001; Riseborough and Jenkins, 2004).

Other problems arose from policy language and hidden assumptions. As Wistow and Henwood (1991) point out, there was scope for confusion between care *in* and care *by* the community. This became evident when reforms were introduced to save money by increasing the burden placed on relatives, neighbours, friends and the voluntary sector in providing informal help for vulnerable people. While older people often had good informal networks of people providing support and dignity, these were not a substitute for decent services (Phillipson *et al.*, 1999). Another example is provided by the term independence, which was often contrasted with the notion of dependence – that people were robbed of control and choice by institutions and practices that prevented them from helping themselves and exercising self-determination. However no one could be truly independent and there was interdependency in most social relationships. People might choose to be looked after, and this choice might be denied if care models were mainly driven by the promotion of independence (Peace *et al.* 1997).

Supporting People

The Supporting People programme formalized the distinction between housing, care and support. After the 1997 High Court judgement referred to earlier the government introduced a transitional Housing Benefit scheme to pay for housing-related support and housing costs until Supporting People was enacted. After April 2003 housing-related support costs were paid either in the form of grants to providers or directly to leaseholders and owners from locally held Supporting People budgets.

Housing-related support services included accommodation-based support services and non-accommodation-based services that aimed to help people remain independent, but excluded housing management functions. They also included services such as information and advice for people who were housebound. The aims of Supporting People were as follows (DTLR, 2001a):

- To replace unrelated, overlapping revenue streams with a single budget.
- To create a stable funding environment and a system to enable support services to develop.
- To separate housing management from housing-related support costs.
- To achieve a closer fit between the services that people needed and those which were commissioned.
- To develop processes to commission better support services.
- To integrate support with care provision and other strategic initiatives, such as community safety.
- To encourage cost-effective and transparent planning, funding and accountability arrangements.
- To complement a range of other government policy objectives.

The Supporting People 'single pot' replaced six separate funding streams:

- Housing Benefit for tenancy-related support services.
- The portion of income support paid by the Department for Work and Pensions for support services for low-income leaseholders/owner-occupiers in specialist housing.
- Probation accommodation grants (Home Office funding for accommodation and support).
- Government and local authority grants for aspects of the running costs of home improvement agencies.
- The supported housing management grant, which was paid by the Housing Corporation to housing associations for supported housing and services.
- Local authority housing revenue account funding for council tenants, which was used to provide housing-related support.

The policy process

Between 1998 and 2001 the government consulted with stakeholders on the content of the Supporting People policy, including options for charging arrangements and setting standards for services, and on the many drafts of written guidance. This was designed to keep stakeholders informed about the evolving policy and to bring about a shared understanding (DTLR, 2001a).

From late 2000 the government worked closely with local authorities to ensure that the procedures, personnel, administrative systems and information technology would be in place for the implementation of Supporting People in 2003. A national 'team' was set up to lead the process. Local authorities (a nominated district or the county in areas where there was two-tier local government, and unitary authorities elsewhere) received funds to employ staff and develop procedures. Conferences and training events at the national, regional and local levels were funded by the DTLR. Local team leaders had to ensure that their areas made good progress against national milestones.

Implementation structures

Shadow structures were in place in most local authority areas from 2001, comprising five main elements:

- *The Supporting People team*: the officers who administered the local programme, as outlined in their Supporting People strategy.
- *The inclusive forum*: a series of consultative bodies whose members had to include service users, service providers and community and voluntary organizations, and was required to meet at least twice a year.
- *The core strategy development group*: this group proposed the draft strategy to the commissioning body and oversaw the Supporting People team's work. Members included service providers, partner organizations such as health and local councillors.
- *The commissioning body*: this body took key decisions, set priorities and presented the strategy for approval by elected members. It was composed of partner organizations and representatives of the health, probation, local authority housing and social services.
- *The administering authority*: this authority received the Supporting People grant, set up financial procedures and audit arrangement to account for the grant which it administered on behalf of the commissioning body.

There were slight variations among local structures and some differences among local authority areas in respect of their arrangements to involve councillors. The DTLR checked to ensure that local functions and respon-sibilities met the national guidlines and that there was a clear split between consultation and decision making (Anchor Trust and Housing Corporation 2002).

Before full implementation local Supporting People teams were required to:

- Analyze the need for support services.
- Map the existing supply of support services.

- Describe each service.
- Ask existing providers to apply to become accredited providers.
- Devise a service user strategy.
- Set up information technology systems to store data on services.
- Prepare contracts for services that were linked to payment arrangements.
- Work out how much money would be spent locally on support.
- Identify and separate support costs from other costs, such as the cost of housing management.

Organizations that provided housing-related support services were advised on how to separate support costs from housing and other service costs. The task was complicated by the fact that support costs were often hidden in the local authority Housing Revenue Account. Each local Supporting People team had to prepare and submit a shadow Supporting People strategy to the Office of the Deputy Prime Minister by the end of September 2002, containing information on all the above elements and their plans for the future. The teams subsequently submitted one-year strategies for 2003 and 2004, followed by a five-year strategy for 2005–10. Liaison was established between the teams and the Regional Housing Boards, which often involved the establishment of commissioner and provider forums at the regional level.

Some elements of Supporting People developed more slowly than others. For example it took some time for links between Supporting People and community care assessments to be developed and for charging arrangements to be agreed. Cross-authority and regional arrangements took even longer to develop since the services had not been considered on a regional basis prior to the establishment of Regional Housing Boards.

The development and implementation of Supporting People was characterized by more openness and greater stakeholder consultation than was usual in many social welfare policies. A dedicated government website – the Supporting People Knowledge website or SPKweb – was open to all throughout the process and after implementation. Unlike Housing Benefit, Supporting People had minimal formal national requirements and no regulations. However the administering authorities soon became overwhelmed by paperwork. Guidance was provided in *Supporting People: Policy into Practice* (DTLR, 2001a) and *Supporting People. The Administrative Guidance* (DTLR, 2001b).

Concerns and uncertainties

Following the open policy development process, more prescriptive procedures were developed for matters such as monitoring and quality. Audit Commission inspection was introduced in 2003 and Supporting People became subject to the 'payments by results approach'. For example if a commissioning body identified a need for a service in the area but failed to say how it planned to meet that need in its strategy (perhaps over a number of years) there was likely to be a financial penalty.

The overall budget for Supporting People was a constant concern. The initial method of estimating the national pot involved a formula to predict expenditure, which included some factoring in of existing needs for services plus some additional funds. However the estimated size of the national pot grew from an initial £0.75 billion to £1.8 billion. When the policy was implemented in 2003 the government announced a provisional national pot of £1.4 billion: less than the higher estimates but more than the government had originally envisaged (Association of Local Government, 2003). During 2003 there were some adjustments and new funding for pilot programmes and short projects, but some administering authorities received far less than they had expected.

The government had not found an appropriate formula to allocate funds to local areas based on need. Two attempts were made to find a method in 2003, and in 2004 a study was commissioned by the Office of the Deputy Prime Minister, with an announcement expected in mid-2005. In the meantime local administering authorities worked with budgets based partly on past history. While the final distribution formula was awaited a spending review identified savings to be made during the period 2005–08. All local areas were advised on the savings they were expected to make, ranging from nothing to 7.2 per cent. They were given indications of the likely impact on their budgets of these savings and of the new distribution formula.

Commissioners had to adjust the plans in most areas. For example new capital projects for supported housing were unable to proceed without guaranteed revenue funding. In the West Midlands the shortfall in Supporting People funding resulted in a reduction in supported housing's share of the regional housing capital programme which fell from 20 per cent in 2003–4 to 7 per cent in 2004–6, thus preventing some temporary accommodation schemes for the homeless from proceeding (West Midlands Voluntary and Community Housing Network, 2005). This was partly the result of new thinking on the appropriateness of supported housing, rather than of overcommitted budgets. Support that was not linked to special needs housing was now favoured and in most areas there was an increase in the funds for support that was not linked to a particular form of housing.

The first change that service providers experienced was the formalization of service contracts and contracting. This was followed by reviews of their services and audits of service quality. The draft five-year plans required providers to adjust their services or provide new services in line with locally identified needs. Prices were heavily scrutinized and commissioners planned to drive down costs by terminating contracts for services that were inappropriate, too expensive or of poor quality. In a dramatic break with the past, some commissioners introduced tendering arrangements to encourage more flexible services. All of these changes required well-considered strategic responses by providers, but there were variations in their capacity to do this.

Impacts on older people

The Supporting People guidance (DTLR, 2001a) included services that generally (but not exclusively) catered to older people, including:

- Community alarm services.
- Support services to enable people to live independently in housing, rather than in care institutions. For example support by visiting wardens or scheme managers.
- Low-level support services that removed the need for people to leave their homes and go into long-term residential care, and low-level services to enable people to leave hospital or a care facility and return home.
- Part funding for Home Improvement Agency support services (sometimes called 'staying put' or 'care and repair')

The guidance emphasized the importance of linking the Supporting People plans and commissioning strategies to strategic plans for the older population as a whole. Sections of the guidance dealt with improving access to sheltered housing so that older people could make informed decisions and move across tenure and geographical boundaries. Commissioners were encouraged to fund more support services for older BME people and other groups whose needs were not being met.

In general Supporting People promised to provide more older people with support services than in the past, and more appropriate services to meet the needs of an increasingly diverse older population. It was expected that the existing services would be rationalized and that better quality services that would enable people to live independently would be provided. If a need for services was identified and the existing provisions were poor or non-existent, organizations accredited as Supporting People providers would be invited to bid for new service contracts. This process of considering needs and supply was intended to form the basis of formal commissioning and contracting and to be linked to other processes for change. In the case of older people's services, links were made through integrated Best Value reviews, Local Strategic Partnership priorities and integrated strategies. These higher-level strategies were designed to achieve a better match between needs and resources.

Other changes were occurring in expectations and practice. Most sheltered housing providers had realized that the public demand for sheltered housing had changed along with consumers' expectations. This form of housing was less popular with older people than in the past and there was greater sensitivity to location, design and quality. Supporting People was expected to address these changes in demand by developing more flexible and responsive services, such as 'floating' support – that is, not restricted to people who lived in social housing. This was good news for many older people, particularly if Supporting People funds were used to provide a package of services that came closer to their wishes. Older people often required a package that included help with shopping, staying mobile, maintaining social and leisure interests, keeping healthy, and transportation. Supporting People on its own could not fund all these services, but it could contribute to them.

In the lead-up to the implementation of Supporting People in 2003 there was fear that services for older people would worsen because of a shortfall in care and support staff. Confusing definitions, arbitrary divisions between services and gaps in provision were key problems. Moreover some older people who had not paid for services before 2003 would now be charged.

The impact on providers was mixed. There were opportunities to develop new services but Supporting People would not even fund all the current services. Service providers that had operated prior to 2003 received interim contracts to continue to provide services until the first review; all services were to be reviewed within three years. There was apprehension that these reviews would result in major changes. Some providers of traditional services were already aggrieved because Supporting People commissioners were seeking to drive down costs and improve quality, and in some cases to withdraw from existing contracts in favour of new and 'better' services. The pattern of change was similar for other groups but it was particularly marked for services for older people because older people received a larger share of the overall budget in all areas. Funds that had hitherto been used for services in the social housing sector, such as sheltered housing or community alarms, were increasingly used to provide general services for older people regardless of their form of tenure.

Conclusions

This chapter has described policy changes that have affected social care, housing, health and support services and their funding. These changes reflected policy moves to promote care in the community and control welfare budgets.

The use of a whole systems approach – involving joint working and service integration – has been a key objective in social care, health and housing. Observations of the implementation of the Care Standards Act and Supporting People indicate that implementing this approach has been challenging. One of the early criticisms of the Supporting People proposal was that it assumed there was currently more joint working than actually existed. There have been significant developments since then, but there is still a long way to go. Housing organizations continuously struggle to be included in policy making and planning in many areas.

Real changes have occurred in the various professions and institutions that deliver social welfare services in the UK. What used to be called special needs housing is now more likely to be treated as ordinary housing and support and care is tailored to the individual. Decent housing is seen as a fundamental requirement in social care, and health and professional practices have been adjusted accordingly. There is greater attention to the diverse needs and wishes of the population and there is more imagination in the design of housing and in health and care practices. It is at the practice interface that transformations are most likely.

Supporting People promised greater access to support services and more flexible services regardless of tenure. Despite all the problems there is a genuine commitment amongst Supporting People commissioners and their counterparts in health, housing and social care to deliver better and more appropriate support services. However care in the community was introduced with similarly high hopes and they were subsequently scaled down.

Ideals such as independence can be difficult to realize in practice. Supporting People was intended to provide low-level and housing-related support to vulnerable people so that they could continue to live independently. While it has introduced more flexibility into the system to facilitate this, the range of services available is not extensive enough to address all individuals' lives and needs (Herbert and Sawyer, 2005).

The impact of policy change on the roles, styles of working and in some cases survival of organizations has already been dramatic. Contrary to the stable financial outlook promised by Supporting People, financial uncertainty emerged. Providers of support services were faced with the possibility that contracts would not be renewed or payments would be reduced, and they were exposed to tough regulation through quality audits of their services. There was speculation that some smaller providers would cease to operate and that some general needs housing associations would choose to reduce their involvement in supported housing provision. To some extent this happened, but Supporting People commissioners also proposed new services by different providers for groups of people whose needs had not previously been met. These changes can be seen in almost all the Supporting People five-year strategies published in 2005.

Supporting People was intended to complement other policies to develop better care and preventive services for a diverse range of people. However joint commissioning and integrated approaches are only just emerging and need more time to develop (Riseborough and Fletcher, 2004). Supporting People is only one of a number of approaches to deal with instability in supported housing and tackle demands on welfare budgets. A more radical method partly embraced in the Community Care (Direct Payments) Act of 1996 and recent Housing Benefit reforms (see Chapter 8) is to give money for care and accommodation directly to eligible older people so that they can purchase the services they consider they need.

Chapter 12

Social Exclusion, Housing and Neighbourhood Renewal

When the Labour government took office in 1997 it developed a new policy agenda to tackle social exclusion. This agenda focused on neighbourhoods with a high concentration of deprived households and this connected it with questions of housing access and choice, residential mobility and housing and neighbourhood management. The term social exclusion refers to the mechanisms and processes that exclude citizens, focusing 'primarily on relational issues, in other words inadequate social participation, lack of social integration and lack of power' (Room, 1995a, p. 105). It refers to 'the dynamic process of being shut out, fully or partially, from any of the social, economic, political and cultural systems which determine the integration of a person in society' (A. Walker, 1997, p. 8). It is distinguished from poverty in that it 'goes beyond economic and social aspects of poverty and embraces the political aspects such as political rights and citizenship which outline a relationship between individuals and the State as well as between the society and the individual' (Rodgers *et al.*, 1995, pp. 6–7).

Four key 'symptoms' of social exclusion were identified at that time:

- *Concentration*: social deprivation and poverty were concentrated in certain parts of cities and disadvantaged groups in these areas were cut off from the mainstream, contributing to social exclusion.
- *Persistence*: social exclusion was experienced when there was long-term exposure to poverty and social deprivation.
- *Compounded (by interlocking processes)*: the persistence of social exclusion was reinforced by interlocking processes that reinforced one another, for example through the 'poverty trap' or the failure of providers to coordinate their services (for example social services and housing).
- *Resistance*: traditional policy solutions were not effective because the welfare system – designed according to different assumptions about household formation and the role of citizens – was not flexible enough to respond adequately (Room, 1995b).

Commentators who criticized the concept of social exclusion claimed that it had no more potential to explain divisions in society than existing concepts such as marginalization, polarization or poverty. They suggested that the concept was an ill-defined political fudge arising from the inability to agree a clear definition of poverty. The term social exclusion could, in this view, satisfy the political ambitions of those who appeared to be concerned with poverty reduction but had avoided past debates about poverty thresholds (Townsend, 1979).

Nevertheless the concept of social exclusion did advance understanding by emphasizing processes and dynamics rather than measuring the number of households that fell below some income or consumption standard at a particular time. This raised questions about the effectiveness of state services. The term 'poverty trap' is not new but it illustrates the way in which various social benefits are inadequately coordinated with tax regulations, and the consequences of this for individuals can be damaging. The failure to coordinate policy is an important element in understanding the process of social exclusion. Often policies have not been sensitive to the effects on groups such as lone parents, rough sleepers or BME groups. This chapter focuses on some of the connections between housing and social exclusion, including the direct and indirect effects of housing on social exclusion, housing tenure and social exclusion, and policy responses to social exclusion.

Social exclusion and housing

Most discussions of social exclusion start with reference to where people live – that is if they have a home – and the spatial concentration of disadvantage. Housing processes are central to any discussion of these issues, and neighbourhood effects are important factors in the persistence of social exclusion over time and how local services respond to need.

Housing can make both direct and indirect contributions to poverty and social exclusion (Table 12.1). Direct contributions include insufficient provision of shelter (homelessness and rooflessness), inadequate housing (poor physical conditions and overcrowding) and unresponsive housing policy and practices. Indirect contributions arise when housing circumstances increase the risk of social exclusion, for example because of the location of housing or the relationship with local environments and services.

Substandard housing has a direct impact on health, especially amongst vulnerable groups such as older people, children, disabled people and pregnant women. Dwelling conditions have improved over the past 30 years – around 200 000 homes were in an unsatisfactory condition in 1991 compared with three million in 1971 (Leather and Morrison, 1997). Dwellings that lack a bath or shower account for around 1 per cent of all properties in England and Wales (HMSO, 1992). Damp housing has the most far-reaching implications for health and is linked to high rates of asthma and respiratory illness, especially among children – dampness is present in one in 15 properties

Table 12.1   *Direct and indirect impacts of housing on social exclusion*

	Direct	*Indirect*
Compound	Homelessness directly affects access to services and jobs. Homelessness, overcrowding and temporary housing can disrupt education and affect health	Exclusion is compounded when there is fuel poverty and poor housing conditions. Access to jobs and services is affected when housing is located in peripheral or remote areas and when services are under pressure because of lack of coordination or effective joint working
Persistent	The impact of poor housing conditions and overcrowding is enhanced by duration and failure to remed the situation	Health and long-term unemployment, low incomes and institutional discrimination in the market contribute to lack of choice and inability to move
Resistant	Fragmentation of public policy and shortcomings in housing management can result in a slow response. Property- or estate-based actions may be insufficient to tackle exclusion. The operation of the Housing Benefit system can compound money problems	Estate-based initiatives can move problems around and insulate areas in the short term, but may be ineffective in the long term. This may reflect inadequate and uncoordinated investment and regeneration strategies
Concentrated		Residualization of council housing and low demand in parts of the market result in geographical concentrations of poor households with little choice. This increases the risk of local services being poor and under pressure. Urban 'white flight', changes in aspirations and the broadening of housing choices may further increase polarization and the pressure on local services

Source: Adapted from Room (1995a).

(7 per cent) (Smith, 1989b). In 1993, 15.4 per cent of the pre-1919 stock in England was unfit and 39 per cent was in a state of disrepair; for stock built after 1963 the figures were 2.2 per cent and 4.6 per cent respectively (Leather and Morrison, 1997). Terraced houses and flats accounted for 54 per cent of all unfit dwellings in 1993 (ibid.)

Overcrowding is correlated with increased vulnerability to airborne infections, respiratory diseases and diarrhoea. There are also strong effects on mental health, stress-induced morbidity and educational attainment (Byrne and Keithley, 1993; Kellett, 1993). Overcrowding is more likely to be found in inner city areas, where residents are more likely to be unemployed or from BME groups (Ineichen, 1993; Howes and Mullins, 1999). Between 1971 and 1990 the percentage of overcrowded households declined from 9 per cent to 3 per cent (HMSO, 1992).

Homelessness and temporary accommodation affect the health and development of adults and children. People who suffer prolonged periods of homelessness or rooflessness face severe disruption of education, work and health (Bines, 1994; Connelly and Crown, 1994). In the 1990s the government sought to reduce the incidence of rough sleeping to an absolute minimum through the Rough Sleepers Initiative, which was launched in London in 1990 and subsequently extended to other major cities. It continued under the Labour government following a review by the Social Exclusion Unit (1998c). This programme was successful in reducing the number of people sleeping on the streets and in providing access to supported housing and health and support services, but it failed to address the wider problems of single homelessness and insecure housing (Fitzpatrick *et al.*, 2000).

Homelessness continued to rise in the 1990s. The Homelessness Act of 2002 amended the statutory duties of local authorities (see Chapter 4) and promoted joined-up working at the local level through the requirement for interagency homelessness strategies. In some places this led to the involvement of health, social care, criminal justice and employment agencies in preventing homelessness and providing support (Office of the Deputy Prime Minister, 2004.) There were also more joined-up national policies. For example the Department of Health and the Homelessness Directorate produced joint guidance to improve health care for families in temporary accommodation, provide homeless people with better access to primary health care, mental health services and substance misuse treatment, and prevent homelessness through targeted health support (Department of Health and Office of the Deputy Prime Minister, 2004).

The links between homelessness and poor health are as follows:

- Difficulty with access to primary care and treatment (for example drug rehabilitation), increased mental, physical and obstetric ill-health, and behavioural problems amongst children.

- Temporary housing raises social costs by disrupting social networks; overcrowding and unsafe housing result in a higher risk of accidents; poor nutrition is associated with poor amenities and child development problems.
- A vicious circle is associated with 'no home, no job', so homeless people should be prime targets for employment access training; insecure and low-wage employment can also limit access to good-quality secure housing.

Older people are more likely than others to be living in unfit housing (Leather and Morrison, 1997), which makes them vulnerable to extreme changes in weather. For example the number of domestic accidents increases in winter due to the effect that cold weather can have on older people's cerebral functioning (Wilkinson, 1999). Fuel poverty exacerbates this risk: the poorest 30 per cent of households spend twice as much of their income on heating unfit housing than the remaining 70 per cent (Boardman, 1991). It is notable that older people comprise 15 per cent of the general population but 40 per cent of the poorest decile (HMSO, 1992).

A key consideration when discussing social exclusion is whether exposure to disadvantage is short term or sustained. Long-term or repeated periodic exposure to damp or overcrowded conditions is likely to have a greater impact on life chances than a single short exposure. Counting numbers at a particular time treats each case the same irrespective of duration. For example a reduction of the accounting period from 12 months to one month increases the poverty rate by almost a quarter (Walker, 1995). Looking at life-time earnings rather than relying on cross-sectional analysis of earnings reduces the polarization effect of earnings and income structures. Therefore extending the accounting period reduces the number found to be in poverty, but brings us closer to identifying those who are most affected by social exclusion. This perspective can be applied to the analysis of housing and its interaction with other policy areas. Students living in poor-quality housing, for example, are not normally considered to be disadvantaged by this because the situation is temporary, they have other services and facilities to draw on and they will probably have the opportunity to move on to better accommodation.

The type of household suffering housing deprivation has changed in recent years, with young single-person households accounting for a larger share of multiple housing deprivation than in the past. Between 1981 and 1991 the proportion of single-person households living in substandard multiple housing (lacking amenities and overcrowded) doubled from 18 per cent to 35 per cent of all such households, whereas the share of couples with children fell from 46 per cent to 27 per cent (Dale *et al.*, 1996). Some sections of the housing market have very high turnover rates and it is likely that many of those in the worst housing move to similar housing elsewhere, with no reduction in long-term housing deprivation. Increased turnover (known as churning) in the same part of the market (especially within and between the social rented sector and the lower end of the private rented sector) may be a symptom of exclusion rather than signifying opportunities to move away from housing deprivation. Analysis of social exclusion therefore requires an understanding of the functioning of sections of the housing market, household formation, housing pathways an individual's (pattern of movement from home to home in their 'housing career') and the length of time that relative housing deprivation is experienced.

Housing situations that evidently have direct consequences for health are much less common than in the past. However this does not mean that they are any less important for those who are exposed to them, and it may mean that they are being neglected. The social exclusion agenda highlights the indirect effects of housing and complex interactions between housing and other services. This has implications for policies to address the role of housing in social exclusion and for joined-up health and housing policies.

Housing tenure and social exclusion

Some of the early statements by ministers about social exclusion suggested an assumption that the problem of social exclusion was synonymous with large council estates. The evidence suggests a more complex situation. As the housing tenure structure has changed, so has the social composition of people in different tenures. With the growth of home ownership and the contraction of social renting there has been a growing concentration of economically inactive, less skilled, unemployed and low-income people in social housing. The distribution of economic activity and socioeconomic groups by tenure is shown in Table 12.2.

Whilst there was already a distinct difference between the social composition of home owners and tenants in the social rented sector in 1981, this had greatly intensified by 1996. In 1981, 42 per cent of council tenants and 51 per cent of housing association tenants were economically inactive, compared with 3 per cent of the owners of mortgaged homes and 54 per cent of outright home owners (most of whom were retired) and 32 per cent of all household heads. By 1996 the proportion of economically inactive household heads in all tenures had risen to 41 per cent, and the proportion of economically inactive household heads who were outright owners or had mortgages had risen to 70 per cent and 12 per cent respectively. Meanwhile the proportion of economically inactive social renters had risen to 63 per cent.

Economic inactivity had increased across the board, but particularly in the council sector. In 1996, 32 per cent of home owners were in the top

Table 12.2 *Socioeconomic group and economic activity by housing tenure of head of household*

	Owner occupiers outright ownership	Mortgaged	Social housing local authority	Housing association	All
1981					
Professional	2	8	0	0	3
Employer or manager	12	24	3	3	11
Intermediate non-manual	5	14	3	7	7
Junior non-manual	5	9	4	6	6
Skilled manual and own account non-professional	15	33	27	16	25
Semiskilled manual and personal services	7	8	16	11	11
Unskilled manual	2	1	6	5	3
Economically inactive household heads	54	3	42	51	32
1996					
Professional	1	8	0	0	4
Employer or manager	6	25	2	5	14
Intermediate non-manual	3	12	2	4	7
Junior non-manual	3	8	5	4	6
Skilled manual and own account non-professional	11	25	13	12	18
Semiskilled manual and personal services	4	9	11	11	8
Unskilled manual	1	2	4	4	2
Economically inactive household heads	70	12	63	62	41

Source: General Household Survey (1981, 1998).

three socioeconomic categories, compared with only 5 per cent of tenants in the social rented sector. Conversely just 8 per cent of home owners were in the semiskilled and unskilled categories but in the social rented sector the proportion was almost double (15 per cent).

Whilst this increasing concentration of economically inactive, less-skilled and unemployed people in social housing is striking, home ownership was not immune from these trends. The broader base of home ownership and the differentiation of the private sector resulted in a more fragmented pattern of exclusion in UK cities. Research on housing tenure and social exclusion shows that the distribution of deprivation by tenure varied considerably by region (Lee and Murie, 1997). Hence the way in which social exclusion was concentrated, persisted and compounded depended on local circumstances.

Table 12.3 shows regional differences in the relationship between race, deprivation and tenure. According to the national census, Birmingham, Bradford and Liverpool non-white households in a number of deprived categories were less likely than the population as a whole to be living in council housing. In Bradford 9.5 per cent of non-white households and 35.2 per cent of white households without a car lived in council housing. In Tower Hamlets the figures were 79.8 per cent and 66.4 per cent respectively. It was only in Tower Hamlets that council housing catered for the majority of non-white households in deprived categories. In Bradford less than 10 per cent of deprived non-white households were in council housing, in Liverpool the proportion was 30.3 per cent and in Birmingham it was 33.7 per cent.

This analysis showed that policies to target social deprivation and income inequality needed to be more sensitive to difference. The extent to which poorer households were found in social rented housing varied considerably between ethnic groups and areas. And policy was not

Table 12.3   *Percentage of all white and non-white deprived households living in council housing, 1991*

Deprivation indicator	Percentage of each category living in council housing			
	Tower Hamlets	*Birmingham*	*Liverpool*	*Bradford*
Household has no car				
Non-white	79.8	33.7	30.3	9.5
White	66.4	45.7	42.3	35.2
Household has no wage earner				
Non-white	83.9	35.8	23.0	7.8
White	70.0	41.2	41.4	30.6
Long-term illness in household				
Non-white	84.7	22.0	18.2	8.7
White	71.0	36.8	39.3	28.1
Household head unemployed				
Non-white	82.1	29.9	27.8	9.6
White	67.1	47.4	43.1	38.4

Sources: Population Census (1991). Reproduced from table 12.3 in Lee and Murie (1997) (*Poverty, Housing Tenure and Social Exclusion*) by kind permission of The Policy Press.

attuned to different experiences of BME communities, as Harrison (1995, p. 6) puts it, 'in the UK social policy interventions have offered less than expected to minority ethnic communities'.

New Labour's responses to social exclusion

Social exclusion was a key element of the political agenda during the 1997 election campaign, and when the Labour government took office its approach marked a significant departure from that of the previous Conservative administration. There was a commitment to tackle the traditional Labour concern about poverty and to address social exclusion.

The importance of social inclusion to New Labour was signalled by the venue of Tony Blair's first public speech as prime minister: outside the Aylesbury Estate in the London Borough of Southwark. There he stated that 'for 18 years, the poorest people in our country have been forgotten by government. They have been left out of growing prosperity, told that they were not needed, ignored by the Government except for the purpose of blaming them. I want that to change. There will be no forgotten people in the Britain I want to build' (Social Exclusion Unit, 1998a).

It was clear that the government's policy on social exclusion would contain elements that related directly to the frameworks of exclusion discussed earlier. The venue of the speech and its emphasis on 'forgotten people' implied that social exclusion was restricted to a poor underclass concentrated in the poorest council housing estates. The establishment of the Social Exclusion Unit (SEU) confirmed this viewpoint as it initially focused on the problems of the 'worst estates' (in addition to school truancy, homelessness and teenage pregnancy).

A twin track approach was developing across Whitehall. The SEU – with support from ministerial departments located in the Cabinet Office – was charged with 'joining up' government policy on social exclusion. Meanwhile the Department of Education and Employment was developing the 'new deal' programme to bring long-term unemployed people back into the labour market. Initially the programme was targeted at young people (under 25) who had been unemployed for six months or more (New Deal for Young People, NDYP). Later the programme was extended to include over 25s, older people (50 plus), the disabled and partners of people claiming the job seekers' allowance. Between April 1998 and January 2002, 753 600 young men and women participated in the NDYP. The National Institute of Economic and Social Research estimated that the long-term youth unemployment rate was halved to 45 000 during the period covered, with a net gain to the national economy of £500 million (Department for Work and Pensions, 2002b). The principle of the new deal, therefore, was to reduce government expenditure by offering the right to employment and imposing a duty on unemployed people to take up that right through the new deal.

Existing policy vehicles on regeneration were adapted to fit the social inclusion agenda. Criteria for Single Regeneration Budget (SRB) funding were revised to give priority to projects from the most deprived areas according to an Index of Local Deprivation (ILD)(DETR, 1998b). This was in contrast to the competitive bidding process that had existed under the conservatives. In the most deprived local authority areas new spatial policies were introduced to tackle problems associated with health and education, and programmes were launched to join up existing strategies in the longer term:

- The New Deal for Communities initially involved 17 pathfinder partnerships (announced in the autumn of 1998), followed by a further 22 partnerships in 1999. Over £1.9 billion was committed to 39 partnerships in 38 local authority districts in England.
- Eleven Health Action Zones were designated in England in April 1998, followed by a further 15 in April 1999. The zones covered areas of deprivation and poor health and the aim was to tackle health inequalities and modernize services through local innovation.
- Seventy-three Education Action Zones were set up between September 1998 and January 1999 to work with local partners (schools, parents, the community, businesses and local authorities) to find innovative solutions to their problems.

These initiatives varied in the extent to which housing was given explicit attention: some were highly tenure specific, others paid relatively little attention to the role of housing. However, it was clear that the Labour government it intended to tackle exclusion at the neighbourhood level through intensive management of pockets of poverty rather than by addressing market differentiation and urban social stratification.

Perhaps the most prominent early housing-based approach was the SEU's 'worst estates' agenda. 'Worst estates' referred to 1370 council estates in England that were deemed to have the worst concentrations of deprivation (Mandelson, 1997). The research underpinning the identification of these estates had been commissioned by the previous Conservative government, overseen by the Department of the Environment and published in January 1997. The official government Index of Local Conditions (ILC) had been used to identify the worst estates and the exercise had involved three stages:

- Identifying the most deprived (5 per cent) of enumeration districts (EDs) in England according to the ranking of the 121 933 EDs on the index.
- Identifying those in which more than half of households were in council housing and eliminating those with less than 50 per cent council housing.
- Combining EDs with similar tenure characteristics, so that EDs that were adjacent to 'non-deprived' council housing EDs formed a single estate.

The resulting 'worst estates' were areas of deprivation in which the majority of tenants lived in council housing. This approach to measuring deprivation and linking it to housing had a number of weaknesses. For example the choice of indicator (the index of local conditions) tended to skew the areas identified towards council estates in London, which were often relatively homogeneous but small-scale concentrations of households with children. Also, assumptions were made about the relationship between housing tenure and deprivation. A false dichotomy was created between excluded council housing tenants (non-citizens) and the included citizens living in other tenures. These criticisms (see Lee, 1998) were addressed by means of a revised index (DETR, 1998b) but it was too late for this to be incorporated into the mapping of the worst estates.

In 1999 the SEU commissioned 18 policy action teams to report on a variety of themes, one of which was 'unpopular housing' and the previous thinking on worst estates was subsumed under a broader framework for understanding the process and dynamics of social exclusion.

A different approach was taken to targeting areas for the New Deal for Communities programme. Few guidelines were laid down by the DETR to local authorities on how to select pathfinder neighbourhoods, apart from restricting the size of neighbourhoods to approximately 4000 households requiring evidence that viable partnerships could be developed with local communities. This was a significant departure from the thinking that had informed the identification of the worst estates.

The two pathfinder neighbourhoods chosen in Birmingham were a peripheral council housing estate (Pool Farm) and an inner city, mixed tenure neighbourhood with a large BME population (Aston). In the adjacent authority of Sandwell an inner city neighbourhood with mixed tenure and a significantly high proportion of BME households was chosen (Greets Green). The majority of neighbourhoods selected pathfinder outside London were of mixed tenure – but single tenure council housing estates were selected in Hull and Norwich. In Beswick (East Manchester) new house building in the area chosen had been abandoned and the new deal strategy was closely linked to the economic development potential of the area.

While all the pathfinder neighbourhoods had severe deprivation problems, their characteristics differed and the solutions needed also differed. The abandonment of new building in Beswick suggested that the physical condition of housing stock was not always a predictor of the popularity of an area (Lowe *et al.*, 1998; Murie *et al.*, 1998) and that similarly deprived areas differed in their degree of popularity and social cohesion (Lee, 1998). This implied that deprivation did not necessarily result in social exclusion, with some deprived areas being popular and well-functioning and others exhibiting signs of unpopularity, high turnover, abandonment and low social cohesion. Thus the focus for investment decisions shifted to the long-term viability of neighbourhoods. This required greater attention to low and changing demand for housing and the operation of markets and aspirations rather than the traditional 'pockets of poverty' approach.

The Social Exclusion's Unit (1998) report drew attention to the complexity of regeneration over the preceding two decades and the failure to coordinate with mainstream public expenditure to tackle poverty and social exclusion. It argued that mainstream funds needed to be used more effectively since mainstream spending represented a huge proportion of total incomes in most poor neighbourhoods (Bramley *et al.*, 1998). There was a need to coordinate the large number of overlapping initiatives (for example the Inner City Task Force, Estate Action, City Challenge, Estates Renewal Challenge Fund, Capital Challenge and the Single Regeneration Budget) with differing rules and administrative boundaries. It was considered that physical regeneration had been elevated above social regeneration in that there had been too little investment in social and human capital and community commitment had not been harnessed effectively. There was a need to join up the strategies in neighbouring areas and guard against the displacement of problems. Finally, it was necessary to build better links between deprived neighbourhoods and areas of employment, leisure and facilities.

This thinking was highly influential, not least in steering the 18 Policy Action Teams, which between 1999 and 2001 reported on such matters as neighbourhood management, local services and unpopular housing. The resulting action plan (Social Exclusion Unit, 2001) set out the government's proposed measures for narrowing the gap between deprived neighbourhoods and other areas:

- The strategy was to be over seen at the national level by the Neighbourhood Renewal Unit (NRU, part of the Office of the Deputy Prime Minister)
- Neighbourhood renewal teams would be set up in the nine government offices to provide a direct channel of communication from neighbourhood/community groups to the NRU.
- Local communities would be put at the centre of regeneration and would have a seat on Local Strategic Partnerships (LSPs), which would coordinate the Neighbourhood Renewal Fund with existing public expenditure on behalf of the NRU.
- A community empowerment fund would be established to create community empowerment networks that would communicate directly with the NRU.
- To facilitate the monitoring of this process and to chart progress, 'floor targets' (or public service agreements) for employment, crime, education, health, housing and the environment would be established to enable comparisons over time.
- Neighbourhood management would help bridge the gap between the country's most deprived neighbourhoods and the average neighbourhood, and improve deprived neighbourhoods in terms of reduced long-term unemployment and crime, and better health and qualifications.

This strategy constituted a huge change in the pace and scale of the government's attack on deprivation, with an emphasis on mainstreaming. The strategy put communities at the heart of regeneration by combining mainstream expenditure with neighbourhood renewal funding, and elevated the role of communities by including them in local strategic partnerships and community empowerment networks. More fundamentally, it was acknowledged that previous regeneration policies had failed because they had been too limited in scale or focused too narrowly on the physical aspects of regeneration. When policies had been spatially targeted there had generally been insufficient understanding of the causes of poverty at the area level, leading to the displacement of problems to other areas.

Key changes of approach

During this period there was a switch of emphasis from the worst estates and the failure of housing management to a more comprehensive neighbourhood and housing market agenda. The policy implication was that it was necessary to manage urban systems and markets rather than just smaller areas. The debate moved on from focusing on outcomes at the council estate level to understanding, monitoring and designing policies to modify cross-tenure and market-related effects. This change in thinking was in recognition of the new patterns of differentiation and the fragmentation of housing tenure (see Chapters 5 and 6). The importance attached to tenure in explanations of social exclusion and social cohesion was reduced, despite the concentration of lower-income groups in the council sector. Debates on low and changing demand and sustainable housing further modified these views. The SEU also accepted the argument that 'too much emphasis was placed on physical regeneration and not enough on communities themselves' (Neighbourhood Renewal Unit, 2002, p. 3). These sentiments justified limiting the focus on housing and combining neighbourhood management with resident involvement to bring about sustainable and stable neighbourhoods. However the evidence on low and changing demand subsequently provoked questions about the capacity of communities to be at the centre of regeneration and to make a significant impact on managing neighbourhoods. In Liverpool, for example, a significant part of the city was subject to high turnover and churning, abandonment and low demand. Those left behind might be loyal to the area, but they alone could not provide the basis for the long-term regeneration of the neighbourhood.

Low demand also contributed to the bifurcation of housing policy along north–south lines. In parts of the North and Midlands there was evidence of market blight and an exponential increase of problems associated with high turnover and abandonment. Slowly there was recognition that regeneration and renewal policies that focused on small areas and were not integrated into wider regeneration strategies were likely to fail.

The changing demand for housing

In the 1990s it became apparent that there were higher turnover rates and a growing number of empty properties available for letting. Concern about this first emerged in Scotland, when local authorities lost housing subsidy where vacancy levels were excessive. The justification for this was that high vacancy rates were seen to reflect management failures and inefficiencies. Research evidence suggested a different picture that was related to the impact of declining demand in areas severely affected by economic and demographic changes. These same issues subsequently emerged elsewhere following an examination of trend in the social rented sector, especially in the North of England. Turnover and vacancies increased considerably in the 1990s in both the housing association sector and council housing (Lowe *et al.*, 1998; Murie *et al.*, 1998).

Subsequent analyses of what was happening in these parts of the market confirmed the increase in turnover and vacancies and suggested that it was not simply a short-term blip but reflected a significant and sustained change in the overall housing markets at the national, regional, subregional, local and neighbourhood levels.

In England the SEU policy action team set up to investigate unpopular housing concluded that the problem of low demand had different causes in different areas (DETR, 2000a). Low demand and unpopular housing were found to occur in social housing where:

- There was a small or non-existent waiting list.
- Tenancy offers were frequently refused.
- A large number of empty properties were available to let.
- There was a high tenancy turnover.

In the private sector demand was low where:

- There were particularly low and/or falling property values.
- There was a large number of empty properties.
- There was a high tenancy turnover.
- There were many long-term empty or abandoned properties.
- There was a visibly large number of properties for sale or let.

Other accounts suggested that not all of these factors indicated low demand, but rather that the pattern of demand had changed. Changing demand included situations where higher turnover reflected a change in what tenants were seeking (e.g. shorter term housing), or where they were using social rented housing as a transitional or temporary option before moving on to other housing. This reflected a change in expectations and aspirations. Some of the explanatory factors in changing demand were national and some were local. Some were long-established and some were much more immediate. The longer-term factors included demographic change, economic change, changes in housing markets, residualization, changing aspirations, obsolescence, neighbourhood decline, poverty and affluence. The starting point for many analyses of changing demand was the neighbourhood, as problems were often most apparent at the estate or neighbourhood level. However the underlying causes often lay outside the neighbourhood at the national, regional or subregional level.

Sustainable communities

A new phase in area based housing policy was heralded by the Sustainable Communities Plan (Office of the Deputy Prime Minister, 2003). While earlier Conservative governments had talked about sustainable home ownership and the term sustainability had already entered the policy vocabulary, the key dimensions of the 2003 policy were relatively new and combined proposals to deal with the housing shortage and affordability problems in the South-East of England with proposals for Housing Market Renewal Areas HMRAs in parts of the Midlands and the North.

In this section we present the proposal for HMRAs as an example of evidence-based policy making, which is relatively unusual in the housing field. The proposal was in part triggered by evidence that challenged long-held assumptions. For a long time changes in the housing market in the Midlands and the North of England were not recognized as fundamental. The growing number of empty properties and the higher turnover and abandonment rates were interpreted either as reflecting poor housing management or as purely local problems. The view of the government was that there was no need for new programmes since policies were already in place to address these problems. For example research by the policy action team established by the Social Exclusion Unit (DETR, 2000a) labelled the problem as one of low demand or unpopular housing. The methodology used for the research consisted of surveys of local authorities that were thought to have an understanding of the issues, household interviews and a series of local case studies. There was no market-based analysis with a subregional or regional element and the focus was principally on the council housing sector. The Social Exclusion Unit made no mention of housing market renewal and generally underplayed the significance of housing.

Around that time other reports emphasized the links between deprivation and housing on a much larger scale for all types of tenure (see for example

Lee and Murie, 1997; Keenan *et al.*, 1999; Cole *et al.*, 1999; Holmans and Simpson, 1999). The government's index of local deprivation was seen to be more applicable to problems in council estates than to multitenure areas, whereas the problems lay with the operation of regional and subregional housing markets rather than with housing management failures by local authorities. Therefore concern began to be expressed about the extent to which the government had framed the issues as primarily associated with large council estates.

New research began to provide the evidence upon which the HMRAs would be based. This research was commissioned by consortia of local authorities and housing associations in the Midlands and the North as they felt that the profound changes affecting their operations were not being given due attention. Then a study carried out for the Housing Corporation suggested that the rising vacancy levels and high turnover in parts of the Midlands and the North were due to changing demand in response to a variety of factors that were severely affecting particular subregions (Murie *et al.*, 1998). Forty-six organizations in the North-West then commissioned the Centre for Urban and Regional Studies (CURS) to research the nature of changing demand and to make recommendations for regeneration (Nevin *et al.*, 2001). There was a consistent dialogue between the CURS research team and these organizations. The methodology included an examination of local authority and other data, a spatial analysis to identify neighbourhoods at risk, social survey data obtained from interviews with households living in new dwellings and a linked study of vacancies, and interviews with households in older, poor neighbourhoods where there was a reduction in demand for private sector accommodation.

The results revealed the scale of the problem in the North-West and its cross-tenure cross-boundary dimensions. It was argued that the latter features meant that existing policy vehicles were not capable of dealing with the problem. The number of areas that were at risk because of changing demand, taken together with areas where the market was already dysfunctional, presented a major challenge for policy. Moreover the resources available to local authorities from their housing investment funds the Housing Corporation and other sources, including the private sector, would be insufficient to deal with so large a problem.

This stream of research and consistent lobbying by local authorities and housing associations brought home to the government the need for a new approach. Focusing resources on small areas was no longer sufficient to deal with the problems emerging in older neighbourhoods in major urban areas or in council estates on the fringes. In November 2001, 120 housing agencies in the North and the Midlands pressed for stronger measures to be taken. In a submission to the government's comprehensive spending review they suggested that a housing market renewal fund be set up to improve areas with populations of over 120 000 that showed signs of market failure (Cole and Nevin, 2004). This Fund, it was argued, should be used to transform areas rather than maintain neighbourhoods that did not have a sustainable future.

In 2003 nine housing market renewal areas were designated: Birmingham and Sandwell, East Lancashire, Humberside, Manchester and Salford, Merseyside, Newcastle and Gateshead, North Staffordshire, Oldham and Rochdale, and South Yorkshire. In total these areas contained over 800 000 properties and the Office of the Deputy Prime Minister allocated £500 million to them over the next three years.

Why was this decision taken? There is strong evidence that the relevant governmental players were persuaded that they had to adopt a different policy approach. Certainly the solution proposed bore a direct relation to the recommendations that emerged from the research. Because this research had not been commissioned by the government it was more likely to challenge the latter's predilections than to legitimate its convictions.

However it would be naive to place the credit purely upon the research alone. Effective lobbying by the National Housing Federation and others and their support by local MPs and other people with the ability to persuade ministers were also crucial. Another important factor was the coincidence of these proposals and pressure on the government to address the housing affordability and shortage problems in the South-East. If it responded only to the problems in the South-East there would be a major risk that MPs and local authorities in other parts of the country would complain that their needs were being ignored and their resources creamed off. By packaging the two issues of affordability and changing demand into the communities plan (Office of the Deputy Prime Minister, 2003a) the government was able to give the impression of a coherent national approach to sustainable communities throughout England and to balance the political accounts. Thus even when evidence was the dominating factor the politics of policy making would not go away.

In summary, evidence-based policy making seems most likely to work when the evidence is strongly supported by influential organizations and its emergence coincides with political and policy developments. Hence timing may be as important as the quality of evidence in explaining why major policy changes occur.

Conclusion

It can be argued that New Labour's early policy approach to social exclusion underestimated the role of housing and mistakenly conceptualized housing mainly in terms of management of the worst estates. Over time its approach was refined to take on board the lessons of early interventions and research evidence. This led to a period of debate in which the part played by housing in sustaining neighbourhoods and maintaining their cohesion was central.

Neighbourhood management, however, will fall into 'management by tenure' in the absence of a framework for analysis that is less dependent on divisions between tenures and takes account of broader influences on the spatial patterns of social division. The policy implications arising from tenure change, housing market change and differentiated and fragmented spatial patterns are different from those in the past. It is essential for policy makers to recognize the role of housing in social exclusion, to avoid seeing neighbourhood management as synonymous with housing management, and to recognize the importance of subregional, regional and national dimensions of social exclusion.

The ways in which social exclusion is defined have an obvious impact on how housing is perceived as contributing to poverty. If social exclusion is defined as exclusion from work, housing's role will be seen as secondary to that of supply and demand employment issues such as business practices, skills and training. If housing is placed in a more central position it can be viewed as contributing to the experience of poverty, both directly for example where overcrowding and poor housing conditions result in poor health, and indirectly where sociotenurial polarization and the residualization of council housing, result in inequalities between neighborhood. The importance of tenure as an explanatory housing variable is a prominent feature of accounts of social exclusion in the UK and is partly driven by the significant size and share of housing that is not provided through the market. However such accounts reduce the significance of the part played by housing in the experience and distribution of social exclusion. Moreover their restrictive view means that the excluded are portrayed as residents of the worst estates in manageable pockets of deprivation.

Recent approaches to problems in regional and subregional housing markets have led to new forms of intervention in which housing policies such as selective clearance and the strategic construction of new types and sizes of home are much more prominent. The introduction of the nine housing market pathfinder areas (HMRAs), as described in this chapter, is a fascinating case of policy formulation in which evidence played an unusually significant part but policy networking, lobbying and political calculation remained central. An even more fascinating account remains to be written of the implementation of the HMRAs, in which the lessons learnt from the social inclusion debates in respect of joined-up policy and the interaction between housing, economic development, civil engagement and public service investment will surely play a continued role. Success will be measured not just in terms of turning around failing markets but also in securing the inclusion of groups such as asylum seekers, refugees and homeless people who were strongly represented in such areas before turnaround.

Chapter 13

Private Sector Housing Renewal

Policies on the renewal of private housing have long varied among the constituent parts of the UK. In Scotland, Wales and Northern Ireland public funding per private dwelling is higher than in England (Leather and Revell, 2000). This became marked after 2002, when England moved further away from a public investment model for private housing renewal. Scotland had distinctive policies and higher expenditure, partly because poor conditions were concentrated in the country's large number of tenement houses, which were less common elsewhere in the UK. Northern Ireland had a significantly different approach before 1980, but since then legislation has generally followed that of England, with a time lag to allow some adaptation to local circumstances. Prior to devolution the policies of England and Wales were similar, but have since diverged.

In England, between 1969 and 2002 a series of Housing Acts set out a closely circumscribed framework of interventions that local authorities were empowered, or in some cases obliged, to undertake. In 2002, however, this framework was dismantled and local authorities were expected to develop their own strategies and policy instruments to suit local circumstances. To some extent this made sense since there were marked differences in private housing conditions and in factors such as house prices, which influenced the level of investment in housing. However the principal driver of the change was public expenditure on private sector renewal, which had been in decline since the early 1990s. The mismatch between powers and resources reached crisis point between 1990 and 1996, when for the first time a number of forms of grant aid were made available as of right. The government resolved this mismatch by abolishing the entitlements and making individual local authorities responsible for the task of balancing needs and resources, and by persuading individual property owners to invest more of their own resources in addresing poor housing conditions.

Wales and Northern Ireland took a similar but less radical approach. Resources for private sector renewal declined less steeply there, and local authorities and the Northern Ireland Housing Executive were able to modify or adapt their existing mechanisms more easily, with less emphasis on generating private investment. In Scotland policy remained more or less unchanged, but a series of inconclusive reviews suggested that change was likely in the future.

At the same time as the new arrangements were being introduced in England and Wales, broader developments in the housing market posed a major challenge to policy. From the late 1990s there was growing awareness that in some of the older private housing areas renovation was failing to generate demand, house prices were static or even falling, vacancy rates were increasing and housing associations that had acquired properties were having difficulty letting them. The implications for private sector renewal were enormous. According to Bramley *et al.* (2000), 375 000 privately owned dwellings were affected by low demand. In low-demand areas even private properties in good condition, including some that had recently been renovated with grant aid, were affected.

This followed the growth of private renting after the decontrol of rents and the weakening of security of tenure in 1988 (see Chapter 6). However the private rented sector had poorer quality housing than any other housing sector and this situation has continued (Office of the Deputy Prime Minister, 2003c). The expansion of private renting prompted the construction of some purpose built new dwellings, but it also resulted in older dwellings being transferred from home ownership. In areas of low or changing demand, speculative purchase by private landlords who were unwilling to invest in improving their properties or manage them adequately accelerated the market depression. Local authorities found it more difficult to persuade such landlords to invest in their properties than to influence home owners.

History of housing renewal in the UK

The UK has an ageing housing stock and consequently the problems associated with poor housing conditions have always been prominent in policy. In England 39 per cent of dwellings are over 50 years old and 21 per cent (4.4 million dwellings) are over 85 years old (Office of the Deputy Prime Minister, 2003c). About 95 per cent of the housing stock built prior to 1919, together with the responsibility for its repair, maintenance and improvement, is in the hands of private owners.

In the 1950s and 1960s the poor condition of much private housing built in the nineteenth century meant that demolition was the only practical solution, but after the 1970s demolition fell to a negligible level, partly because of its high cost and partly because of increasing opposition by private owners. Instead refurbishment became the chief means of dealing with poor housing conditions. This was largely achieved by the provision of grant aid to owner-occupiers and private landlords, and to a lesser degree by the acquisition and renovation of dwellings by housing associations and local authorities for subsequent rental.

The principal policy changes in the postwar period are summarized in Table 13.1. Significant shifts occurred during this period in respect of the

274

Table 13.1 *Housing renewal policies in the postwar period*

1950–69: slum clearance	After the postwar construction boom ended the emphasis shifted to the removal of slum housing. Renovation was mainly seen as a stop-gap measure until substandard dwellings were cleared.
1969–89: publicly funded private sector renewal	The rise in owner-occupation of older stock, growing criticism of clearance and municipal rehousing led to shift in focus to area renewal and renovation. Successive governments provided grant aid to owner-occupiers and private landlords to assist them with renovation work. • The scope of grant aid was broadened to cover repairs as well as improvements (such as the installation of bathrooms and kitchens), and eventually to include adaptations to make dwellings suitable for people with disabilities. • Subsidies were increased to enable low-income home owners to benefit. • Area-based focus developed through the designation of Housing Action Areas and General Improvement Areas. • Enveloping and block repair schemes for groups of houses were stimulated by higher grant payments.
1989–2002: means tested and targeted private renewal	A housing green paper asserted that 'homeowners must...carry the primary responsibility for keeping their property in good repair' (DETR, 1985, p. 1). The Local Government and Housing Act introduced a means test to restrict public funding but also introduced mandatory grants to make dwellings 'fit for human habitation' (which increased funding demand). In 1996 mandatory grants were discontinued, apart from disabled facilities grants (DFGs). Overall grant expenditure fell and DFGs accounted for an increasing proportion of the total.
2002 onwards: public–private framework harnessing private investment in renewal	A regulatory reform order repealed the framework of grants and assistance to home owners and required all local authorities to develop strategies to improve local housing conditions and to invest a mixture of public grants and private funds in renewal. This led to initiatives to attract private funding. Housing Market Renewal Areas were designated (this new public investment stream was limited to seven areas nationally). The decent homes target and the health and safety hazard rating set standards for local strategies.

Sources: Merrett (1979); Moore (1980); Gibson and Langstaff (1982); Gibson (1986); Leather and Mackintosh (1994, 1997).

types of intervention (renovating or demolishing substandard homes), sources of funding (discretionary and mandatory public grants, private borrowing), the extent of targeting (area focus or means testing) and the scale of public expenditure on renewal. Throughout the period changes in the housing market – for example tenure changes, house price cycles and mortgage lenders' policies – were at least as important as public policies in influencing the process of renewal.

Implementing the regulatory reform order

The repeal of various pieces of legislation that provided the framework for grants and other housing renewal assistance to home owners was achieved through a new parliamentary mechanism – a regulatory reform order – that avoided the need for primary legislation. The Regulatory Reform (Housing Assistance) (England and Wales) Order of 2002 was the first example of this. Its main provisions were as follows:

- A new general power that enabled local housing authorities to provide assistance for housing renewal. They could do so directly or provide finance to enable third parties such as housing associations to do so.
- Repeal of the provisions in the Housing Grants, Construction and Regeneration Act of 1996 that related to renovation grants, common parts grants, grant for Houses in Multiple Occupation, group repair and home repair assistance.
- Repeal of the provisions in the 1985 Housing Act that related to loans by local housing authorities for housing renewal.
- Streamlined provisions governing the designation and operation of renewal areas.

All local authorities were given a maximum of one year to draft a new policy on private sector housing renewal, and publication of this policy triggered the end of the old powers and the start of the new. The local authorities were expected to consult widely with other organizations and the public about their new policy, and to develop a wide range of partnerships to ensure that the policy would be effective (Office of the Deputy Prime Minister, 2003e). They were urged to consider ways of encouraging home owners to borrow or use their own resources to finance repairs and improvements. These could include measures to make commercial loan finance more attractive, including the use of grant aid as an incentive for borrowing. The local authorities were also urged to increase awareness of the need for investment in repairs and improvements, and to provide practical help in getting the work done, especially in the case of vulnerable people.

Measures to stimulate borrowing

One of the most controversial aspects of the new policy framework was that home owners were expected to borrow in order to finance repairs and improvements. With the average dwelling price standing at over £150 000, many home owners had the capacity to borrow. However properties in poor condition tended to be of lower value and therefore there was less scope for borrowing, especially when there was an outstanding mortgage. Furthermore consumer debt was at a record level and even home owners with unmortgaged properties often had too low an income to make loan repayments. Older people were the most obvious group to suffer from this equity rich–income poor syndrome.

Other obstacles to borrowing were the cost of property surveys (to assure the lender of the value of the security) and the cost of the legal work required to set up the mortgage. On a large loan for house purchase these costs were proportionately small, but on a small repair loan they amounted to a significant overhead, even when incorporated into the loan. Loans of under £25 000 also fell under the provisions of consumer credit legislation, which further increased the administrative costs. Many commercial lenders would not provide small loans, and others had a lower limit on borrowing that excluded most small repair loans. Therefore home owners were more likely to use their savings or income, or to neglect major but important jobs such as roof repair in favour of smaller, more affordable works. This was a considerable problem since unless borrowing could be stimulated the policy of shifting funding responsibility from the public sector to home owners would result in a worsening of poor conditions in the private sector.

There were two main ways of addressing these problems. First, local authorities had the power to grant loans directly and to subsidize loan set-up costs, and they were exempt from most consumer credit legislation. However such loans were subject to the same constraints as capital grants and any benefits to local authorities from recycling receipts through loans would only emerge gradually as the loans were paid off. As a result few authorities used this option unless they had access to a special pool of capital.

The second approach was to establish a new lending vehicle outside the local authority to tap into other sources of capital. ART Homes in Birmingham is the best known example of such a vehicle (ART Homes, 2000; Groves and Sankey, 2004). Originally part of the Aston Reinvestment Trust, a charitable body set up to lend to new businesses in the Aston area of Birmingham that could not acquire traditional funding, ART Homes later became part of a housing association. It overcame a series of hurdles, including gaining a licence to lend and regulatory approval for its products.

However it found it difficult to obtain capital from sources other than local authorities. In particular it found it hard to persuade commercial lenders such as banks and building societies to provide capital for onward lending at sufficiently attractive terms.

To overcome the loan repayment problems of low-income households, ART Homes developed an equity share loan. Under this arrangement the borrower did not make interest repayments (thus making the loan affordable) but instead gave up a share of the equity in the property. The lender thus obtained a return from any gain in the value of the equity share, rather than from interest repayments. But obtaining capital for lending on these terms proved even more difficult.

Developing alternative loan mechanisms of this type was complex and time-consuming (for details see Groves and Sankey, 2004). Most local authorities lacked the capacity to develop such mechanisms from scratch and small bodies such as ART Homes could not provide a national service. There remains a clear need for larger-scale approaches involving input from the government as a catalyst, facilitator and provider of start-up funding.

Dealing with private landlords

In 2001 in England, 10 per cent of households in the private rented sector and 3 per cent of owner-occupiers lived in dwellings that were unfit for human habitation, (Office of the Deputy Prime Minister, 2003c) In the private rented sector, conditions were worst in older terraced houses, and Houses in Multiple Occupation (HMOs), that is, dwellings that had been converted into flats or bedsits with shared facilities and amenities. The risk of fire in HMOs tended to be greater than in other types of dwelling.

A wide and often confusing range of powers existed under legislation to control conditions in private rented housing, with further powers for HMOs. For many years local authorities attempted to improve conditions in private rented accommodation by exercising these powers, but with the growth of private renting in the 1990s and a reduction of local authority staffing levels it became apparent that an alternative approach was necessary.

From the mid 1990s some authorities introduced schemes whereby landlords could volunteer their properties, and themselves as managers, for accreditation by the local authority. Student accommodation was an early candidate for accreditation and it subsequently spread to much of the private rented sector. There were various incentives, including grants for repair work, conferment of a higher status and help in finding suitable tenants. The incidence of accreditation schemes increased substantially, helped by the formation of a national network to promote good practice.

But their impact was limited in areas of high demand, where landlords could find tenants without accreditation, and in general the schemes attracted landlords who were already providing reasonably managed accommodation and meeting the required standards.

Some argued that voluntary schemes of this type were insufficient to drive up standards in the worst parts of the sector. For example the Chartered Institute of Housing argued that all accommodation in the private rented sector should be licensed, and that failure to meet the housing condition and management standards should be a ground for refusing or revoking licences (Chartered Institute of Housing, 2002). The government rejected this proposal as unnecessary and unworkable, but did move towards licensing HMOs and considered wider licensing in areas of low demand. The former dealt with that part of the private rented sector with greatest problems and serious risks, including fire hazards. The proposal for licensing of all private lettings in selected areas was a response to evidence of increased private renting by bad landlords in areas of low and changing demand. The government supported a series of pilot projects to make enforcement action more effective.

Finally, there was a proposal to restrict Housing Benefit payments to properties that met the required standards. However it was anticipated that this would affect supply in high-demand areas and there was a danger that landlords would move out of the Housing Benefit market rather than pay for improvements.

Low and changing demand

The issue of low and changing demand for housing and the establishment of Housing Market Renewal Areas (HMRAs) was discussed in Chapter 12. The pathfinder HMRAs were substantial, containing between 40 000 and 120 000 dwellings and spanning more than one local authority area, and in some cases several areas. This set a significantly different context for renewal policy in these areas. While no additional HMRAs were designated there was interest in applying a similar approach in other areas of changing demand (such as the Black Country and Telford), and Regional Housing Boards were expected to identify such areas more precisely and to target resources at them.

Low and changing demand affected private sector renewal programmes in a number of ways. For example the continued problems faced in areas that had been subject to extensive renewal in the recent past put into doubt the effectiveness of the programmes. Some commentators argued that area-based programmes had a time-limited impact and that problems re-emerged after the 'lifetime' of the improvements had expired. Others considered that changing demand was the result of economic and demographic change and people's growing aspirations, and therefore a narrow focus on housing conditions was unlikely to remedy the demand problem (Murie *et al.*, 1998).

While the declaration of HMRAs appeared to indicate acceptance of the broad economic and demographic drivers of changing demand, implementation of the programme still tended to focus mainly on housing capital investment. Traditional housing renewal interventions were prominent in the pathfinder HMRA prospectuses published in 2004 and 2005, with less attention to broader economic and demographic change.

A major divergence from renewal activities was also evident in an increase in demolition. In some areas, very substantial demolition programmes were proposed in order to change the character of the area and make space for the construction of a wider mix of housing types. However it was questionable whether these demolitions would all go ahead, especially in light of the rapid rise in house prices in inner city areas across the North of England in 2003–4. Speculative purchases by investors, some motivated by the prospect of capital gains from compulsory purchase, posed a serious threat to the demolition strategy by increasing unit costs. This challenged the viability of large-scale demolitions since budgets were inadequate to accommodate the higher unit costs. As the plans became more public there was high-profile opposition to clearance on heritage grounds (notably in Liverpool, where Ringo Starr lent his support to the opponents) and in the context of a continuing national shortfall in the housing supply.

Demolition was also made more difficult by growing concern about individual rights. The clearance programmes of the 1950s and 1960s had been implemented with little concern for these rights, especially in the case of private landlords, many of whom had received little compensation on the ground that their properties were unfit for human habitation. Since then the introduction of legislation to improve compensation for owners and to deal with other adverse effects of compulsory purchase, such as disturbance, had not only made clearance more expensive but also delayed its implementation.

As we have seen, general funding for renewal declined from 1996 and there was belated recognition that previous public grant commitments had not been budgeted for. The earmarking of substantial funds for the HMRAs from regional housing budgets highlighted the contrast between the resourcing of area-based initiatives and private sector renewal elsewhere.

Changing standards

For most of the twentieth century the principal standard that properties were expected to meet was fitness for human habitation. In 2001 the government introduced the Decent Homes Standard, which broadened the concept of fitness to take account of factors such as energy efficiency and the standard of kitchens and bathrooms in both the social and the private sector. A decent home would:

- Meet the current statutory minimum standard for housing (at that time the fitness standard).
- Be in a reasonable state of repair.
- Have reasonably modern facilities and services.
- Provide a reasonable degree of thermal comfort.

In July 2002 a public service agreement target was announced for housing in the private sector. This applied only to dwellings occupied by vulnerable households (defined as those on income support, Housing Benefit, council tax benefit, disabled persons tax credit, income-based job seekers' allowance, working family tax credit, attendance allowance, disability living allowance, industrial injuries, disablement benefit on war disablement pension). The goal was to increase the proportion of vulnerable households living in homes in a decent condition.

The consequences of this are only just beginning to emerge, but it is apparent that it may discourage focusing resources on the worst housing. A cost-effective way of ensuring that more vulnerable households are provided with decent homes is to improve the energy efficiency of dwellings that otherwise meet the Decent Homes Standard, or dwellings that only just fail to meet the standard and so are easy to improve. There is also growing interest in targeting investment at vulnerable groups. This reflects a broader trend over many years to target investment at specific problems that affect specific client groups, rather than renovating properties in the poorest condition.

One major objection to the concept of unfit for human habitation was its vagueness and incomprehensibility to all but a small number of specialist professionals. In 2001 over 630 000 households lived in private sector dwellings that were deemed unfit, and unfit houses had been occupied for many years. Such houses changed ownership without any awareness on the part of buyers or sellers of the houses' (apparently) serious defects. This suggests that the standard was not always sufficiently meaningful to owners and residents. A further problem was it did not take account of some potentially very serious matters (such as the presence of radon gas) or matters that had come to prominence since the standard was last revised (such as energy efficiency). To remedy this the government developed a rating based on the assessment of a range of risks to health and safety. The Housing Health and Safety Rating System was introduced under the Housing Act of 2004 and if it is successful it will replace the fitness standard (Office of the Deputy Prime Minister, 2004e). The rating will inevitably cause a shift of local authority housing renewal spending towards addressing the major risks identified in dwellings.

Conclusion

Private sector housing renewal policy in England has changed dramatically since 2002, although many of the effects of these changes remain to be seen. There has been a move away from the long-term programme of grant-funded renewal and towards public–private arrangements to finance the improvement of poor-quality housing. This approach has been slower to develop in other parts of the UK where a public funding framework has been retained.

This policy change followed changes in the external environment. From the 1970s to the late 1990s areas consisting of older terraced housing, which were the main focus of housing renewal policy, increasingly came into owner-occupation. Although property prices in many of these areas were low they rose in line with overall price rises. Over the last ten years many of the houses in question have been put up for rent, with owners seeking a return on their capital rather than achievement of a sustainable neighbourhood. The new occupants often lack a long-term commitment to the community. These changes have exposed the limitations of policies based on improving housing conditions without considering factors such as local services, the environment and the ability to live in safety without fear of crime.

The government's responses to these changes highlight the ambiguities and uncertainties underlying public policy on the condition of private sector housing. On the one hand the framework for private sector renewal has been modified by the Regulatory Reform Order of 2002 and its stress on self-reliance, with public resources being targeted at housing that poses a risk to health and well-being and at people who are least able to help themselves. In the short term such targeting may shift resources from houses in the worst condition to those occupied by the most vulnerable people. However, in the longer term it will prove difficult to preserve such improved housing for occupancy by vulnerable groups, since occupancy will be determined by markets.

Alongside this new approach, HMRAs have brought new subsidy and support arrangements to deal with poor housing conditions, but only in geographical areas where housing markets are deemed to be at risk or showing signs of weakness, rather than generally attending to dwellings in poor condition. What is absent is a coherent policy that sets out the respective responsibilities of the state and private owners in relation to housing conditions. There is an understandable reluctance on defining precisely what is expected of home owners in terms of repairs or improvements, and a considerable reluctance to do so for the majority of private landlords.

If there is no standard that owners are obliged to meet, then it is likely that the state will have to meet the costs that will arise when conditions reach the point at which health, safety or other standards are compromised. Measures such as the new health and safety hazard rating are a way of achieving minimal state responsibility. More problematically, wider housing market decline implies an even greater degree of state responsibility, as reflected in the relatively generous resources allocated so far to HMRAs. However it is doubtful whether any government will provide the resources needed to see this programme through in locations where an oversupply of social rented housing and unattractive private stock threaten the long-term sustainability of the market.

Chapter 14

A New Comprehensive Housing Policy: Overcoming Fragmentation or Managing Complexity?

The chapter argues that, while governments will continue to present their housing policies as comprehensive in nature, increasing institutional fragmentation and societal diversity will mean that such policies can best be seen as attempts to manage complexity. Future policy outcomes will be affected by many influences outside direct state control, such as the changing nature of places, markets and communities.

Fragmentation and coordination

A recurring theme in this book has been the recent fragmentation of housing policy and of the institutional framework that had evolved in the first half of the twentieth century to deliver policy. This is evident in the ways in which governance, tenures and policy making have changed over the past 25 years. Institutional arrangements have been reshaped to conform to changing ideas on the management and governance of public services. Today there is much greater fragmentation of control, greater institutional diversity, a larger range of providers and products in the housing market, more competition and a greater managerial focus at all levels. The reduction of the public sector housing stock through the Right to Buy scheme and stock transfer, together with the growth of the non-profit sector, have increased the extent of fragmentation but have been accompanied by attempts to reassert control through regulation.

Fragmentation has led to more invasive central control, with a panoply of targets, performance indicators and inspectorates (Power, 1997). While the growing emphasis on delivery and ensuring that taxpayers' money is prudently invested has provided a significant boost for the regulatory state, doubt remains about the ability of centrally driven strategies to produce the most appropriate outcomes. Incentive structures that reward performance based on 'earned autonomy' are gaining ground, for example in relation to funding for arm's length management organizations in the local authority housing sector, but there is cynicism about the extent to which regulation will be significantly relaxed, despite the rhetoric of proportionality and reduced regulatory burden.

Tenure too has become a more fragmented and uncertain construct as the composition of and part played by each of the main tenures has changed. Some of the past divisions between tenures remain, but changes in the structure of the housing market have resulted in a situation where the bottom end of the owner-occupied sector does not offer advantages that are significantly different from those in the social or private rented sector. The category 'home ownership' embraces diverse subcategories that may merit different policy treatment. Meanwhile in rental housing the replacement of separate subsidy systems by a general Housing Benefit system has reduced the superiority of social rented housing. Private renting can often provide a greater number of options in terms of dwelling type and locations, and the transferability of Housing Benefit affects the choices made. The private rented sector now performs a range of functions and has attracted different patterns of investment and consumption in different parts of cities, as our case studies of Liverpool and Birmingham in Chapter 6 illustrated. Meanwhile many of the past assumptions about social housing no longer hold. Demand does not always exceed supply and policy may be more concerned with marketing than rationing. Despite the introduction of choice-based lettings, access to social housing continues to be partly based on bureaucratic definitions of housing need. However because the quality and reputation of the sector have diminished the power of gatekeepers is less significant than in the past. All of these changes mean that tenure only takes on meaning in the context of specific places, markets and communities, and we shall discuss this further later in this chapter.

Policy responses may also be seen as fragmented. We can view policies as a series of fragmented responses to specific issues and periodic attempts to use more holistic measures in recognition of the interconnections between tenures, between different policy strands and between housing and the wider economy. An academic review of 25 years of English housing policy (Stephens *et al.*, 2005) provides support for this view. It was found that housing policy had concentrated on issues such as deregulation and liberalization, the restructuring of housing subsidies and the restructuring of assets. The review concludes that many of the policies succeeded on their own terms but failed to address the underlying problems. There were significant failures in the supply of housing, complex interactions between housing policies and economic restructuring and a failure of the housing system to become robust and self-sustaining. This is attributed to policies being reactive, narrowly conceived and micro-managed with limited overall vision or coherence.

A new comprehensive housing policy?

In this context the publication of a five-year-plan for housing by the Office of the Deputy Prime Minister (2005) appeared to indicate that the government had confidence in its ability to deliver a comprehensive approach to housing policy. But this approach differed significantly from previous attempts to develop a comprehensive housing policy, for example after the First and Second World Wars and in the 1970s.

The new comprehensive housing policy can be depicted as a managed approach to making home ownership a universal form of tenure. It comprises a plethora of schemes to assist ever more households to enter home ownership. Social housing is now even more explicitly cast as a safety net for those who are unable to follow any of the routes to home ownership and to meet the short-term needs of those who intend to purchase a home at a later date. The more interventionist framework introduced by the Sustainable Communities Plan (Office of the Deputy Prime Minister, 2003a) to provide more affordable homes in high-growth areas in the South of England and to sustain and restore markets in selected locations the North and Midlands has become embedded. But there is a determination to place greater emphasis on private sector delivery, for example through the expansion of private finance initiatives, by allocating Social Housing Grant to developers, and introducing new shared ownership schemes with lending institutions without non-profit partners. The tensions at the heart of this new comprehensive housing policy relate to the ability of the state to steer private institutions and to influence market processes.

This fragmented, marketized approach relies on the incorporation of key institutions into the policy process and appropriate governmental levers to control the overall shape of the housing system. Incorporation is exemplified by the direct involvement of private financial institutions in the provision of social housing, and by the emergence of new means of control in the non-profit housing sector, with power increasingly vested in group parents and 'lead Investment Partners' who work closely with government the national and regional levels (see Chapter 9).

Governmental leverage is more problematic, although for electoral purposes there has certainly been an interest in appearing to be in control. The power of regulatory bodies such as the Audit Commission has been increased in an attempt to secure national conformity to certain standards. Even local authorities, whose ability to deliver comprehensive housing services has been steadily eroded since the 1970s, have been exhorted to take a greater strategic role, and their influence continues to be significant in respect of land use planning and securing sites for affordable housing (see Chapter 5).

While there are attractions in this vision of greater coordination there are significant weaknesses in the institutional capacity to deliver, and considerable powerlessness in relation to market forces. Chapter 13 highlighted the restricted ability to raise private sector housing standards by relying on owners and private lenders to finance work previously paid for by public grants. This limitation appears to have been acknowledged in that a weaker version of the decent homes target has been applied to the private sector than to social housing. Another area in which policy might be seen as steering change rather than controlling delivery is the introduction of allowances (see Chapter 8). In this example the concept of 'shopping incentives' has been applied in an attempt to influence consumer behaviour, yet the underlying motivations of tenants are not fully understood (Marsh, 2004). In the end there are limits to the extent to which the government, be it at the central, regional or local level, can implement a comprehensive housing policy in an environment where so many of the key drivers of change are related to market forces, social and demographic change and consumer behaviour.

Complexity and change

We believe that this situation calls for a significantly different framework for understanding housing and housing policy than is provided by traditional models of central – local relations and principal – agent models of economic analysis, because these models imply a degree of certainty in the policy process that is rarely present in practice.

The importance of both policy and non-policy drivers of change is now widely recognized. Stephens *et al.* (2005) identify four main influences on the housing system: demographic trends, social change, macroeconomic variables and housing policy. Our account has shown how non-policy influences have often been the more powerful in determining housing outcomes, for example in relation to the problems that arose in the home-ownership market in the late 1980s and early 1990s (see Chapter 3). The continuous interaction between policy and non-policy drivers of change suggests a need for more holistic explanations of housing outcomes and housing policy.

One such mode of explanation is the 'whole systems approach' to policy. This has gained considerable support as a result of the growing emphasis on joined-up government to address the fragmentation caused by the new public management reforms (Minogue *et al.*, 1998). Whole-system thinking has been important in policy making and implementation in highly connected areas such as social care, health and housing (see Chapter 11). Systems theory has been drawn on since the 1970s to explore complex patterns of influence within and between organizations, allowing greater attention to the contextual and contingent factors underlying change (Ackoff and Emery, 1972). Other approaches to understanding complex systems are chaos theory and complexity theory. These are particularly appropriate when change involves an interplay between diverse external and internal influences where boundaries between organizations are permeable, and where charge is non-linear (Haynes, 2003).

Complexity theory was used in Chapter 10 to account for changes in the 'attractor pattern' for social housing in respect of choice-based lettings, and we believe that it is capable of much wider application. It can help us to understand the nature of change in complex policy systems such as housing where institutional relationships are negotiated and to a large extent self-organizing, and can therefore only be influenced or steered, rather than controlled, by external or internal intervention. In general housing policy has, like social housing lettings, been through long periods of apparent stability interspersed by periods of dramatic change, when tensions between competing beliefs and behaviours become very strong and a new pattern takes hold. Examples include the use of tax incentives to promote home ownership and the use of local authorities as the main agents for subsidized rental housing. Both strategies held sway for long periods in the twentieth century but were then progressively challenged, destabilized and eventually replaced by new approaches. Complexity theory encourages us to ask questions about the forces that lock institutions into existing 'attractor patterns'. Proponents of the theory suggest that the climate for change can be actively managed to shift the pattern of attractors and stimulate feedback, and thereby generate a process of self-supporting change.

Explaining policy shifts

One factor supporting the complexity approach is that conflicts of view and interest have existed throughout the period considered in this book. Problems have been viewed differently by individuals and households in different organizations and situations. Periods of apparent stability of view have tended to disguise the potential for radical change to emerge.

The early chapters of this book identified distinctive periods of housing policy when the political coalitions on housing issues and the dominant concerns, aims and methods of policy differed. The further back we go the simpler the agendas and explanations appear. The neglect of housing in the nineteenth century was associated with a lack of institutional capacity limited political franchise, with powerful vested interests and moral crusaders opposing state intervention. The introduction of a modern housing policy in the early twentieth century can be explained by the withdrawal of private investors from housing, emerging leadership and institutional capacity in local government, growing working-class political pressure the emergencies created by the First World War and its aftermath, and the fear of disturbances and revolution. The continuity and maturation of housing policy in the middle of the century can be explained by continuing working-class pressure and support for a new welfare state, new wartime emergencies, more mature institutional capacity in local government and the decline of the private landlord.

Once the worst of the housing problem had been dealt with in the postwar 'numbers game' there was less political interest in the problems that remained, and those who were experiencing those problems were increasingly marginalized, both politically and economically. The shift in UK housing policy after 1979 can be partly explained by the success of previous policies and economic and social changes in removing the worst housing problems, the absence of a major emergency with an impact on housing and the break up of the political coalitions that had supported the parallel development of council housing and home ownership. The institutional capacity of the local authority housing sector began to diminish as public expenditure was run down and responsibilities transferred to other agencies.

Destabilization of the welfare state attractor for housing policy in the later part of the twentieth century was partly a result of the aspiration of the growing middle class to own their homes and to obtain housing that was commensurate with their increased affluence and power as consumers. Changes in the economy, employment patterns and income levels, and in what the housing market had to offer, fractured the policy agenda. More of the middle mass saw their housing problems as individual rather than collective and used market processes rather than council housing to resolve them. As in other spheres, the politics and economics of mass production and the redistributive welfare regime were replaced by a post-industrial, consumption-driven society. Against this background there was growing antagonism to state intervention and subsidies, public bureaucracy and municipalism, the 'undeserving poor' and council tenants who could not afford market housing.

A new attractor pattern was provided by a residual housing policy, a drift in the welfare state away from universal provision and towards means tested provision, a shift from bricks and mortar to personal subsidies and the adoption of new public management recipes. Some accounts of this shift have referred to the 'end of housing policy' or to a residual policy preoccupied with housing the poor. Both of these perspectives are flawed (Lowe, 2004). Although an examination of the contents of legislation might appear to support the view that the main concerns were with social rented housing, supported housing and vulnerable groups, this picture would be misleading.

The consistently dominant concern in policy was now to support sustainable home ownership, and when the sustainability of the sector was threatened (as in the early 1970s and early 1990s) the government stepped in to stabilize the market. Public policies, notably the Right to Buy scheme, fuelled the demand for home ownership and undermined the sustainability of other tenures. There was further intervention to expand home ownership through the planning system, shared equity and help for first-time buyers. The role of the state in providing finance to maintain home ownership also changed. The general tax relief associated with previous phases and the major advantages conferred on high-income, high-tax groups were significantly eroded. Effective management of the economy, high employment, rising incomes and low interest rates became more important to home owners than tax relief.

Increasingly home ownership became a key means of accumulating and storing wealth as well as providing shelter. In this situation the mass housing policy became a housing tenure policy rather than a housing need policy. State housing was no longer purely associated with shelter but also with the opportunity to purchase a commodity that would increase in value. Against this backdrop the idea of providing tenants with equity stakes attracted interest, and is likely to develop further.

It should be noted that the representation of policy phases set out above is a little too simple in that the phases overlapped and the shifts in agenda were not crystal clear. For the present phase of policy it also implies a more coherent approach than exists in reality. An alternative version of the 'end of housing policy' was discussed in Chapter 4, where it was argued that housing policy as we knew it might be at an end but that it had offspring that continue to affect the operation of the housing market: neighbourhood renewal, assistance with housing costs, housing taxation, Supporting People and neighbourhood management. The new housing policy involves a wider range of agencies with differing ambitions. It is a more complex and fragmented part of social, economic and environmental policies, of urban and rural policies and of policies influenced by the European, national, regional, local and neighbourhood levels. Different agencies have specific targets and missions and a plethora of strategies struggle to provide synergy and coherence for joined-up projects. In this context the new housing policy will struggle to be comprehensive in impact.

Places, markets and communities

The differentiation of places, markets and communities has been a key element of the complexity that we have attempted to describe and is essential to understanding the diversity of housing outcomes and experiences in different parts of the UK and for different social groups. In considering places it is appropriate to consider the neighbourhood, regional and national levels.

With the fragmentation of tenure outlined earlier in this chapter, the real housing divisions today lie between neighbourhoods rather than types of tenure and relate to opportunities for capital accumulation and associated lifestyle factors such as the quality of local schools and leisure opportunities. These divisions have been recognized by the marketing and consumer service sectors, which now use sophisticated classifications based on postcodes or small census areas to target different lifestyle groups. Public policy too is beginning to address the complexity of neighbourhood differentiation and in doing so it has realized that housing markets and submarkets may cut across the administrative boundaries through which policies were previously delivered.

The Sustainable Communities Plan (Office of the Deputy Prime Minister 2003a) is an example of a shift in policy following recognition of the fact that radically different approaches would be required to address the issues arising from different types of housing market. There were housing problems associated with high demand and economic buoyancy, but there were also problems associated with economic decline and lack of demand. High demand for housing created particular problems for those with the lowest incomes, while economic buoyancy generated high capacity to invest in housing. Economic decline presented different but no less difficult circumstances. Analysis indicated that a variety of approaches were needed in neighbourhoods with changing demand, depending on the function played by these neighbourhoods. In some neighbourhoods high turnover was associated with their function as an entry point to the housing market or the provider of short-term accommodation from which people would move on rapidly. Other neighbourhoods were clearly failing or at risk of failure, and in their case it was necessary to ensure that the provision of new housing in adjacent neighbourhoods did not tip them into terminal decline.

The plan also recognized that providing adequate housing alone was not sufficient to improve opportunities and life chances. Indeed as social rented housing became increasingly residualized and some mixed tenure neighbourhoods became 'poverty neighbourhoods', some of the earlier assumptions about housing provision were revised. It was recognized that means of choice and mobility as well as good quality housing were needed. A broader neighbourhood management approach was advocated to improve services and restore the confidence of residents and potential investors.

As Chapter 12 noted, implementation of the Sustainable Communities Plan brought a rapid change in the administrative framework for housing policy in England. The nascent regional assemblies began to work through new institutions, including housing and planning boards to coordinate strategies at the regional level. In response to this other key institutions such as housing associations and support providers began to regroup at regional level to influence policy and secure resources (see Chapter 11). Markets and submarkets rather than local authority boundaries would form the basis of strategy and investment. Integration with other regional strategies, notably those promulgated by regional development agencies, became a key rationale for housing policy. The superimposition of growth areas (where new housing investment would be concentrated) and Housing Market Renewal Areas (with concerted action to transform housing markets) on to this new regional geography provided the basis for growing differentiation in housing policy between different parts of England.

National assemblies had been established for a longer period in other parts of the UK, and as discussed in Chapter 1 they had developed some distinctive approaches to policy, reflecting significantly different starting points, administrative and legal institutions and national priorities. The most notable differences were the higher expenditure on housing in Scotland and Northern Ireland, the more rapid process of integrating the local authority and housing association regimes in Scotland and Wales, the more generous approach to funding long-term personal care in Scotland and the centralization of housing and support functions in Northern Ireland due to the limited powers of local authorities there. There were also some important differences related to distinctive dwelling types, for example Glasgow tenements, and to rural–urban differences in housing markets and tenure mix that may also be found in the English regions.

Although local, regional and national differences remain there has been some convergence. For example there has been a levelling up of housing quality and condition, and higher home ownership has been promoted throughout the UK. The remaining policy differences may simply slow the pace of convergence rather than reverse it. The switch to personal housing subsidies has promoted convergence since Housing Benefit and the proposed housing allowances operate on the same basis across the UK. Finally it is likely that the differences between the UK and other European countries will diminish to some extent.

Differences within society

Different housing experiences among societal groups have been an important aspect of differentiation. In many cases the housing system has exacerbated social inequality, while in others housing interventions have improved the circumstances of poor or socially excluded groups. Housing inequality interacts with other forms of inequality in complex ways, as the following examples illustrate.

Residential segregation has intensified in many areas and neighbourhood change has had different effects on different groups in society (see Chapter 12). According to Harrison and Phillips (2003, p. 7), 'after five decades of settlement Britain's BME population is still disproportionately concentrated in the poorest urban, usually inner city, locations and in the most deprived housing'. This is also the case for many of the minority groups that have settled in the UK under the asylum system. Certain neighbourhoods have assumed a 'reception function' following the procurement of private rented accommodation in these areas by the National Asylum Support Service (NASS) as part of its dispersal programme, and refugees with leave to remain have later tended to take up residence in these neighbourhoods. Without effective planning, the housing options of refugees and others could be adversely affected by policy interventions to revitalize the housing markets in these neighbourhoods (West Midlands Regional Assembly, 2005).

A second example of differentiation relates to the housing, care and support of older people. As discussed in Chapter 11, demographic change, changing aspirations and the restructuring of public funding mechanisms have led to profound changes in housing outcomes. Sheltered housing, whose provision was favoured for a long period (as a result of perverse incentives such as exclusion of sheltered housing tenants from the Right to Buy, and of an ideological predisposition to provide social welfare for 'deserving' groups such as older people), failed to keep pace with changing expectations. Policy moves to separate care, support and housing have hastened the demise of this relatively inflexible form of provision by enabling older people to select from a wider range of options to meet their care and support needs.

A third example is the continued difficulty faced by larger households on low incomes in securing accommodation. In the 1960s and 1970s larger households were among the groups whose needs were sometimes seen as less legitimate by housing providers (Henderson and Karn, 1985). Such value judgements and financial restrictions, for example on construction subsidies, led to inadequate provision for the relatively small number of households that required large dwellings. For 25 years research on the housing needs of BME people has consistently highlighted the institutional racism involved in failure to provide larger accommodation, with *ad hoc* solutions, such as knocking together adjacent properties, occasionally being taken up by social landlords (Mullings, 1991). Yet still, the most recent review of English housing policy notes, 'a particular difficulty in current policy has been the disincentives to provide larger dwellings within the social housing sector, which may well be exacerbated by emphasis on Section 106 agreements' (Stephens *et al.*, 2005, p. 68)

The final example, and one of the most important to the new comprehensive housing policy, is the significant difference in equity and capital accumulation among home owners in different housing submarkets. An important assumption bolstering policies to support the extension of home ownership is the contribution that such policies make to asset-based welfare rather than simply meeting housing needs. The significant growth of equity extraction from housing to fund home improvements and general expenditure has underpinned housing interventions such as the provision of agency services for older home owners (see Chapter 13). Yet it is clear that the ability to extract equity from housing varies enormously among social groups and regions. Joseph (2005) highlights the varied experiences of housing wealth accumulation among migrants from the Caribbean to the UK in the 1950s to 1970s, with variations being associated with patterns of migrant settlement and strategies in the face of discrimination and growing market differentiation.

What next? Complexity and future change

So how will housing policy in the UK evolve in the future? It is important to emphasize that currently there is little overt party political disagreement over housing, and interparty competition is still about the promotion of home ownership and the devising of new routes into it. This is likely to mean further privatization, subsidized home ownership and equity sharing. The political test for housing policy is likely to be whether it facilitates the management of housing and urban problems, makes cities and the residential system work and halts decline, rather than whether it effectively addresses inequality. But policy is not applied to a common base. There are very large variations in the resources and capacities of different places and organizations, and this will determine the scope for innovation and action and the ability to benefit local communities and households.

Big questions remain about the most appropriate delivery mechanism for social housing. The housing association sector has steadily grown at the expense of local authority housing and will probably continue to do so, although the growth of Arm's-Length Management Organizations has accelerated in the past few years, resulting in a significant hybrid sector with its own institutions. Housing associations vary even more widely in size than did local authorities, and their diverse origins mean that their legal, territorial, management, financial and policy profiles are also diverse. There are strong pressures for housing associations to increase the scale of their operations, and these have been reinforced by the 'partnering' approach to grant allocations (see Chapter 9). In the next few years there are likely to be several English housing association groups with over 50 000 homes in ownership.

Size and geographical spread will challenge such associations to devise effective ways to provide locally accountable services.

The regionalization of policy and resource allocation has provided an incentive for this sector to restructure at the regional level. Meanwhile local accountability and neighbourhood delivery has been emphasized by government policy and the sector's own slogan: 'In Business for Neighbourhoods'. Support for mutual organizations has never been strong, apart from a few notable exceptions such as Glasgow's community-based housing association programme in the 1970s. Nonetheless mutuality offers an attractive alternative to some of the more paternalistic forms of provision, and the community gateway model of stock transfer (the community mutual model in Wales) is likely to preserve the mutual tradition, albeit on a very small scale compared to the sector as a whole. Finally, recognition that there is a need for more than just housing and some housing organizations' desire to generate revenue from sources other than rent has encouraged them to specialize in niche markets such as housing and care, neighbourhood regeneration and submarket renting. This has also challenged some of the putative advantages of single-purpose housing organizations. All of the above suggest that there will be continued diversity of organizational forms with distinct purposes, functions, structures and delivery mechanisms.

Beyond this there are four major challenges. The first relates to homelessness and exclusion. The harder stance on antisocial behaviour could develop into resistance to behavioural differences more generally and reinforce the tendency to stereotype and exclude certain groups. This could add to the social control functions that social landlords are increasingly expected to play and could weaken their social welfare ethos. The second challenge relates to segregation and the ability of different groups to obtain good-quality housing and share in the promise of home ownership. Despite the emphasis given to choice in policy pronouncements, we are still a long way from enabling some citizens from exercising real choice. The third is to do with the flawed nature of the owner-occupied sector more generally and the divisions within home ownership. The operation of the planning system and housing market too often serve to preserve historic benefits, while denying new consumers the opportunity to enjoy the promises of their own home. The fourth concerns the shortage of decent alternatives to home ownership, especially in areas of high demand and in view of the reduced status of social rented housing. All of these factors mean that there is a need not just to redevelop a high-quality, high-status social rented sector but also to design a more coherent policy to address the divisions within home ownership and increase the choices available to different social and ethnic groups within and between types of housing tenure.

In conclusion, the next phase of policy is likely to involve the playing out of the various interests currently represented in the housing policy community in different places. We have noted that the housing policy community has become less influential in the regulation and funding of social housing. While regulation is likely to remain strong, 'regulatory capture' may continue to weaken, with change becoming less predictable and decisions that affect housing becoming subject to a wider range of external influences (see Chapter 7). The growing influence of macroeconomic, demographic and technological developments means that the results of policy interventions are likely to become increasingly contingent on external factors, many of which will play out in different ways in different places. In this context we should attach as much significance to the emergent as to the intended effects of policy. This confirms the importance for future studies to explore local contexts in different parts of the UK as well as the policy and non-policy factors that will shape the nation's future housing system. In this respect the new comprehensive housing policy is more likely to be about managing complexity than truly overcoming fragmentation.

References

Ackoff, R. and Emery, F. (1972) *On Purposeful Systems* (London: Tavistock).

Aldbourne Associates (2000) *National Study of Tenant Participation in RSLs* (London: Housing Corporation).

Aldrich, H. (1976) 'Resource dependence and inter-organisational relations', *Administration and Society*, 7(4), 419–54.

Allen, J. and McDowell, L. (1989) *Landlords and Property: Social Relations in the Private Rented Sector* (Cambridge: Cambridge University Press).

Anchor Trust and Housing Corporation (2002) *Implementing Supporting People: A Guide for Support Providers* (Oxford: Anchor Trust).

Arblaster, L. Conway, J., Foreman, A. and Hawtin, M. (1996) *Asking the Impossible? Inter-Agency Working to Address Housing, Health and Social Care Needs of People in Ordinary Housing* (Bristol: Policy Press).

Arnstein, S. (1969) 'A ladder of citizen participation', *Journal of American Institute of Planners*, 35(4), 214–24.

ART Homes (2000) *Stopping the Rot* (Birmingham: ART Homes, Aston Reinvestment Trust).

Ashworth, H. (1954) *The Genesis of Modern British Town Planning* (London: Routledge and Kegan Paul).

Association of Local Government (2003) *Key Issues Updates 2003. Key Issues 7 March 2003* (London: Association of Local Government).

Audit Commission (1986) *Managing the Crisis in Council Housing* (London: HMSO).

Audit Commission (1998) *Home Alone. The Role of Housing in Community Care* (London: Audit Commission).

Audit Commission (1999) *A Balanced Account. The Audit Arrangements for Registered Social Landlords* (London: Audit Commission).

Audit Commission (2002) *Housing After Transfer* (London: Audit Commission).

Audit Commission and Housing Corporation (2001) *Group Dynamics: Group Structures and Registered Social Landlords* (London: Audit Commission and the Housing Corporation).

Bailey, S. J. (1995) *Public Sector Economics – Theory, Policy and Practice* (Basingstoke: Macmillan).

Barelli, J. (1992) *Underoccupation in Local Authority and Housing Association Housing* (London: HMSO).

Barelli, J. and Pawson, H. (2001) *Underoccupation in Social Housing* (London: DETR).

Barker, K. (2004) *Review of Housing Supply, Delivering Stability: Securing our Future Housing Needs Final Report – Recommendations* (London: HMSO).

Begg, I. and Moore, B. (1987) 'The Changing Economic Role of Britain's Cities', in V. A. Hausner (ed.), *Critical Issues in Urban Economic Development*, vol II (Oxford: Clarendon Press).

Better Government for Older People Steering Committee (2000) *All Our Futures. Report from the Better Government for Older People Programme* (London: Department of Health).

Bevan, M., Crouch, K., Fletcher, P. and Riseborough, M. (2005) *The Housing Needs of Older People in the Countryside* (London: Countryside Agency).

Beveridge, W. (1943) *Pillars of Security* (London: George Allen and Unwin).

Bines, W. (1994) *The Health of Single Homeless People* (York: Centre for Housing Policy).

Bines, W., Kemp, P., Pleace, N. and Radley, C. (1993) *Managing Social Housing* (London: HMSO).

Birrell, D. and Murie, A. (1980) *Government and Politics in Northern Ireland* (Dublin: Gill & Macmillan).

Black, J. and Stafford, D. (1988) *Housing Finance and Policy* (London: Routledge).

Boardman, B. (1991) *Fuel Poverty. From Cold Homes to Affordable Warmth* (London: Belhaven).

Booth, P. and Crook, T. (1986) *Low Cost Home Ownership. An Evaluation of Housing Policy under the Conservatives* (Aldershot: Gower).

Bowley, M. (1945) *Housing and the State 1919–1944* (London: George Allen & Unwin).

Boyne, G. A. and Walker, R. M. (1999) 'Social housing reforms in England and Wales: a public choice evaluation', *Urban Studies*, 36, 2237–62.

Bramley, G. (1997) 'Housing Policy: A case of terminal decline?', *Policy and Politics*, 25 (4), 387–407.

Bramley, G., Parson, H., Third, H. and Parter, J. (2000) *Low Demand Housing and Unpopular Neighbourhoods* (London: DETR).

Bramley, G., Evans, M. and Atkins, J. (1998) *Where does Public Spending Go? Report of a pilot study to analyse the flows of public expenditure into local areas* (London: DETR).

Bramley, G., Morgan, J., Dunmore, K. and Cousins, L. (2002) *Evaluation of the Low Cost Home Ownership Programme in England* (London: ODPM).

Bramley, G., Munro, M. and Pawson, H. (2004) *Key Issues in Housing. Policies and Markets in 21st Century Britain* (Basingstoke: Palgrave).

Bramley, G. and Pawson, H. (2002) 'Low demand for housing: incidence, causes and UK national policy implications', *Urban Studies*, 39 (3), 393–422.

Brindley, T. and Stoker, G. (1988) 'Housing renewal policy in the 1980s', *Local Government Studies*, Sept. Oct., 45–67.

Brion, M. (1995) *Women in the Housing Service* (London: Routledge).

Brown, T., Hunt, R. and Yates, N. (2000) *Lettings: A Question of Choice* (Coventry: Chartered Institute of Housing).

Burnett, J. (1986) *A Social History of Housing 1815–1985* (London: Methuen).

Burrows, R. (2003) 'How the other half lives? An exploratory analysis of the relationship between poverty and home ownership in Britain', *Urban Studies*, 40 (7), 223–42.

Butler, S. (1998) *Access Denied: The Exclusion of People in Need from Social Housing* (London: Shelter).

Byrne, D. and Keithley, J. (1993) 'Housing and health in the community', in R. Burridge and D. Ormandy (eds), *Unhealthy Housing: Research, Remedies and Reform* (London: Chapman and Hall).

Cabinet Office (2001) *A New Commitment to Neighbourhood Renewal: National Strategy Action Plan* (London: Cabinet Office).

Cairncross, L., Clapham, D. and Goodlad, R. (1997) *Housing Management, Consumers and Citizens* (London: Routledge).

Cairncross, L., Morrell, C., Darke, J. and Brownhill, S. (2002) *Tenants Managing. An Evaluation of Tenant Management Organisations in England* (London: ODPM).

Cairncross, L. and Pearl, M. (2003) *A baseline survey of housing association board members* (London: Housing Corporation).

Carroll, C., Cowans, J. and Darton, D. (1999) *Meeting Part M and Designing Lifetime Homes* (York: Joseph Rowntree Foundation).

Centre for Public Services (2004) *The Case for the 4th Option for Council Housing and a Critique of Arms Length Management Organisations* (Sheffield: Centre for Public Services).

Chaplin, R., Martin, S., Yang, J. H., and Whitehead, C. (1994) *Affordability: Definitions, Measures and Implications for Lenders*, Discussion Paper 45 (Department of Land Economy, and University of Cambridge).

Charity Commission and Housing Corporation (2002) *Guidance for Charitable Registered Social Landlords* (London: Charity Commission and Housing Corporation).

Chartered Institute of Housing (1997) *More than Bricks and Mortar* (Coventry: Chartered Institute of Housing).

Chartered Institute of Housing (2002) *Selective Licensing of Private Landlords. Response Paper* (Coventry: Chartered Institute of Housing).

Chartered Institute of Housing (2003) *Regional Housing Strategies. Advice Notes* (Coventry: Chartered Institute of Housing).

City of Liverpool (1986) *Liverpool's Population: Population, social and housing stock changes and trends 1971–1991* (Liverpool: Liverpool City Council).

Clapham, D. (1997) 'A Woman of her Time', in J. Goodwin and C. Grant (eds), *Built to Last? Reflections on British Housing Policy* (London: Shelter).

Clapham, D. and Evans, A. (1998) *From Exclusion to Inclusion* (London: Hastoe Housing Association).

Clapham, D. and Kintrea, K. (1994) 'Community ownership and the break up of council housing in Britain', *Journal of Social Policy*, 23 (2), 210–45.

Clapham, D. and Kintrea, K. (2000) 'Community-based housing organisations and the local governance debate', *Housing Studies*, 15 (4), 533–59.

Clarke, J., Gerwutz, S. and McLauglin, E. (2000) (eds) *New Managerialism, New Welfare?* (London: Open University, Sage).

Clarke, J. and Newman, J. (1997) *The Managerial State* (London: Sage).

Cole, I. and Furbey, R. (1994) *The Eclipse of Council Housing* (London: Routledge).

Cole, I., Kane, S. and Robinson, D. (1999) *Changing Demand, Changing Neighbourhood. The Response of Social Landlords* (Sheffield: Sheffield Hallam University).

Cole, I. and Nevin, B. (2004) *The Road to Renewal: The Early Development of the Housing Market Renewal Programme in England* (York: York Publishing Services).

Coleman, D. and J. Salt, (1992) *The British Population* (Oxford: Oxford University Press).

Commission for Racial Equality (1984) *Race and Council Housing in Hackney* (London: CRE).

Community Housing Task Force (2003a) *Option Appraisals Advice Note on Communications and Consultation Strategies* (London: ODPM, CHTF).

Community Housing Task Force (2003b) *Tenant Empowerment Strategies in Option Appraisal* (London: ODPM, CHTF).

Confederation of Construction Clients (2003) *The Client Charter* (London: Confederation of Construction Clients).

Confederation of Co-operative Housing (2001) *Stock Transfer. Creating community controlled housing* (Birmingham: Confederation of Co-operative Housing).

Connelly, J. and Crown, J. (1994) *Homelessness and Ill Health. Report of a Working Party of the Royal College of Physicians* (London: Royal College of Physicians).

Conservative Party (1979) *Election Manifesto.*

Cooper, C. and Hawtin, M. (1998) *Resident Involvement and Community Action. Theory to Practice* (Coventry: Chartered Institute of Housing).

Cope, H. (1999) *Housing Associations. The Policy and Practice of Registered Social Landlords* (Basingstoke: Macmillan).

Crook, A. D. H., Hughes, J. and Kemp, P. A. (1995) *The Supply of Private Rented Homes* (York: Joseph Rowntree Foundation).

Crook, A. D. H., Kemp, P. A., Anderson, I. and Bowman, S. (1991) *Tax Incentives and the Decline of Private Renting* (York: Cloister Press).

Cullingworth, B. (1963) *Housing in Transition* (London: Heinemann).

Cullingworth, B. (1966) *Housing and Local Government* (London: George Allen & Unwin).

Cullingworth, B. (1969) *Council Housing Purposes, Procedures and Priorities* (London: DoE).

Cullingworth, B. (1979) *Essays on Housing Policy* (London: George Allen and Unwin).

Dale, A., Williams, M. and Dodgeon, B. (1996) *Housing Deprivation and Social Change*, Series LS No. 8, Office for National Statistics (London: HMSO).

Davis, C. (2003) *Housing Associations – Rehousing Women Leaving Domestic Violence. New challenges and good practice* (Bristol: Policy Press).

Davis, H. and Spencer, K. (1995) *Housing Associations and the Governance Debate* (Birmingham: Birmingham University, School of Public Policy).

Department for Work and Pensions (2002a) *Building Choice and Responsibility: A Radical Agenda for Housing Benefit* (London: DWP).

Department for Work and Pensions (2002b) *Findings from the macro evaluation of the New Deal for Young People* (London: HMSO).

Department for Work and Pensions (2003) *Housing Benefit Local Housing Allowance Guidance Manual* (London: DWP).

Department for Work and Pensions (2004) *The Nine LHA Pathfinder Areas: A summary of the baseline position before the introduction of the LHA* (London: DWP).

Department of Health (1998) *Modernising Social Services* (London: Department of Health).

Department of Health (2001) *Integrating Community Equipment*, DH Circular HSC (2001), 008 LAC (2001), 013 (London: Department of Health).

Department of Health (2005) *Independence Well Being and Choice – Our Vision for the Future of Social Care for Adults in England* (London: HMSO).

Department of Health and DTLR (1999) *Better Care, Higher Standards – the Long Term Care Charter* (London: Department of Health and DTLR).

Department of Health and Office of the Deputy Prime Minister (2004) *Achieving Positive Shared Outcomes in Health and Homelessness* (London: DoH and ODPM Homelessness and Support Directorate).

Department of Social Security (1998a) *New Ambitions for our Country: A New Contract for Welfare* (London: DSS).

Department of Social Security (1998b) *Supporting People: A New Policy and Funding Framework for Support Services* (London: DSS).

Department of the Environment (1971) *Housing Associations* (London: DOE).

Department of Environment (1977) *Housing Policy: Technical Volume Part* 1, Cmnd 6851 (London: HMSO).

Department of Environment (1971) *Fair Deal for Housing Cmnd 4728* (Lava: HMSO).

Department for the Environment (1987) *Housing: The Government's Proposals*, Cm 214 (London: HMSO).

Department of the Environment (1983) *English House Condition Survey 1981. Part 2: Report of the interview and local authority survey* (London: HMSO).

Department of the Environment (1987) *Finance for Housing Associations: The Government's Proposals* (London: DoE).

Department of the Environment (1997) *Mapping Local Authority Estates using the Index of Local Conditions* (London: DoE).

DETR (1985) *Home Improvement – A New Approach*, Cmnd 9513 (London: HMSO).

DETR (1997) *Regeneration: The Way Forward, A Consultation Paper* (London: DETR).

DETR (1998a) *Supporting People. A New Funding Framework for Support Services* (London: DETR).

DETR (1998b) *The 1998 Index of Local Derivation: A Summary of Results* (London: DETR).

DETR (1999) *Supporting People. A New Funding Framework for Support Services. Summary of analysis of responses to the 'Supporting People' consultation document* (London: DETR).

DETR (2000a) *Unpopular Housing – Policy Action Team 7 Report* (London: DETR).

DETR (2000b) *Our Towns and Cities: The Future – Delivering an Urban Renaissance* (London: HMSO).

DETR and DSS (2000a) *Quality and Choice: A Decent Home for All. The Housing Green Paper* (London: DETR and DSS).

DETR and DSS (2000b) *Quality and Choice: A Decent Home for All. The Housing White Paper* (London: DETR and DSS).

DETR and DSS (2000c) *Guide to Social Rent Reforms* (London: DETR and DSS).

DTLR (2001a) *Supporting People: Policy into Practice* (London: DTLR).

DTLR (2001b) *Supporting People. The Administrative Guidance* (London: DTLR).

DTLR (2001c) *Quality and Choice for Older People's Housing. A Strategic Framework* (London: DTLR).

DETR (2001d) *Year 2000 Review of the Housing Corporation: Prior Options Report* (London: DETR).

Donnison, M. (1967) *The Government of Housing* (Harmondsworth: Penguin).

Duclaud-Williams, R. (1978) *The Politics of Housing in Britain and France* (London: Heinemann).

Duizendstraal, A. and Nentjes, A. (1994) 'Organizational slack in subsidised non-profit institutions', *Public Choice*, 81 (3–4), pp. 297–321.

Dunleavy, P. (1981) *The Politics of Mass Housing in Britain 1947–1975* (Oxford: Clarendon Press).

Egan, J. (1998) *Rethinking Construction. Report of the Construction Task Force to Deputy Prime Minister* (London: Department of Government Transport and the Regions).

Egan, J. (2004) *Skills for Sustainable Communities* (London: Office of the Deputy Prime Minister).

Englander, D. (1983) *Landlord and Tenant in Urban Britain 1838–1918* (Oxford: Clarendon Press).

Esping-Andersen, G. (1990) *The Three Worlds of Welfare Capitalism* (Cambridge: Polity Press).

Fenter, M. (1960) *COPEC Adventure. The Story of the Birmingham COPEC House Improvement Society* (Birmingham: Butler and Webb).

Ferlie, E., Ashburner, L., Fitzgerald, L. and Pettigrew, A. (1996) *The New Public Management in Action* (Oxford: Oxford University Press).

Fitzpatrick, S., Kemp, P. and Klinker, S. (2000) *Single Homelessness. An Overview of Research in Britain* (Bristol: Policy Press).

Fletcher, P., Riseborough, M., Humphries, J., Jenkins, C. and Whittingham, P. (1999) *Citizenship and Services in Old Age: The Strategic Role of Very Sheltered Housing* (Beaconsfield: Housing 21).

Fletcher, P., M., Riseborough, C., Jenkins and S. Spencer (2001) *A Supported Housing Strategy for Liverpool* (Liverpool: Liverpool City Council).

Fletcher, P., Riseborough, M., Jenkins, C., Spencer, S. and Rose-Troup, M. (2003) *A supported housing and support service strategy for Liverpool* (Northumberland: Peter Fletcher Associates and Liverpool Health, Housing and Care Partnership).

Ford, J. and Wilcox, S. (1992) *Reducing Mortgage Arrears and Repossessions* (York: Joseph Rowntree Foundation).

Forrest, R., Lansley, S. and Murie, A. (1984) *A Foot on the Ladder* (Bristol: School for Advanced Urban Studies, University of Bristol).

Forrest, R. and Murie, A. (1988) *Selling the Welfare State* (London: Routledge).

Forrest, R. and Murie, A. (1994) 'Home Ownership in Recession', *Housing Studies* 9 (1).

Forrest, R., Murie, A. and Gordon, D. (1995) *The Resale of Former Council Homes* (London: Department of the Environment and HMSO).

Forrest, R., Murie, A. and Williams, P. (1990) *Home Ownership* (London: Unwin Hyman).

Foster, S. (1992) *Mortgage Rescue. What does it add up to?* (London: Shelter).

Francis, J. (1993) *The politics of regulation. A comparative perspective* (Oxford: Blackwell).

Franklin, B. (1998) 'Constructing a Service: Context and Discourse in Housing Management', *Housing Studies*, 13 (2), pp. 201–16.

Franklin, B. (2000) 'Demands, Expectations and Responses: The Shaping of Housing Management', *Housing Studies*, 15 (6), pp. 907–27.

Fraser, M. (1996) *John Bull's Other Homes. State Housing and British Policy in Ireland 1883–1922* (Liverpool: Liverpool University Press).

Galster, G. (1997) 'Comparing demand-side and supply-side housing policies: sub-market and spatial perspectives', *Housing Studies*, 12 (4), pp. 561–77.

Garside, P. (2000) *The Conduct of Philanthropy: William Sutton Trust 1900–2000* (London: Cambridge University Press).

Gauldie, E. (1974) *Cruel Habitations* (London: Allen and Unwin).

Gibb, K. (1995) 'A Housing Allowance for the UK: Pre-conditions for a Tenure-Neutral Income-Related Housing Allowance', *Housing Studies*, 10 (4), pp. 517–32.

Gibb, K. (2003) 'Transfering Glasgow's Council Housing: Financial, Urban and Housing Policy Implications', *European Journal of Housing Policy*, 3(1), pp. 89–114.

Gibb, K., Munro, M. and Satsangi, M. (1999) *Housing Finance in the UK: An Introduction*, 2nd edn (Basingstoke: Macmillan).

Gibson, M. (1986) 'Housing renewal: privatisation and beyond', in P. Malpass (ed.), *The housing crisis* (London: Routledge).

Gibson, M. and Langstaff, M. (1982) *An Introduction to Urban Renewal* (London: Hutchinson).

Gilbert, B. B. (1970) *British Social Policy 1914–1939* (London: Batsford).

Goodlad, R. (1993) *The Housing Authority as an Enabler* (Coventry: Chartered Institute of Housing).

Gray P. G. (1947) *The British Household. The Social Survey* (London: Central Office of Information).

Greater London Council (1984) *Going … Going … Almost Gone: What price the private rented sector?* (London: Greater London Council).

Griffith, J. A. G. (1966) *Central Departments and Local Authorities* (London: George Allen & Unwin).

Groves, R. (2004) *Understanding the Private Rented Sector* (Birmingham: CURS, University of Birmingham).

Groves, R. and Murie, A. (2005) *Housing and the New Welfare State* (Aldershot: Ashgate).

Groves, R., Lee, P., Murie, A. and Nevin, B. (2001) *Private Rented in Liverpool* (Liverpool: Liverpool City Council).

Groves, R. and Sankey, S. (2004) *Implementing New Powers for Private Sector Housing Renewal under the Regulatory Reform Order, 2002. Findings of the second survey* (Birmingham: CURS, University of Birmingham).

Groves, R. and Sankey, S. (2005) *Implementing New Powers for Private Sector Housing Renewal* (London: ODPM).

Gulliver, K. (2000) *Social Concern and Social Enterprise. The Origins and History of Focus Housing* (Studley: Brewin).

HACAS Chapman Hendy (2002) *Effects of Rent Reforms on Black and Minority Ethnic Registered Social Landlords* (London: ODPM).

HACAS Chapman Hendy and KPMG (2000) *Assessing the Impact of Housing Green Paper Rent Reforms on Individual Registered Social Landlords* (London: DETR).

Hamnett, C. (1999) *Winners and losers – Home Ownership in Modern Britain* (London: UCL Press).

Harloe, M. (1978) 'The Green Paper on Housing Policy', Chapter 3 in M. Brown and S. Baldwin (eds), *The Yearbook of Social Policy in Britain 1977* (London: Routledge).

Harloe, M. (1985) *The People's Home? Social Rented Housing in Europe and America* (Oxford: Blackwell).

Harriott, S. and Matthews, L. (1998) *Social Housing. An Introduction* (Harlow: Longman).

Harrison, M. (1991) *Achievements and Options. Black and minority ethnic housing organisations in action* (Leeds: Armley).

Harrison, M. (1995) *Housing, 'Race', Social Policy and Empowerment* (Aldershot: Avebury).

Harrison, M. and Davis, C. (2001) *Housing, Social Policy and Difference. Disability, ethnicity, gender and housing* (Bristol: Policy Press).

Harrison, M. and Phillips, D. (2003) *Housing and Black and Minority Ethnic Communities. Review of the Evidence Base* (London: ODPM).

Haynes, P. (2003) *Managing Complexity in the Public Services* (Maidenhead: Open University Press).

Heenan, D. (2001) 'Gender, culture and social housing', in C. Paris (ed.), *Housing in Northern Ireland – and Comparisons with the Republic of Ireland* (Coventry: Chartered Institute of Housing).

Henderson, J., and Karn, V. (1985) 'Race, Class and the Allocation of Public Housing in Great Britain', *Urban Studies*, 21, pp. 115–28.

Henderson, J. and Karn, V. (1987) *Race, Class and State Housing: Inequality and the Allocation of Public Housing* (Aldershot: Gower).

Henney, A. (1985) *Trust the Tenant: Devolving Municipal Housing* (London: Centre for Policy Studies).

Herbert G. and Sawyer L. (2005) *New Approaches to Support Older People at Home* (York: Joseph Rowntree Foundation).

Heywood, F., Oldman, C. and Means, R. (2001) *Housing and Home in Later Life* (Buckingham: Open University Press).

Higgins, J. (1989) 'Defining Community Care: Realities and Myths', *Social Policy and Administration*, 23 (2), pp. 3–16.

Hill, M. (1997) *The Policy Process in the Modern State* (Harlow: Pearson).

Hills, J. (1989) 'The Voluntary Sector in Housing: The role of British Housing Associations', in E. James (ed.), *The Non-Profit Sector in International Perspective* (New York: Oxford University Press).

Hills, J. (1991) *Unravelling Housing Finance: Subsidies, Benefits and Taxation* (Oxford: Clarendon Press).

Hills, J. (1993) *The Future of Welfare: A Guide to the Debate* (York: Joseph Rowntree Foundation).

Hills, J. (2001) 'Inclusion or Exclusion? The role of housing subsidies and benefits', *Urban Studies*, 38 (11), pp. 1887–902.

HMSO (1971) *Fair Deal for Housing*, Cmnd 4728 (London: HMSO).

HMSO (1992) *Social Trends* (London: HMSO).

Hogwood, B. W. and Gunn, L. A. (1981) *The Policy Orientation* (Strathclyde: Centre for the Study of Public Policy, University of Strathclyde).

Holmans, A. E. (1987) *Housing Policy in Britain: A History* (London: Croom Helm).

Holmans, A. E. (1991) *Estimates of Housing Equity Withdrawl by Owner Occupiers in the United Kingdom 1970 to 1990* (London: Department of the Environment).

Holmans, A. and Simpson, M. (1999) *Low Demand. Separating Fact from Fiction* (Coventry: Chartered Institute of Housing).

Home Ownership Taskforce (2003) *Final Report of Brenda Dean's Review* (London: Housing Corporation).

Hood, C. (1995) 'The "New Public Management" in the 1980s: variations on a theme', *Accounting, Organisations and Society* 20, pp. 93–109.

Hood, C., Scott, C., James, O., Jones, G. and Travers, T. (1998) *Regulation Inside Government. Waste Watchers, Quality Police and Sleaze Busters* (Oxford: Oxford University Press).

Houlihan, B. (1988) *Housing Policy and Central Local Government Relations* (Aldershot: Avebury).

Housing Associations Charitable Trust (2004) *Accommodate, The Refugee Housing Partnership Project*, newsletters 1 and 2 (London: Housing Associations Charitable Trust).

Housing Corporation (1998a) *Black and Minority Ethnic Housing Policy* (London: Housing Corporation).

Housing Corporation (1998b) *The 1998 Scheme Development Standards*, 3rd edn (London: Housing Corporation).

Housing Corporation (1999a) *Regulating Diversity. Discussion Paper* (London: Housing Corporation).

Housing Corporation (1999b) *Regulating a Diverse Sector. Consultation Paper* (London: Housing Corporation).

Housing Corporation (2000) *Communities in Control* (London: Housing Corporation).

Housing Corporation (2002a) *The Way Forward. Our Approach to Regulation* (London: Housing Corporation).

Housing Corporation (2002b) *Assessing Financial Viability*, Regulatory Code Good Practice Note 2 (London: Housing Corporation).

Housing Corporation (2002c) *The Way Forward. Inspection: Our Approach to Inspection* (London: Housing Corporation).

Housing Corporation (2002d) *Reviewing the Housing Corporation's Tenant Participation Policy. Discussion Paper* (London: Housing Corporation).

Housing Corporation (2003a) *Understanding our Assets. A Self-Assessment Framework for Boards of Housing Associations* (London: Housing Corporation).

Housing Corporation (2003b) *Involvement Policy. Consultation Paper* (London: Housing Corporation).

Housing Corporation (2004a) *New Partnerships in Affordable Housing. A Pilot Investment Programme Open to Housing Associations and Unregistered Bodies* (London: Housing Corporation).

Housing Corporation (2004b) *Housing Corporation: 40 Years of Affordable Homes* (London: Housing Corporation).

Housing Corporation (2004c) *Making Groups Work*, Good Practice Note 11 (London: Housing Corporation).

Housing Corporation and National Housing Federation (2003a) *Private Finance Monitoring Bulletin*, no 13, March (London: Housing Corporation and NHF).

Housing Corporation and National Housing Federation (2003b) *Global Accounts and Sector Analysis of Housing Associations* (London: Housing Corporation and NHF).

House of Commons Environment Committee (1980) *Enquiry into the Implications on the Government's Expenditure Plans 1980–81 to 1983–84* (London: HMSO).

House of Commons Environment Committee (1982) *The Private Rented Sector* (London: HMSO).

Howe, G. and Jones, C. (1956) *Houses to Let* (London: Conservative Political Centre).

Howes, E. and Mullins, D. (1999) *Dwelling on Difference. Housing and Ethnicity in London* (London: London Research Centre).

Hughes, G., Mears, R. and Winch, C. (1996) 'An Inspector Calls? Regulation and accountability in three public services', *Policy and Politics*, 25 (3), pp. 299–313.

Hughes, O. E. (1998) *Public Management and Administration. An Introduction* (Basingstoke: Palgrave).

Ineichen, B. (1993) *Homes and Health: How Housing and Health Interact* (London: Spon).

Jones, C. (2003) *Exploitation of the Right to Buy Scheme by Companies* (London: Office of the Deputy Prime Minister).

Jones, C. and Murie, A. (1998) *Reviewing the Right to Buy* (Birmingham: CURS, University of Birmingham).

Jordan, B. (1996) *A Theory of Poverty and Social Exclusion* (Cambridge: Polity Press).

Joseph, R. (2005) *Housing Wealth and Accumulation. Experiences of Afro-Caribbean Households of Home Ownership in Birmingham and London, 1950–79* (Birmingham: CURS, University of Birmingham).

Joseph Rowntree Foundation (2004) *From Welfare to Well Being – Planning for an Ageing Society. Report from the Task Group on Housing, Money and Care for Older People* (York: Joseph Rowntree Foundation).

Karn, V. (1993) 'Remodelling a HAT: the implementation of the Housing Action Trust legislation 1987–92', in P. Malpass and R. Means (eds), *Implementing Housing Policy* (Buckingham: Open University Press).

Karn, V., Kemeny, J. and Williams, P. (1985) *Home Ownership in the Inner City–Salvation or Despair?* (London: Croom Helm).

Karn, V. and Sheridan, L. (1994) *New Homes in the 1980s. A Study of Design, Space and Amenities in Housing Association and Private Sector Housing* (York: Joseph Rowntree Foundation).

Keenan, P., Lowe, S. and Spencer, S. (1999) 'Housing abandonment in inner cities – the politics of low demand for housing', *Housing Studies*, 14 (5), pp. 703–16.

Kellett, J. M. (1993) 'Crowding and Mortality in London Boroughs', in R. Burridge and D. Ormandy (eds), *Unhealthy Housing: Research, Remedies and Reform* (London: Chapman and Hall).

Kelman, S. (1986) 'A case for in-kind transfers', *Economics and Philosophy*, 2, pp. 35–73.

Kemeny, J. (1981) *The Myth of Homeownership. Public Versus Private Choices in Housing Tenure* (London: Routledge).

Kemeny, J. (1992) *Housing and Social Theory* (London: Routledge).

Kemp, P. (1992) *Housing Benefit: An Appraisal* (London: HMSO).

Kemp, P. (1998) *Housing Benefit: Time for Reform* (York: Joseph Rowntree Foundation).

Kemp, P. (2000a) *'Shopping Incentives' and the Reform of Housing Benefit* (Coventry: Chartered Institute of Housing).

Kemp, P. (2000b) 'Housing Benefit and Welfare Retrenchment in Britain', *Journal of Social Policy*, 29 (2), pp. 263–79.

Kendall, J. (2003) *The Voluntary Sector: Comparative Perspectives in the UK* (London: Routledge).

Kullberg, J. (1997) 'From waiting lists to adverts: the allocation of social rental dwellings in the Netherlands', *Housing Studies*, 12 (3), pp. 393–403.

Kullberg, J. (2002) 'Consumers' response to Choice Based Letting mechanisms', *Housing Studies*, 17 (4), pp. 549–80.

Lansley, S. (1979) *Housing and Public Policy* (Beckenham: Croom Helm).

Leather, P. and Mackintosh, S. (1992) *Maintaining Home Ownership: The Agency Approach* (London: Longman and Institute of Housing).

Leather, P. and Mackintosh, S. (1994) *The Future of Housing Renewal* (Bristol: SAUS Publications).

Leather, P. and Mackintosh, S. (1997) 'Towards sustainable policies for housing renewal in the private sector', in P. Williams (ed.), *Directions in Housing Policy* (London: Paul Chapman).

Leather, P. and Morrison, T. (1997) *The State of UK Housing* (Bristol: Policy Press).

Leather, P. and Revell, K. (2000) *The State of UK Housing*, 2nd edn (Bristol: Policy Press).

Lee, P. (1998) 'Housing Policy, Citizenship and Social Exclusion', in A. Marsh and D. Mullins (eds), *Housing and Public Policy. Citizenship, Choice and Control* (Buckingham: Open University Press).

Lee, P. and Murie, A. (1997) *Poverty Housing Tenure and Social Exclusion* (Bristol: Policy Press).

Legg, C. (1981) *Could Local Authorities be Better Landlords? An Assessment of How Councils Manage their Housing* (London: Housing Research Group, City University).

Le Grand, J. (2003) *Motivation, Agency and Public Policy: Of Knights and Knaves, Pawns and Queens* (Oxford: Oxford University Press).

Le Grand, J. and Bartlett, W. (1993) *Quasi-Markets and Social Policy* (Basingstoke: Macmillan).

Levitas, R. (1996) 'The Concept of Social Exclusion and the New Durkheimian Hegemony', *Critical Social Policy*, 16, pp. 5–20.

Liverpool Student Homes (2000) *Market Analyses of the Student Market in Liverpool, 1995–2000* (Liverpool: Liverpool Student Homes).

Local Government Training Board (1987) *Getting Closer to the Public* (Luton: LGTB).

Lowe, S. (2004) *Housing Policy Analysis: British Housing in Cultural and Comparative Context* (Basingstoke: Palgrave).

Lowe, S., Spencer, S. and Keenan, P. (1998) *Housing Abandonment in Britain. Case Studies in the Causes and Effects of Low Demand Housing* (York: University of York).

Maclennan, D. (1982) *Housing Economics* (Harlow: Longman).

Malpass, P. (1990) *Reshaping Housing Policy: Subsidies, Rents and Residualisation* (London: Routledge).

Malpass, P. (1998) *Housing, Philanthropy and the State: A History of the Guinness Trust* (Bristol: University of the West Of England).

Malpass, P. (1999) 'Housing associations and housing policy in Britain since 1989', *Housing Studies*, 14 (6), pp. 881–93.

Malpass, P. (2000a) *Housing Associations and Housing Policy. A Historical Perspective* (Basingstoke: Macmillan).

Malpass, P. (2000b) 'The discontinuous history of housing associations in England', *Housing Studies*, 15 (2), pp. 169–95.

Malpass, P. (2004) 'Fifty Years of British Housing Policy: Leaving or Leading the Welfare State?', *European Journal of Housing Policy*, 4 (2), pp. 209–27.

Malpass, P. and Mears, R. (1993) *Implementing Housing Policy* (Buckingham: Open University Press).

Malpass, P. and Mullins, D. (2002) 'Local Authority Stock Transfer in the UK: from local initiative to national policy', *Housing Studies*, 17 (4), pp. 673–86.

Malpass, P. and Murie, A. (1994) *Housing Policy and Practice*, 4th edn (Basingstoke: Macmillan).

Malpass, P. and Murie, A. (1999) *Housing Policy and Practice*, 5th edn (Basingstoke: Palgrave).

Maltby, P. (2003) *In the Public Interest: Assessing the Potential for Public Interest Companies* (London: IPPR).

Mandelson, P. (1997) *Labour's Next Steps: Tackling Social Exclusion* (London: Fabian Society).

Marsh, A. (1998) 'Processes of change in housing and public policy', in A. Marsh and D. Mullins (eds), *Housing and Public Policy. Citizenship, Choice and Control* (Buckingham: Open University Press).

Marsh, A. (2001) 'Restructuring social housing rents', in D. Cowan and A. Marsh (eds), *Two Steps Forward: Housing Policy in the New Millennium* (Bristol: Policy Press), pp. 285–304.

Marsh, A. (2004) 'The Inexorable Rise of the Rational Consumer? The Blair Government and the Reshaping of Social Housing', *European Journal of Housing Policy*, 4 (2), pp. 185–207.

Marsh, A., Cowan, D., Cameron, A., Jones, M., Kiddle, C. and Whitehead, C. (2004) *Piloting Choice Based Lettings: An Evaluation* (London: Office of the Deputy Prime Minister).

Marsh, A. and Walker, B. (forthcoming) 'Getting a Policy to Stick: Centralizing Control of Rent Setting in England', *Policy and Politics*.

Marshall, D. (2003) *The Importance of RSL Group Structures in England* (Cambridge. Centre for Housing and Planning Research).

Marshall, T. H. (1950) *Citizenship and Social Class* (Cambridge: Cambridge University Press).

McCreary, A. (1999) *Making a Difference. The Story of Ulster Garden Villages Ltd* (Belfast: Ulster Garden Villages Ltd).

McLachlan, P. (1997) 'The 1974 Corrymeela Conference and its origins', in *Celebrating 21 Years of Voluntary Housing in Northern Ireland* (Belfast: NIFHA).

Melling, J. (1989) 'Clydeside rent struggles and the making of labour politics in Scotland 1900–39', in R. Rodger (ed.), *Scottish Housing in the Twentieth Century* (Leicester: Leicester University Press).

Merrett, S. (1979) *State Housing in Britain* (London: Routledge & Kegan Paul).

Merrett, S. (1982) *Owner Occupation in Britain* (London: Routledge & Kegan Paul).

Middlemas, K. (1979) *Politics in Industrial Society* (London: Andre Deutsch).

Milner Holland Report (1965) *Report of the Committee on Housing in Greater London* (London: HMSO).

Minogue, M., Polidano, C. and Hulme, D. (1998) *Beyond the New Public Management: Changing Ideas and Practice in Governance* (London: Edward Elgar).

Mintzberg, H. (1994) *The Rise and Fall of Strategic Planning* (London, Prentice-Hall).

Moore, A., Findlay, J., Gibb, K., Kasparova, D. and Mills, C. (2003) *Determined Differences: Rent Structures in Scottish Social Housing* (Edinburgh: Scottish Executive Social Research).

Moore, R. (1980) 'Reconditioning the slums: the development and role of housing rehabilitation', Mimeo.

Morris, J. and Winn, M. (1990) *Housing and Social Inequality* (London: Hilary Shipman).

Morgan, G. (1998) *Images of Organisation* (London: Sage Publications).

Mullings, B. (1991) *The Colour of Money. The Impact of Housing Investment Decision Making on Black Housing Outcomes in London* (London: London Race and Housing Research Unit).

Mullins, D. (1996) *Us and Them* (Birmingham: University of Birmingham).

Mullins, D. (1997) 'From regulatory capture to regulated competition', *Housing Studies*, 12 (3), pp. 301–19.

Mullins, D. (1998) 'More Choice in Social Rented Housing?', in A. Marsh and D. Mullins (eds), *Housing and Public Policy: Citizenship, Choice and Control* (Birmingham: Open University Press) pp. 124–52.

Mullins, D. (1999a) *Baseline Survey of Registered Social Landlords Best Value Activity* (London: National Housing Federation).

Mullins, D. (1999b) *Non-Profit Housing at the Millennium in England, Scotland and Wales* (Birmingham: University of Birmingham, Centre for Urban and Regional Studies, for Zurich Municipal PLC).

Mullins, D. (2000) 'Social origins and transformations: The changing role of English housing associations', *Voluntas*, 11 (3), pp. 255–75.

Mullins, D. (2001) *Tenants Choice. The role of the Housing Corporation*. Report for Department of Environment (Birmingham, CURS, University of Birmingham).

Mullins, D. (2002) 'Redefining "Competition" as "Competitiveness" – the Best Value activities of registered social landlords', *Public Money and Management*, 22 (2), pp. 25–30.

Mullins, D. (2003) 'Involvement of Users in Governance: Some Experiences from the Non-Profit Housing Sector', in J. Warburton and D. Morris (eds), *Charities, Governance and the Law: The Way Forward* (London: Key Haven Press), pp. 95–118.

Mullins, D. (2004a) 'Transforming Social Housing? Forecasting the Future Shape and Structure of the Housing Association Sector in England', paper presented at the Housing Studies Association Conference, Sheffield, April.

Mullins, D. (2004b) 'The Politics of Organisational Concentration. Group Structures in the English Housing Association Sector', paper presented at the European Housing Network Conference, Cambridge, July.

Mullins, D., Beider, H. and Rowlands, R. (2004) *Empowering Communities, Improving Housing: Involving Black and Minority Ethnic Tenants and Communities* (London: ODPM).

Mullins, D., Latto, S., Hall, S. and Srbljanin, A. (2001) *Mapping Diversity. Registered Social Landlords, Diversity and Regulation in the West Midlands* (Birmingham: University of Birmingham).

Mullins, D., Niner, P. (1996) *Common Housing Registers: An Evaluation and Analysis of Current Practice* (London: Housing Corporation).

Mullins, D., Niner, P. and Riseborough, M. (1992) *Evaluating Large Scale Voluntary Transfers of Local Authority Housing. Interim Report* (London: HMSO).

Mullins, D., Niner, P. and Riseborough, M. (1993) 'Large Scale Voluntary Transfers', in P. Malpass and R. Means (1993) *Implementing Housing Policy* (Buckingham: Open University Press).

Mullins, D., Niner, P. and Riseborough, M. (1995) *Evaluating Large Scale Voluntary Transfers of Local Authority Housing* (London: HMSO).

Mullins, D., Reid, B. and Walker, R. M. (2001) 'Modernisation and change in social housing: the case for an organizational perspective', *Public Administration*, 79 (3), pp. 599–623.

Mullins, D., Rhodes, M. L. and Williamson, A. (2001) 'Organizational Fields and Third Sector Housing in Ireland, North and South', *Voluntas*, 12 (3), pp. 257–78.

Mullins, D., Rhodes, M. L. and Williamson, A. (2003) *Non-profit Housing Organisations in Ireland, North and South: Changing Forms and Challenging Futures* (Northern Ireland Housing Executive).

Mullins, D. and Pawson, H. (2005) 'The land that time forgot? Reforming access to social housing in England', *Policy and Politics*, vol. 33, no. 2, pp. 205–30.

Mullins, D. and Riseborough, M. (1997) *Changing with the Times. Critical Interpretations of the Repositioning of Housing Associations*, School of Public Policy Occasional Paper 12 (Brimingham: University of Birmingham).

Mullins, D. and Riseborough, M. (2000) *What are Housing Associations Becoming? Final Report of Changing with the Times Project* (Birmingham, CURS, University of Birmingham).

Mullins, D. and Riseborough, M. (2001) 'Non-profit Housing Agencies: "Reading" and Shaping the Policy Agenda', in M. Harris and C. Rochester (eds), *Voluntary Organisations and Social Policy* (Basingstoke: Macmillan).

Murie, A. (1975) *The Sale of Council Houses*, Occasional Paper No 35 (Birmingham: CURS, University of Birmingham).

Murie, A. (1985) 'What the Country Can Afford? Housing under the Conservatives 1979–83', in P. Jackson (ed.), *Implementing Government Policy Initiatives: The Thatcher Administration 1979–83* (London: Royal Institute of Public Administration) pp. 169–87.

Murie, A. (1989) *Lost Opportunities? Council House Sales and Housing Policy in Britain 1979–89* (Bristol: SAUS, University of Bristol).

Murie, A. and Birrell, D. (1971) *The Northern Ireland Housing Trust 1945–71* (Coleraine: University of Ulster).

Murie, A., Leather, P. and Nevin, B. (1998) *Changing Demand and Unpopular Housing* (London: Housing Corporation).

Murie, A., Niner, P. and Watson, C. (1976) *Housing Policy and the Housing System* (London: Allen and Unwin).

Murie, A. and Priemus, H. (1994) 'Social Rented Housing in Britain and the Netherlands: Trends, Trajectories, and Divergence', *Netherlands Journal of the Built Environment*, 9 (2), pp. 107–26.

National Audit Office (2000) *Housing Corporation: Overseeing Focus Housing Association* (London: National Audit Office).

National Audit Office (2001) *Regulating Housing Associations' Management of Financial Risk*, report by the Comptroller and Auditor General (London: National Audit Office).

National Audit Office (2003) *Improving Social Housing Through Transfer*, report by the Comptroller and Auditor General (London: National Audit Office).

National Audit Office (2004) *An Early Progress Report on the New Deal for Communities Programme* (London: National Audit Office).

National Consumer Council (1986) *Measuring Up: Consumer Assessment of Local Authority Services. A Guideline Study* (London: NCC).

National Consumer Council (2001) *Consumer Involvement and Representation* (London: NCC).

National Federation of Housing Associations (1986) *Inquiry into British Housing.* (London NFAA).

National Federation of Housing Associations (1995) *Submission to Commission on the Future of the Voluntary Sector* (London: National Housing Federation).

National Housing Federation (2002) *Effects of Rent Reforms on Black and Minority Ethnic Registered Social Landlords – Comments* (London: National Housing Federation).

National Housing Federation (2003) *In Business for Neighbourhoods* (London: National Housing Federation).

National Housing Federation (2004a) *Code of Governance* (London: National Housing Federation).

National Housing Federation (2004b) *In Business, In Practice. In Business for Neighbourhoods One Year On* (London: National Housing Federation).

Neighbourhood Renewal Unit (2002) *Changing Neighbourhoods, Changing Lives: The Vision for Neighbourhood Renewal* (London: Neighbourhood Renewal Unit).

Nentjes, A. and Schopp, W. (2000) 'Discretionary profit in subsidised housing markets', *Urban Studies*, 37 (1), pp. 181–94.

Nevin, B., Lee, P., Goodson, L., Murie, A. and Phillimore, J. (2001) *Changing Housing Markets and Urban Regeneration in the M62 Corridor* (Birmingham: University of Birmingham).

Nevitt, A. A. (1966) *Housing Taxation and Subsidies* (London: Nelson).

Nevitt, A. A. (1968) 'Conflicts in British Housing Policy', *The Political Quarterly*, 39, pp. 439–50.

Newcombe, R. (1998) *Not Too Big, Not Too Small: Strategies for Medium-Sized Housing Associations* (York: University of York, Centre for Housing Policy).

Newman, J. (2000) 'Beyond the New Public Management. Modernising Public Services', in J. Clarke, S. Gerwutz and E. McLauglin (eds), *New Managerialism, New Welfare?* (London: Open University, Sage).

Newman, J. (2001) *Modernising Governance. New Labour, Policy and Society* (London: Sage).

NICVA (2000) *The Social Economy in Northern Ireland. Mapping and Tapping the Potential* (Belfast: NICVA).

NIFHA (1999) *Annual Report 1988/9* (Belfast: Northern Ireland Federation of Housing Associations).

NIFHA (2004) *Annual Report 2003/4* (Belfast: Northern Ireland Federation of Housing Associations).

Niner, P. (1975) *Local Authority Housing Policy and Practice* (Birmingham: CURS, University of Birmingham).

Niner, P. and Rowlands, R. (2003) *Involving Black and Minority Ethnic Tenants in Decisions on Housing Investment Options. Report on Postal Surveys* (Birmingham: CURS, University of Birmingham).

Niskanen, W. A. (1971) *Bureaucracy and Representative Government* (Chicago: Aldine-Atherton).

Nolan Committee (1996) *Committee on Standards in Public Life.*

Office of the Deputy Prime Minster (2003a) *Sustainable Communities: Building for the Future* (London: ODPM).

Office of the Deputy Prime Minister (2003b) *Review of the Delivery of the Decent Homes Target for Social Housing (PSA Plus Review)* (London: ODPM).

Office of the Deputy Prime Minister (2003c) *English House Condition Survey 2001* (London: ODPM Publications).

Office of the Deputy Prime Minister (2003d) *Delivering Decent Homes – Option Appraisal* (London: ODPM).

Office of the Deputy Prime Minister (2003e) *Housing Renewal* (London: ODPM).

Office of the Deputy Prime Minister (2004a) *Analysing the Impact of Rent Restructuring* (London: ODPM).

Office of the Deputy Prime Minister (2004b) *Housing Allocation, Homelessness and Stock Transfer: A Guide to Key Issues* (London: ODPM).

Office of the Deputy Prime Minister (2004c) *Local Authorities' Homelessness Strategies. Evaluation and Good Practice Guide* (London: ODPM).

Office of the Deputy Prime Minister (2004d) *Deputy Prime Minister's letter rebutting a 'fourth option' for Decent Homes* (London: ODPM).

Office of the Deputy Prime Minister (2004e) *The Housing Health and Safety Rating System and the Fitness Standard Guidance* (London: ODPM).

Office of the Deputy Prime Minister (2005) *Sustainable Communities: Homes for All, A Five Year Plan* (London: ODPM).

Office of the Deputy Prime Minister and Department of Health (2003) *Preparing Older People's Strategies: Linking Housing to Health, Social Care and Other Local Strategies* (London: ODPM and DoH).

Office of National Statistics (various) *Survey of English Housing* (London: HMSO).

Office of Public Management (2002) *Customer Involvement: Opportunities from the Private Sector?* (London: Housing Corporation).

Olechnowicz, A. (1997) *Working-Class Housing in England between the Wars* (Oxford: Clarendon Press).

Orbach, L. (1977) *Homes Fit for Heroes. A Study of the Evolution of British Public Housing 1915–21* (London: Seeley, Service).

Page, D. (1993) *Building for Communities: A Study of New Housing Association Estates* (York: Joseph Rowntree Foundation).

Paris, C. (2001) *Housing in Northern Ireland – and comparisons with the Republic of Ireland* (Coventry: Chartered Institute of Housing).

Paris, C. and Blackaby, R. (1979) *Not Much Improvement: Urban Renewal Policy in Birmingham* (London: Heinemann).

Parker, R. A. (1967) *The Rents of Council Homes* (London: Bell).

Paterson, L. (1994) *The Autonomy of Modern Scotland* (Edinburgh: Edinburgh University Press).

Pawson, H. (2004) 'Reviewing Stock Transfer', in S. Wilcox, *UK Housing Review 2004/5* (Coventry: Chartered Institute of Housing and Council of Mortgage Lenders).

Pawson, H. and Fancy, C. (2003) *Maturing Assets. The Evolution of Stock Transfer Housing Associations* (Bristol: Policy Press).

Pawson, H., Fancy, C., Morgan, J. and Munro, M. (2004) *Learning Lessons from the Estates Renewal Challenge Fund* (London: ODPM).

Pawson, H. and Mullins, D. (2003) *Changing Places: Housing Association Policy and Practice on Nominations and Lettings* (Bristol: Policy Press).

Pawson, H. and Sinclair, S. (2002) *Evaluation of Department for Work and Pensions Underoccupier Incentive Scheme*, In-house Report 99 (London: Department for Work and Pensions).

Pawson, H. and Sinclair, S. P. (2003) 'Shopping Therapy? Incentive Payments and Tenant Behaviour: Lessons from Underoccupation Schemes in the UK', *European Journal of Housing Policy*, 3 (3), pp. 289–311.

Peace, S. and Holland, C. (eds) (2001) *Inclusive Housing in an Ageing Society. Innovative Approaches* (Bristol: Policy Press).

Peace, S., Kellaher, L. and Willcocks, D. (1997) *Re-evaluating Residential Care* (Buckingham: Open University Press).

Pearl, M. (1997) *Social Housing Management. A Critical Appraisal of Housing Practice* (Basingstoke: Macmillan).

Peters, T. H. and Waterman, R. H. (1982) *In Search of Excellence* (New York: Warner).

Phillips, D. (1986) *What Price Equality?* (London: Greater London Council).

Phillipson, C., Bernard, M., Phillips, J. and Ogg, J. (1999) 'Older people's experience of community life: Patterns of neighbouring in three urban areas', *Sociological Review*, 47 (4), pp. 715–43.

Pooley, C. G. (ed.) (1992) *Housing Strategies in Europe. 1880–1930* (Leicester: Leicester University Press).

Power, A. (1987) *Property Before People* (London: Allen and Unwin).

Power, M. (1997) *The Audit Society. Rituals of Verification* (Oxford: Oxford University Press).

Randolph, B. (1993) 'The re-privatisation of housing associations', in P. Malpass and R. Means (eds), *Implementing Housing Policy* (Buckingham: Open University Press).

Ravetz, A. (2001) *Council Housing and Culture. The History of a Social Experiment* (London: Routledge).

Reid, B. (1995) 'Interorganisational Networks and the Delivery of Local Housing Services', *Housing Studies*, 10 (2), pp. 133–50.

Reid, B. and Hickman, P. (2002) 'Are Housing Organisations Becoming Learning Organisations? Some Lessons from the Management of Tenant Participation', *Housing Studies*, 17 (6), pp. 895–918.

Rex, J. and Moore, R. (1967) *Race, Community and Conflict* (Oxford: Oxford University Press).

Riseborough, M. (1998) 'More choice and control for users? Involving tenants in social housing management', in A. Marsh and D. Mullins (eds), *Housing and Public Policy. Citizenship, Choice and Control* (Buckingham: Open University Press).

Riseborough, M. and Fletcher, P. (2004) *Strategic Moves. Thinking, Planning and Delivering Differently* (London: Housing Learning and Improvement Network, Department of Health).

Riseborough, M. and Jenkins, C. (2004) *Now You See Me Now You Don't. How are Older People Being Included in Regeneration?* (London: Age Concern England).

Riseborough, M. and Srbjlanin, A. (2000) *Overlooked and Excluded: Older People and Regeneration* (London: Age Concern England).

Robson, B., Bradford, M., Dean, I., Hall, E., Harrison, E., Parkinson, M., Evans, R., Garside, P., Harding, A. and Robinson, F. (1994) *Assessing the Impact of Urban Policy* (London: HMSO).

Rodgers, G., Gore, C. and Figueiredo, J. B. (1995) *Social Exclusion: Rhetoric, Reality and Responses* (Geneva: International Institute for Labour Studies, United Nations Development Programme).

Room, G. (ed.) (1995a) *Beyond the Threshold: The Measurement and Analysis of Social Exclusion* (Bristol: Policy Press).

Room, G. (1995b) 'Poverty in Europe: competing paradigms of analysis', *Policy and Politics*, 23 (2), pp. 103–13.

Royal Commission on the Future of Long Term Care (2001) *Final Report. With Respect to Old Age* (London: HMSO).

Salamon, L. and Anheier, H. (1997) *Defining the Non-Profit Sector. A Cross-National Analysis* (Manchester: Manchester University Press).

Sarre, P., Phillips, D. and Skellington, R. (1989) *Ethnic Minority Housing. Explanations and Policies* (Aldershot: Avebury).

Saw, P., Pryke, M., Royce, C. and Whitehead, C. M. (1996) *Housing Associations and the Private Lender* (York: Joseph Rowntree Foundation).

Scott, S. (2001) *Good Practice in Housing Management in Scotland. Review of Progress* (Edinburgh: Scottish Executive Central Research Unit).

Scottish Development Department (1977) *Scottish Housing: A Consultative Document* Cmnd. 6852 (Edinburgh: HMSO).

Scottish Development Department (1987) *Housing: The Government's Proposals for Scotland* Cm 242 (Ediburgh: HMSO).

Scottish Executive (2001) 'Free care for older people to be extended in Scotland', news release SE/01 38 (Edinburgh: Scottish Executive).

Sharples, S. (2002) *Stock Swaps Making Them Work – a Good Practice Guide* (Liverpool: Riverside Housing).

Shelter (2003) *Local Authority Homelessness Strategies* (London: Shelter).

Shelter (2005) 'First time buyers scheme will create housing cash "black hole" ', press release (London: Shelter).

Silver, H. (1995) 'Reconceptualising Social Disadvantage: Three Paradigms of Social Exclusion', in G. Rodgers, C. Gore and J. B. Figueiredo (1995) *Social Exclusion: Rhetoric, Reality and Responses* (Geneva: International Institute for Labour Studies, United Nations Development Programme).

Sim, D. (ed.) (2004) *Housing and Public Policy in Post-Devolution Scotland* (Coventry: Chartered Institute of Housing).

Smith, Andrew (2002) *Housing Benefit Reform* (www.dwp.gov.uk/housingbenefit/publications/2002/building_choice/SoS_statement).

Smith, R., Stirling, T. and Williams, P. (2001) *Housing in Wales: The Policy Agenda in an Era of Devolution* (Coventry: Chartered Institute of Housing).

Smith, S. (1989a) *The Politics of 'Race' and Residence* (Cambridge: Polity Press).

Smith, S. (1989b) *Housing and Health. A Review and Research Agenda*, Discussion Paper 27 (Glasgow: Centre for Housing Research, Glasgow University).

Smith, S. and Mallinson, S. (1996) 'The problem with social housing: discretion, accountability and the welfare ideal', *Policy and Politics*, 24 (4), pp. 339–57.

Social Exclusion Unit (1998a) speech given by the prime minister on 2 June 1997 at the Aylesbury Estate, Southwark (www.open.gov.uk/seu).

Social Exclusion Unit (1998b) *Bringing Britain Together: a National Strategy for Neighbourhood Renewal* (London: The Stationery Office).

Social Exclusion Unit (1998c) *Rough Sleeping Report by Social Exclusion Unit*, Cm 4008 (London: HMSO).

Social Exclusion Unit (2001) *A New Commitment to Neighbourhood Renewal: National Strategy Action Plan* (London: Social Exclusion Unit).

Spencer, S. (2002) *Toolkit for Developing Homelessness Strategies* (Sunderland: Northern Housing Consortium).

Spicker, P. (1985) 'The legacy of Octavia Hill', *Housing*, June, pp. 39–40.

Stephens, M., Burns, N. and MacKay, L. (2002) *Social Market or Safety Net? British Social Rented Housing in a European Context* (Bristol: Policy Press).

Stephens, M., Whitehead, C. and Munro, M. (2005) *Lessons from the Past, Challenges for the Future for Housing Policy* (London: ODPM).

Steuerle, C., Ooms, V., Peterson, G. and Reischauer, R. (2000) *Vouchers and the Provision of Public Services* (Washington, DC: Brookings Institution Press).

Stewart, J. (1988) *The New Management of Housing Departments* (Luton: LGTB).

Stewart, J. and Clarke, M. (1987) 'The Public Service Orientation. Issues and Dilemmas', *Public Administration*, 65, pp. 161–77.

Stewart, J. and Ranson, S. (1988) 'Management in the Public Domain', *Public Money and Management*, Spring/Summer, pp. 13–18.

Stigler, G. (1971) 'The theory of economic regulation', *Bell Journal of Economics and Management Science*, 2, pp. 3–21.

Swenarton, M. (1981) *Homes Fit for Heroes* (London: Heinemann).

Swenarton, M. and Taylor, S. (1985) 'The scale and nature of the growth of owner-occupation in Britain between the wars', *Economic History Review*, 38 (3), pp. 373–92.

Taylor, M. (2000) *Stock Transfer Past and Present. A Summary of Research Evidence* (Edinburgh: Scottish Homes).

Taylor, T. (2000) *Best Value, Adding Value* (London: National Housing Federation and Housing Corporation).

Thomas, A. (1986) *Housing and Urban Renewal: Residential Decay and Revitalisation in the Private Sector* (London: George Allen and Unwin).

Thompson, G., Frances, J., Levacic, R. and Mitchell, J. (1991) *Markets, Hierarchies and networks. The Co-ordination of Social Life* (London: Sage).

Tickell, J. (1996) *Turning Hopes into Homes. A History of Social Housing 1235–1966* (London: National Housing Federation).

Titmuss, R. M. (1950) *Problems of Social Policy* (London: HMSO).

Townsend, P. (1979) *Poverty in the UK* (London: Penguin).

Treasury (1981) *The Government's Expenditure Plans 1981/2 to 1983/4*, Cmmnd 8175 (London: HMSO).

Tulloch, D. (2000) *Tenants Choice: Ten Years On*, Report no. 4 (Stirling: University of Stirling).

Twigg, J. (1997) 'Deconstructing the social bath: help with bathing at home for old and disabled people', *Journal of Social Policy*, 26 (2), pp. 211–32.

Walker, A. (1995) 'The dynamics of poverty and social exclusion', in G. Room (ed.), *Beyond the Threshold: The Measurement and Analysis of Social Exclusion* (Bristol: Policy Press).

Walker, A. (1997) *Britain Divided: The Growth of Social Exclusion in the 1980s and 1990s* (London: CPAG).

Walker, B. (1998) 'Incentives, Choice and Control in the Finance of Council Housing', in A. Marsh and D. Mullins (eds), *Housing and Public Policy: Citizenship, Choice and Control* (Buckingham: Open University Press).

Walker, B. (2004) 'The Effects of Rent Restructuring on Social Housing in English Rural Areas', *Journal of Rural Studies*, 20 (4), pp. 445–60.

Walker, B. and Marsh, A. (1995) *Rent Setting Policies in English Local Authorities* (London: HMSO).

Walker, B. and Marsh, A. (1997) 'Rent Setting in Local Government', *Local Government Policy Making*, 23, pp. 39–46.

Walker, B. and Marsh, A. (1998) 'Pricing Public Housing Services: Mirroring the Market?', *Housing Studies*, 13 (4), pp. 549–66.

Walker, B. and Marsh, A. (2000) *Rent Setting Policies in English Local Authorities, 1998/99* (London: DETR).

Walker, B. and Marsh, A. (2003) 'Setting the Rents of Social Housing: The Impact and Implications of Rent Restructuring in England', *Urban Studies*, 40 (10), pp. 2023–47.

Walker, B., Marsh, A. and Niner, P. (2002) *Modelling the Impact of Rent Restructuring: A Case Study Analysis* (London: ODPM).

Walker, B., Mullins, D., Jones, A., Niner, P. and Spencer, K. (2000) *Evaluation of the RSL Best Value Pilots* (London: Housing Corporation).

Walker, B. and Murie, A. (2004) 'The Performance of Social Landlords in Great Britain: What Do We Know and What Does it Show?', *Housing Studies*, 19 (2), pp. 245–67.

Walker, R. M. (1998) 'New public management and housing associations: from comfort to competition', *Policy and Politics*, 22, pp. 71–87.

Walker, R. M. (2001) 'How to abolish public housing: implications and lessons on management reform', *Housing Studies*, 16, pp. 676–96.

Walker, R. M., Jeanes, E. L. and Rowlands, R. O. (2001) *Managing Public Services Innovation. The Experience of English Housing Associations* (Bristol: Policy Press).

Walker, R. M., Pawson, H. and Mullins, D. (2003) 'Devolution and Housing Associations in Great Britain: Enhancing Organisational Accountability?', *Housing Studies*, 18 (2), pp. 177–99.

Walsh, K. (1991) 'Citizens and Consumers: Marketing and Public Sector Management', *Public Money and Management*, Summer, pp. 9–15.

Walsh, K. (1995) *Public Services and Market Mechanisms. Competition, Contracting and the New Public Management* (Basingstoke: Macmillan).

Weber, M. (1947) *The Theory of Social and Economic Organisation* (New York: Free Press).

West Midlands Regional Assembly (2005) *Delivering a Housing Vision for the West Midlands in the 21st Century: Pathways of Choice, West Midlands Regional Housing Strategy 2005* (Birmingham: WMRA).

West Midlands Voluntary and Community Housing Network (2005) *Regional Homelessness Strategy* (Birmingham: WMVCHN).

White, J. (1980) *Rothschild Buildings: Life in an East End Tenement Block 1887–1920* (London: Routledge & Kegan Paul).

Whitehead, C. (1991) 'From need to affordability: an analysis of UK housing objectives', *Urban Studies*, 28 (6), pp. 871–87.

Whitehead, C. (1999) 'The Provision of Finance for Social Housing', *Urban Studies*, 36 (4), pp. 657–72.

Whitehead, C. (2003) 'Financing Social Housing in Europe', *Housing Finance International*, 17 (4), pp. 3–8.

Whitehead, C. and Crook, A. (2000) 'The Achievement of Affordable through the Planning System', in S. Monk and C. Whitehead (eds), *Restructuring Housing Systems* (York Publishing Services Limited).

Whitehead, C. M. E. and Kleinman, M. (1986) *Private Rented Housing in the 1980s and 1990s* (Cambridge: Granta).

Wilcox, S. (1993) *Housing Finance Review, 1993/94* (York: Joseph Rowntree Foundation).

Wilcox, S. (1995) *Housing Finance Review, 1995/96* (York: Joseph Rowntree Foundation).

Wilcox, S. (1997) 'Incoherent rents', in *Housing Finance Review 1997/98* (York: Joseph Rowntree Foundation).

Wilcox, S. (2001) *UK Housing Finance Review 2001/2* (Coventry: Chartered Institute of Housing and Council of Mortgage Lender).

Wilcox, S. (2002) *UK Housing Finance Review 2002/3* (Coventry and London: Chartered Institute of Housing and the Council of Mortgage Lenders for the Joseph Rowntree Foundation).

Wilcox, S. (2004) *UK Housing Review 2004/5* (Coventry: Chartered Institute of Housing and Council of Mortgage Lenders).

Wilding, P. (1972) 'Towards Exchequer Subsidies for Housing, 1906–1914', *Social and Economic Administration*, 6 (1), pp. 3–18.

Wilkinson, D. (1999) *Poor Housing and Ill Health: A Summary of Research Evidence* (Edinburgh, The Scottish Office Central Research Unit).

Williams, P. (2003) 'Private Finance for a Social Purpose: Mortgage Lenders and Housing Associations in the UK', *Housing Finance International*, 17 (4), pp. 9–16.

Wistow, G. and Henwood, M. (1991) 'Caring for People: Elegant Model or Flawed Design?', in N. Manning (ed.), *Implementing Community Care* (Buckingham: Open University Press).

Wohl, A. (1977) *The Eternal Slum* (London: Edward Arnold).

Woods, R. (2000) 'Social Housing. Managing Multiple Pressures', in J. Clarke, S. Gerwutz and E. McLauglin (eds), *New Managerialism, New Welfare?* (London: Open University and Sage).

Wuthnow, R. (1991) 'The voluntary sector: legacy of the past, hope for the future?', in R. Wuthnow (ed.), *Between States and Markets. The Voluntary Sector in Comparative Perspective* (Princeton, NJ: Princeton University Press).

Yates, J. and Whitehead, C. (1998) 'In defence of greater agnosticism: a response to Galster's "Comparing Demand-side and Supply-side Housing Policies"', *Housing Studies*, 13, pp. 415–24.

Zitron, J. (2004) *Towards Investment Partnering* (Coventry: Chartered Institute of Housing).

Index